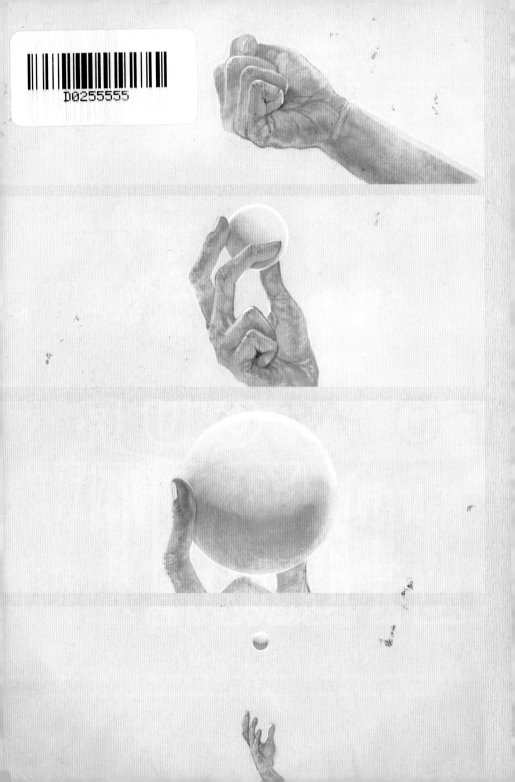

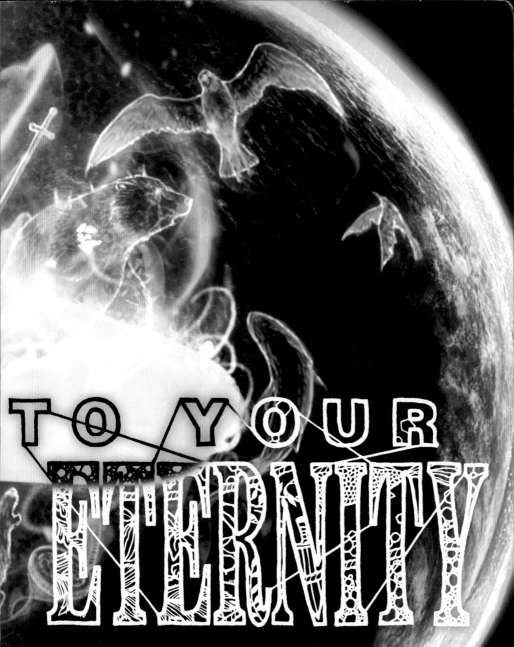

TO YOUR ETERNITY

YOSHITOKI OIMA

I

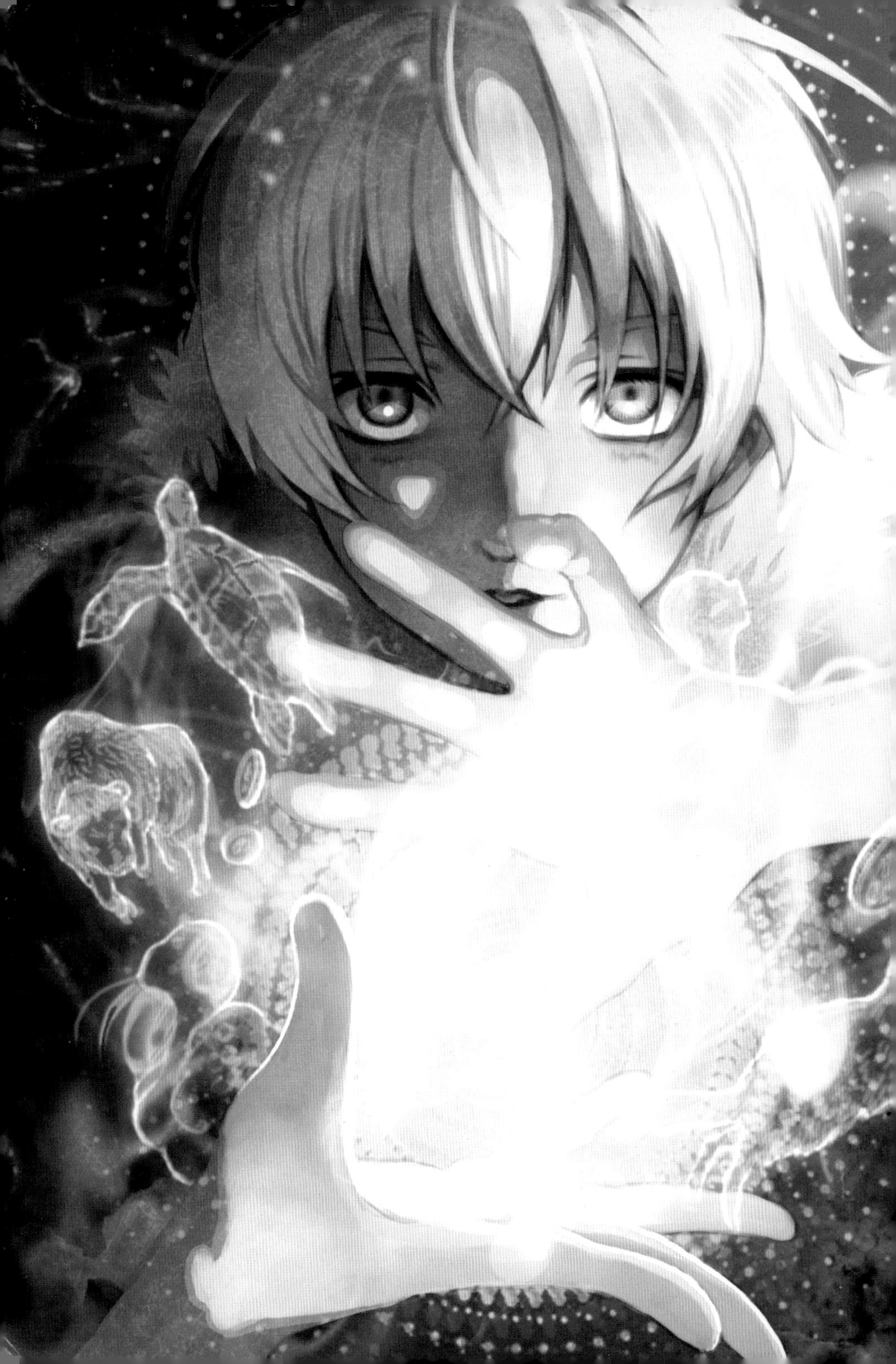

CONTENTS

#1 The Final One

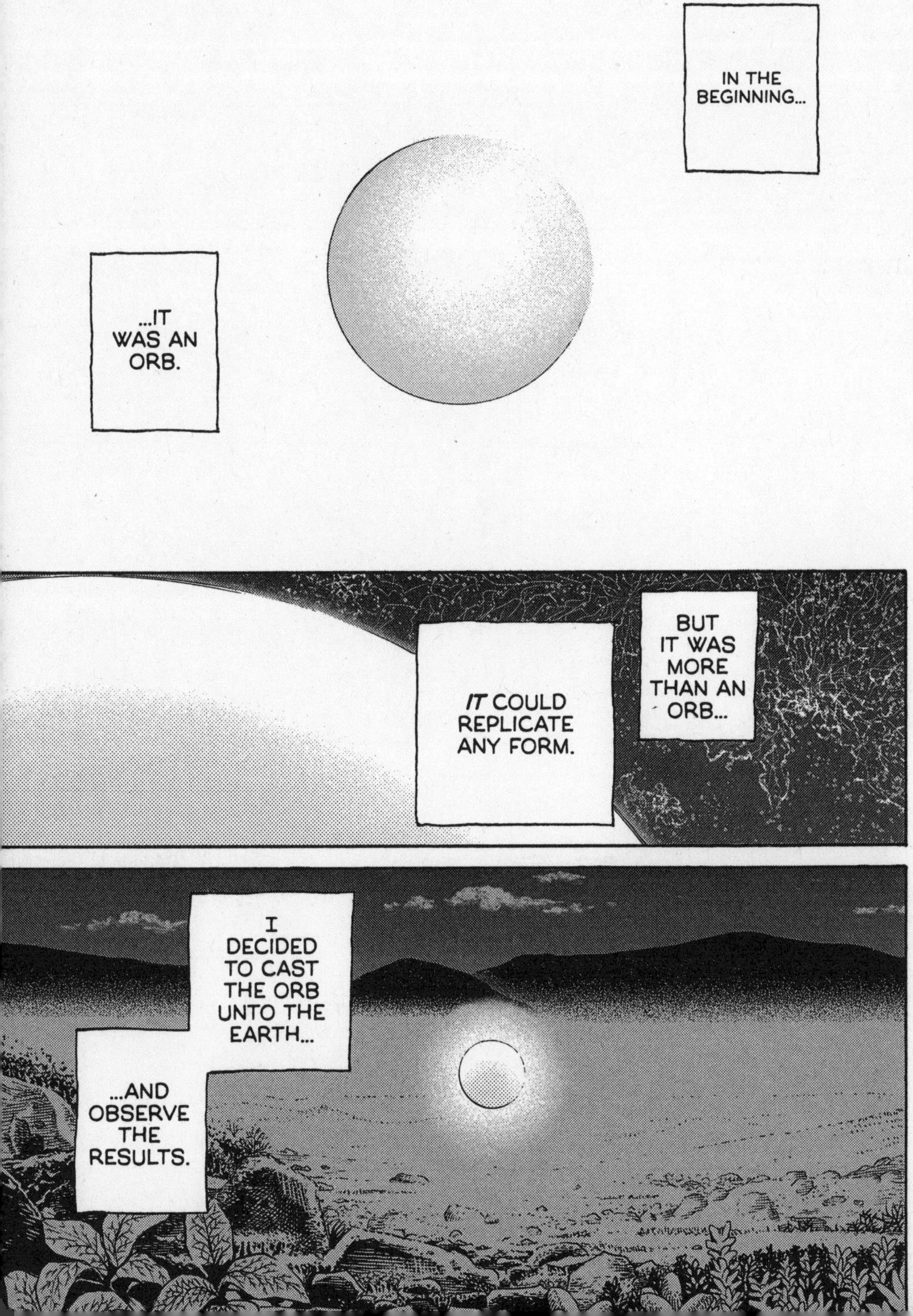
IN THE BEGINNING...
...IT WAS AN ORB.
BUT IT WAS MORE THAN AN ORB...
IT COULD REPLICATE ANY FORM.
I DECIDED TO CAST THE ORB UNTO THE EARTH...
...AND OBSERVE THE RESULTS.

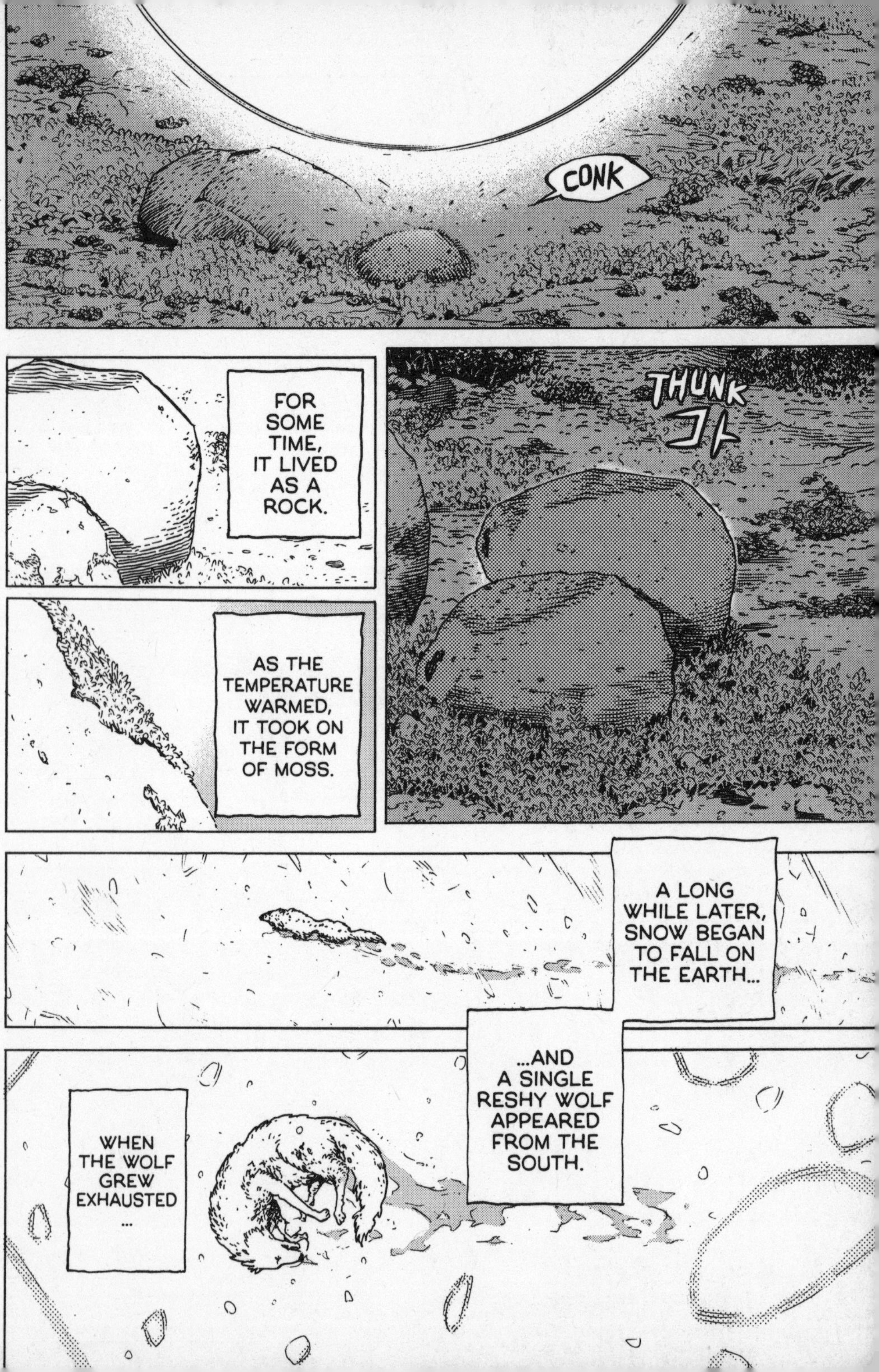
CONK
THUNK
コト
FOR SOME TIME, IT LIVED AS A ROCK.
AS THE TEMPERATURE WARMED, IT TOOK ON THE FORM OF MOSS.
A LONG WHILE LATER, SNOW BEGAN TO FALL ON THE EARTH...
...AND A SINGLE RESHY WOLF APPEARED FROM THE SOUTH.
WHEN THE WOLF GREW EXHAUSTED ...

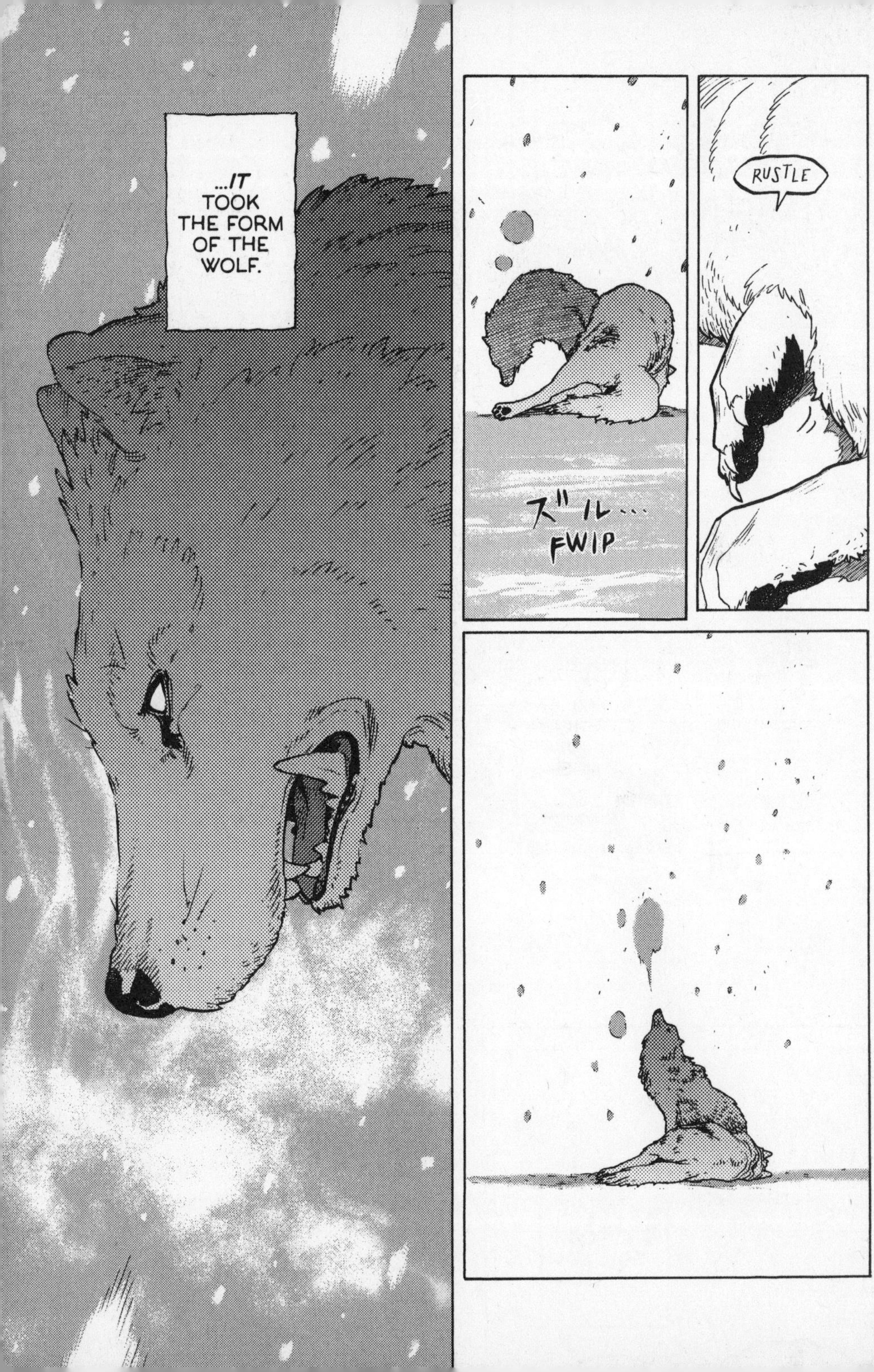
RUSTLE
ズル…
FWIP
...IT TOOK THE FORM OF THE WOLF.

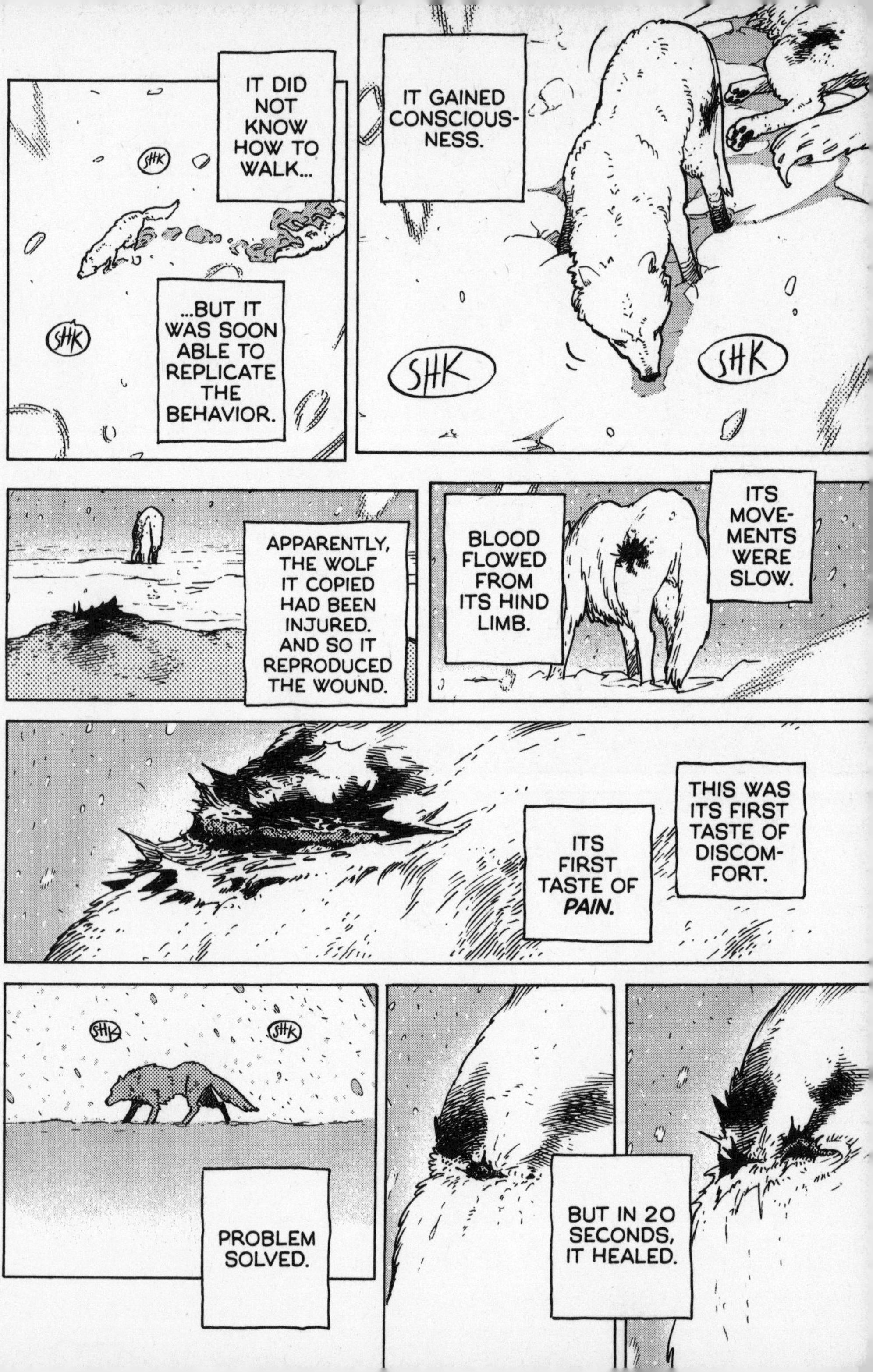
IT GAINED CONSCIOUS-NESS.
SHK
SHK
IT DID NOT KNOW HOW TO WALK...
SHK
SHK
...BUT IT WAS SOON ABLE TO REPLICATE THE BEHAVIOR.
ITS MOVE-MENTS WERE SLOW.
BLOOD FLOWED FROM ITS HIND LIMB.
APPARENTLY, THE WOLF IT COPIED HAD BEEN INJURED. AND SO IT REPRODUCED THE WOUND.
THIS WAS ITS FIRST TASTE OF DISCOM-FORT.
ITS FIRST TASTE OF *PAIN.*
BUT IN 20 SECONDS, IT HEALED.
SHK
SHK
PROBLEM SOLVED.

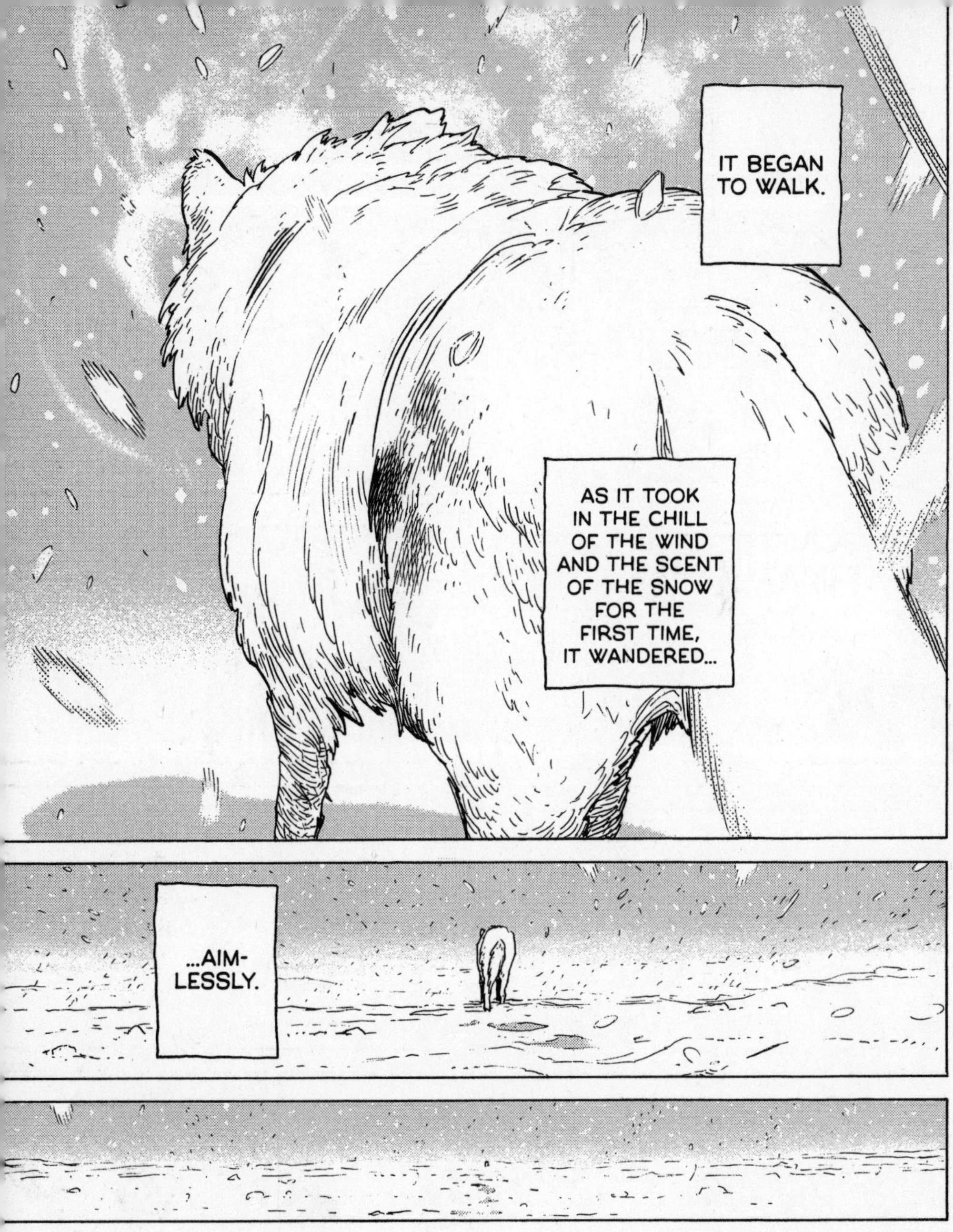
IT BEGAN TO WALK.
AS IT TOOK IN THE CHILL OF THE WIND AND THE SCENT OF THE SNOW FOR THE FIRST TIME, IT WANDERED...
...AIM-LESSLY.

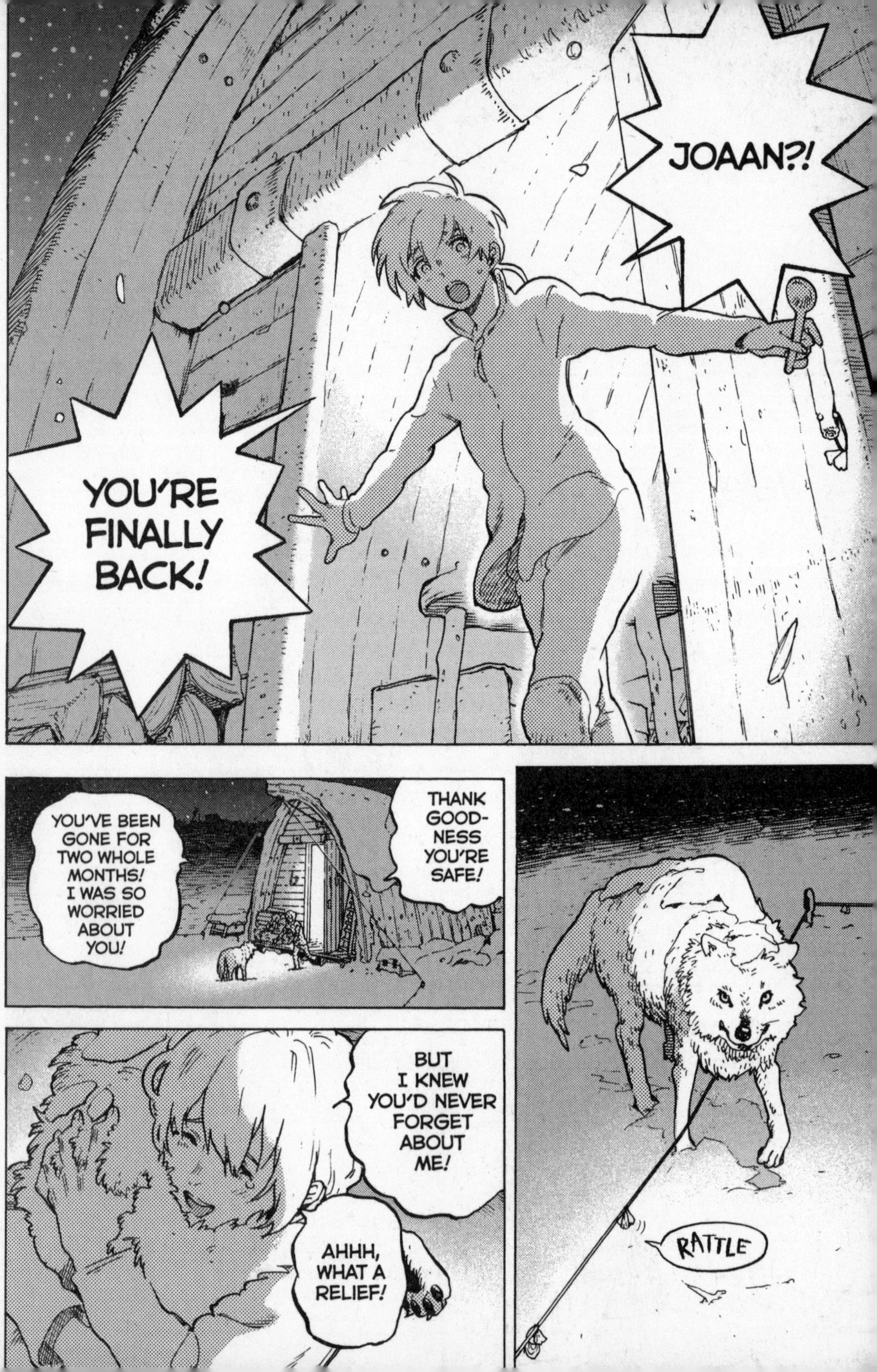
JOAAN?!
YOU'RE FINALLY BACK!
RATTLE
THANK GOOD-NESS YOU'RE SAFE!
YOU'VE BEEN GONE FOR TWO WHOLE MONTHS! I WAS SO WORRIED ABOUT YOU!
BUT I KNEW YOU'D NEVER FORGET ABOUT ME!
AHHH, WHAT A RELIEF!

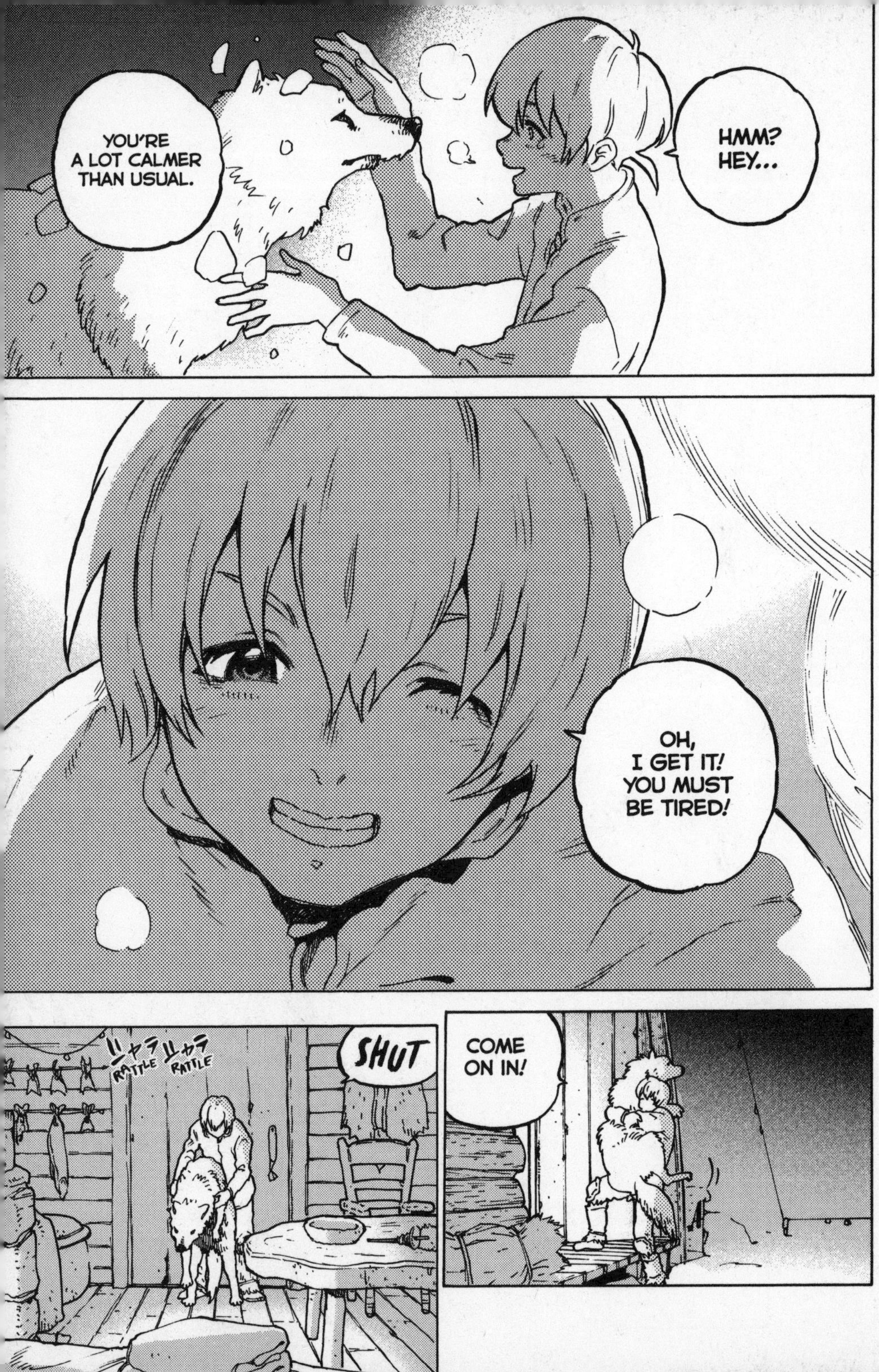
HMM? HEY...
YOU'RE A LOT CALMER THAN USUAL.
OH, I GET IT! YOU MUST BE TIRED!
COME ON IN!
SHUT
RATTLE RATTLE

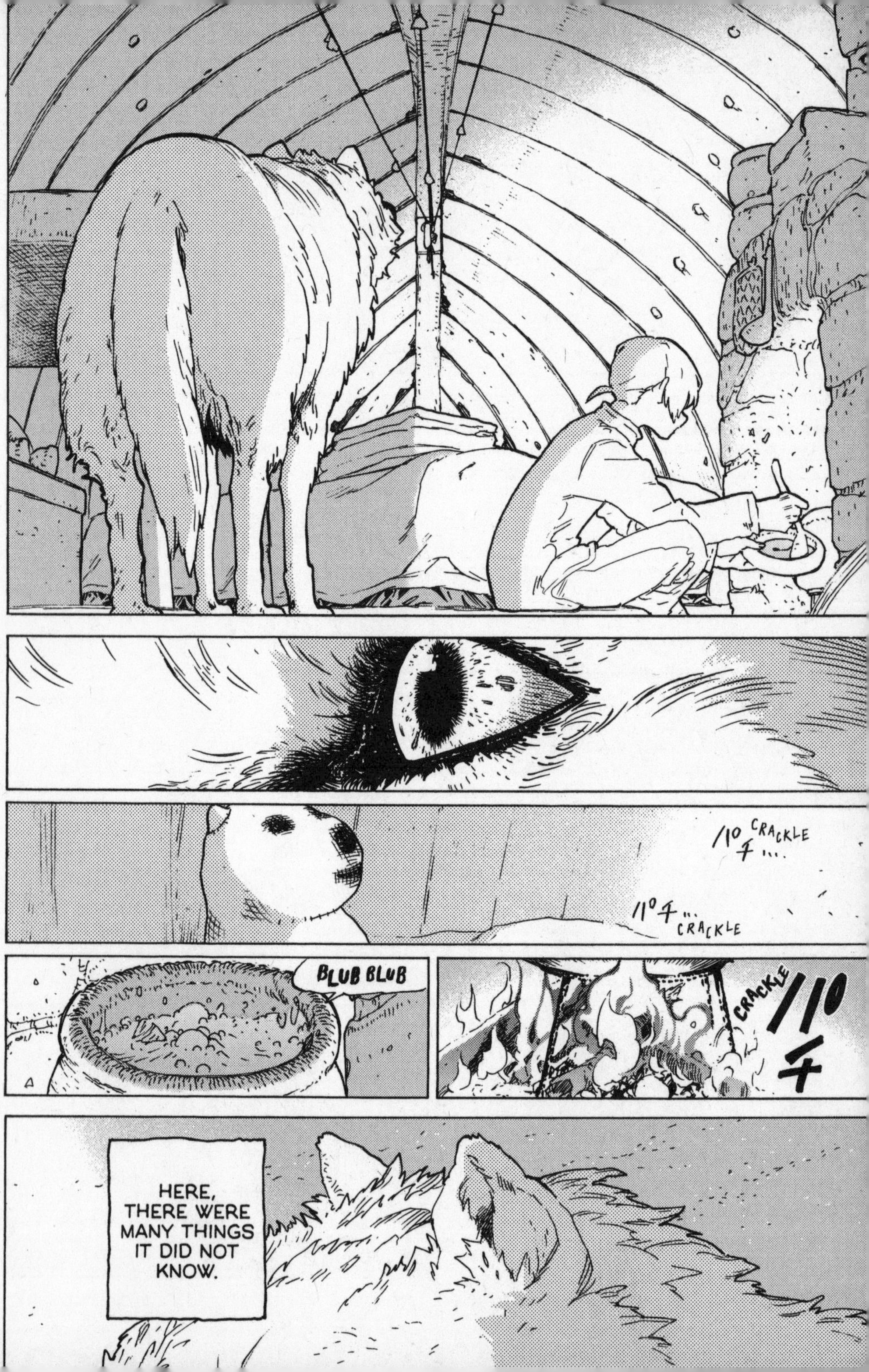
パチ... CRACKLE
パチ... CRACKLE
CRACKLE パチ
BLUB BLUB
HERE, THERE WERE MANY THINGS IT DID NOT KNOW.

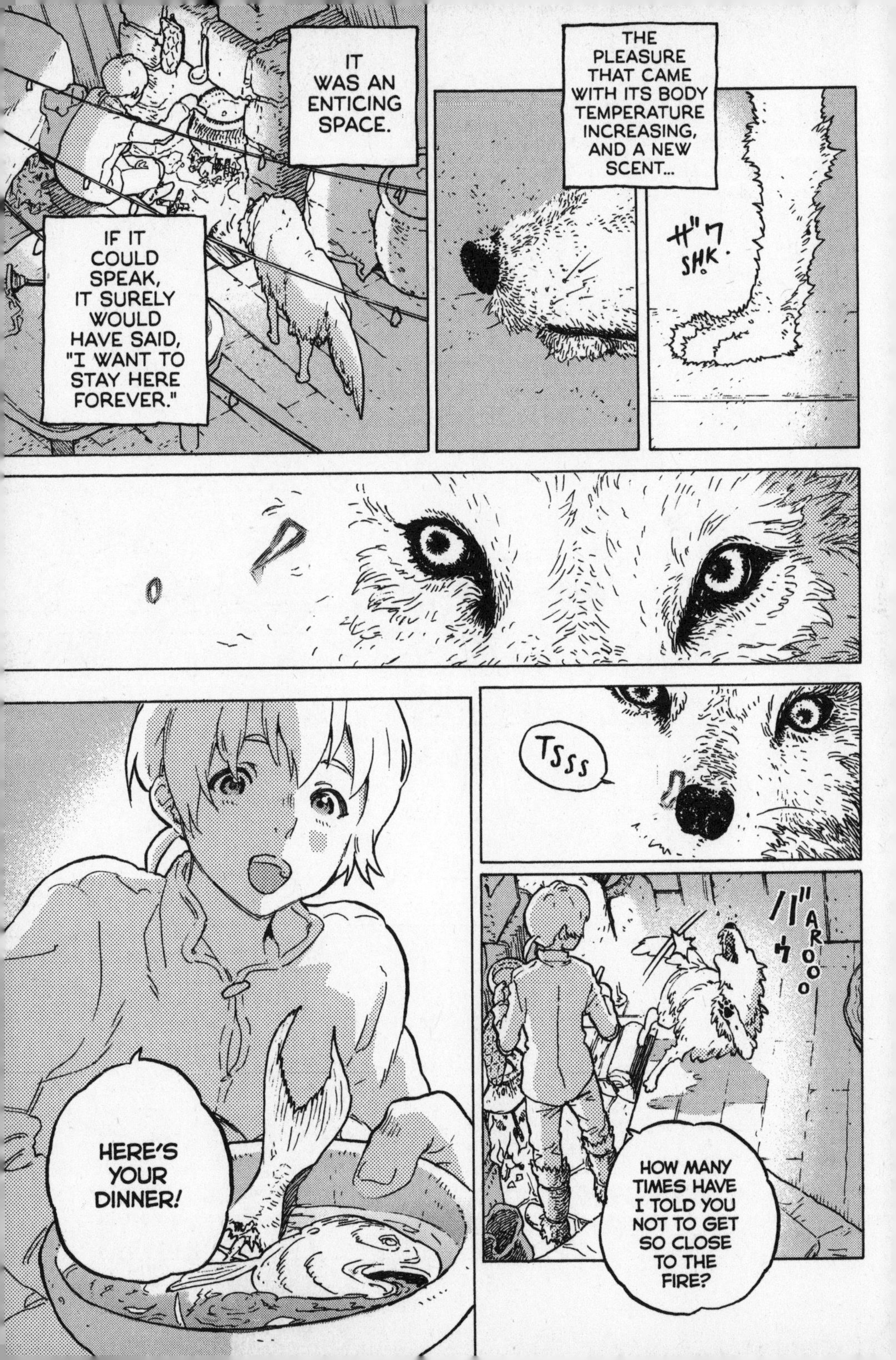

THE PLEASURE THAT CAME WITH ITS BODY TEMPERATURE INCREASING, AND A NEW SCENT...
SHK
IT WAS AN ENTICING SPACE.
IF IT COULD SPEAK, IT SURELY WOULD HAVE SAID, "I WANT TO STAY HERE FOREVER."
TSSS
AROOO
HOW MANY TIMES HAVE I TOLD YOU NOT TO GET SO CLOSE TO THE FIRE?
HERE'S YOUR DINNER!

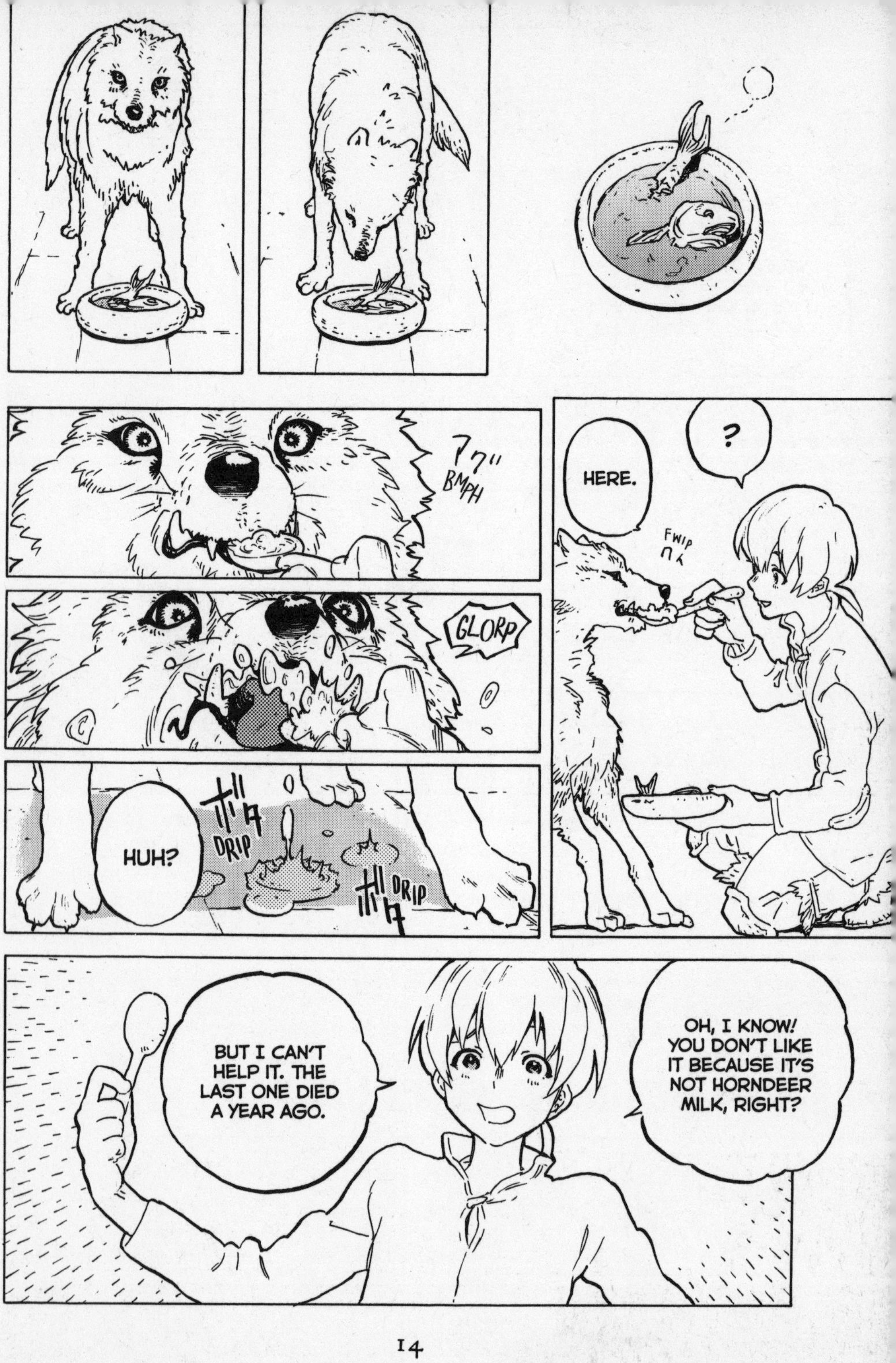
?
HERE.
FWIP
BMPH
GLORP
DRIP
HUH?
DRIP
OH, I KNOW! YOU DON'T LIKE IT BECAUSE IT'S NOT HORNDEER MILK, RIGHT?
BUT I CAN'T HELP IT. THE LAST ONE DIED A YEAR AGO.

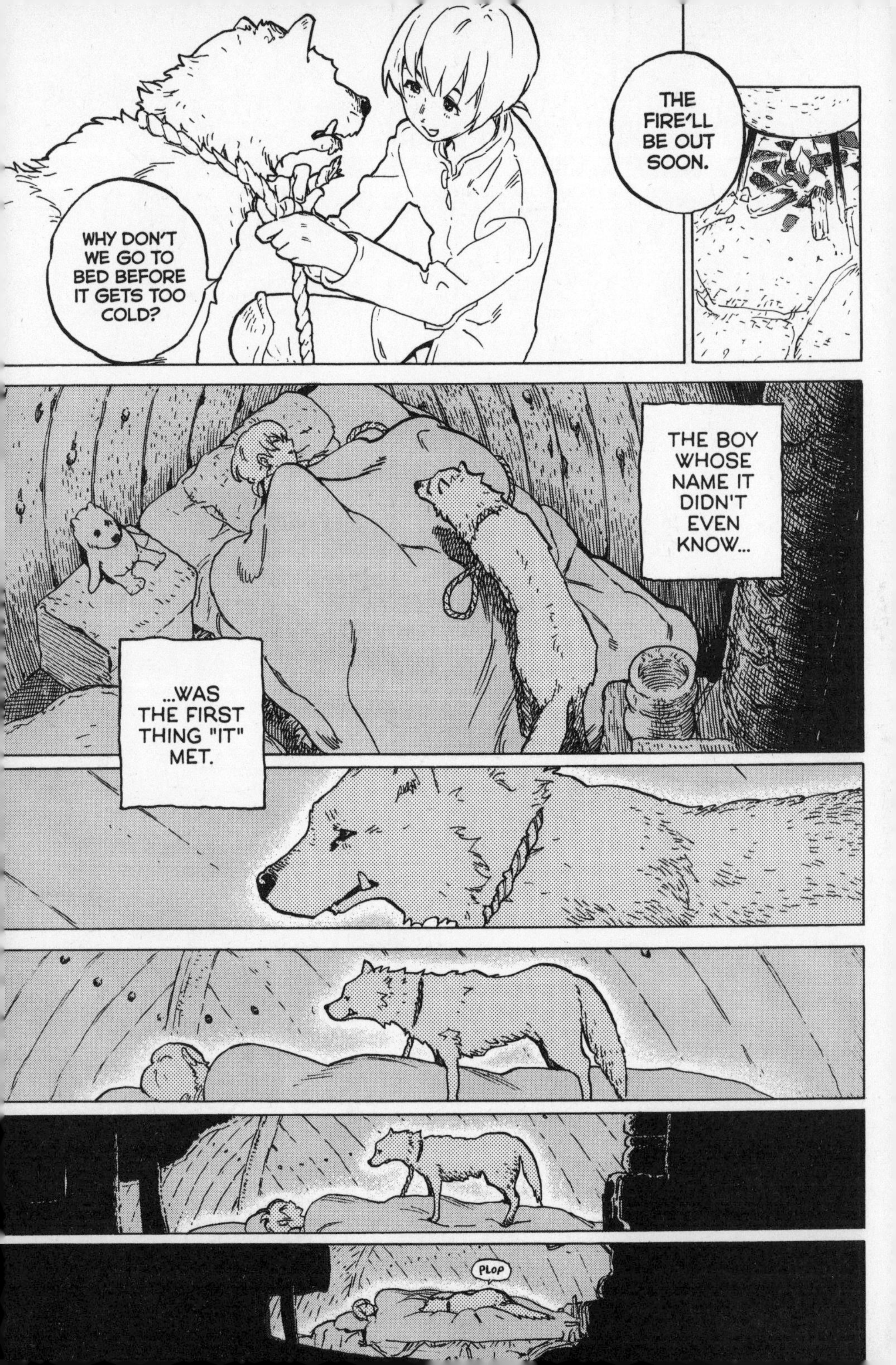
THE FIRE'LL BE OUT SOON.
WHY DON'T WE GO TO BED BEFORE IT GETS TOO COLD?
THE BOY WHOSE NAME IT DIDN'T EVEN KNOW...
...WAS THE FIRST THING "IT" MET.
PLOP

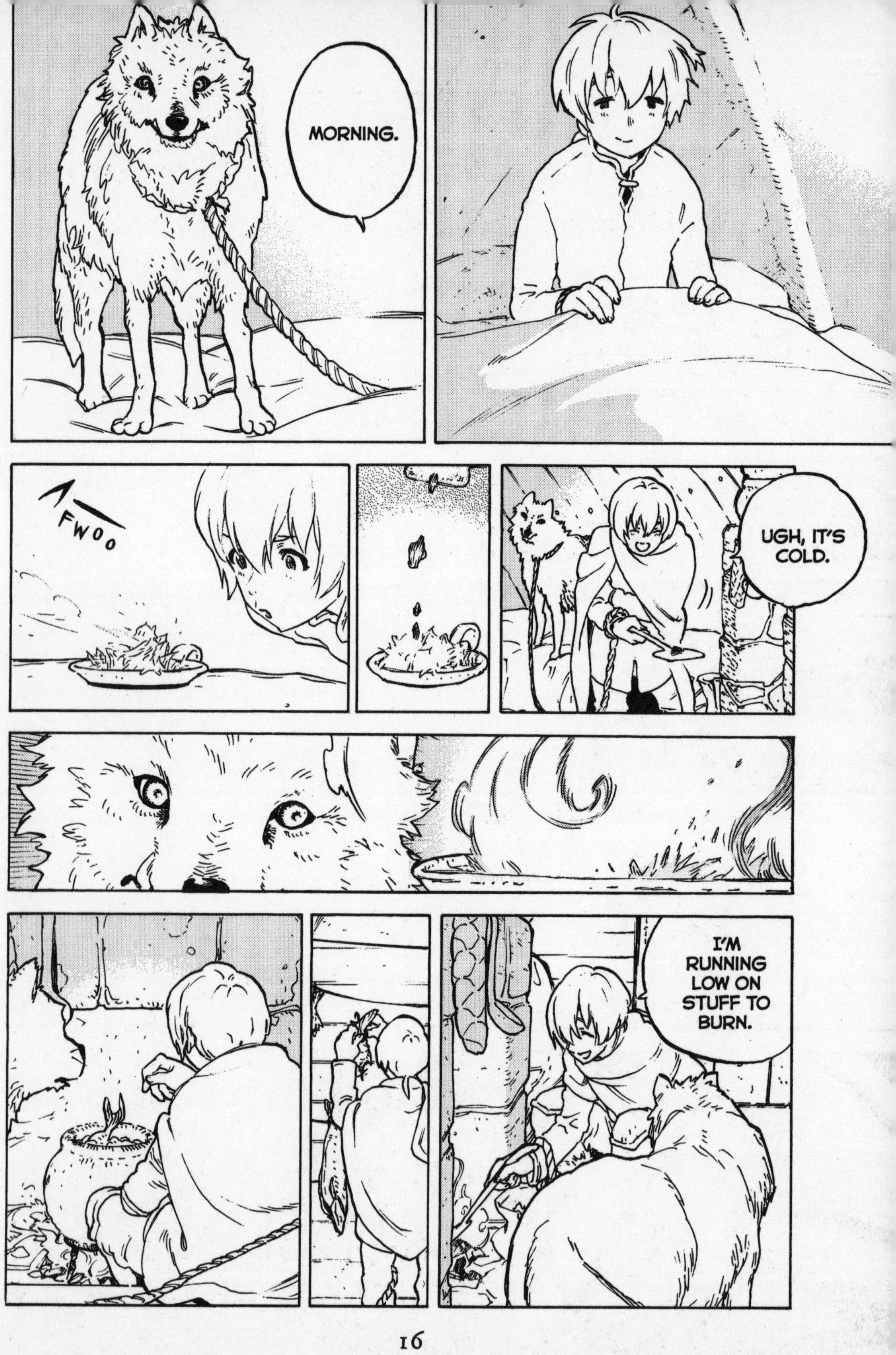
MORNING.
UGH, IT'S COLD.
FWOO
I'M RUNNING LOW ON STUFF TO BURN.

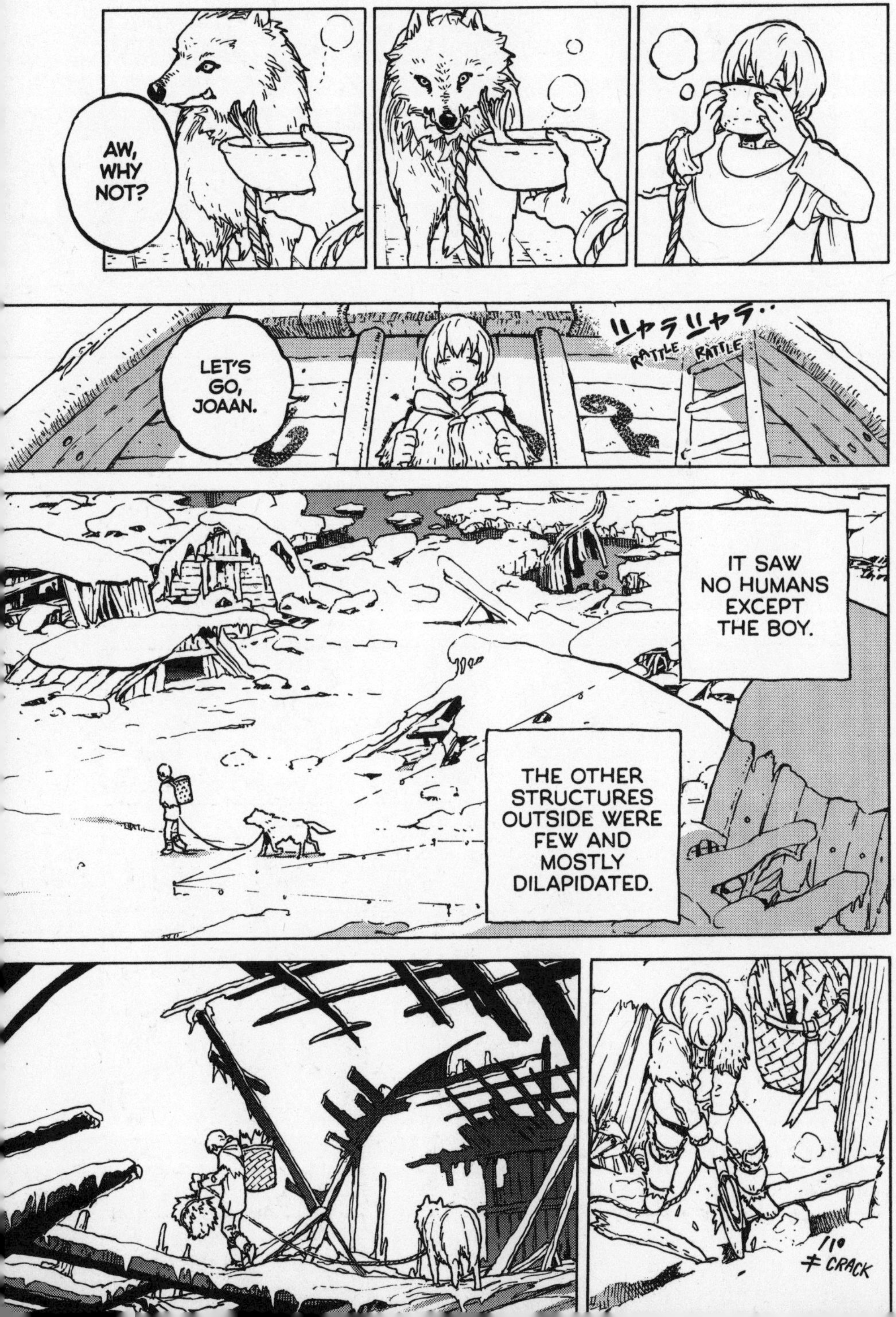
AW, WHY NOT?
RATTLE RATTLE
LET'S GO, JOAAN.
IT SAW NO HUMANS EXCEPT THE BOY.
THE OTHER STRUCTURES OUTSIDE WERE FEW AND MOSTLY DILAPIDATED.
CRACK

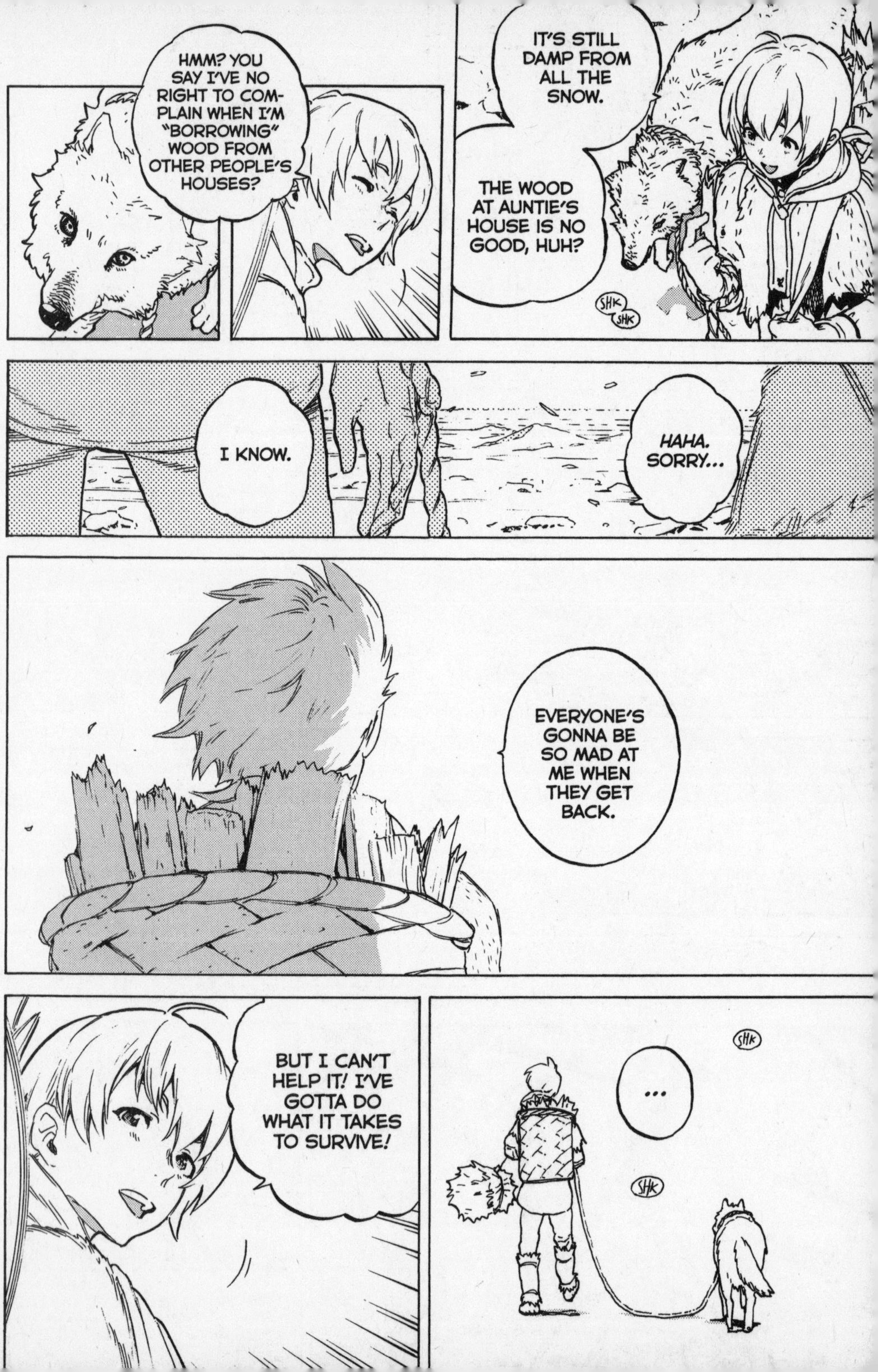
IT'S STILL DAMP FROM ALL THE SNOW.
THE WOOD AT AUNTIE'S HOUSE IS NO GOOD, HUH?
SHK
SHK
HMM? YOU SAY I'VE NO RIGHT TO COM-PLAIN WHEN I'M "BORROWING" WOOD FROM OTHER PEOPLE'S HOUSES?
HAHA. SORRY...
I KNOW.
EVERYONE'S GONNA BE SO MAD AT ME WHEN THEY GET BACK.
SHK
...
SHK
BUT I CAN'T HELP IT! I'VE GOTTA DO WHAT IT TAKES TO SURVIVE!

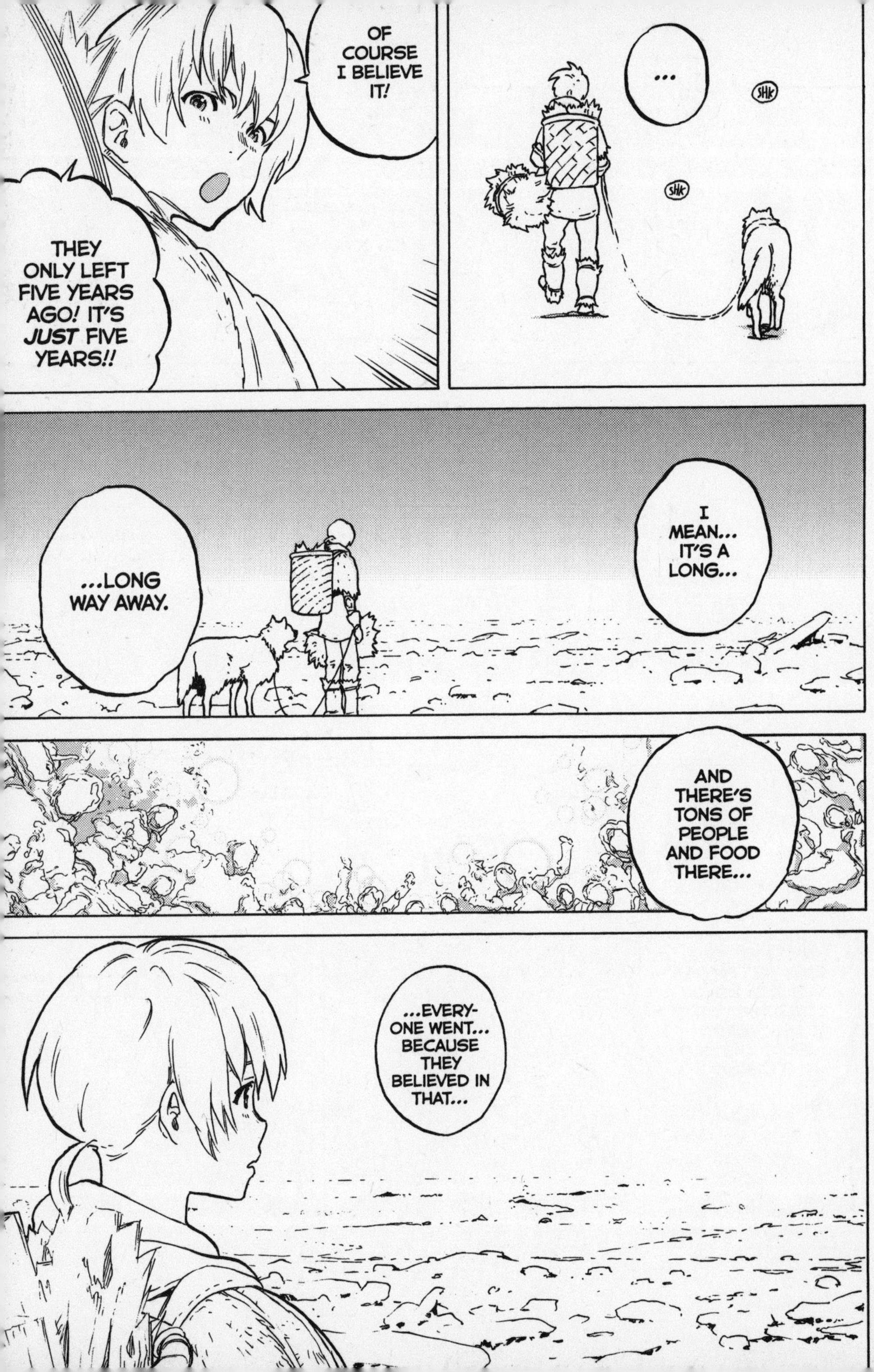
...
SHK
SHK
OF COURSE I BELIEVE IT!
THEY ONLY LEFT FIVE YEARS AGO! IT'S *JUST* FIVE YEARS!!
I MEAN... IT'S A LONG...
...LONG WAY AWAY.
AND THERE'S TONS OF PEOPLE AND FOOD THERE...
...EVERY-ONE WENT... BECAUSE THEY BELIEVED IN THAT...

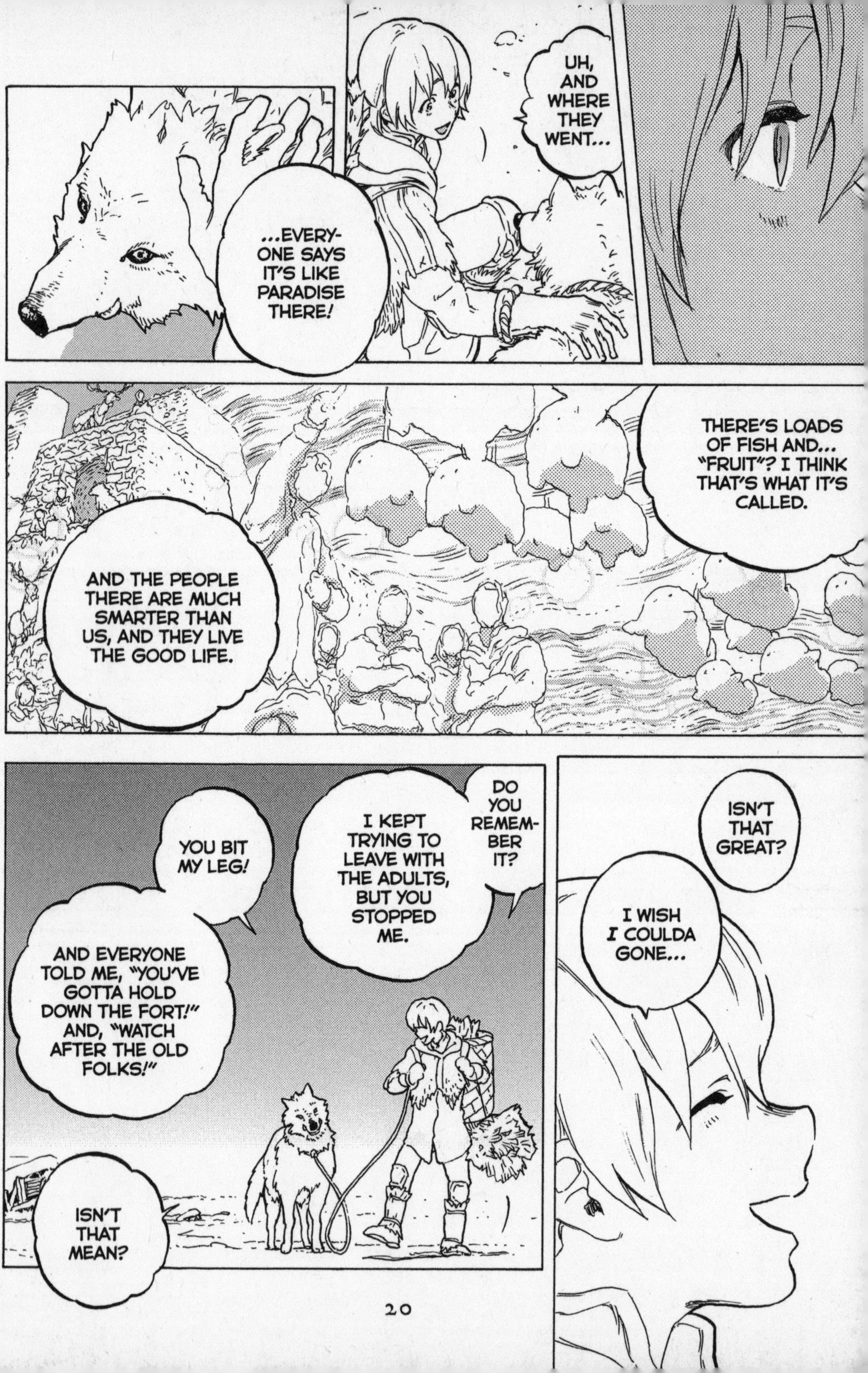
UH, AND WHERE THEY WENT...
...EVERY-ONE SAYS IT'S LIKE PARADISE THERE!
THERE'S LOADS OF FISH AND... "FRUIT"? I THINK THAT'S WHAT IT'S CALLED.
AND THE PEOPLE THERE ARE MUCH SMARTER THAN US, AND THEY LIVE THE GOOD LIFE.
ISN'T THAT GREAT?
I WISH *I* COULDA GONE...
DO YOU REMEM-BER IT?
I KEPT TRYING TO LEAVE WITH THE ADULTS, BUT YOU STOPPED ME.
YOU BIT MY LEG!
AND EVERYONE TOLD ME, "YOU'VE GOTTA HOLD DOWN THE FORT!" AND, "WATCH AFTER THE OLD FOLKS!"
ISN'T THAT MEAN?

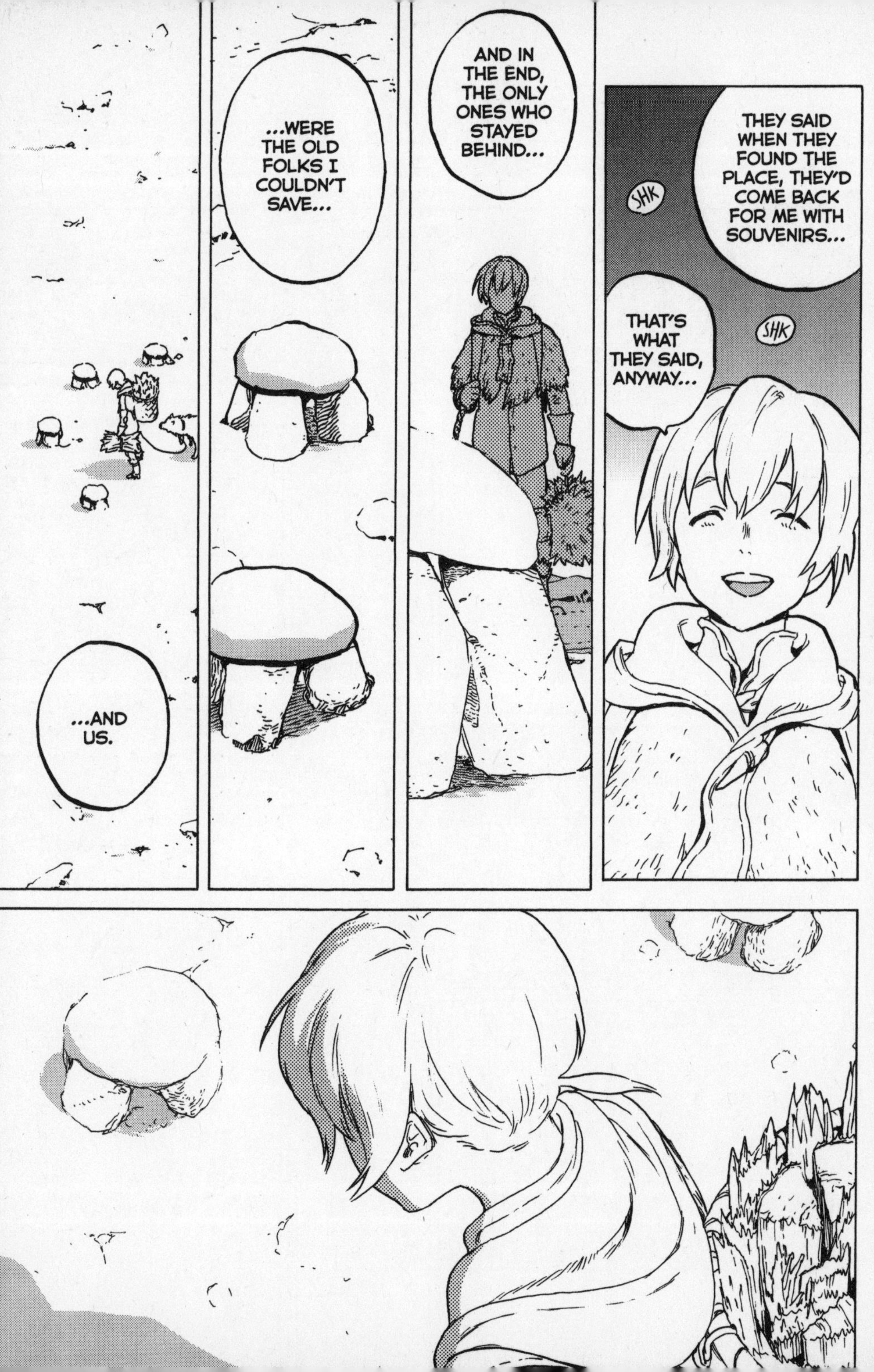
THEY SAID WHEN THEY FOUND THE PLACE, THEY'D COME BACK FOR ME WITH SOUVENIRS...
SHK
SHK
THAT'S WHAT THEY SAID, ANYWAY...
AND IN THE END, THE ONLY ONES WHO STAYED BEHIND...
...WERE THE OLD FOLKS I COULDN'T SAVE...
...AND US.

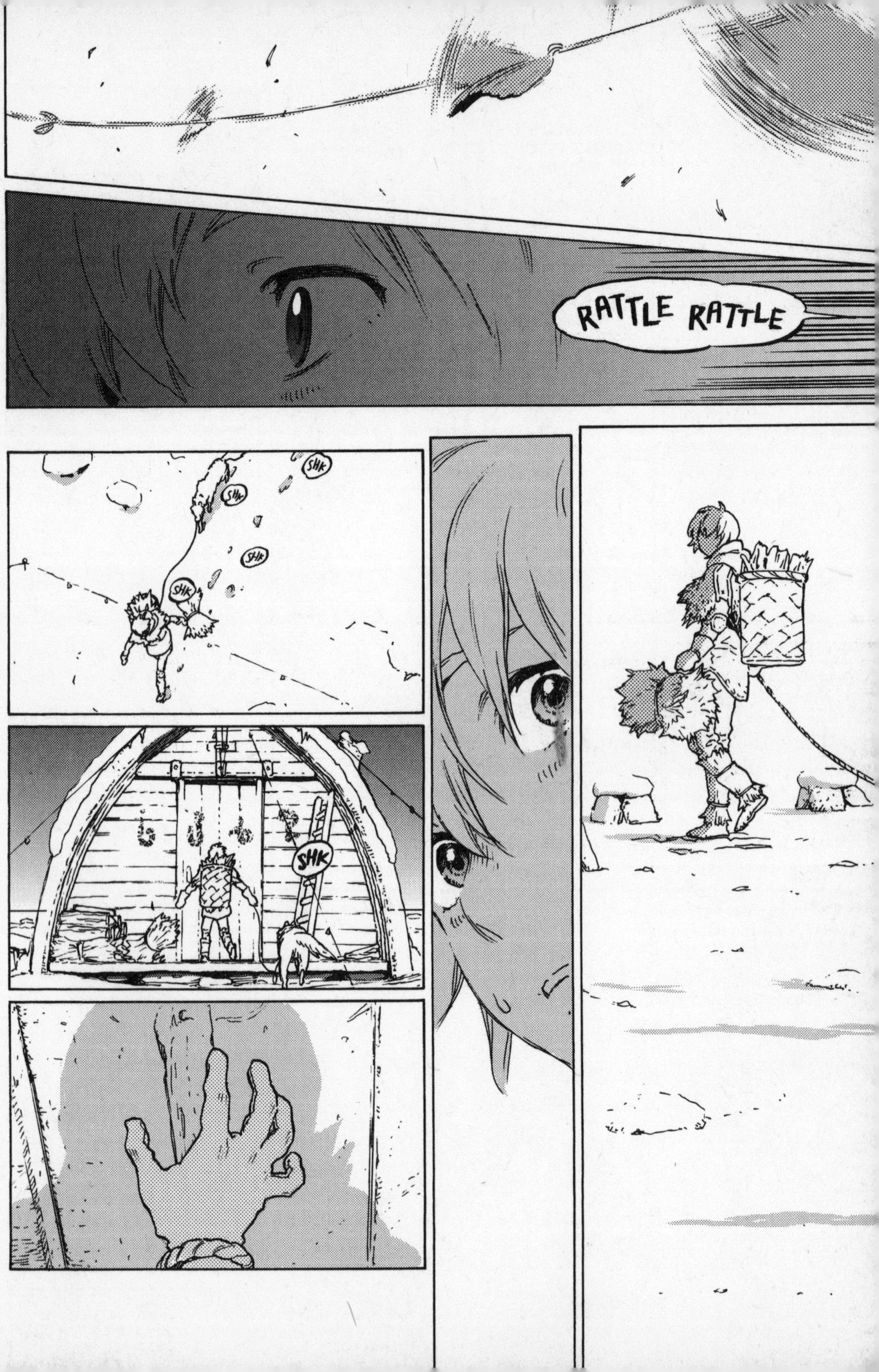
RATTLE RATTLE
SHK
SHK
SHK
SHK
SHK

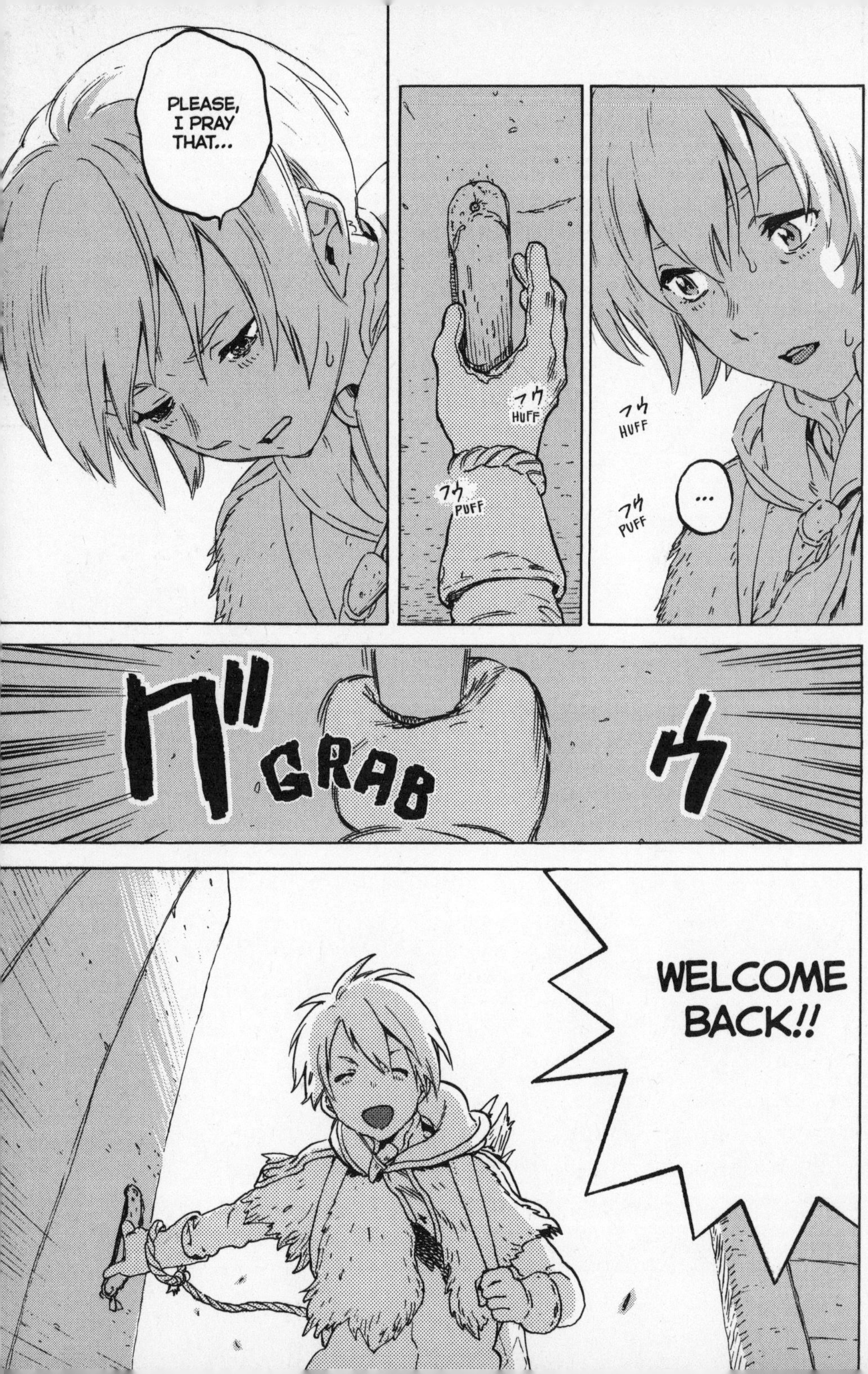

フウ
HUFF
...
フウ
PUFF
フウ
HUFF
フウ
PUFF
PLEASE, I PRAY THAT...
GRAB
WELCOME BACK!!

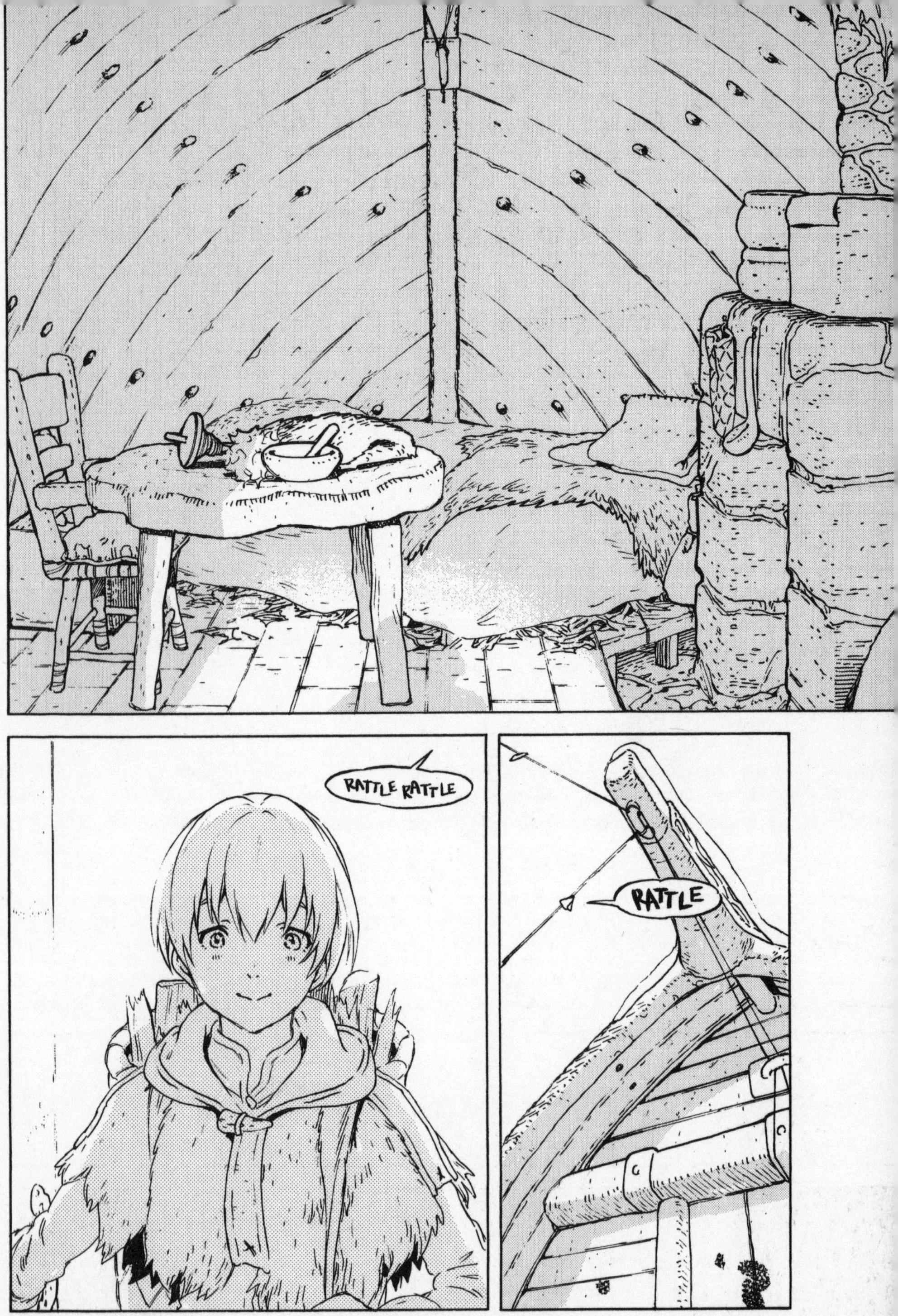
RATTLE
RATTLE RATTLE

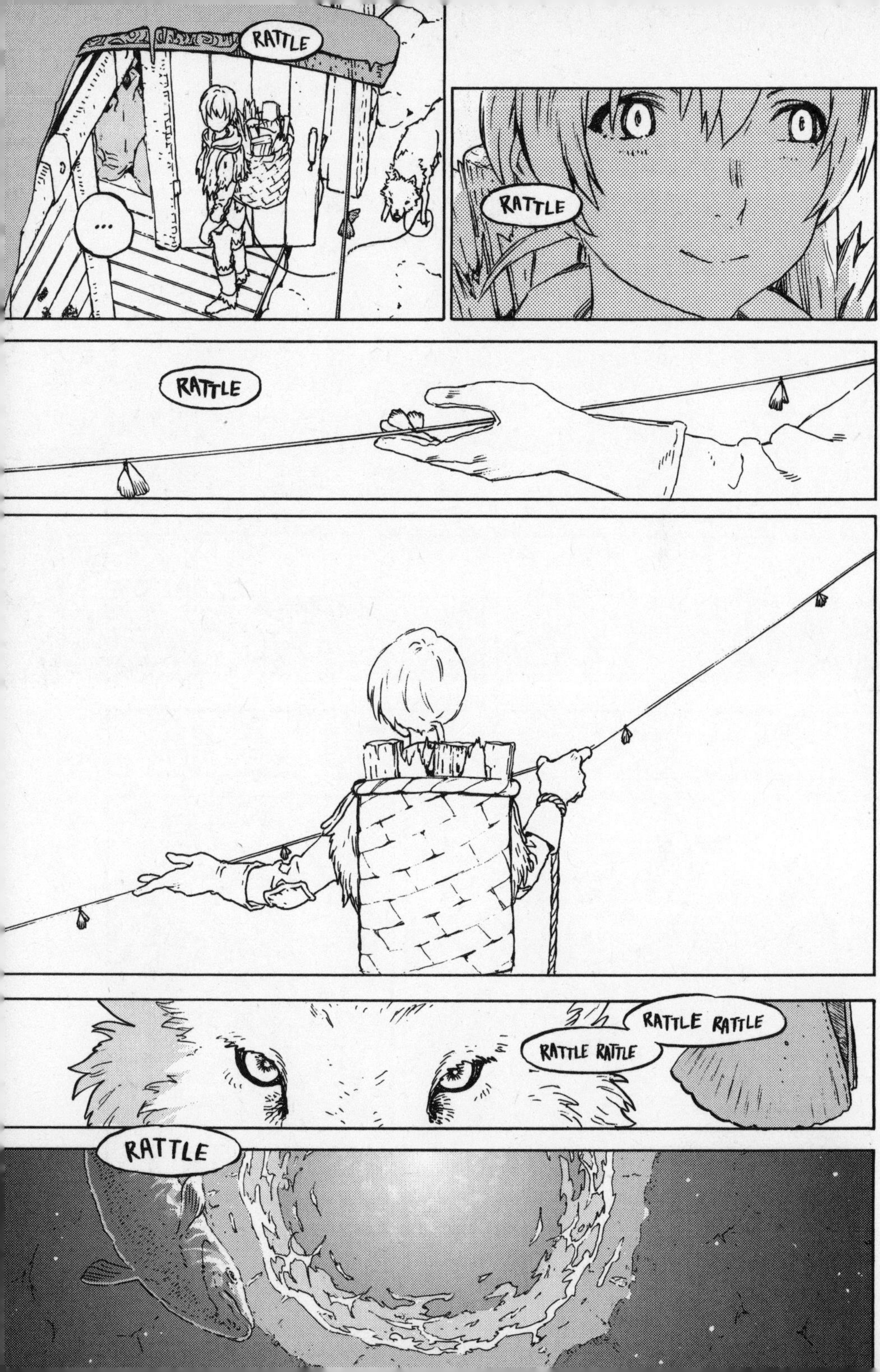
RATTLE
RATTLE
...
RATTLE
RATTLE RATTLE
RATTLE RATTLE
RATTLE

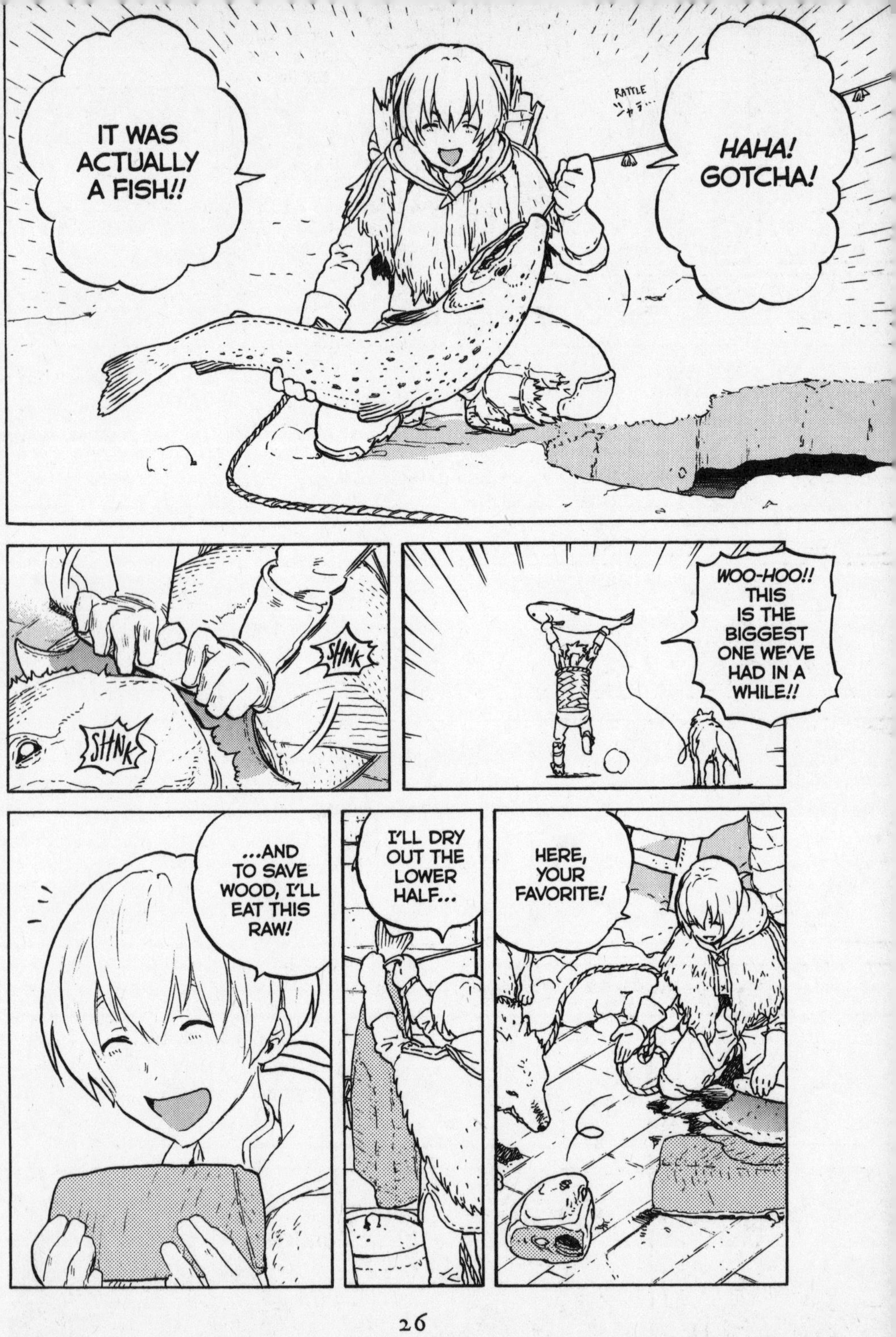
HAHA! GOTCHA!
RATTLE
IT WAS ACTUALLY A FISH!!
WOO-HOO!! THIS IS THE BIGGEST ONE WE'VE HAD IN A WHILE!!
SHNK
SHNK
HERE, YOUR FAVORITE!
I'LL DRY OUT THE LOWER HALF...
...AND TO SAVE WOOD, I'LL EAT THIS RAW!

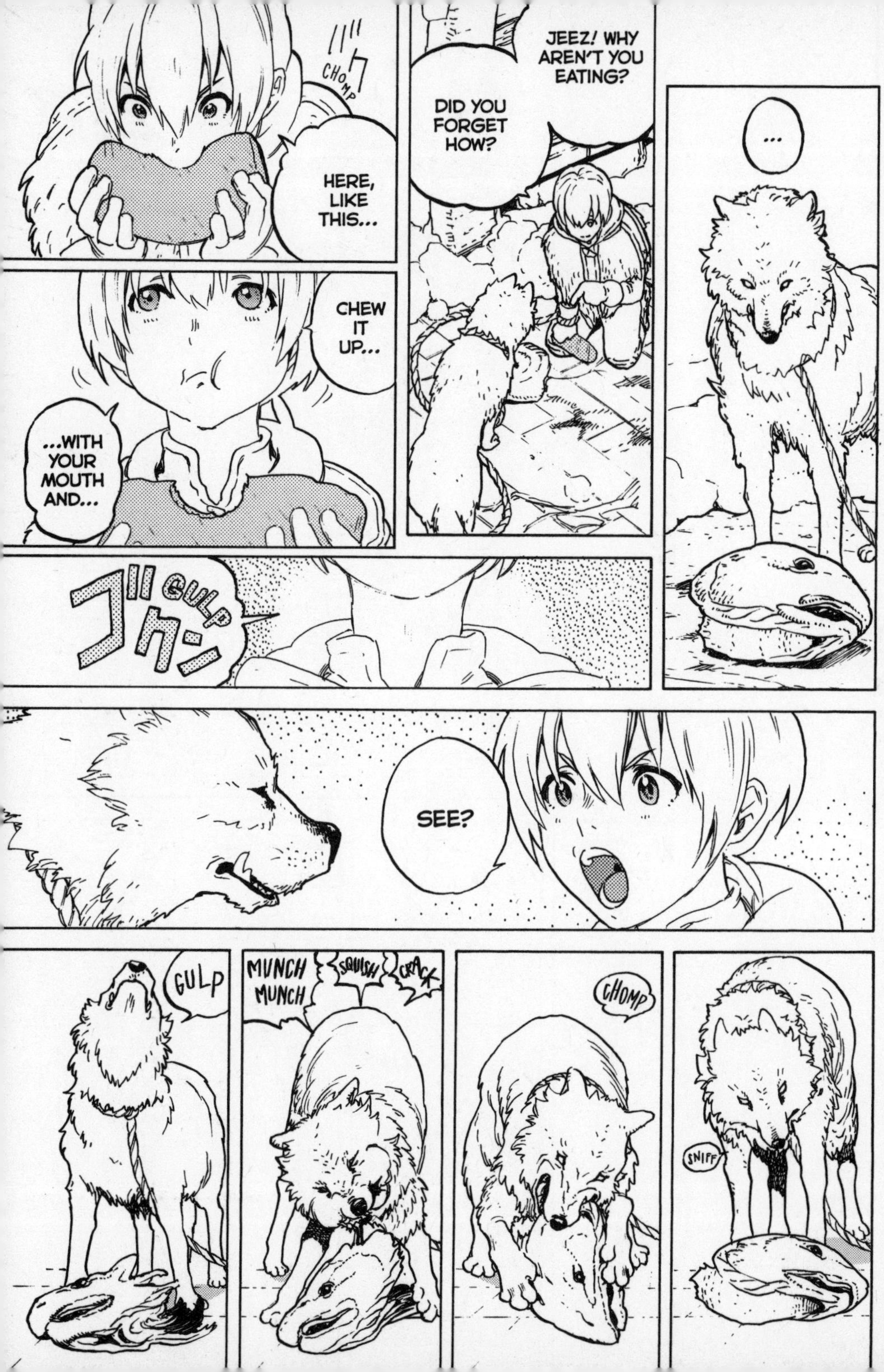
JEEZ! WHY AREN'T YOU EATING?
DID YOU FORGET HOW?
...
CHOMP
HERE, LIKE THIS...
CHEW IT UP...
...WITH YOUR MOUTH AND...
GULP
SEE?
SNIFF
CHOMP
MUNCH MUNCH
SQUISH
CRACK
GULP

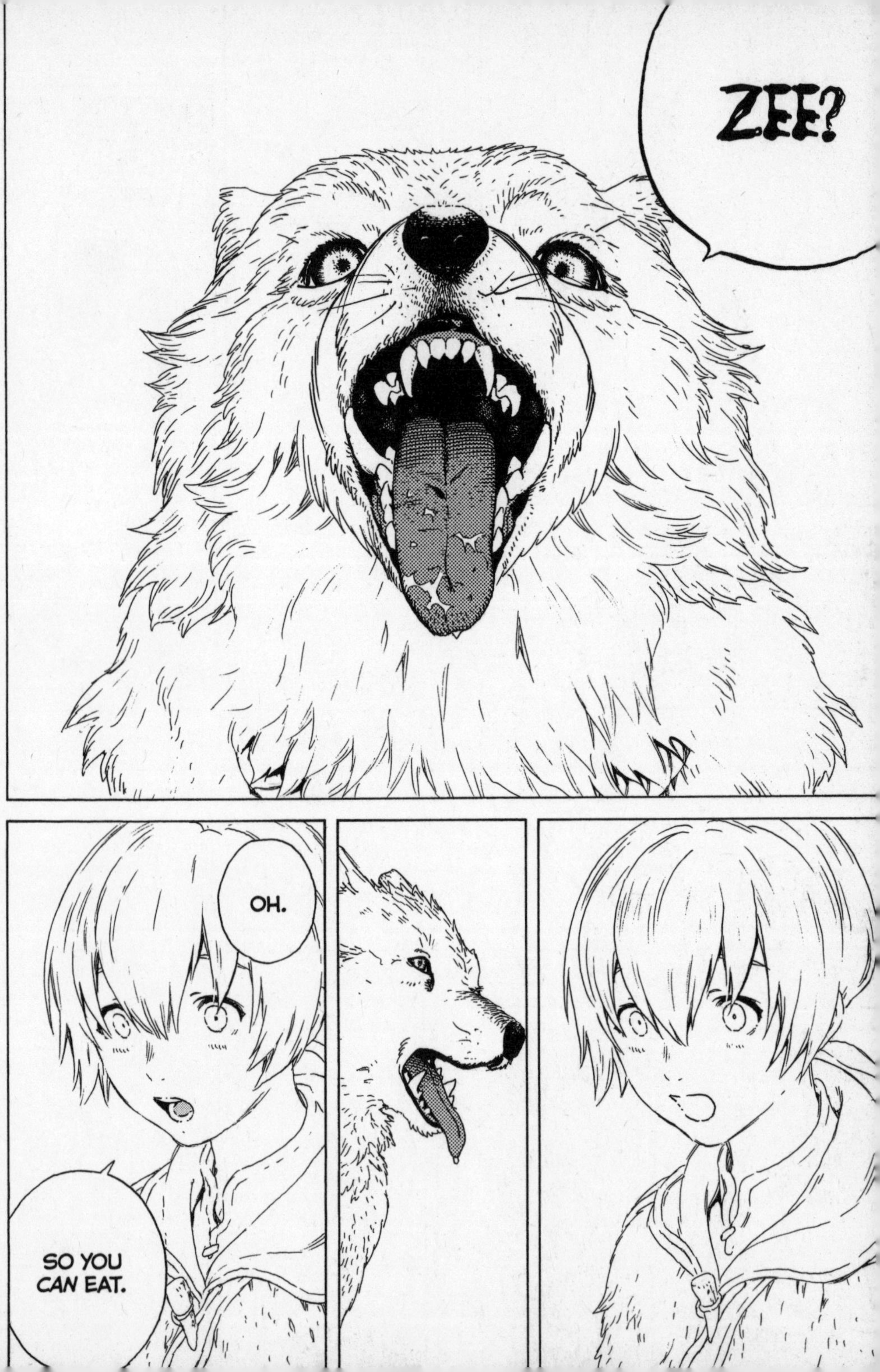
ZEE?
OH.
SO YOU CAN EAT.

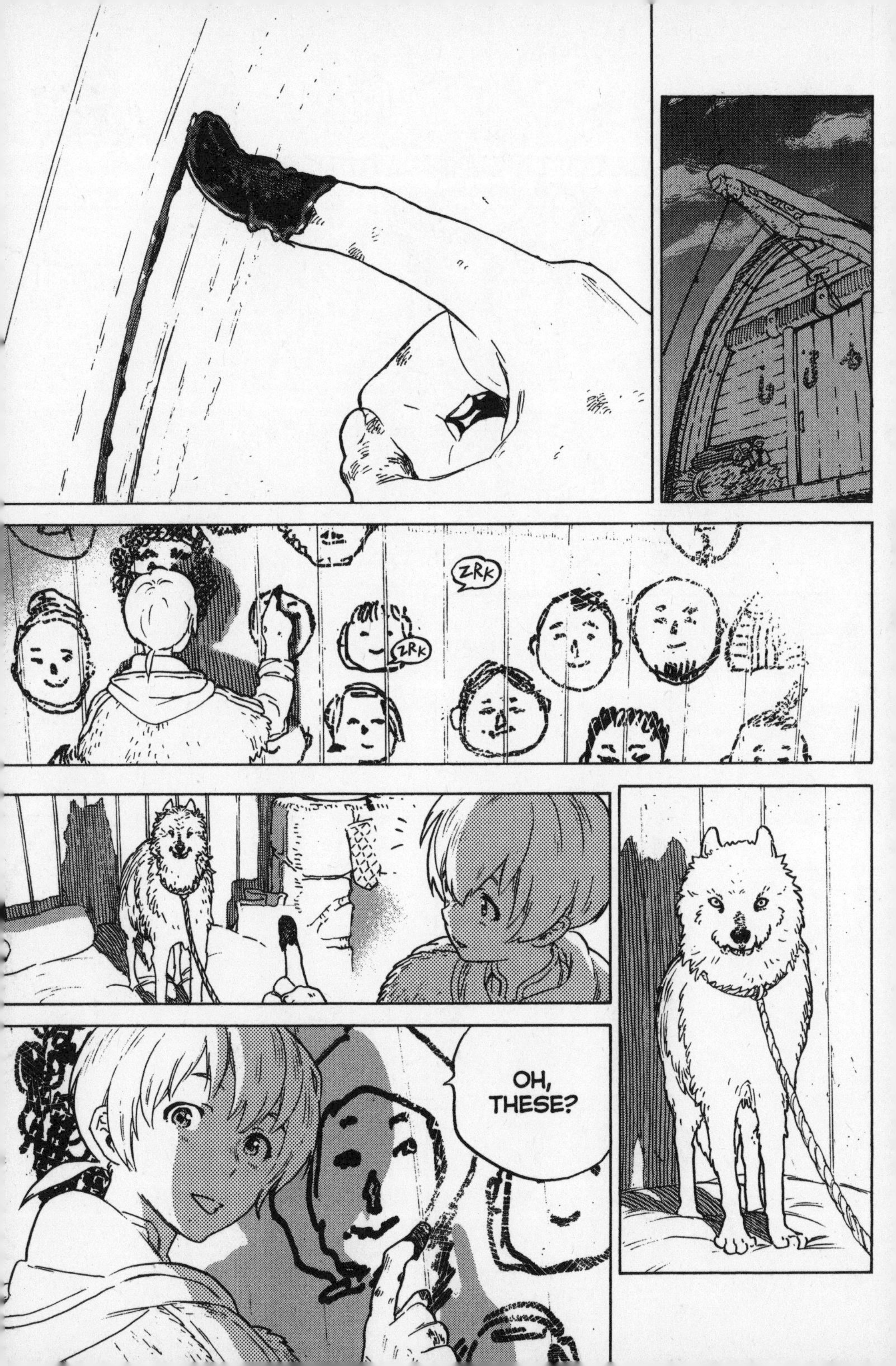
ZRK
ZRK
OH, THESE?

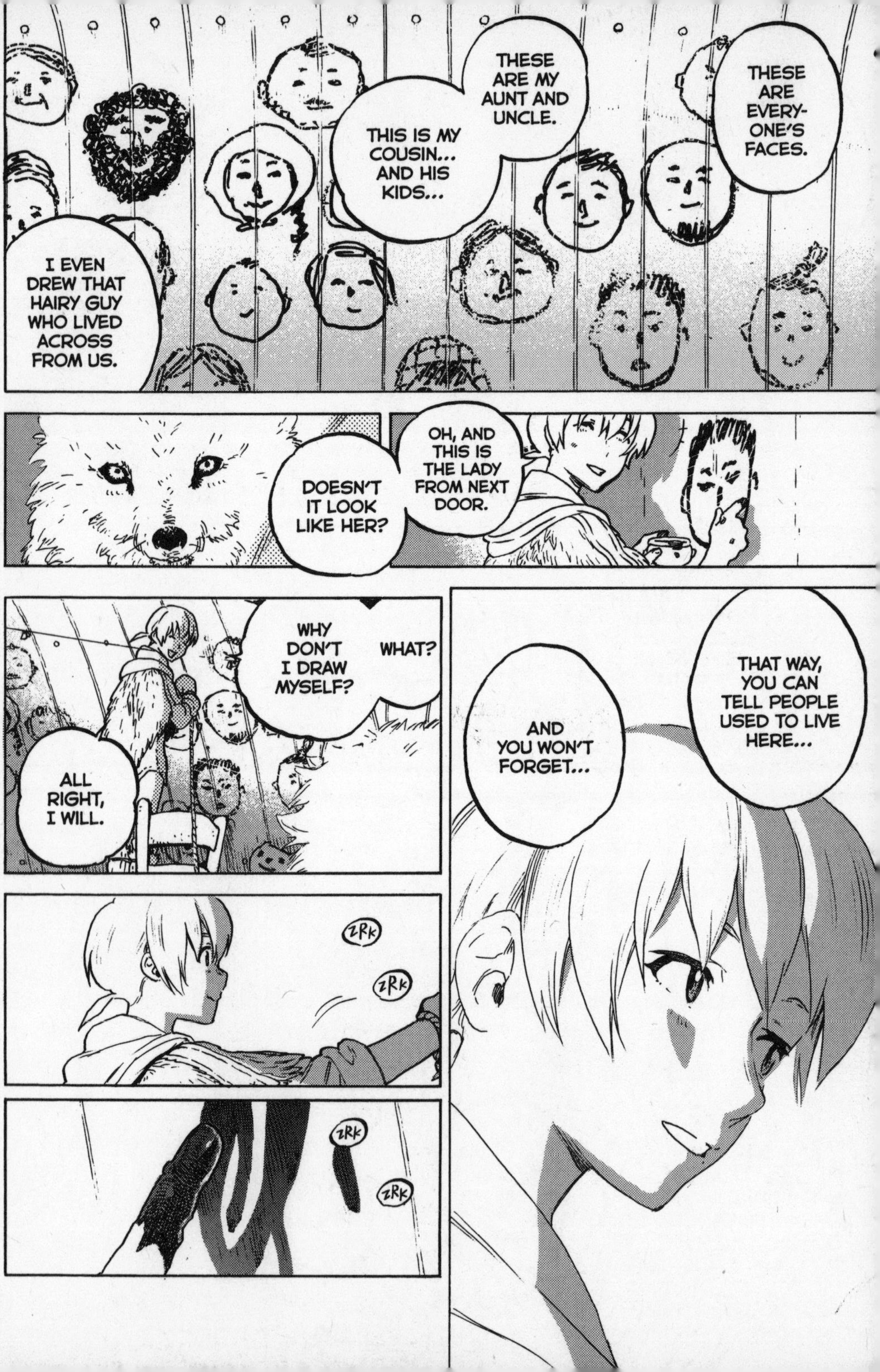
THESE ARE EVERYONE'S FACES.
THESE ARE MY AUNT AND UNCLE.
THIS IS MY COUSIN... AND HIS KIDS...
I EVEN DREW THAT HAIRY GUY WHO LIVED ACROSS FROM US.
OH, AND THIS IS THE LADY FROM NEXT DOOR.
DOESN'T IT LOOK LIKE HER?
THAT WAY, YOU CAN TELL PEOPLE USED TO LIVE HERE...
AND YOU WON'T FORGET...
WHAT?
WHY DON'T I DRAW MYSELF?
ALL RIGHT, I WILL.
ZRK
ZRK
ZRK
ZRK

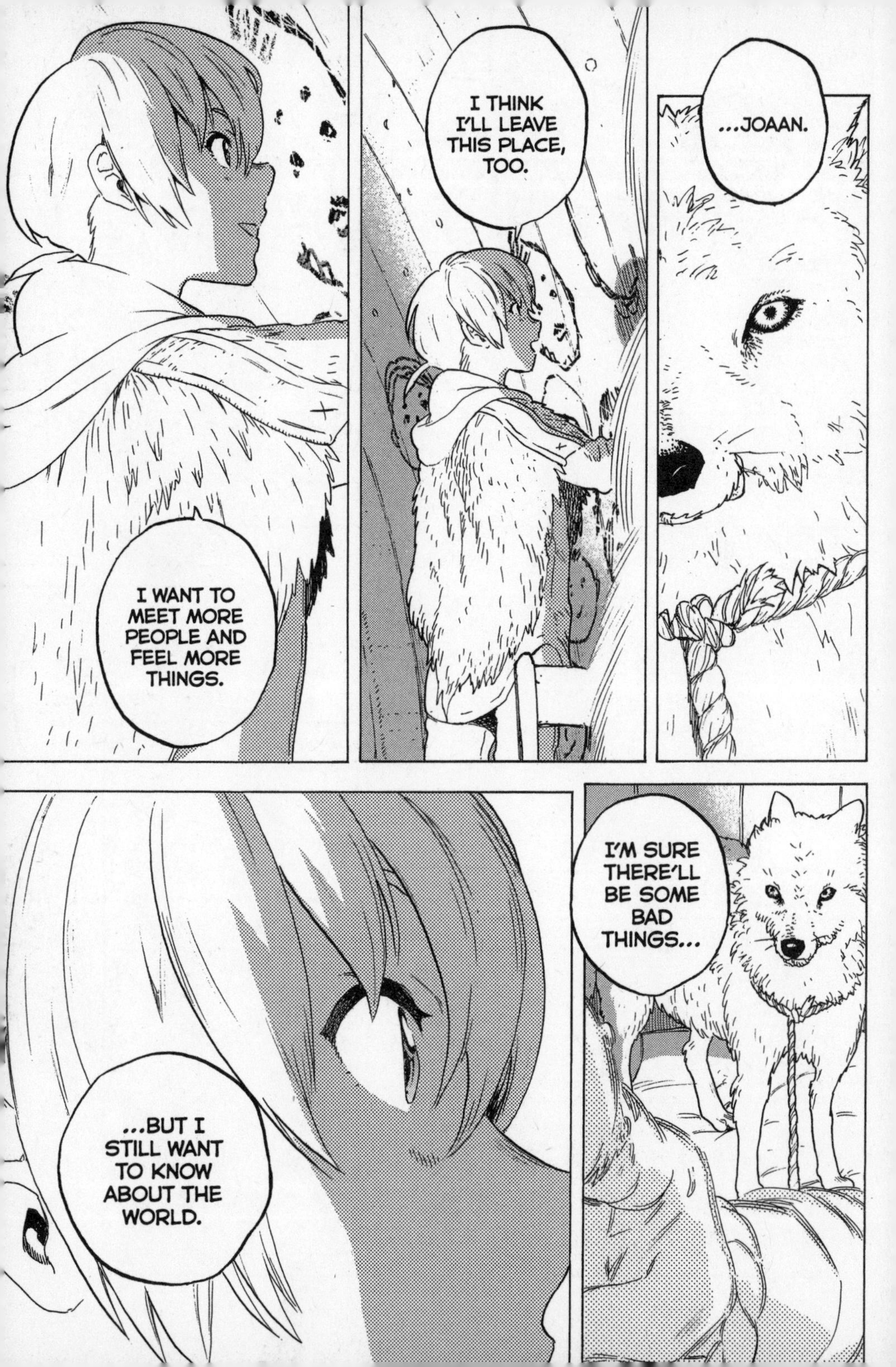
...JOAAN.
I THINK I'LL LEAVE THIS PLACE, TOO.
I WANT TO MEET MORE PEOPLE AND FEEL MORE THINGS.
I'M SURE THERE'LL BE SOME BAD THINGS...
...BUT I STILL WANT TO KNOW ABOUT THE WORLD.

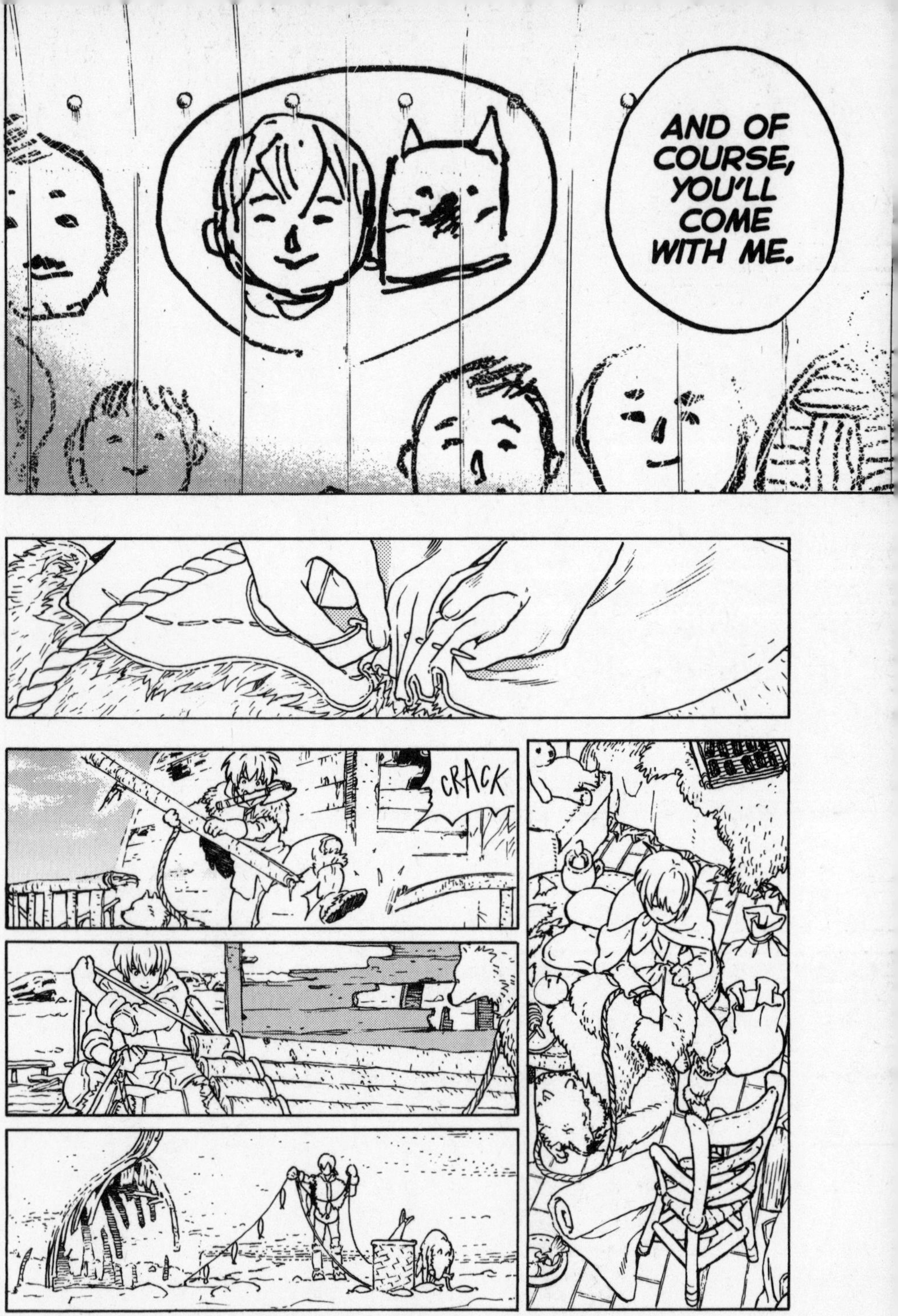
AND OF COURSE, YOU'LL COME WITH ME.
CRACK

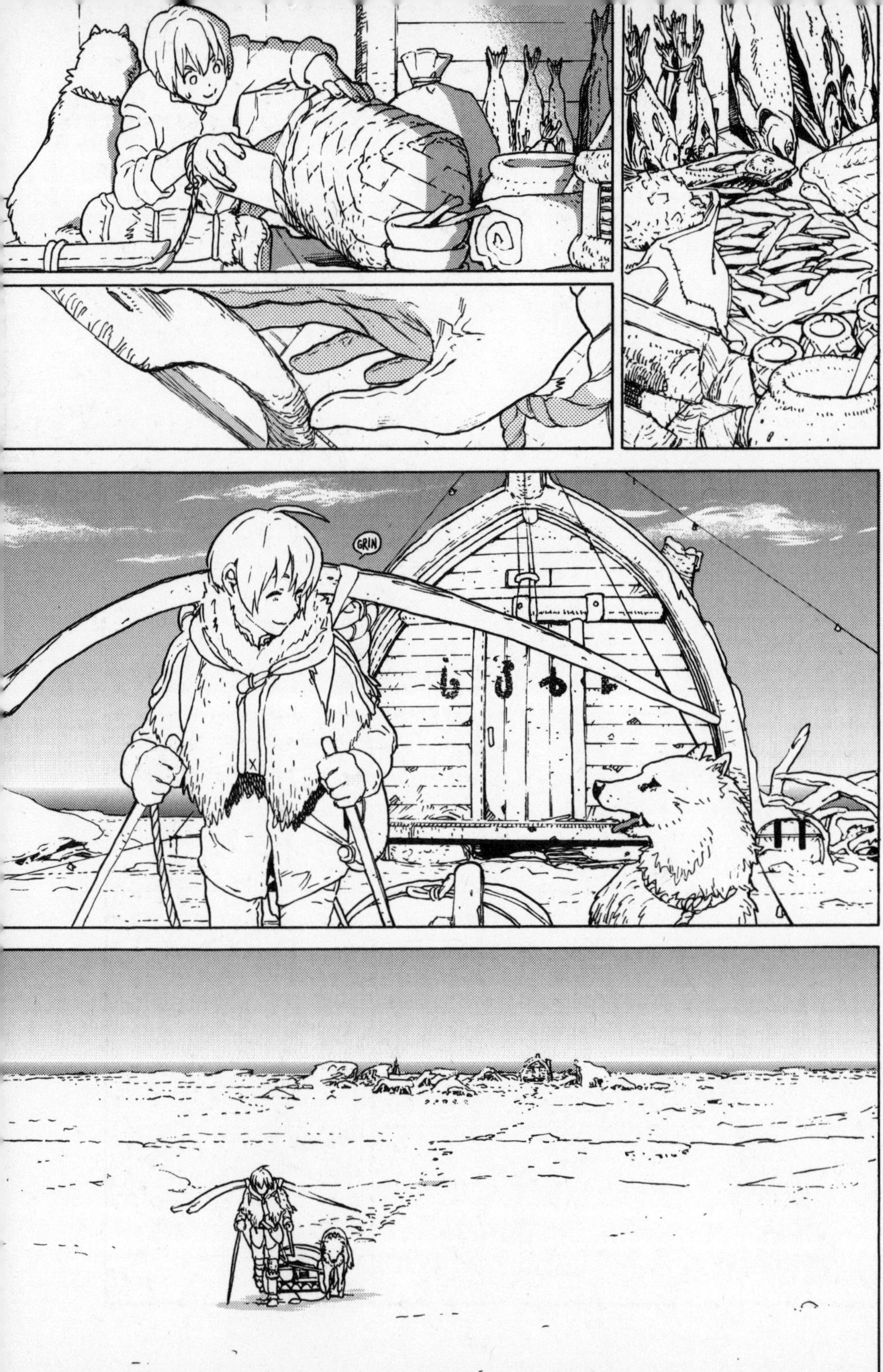
GRIN

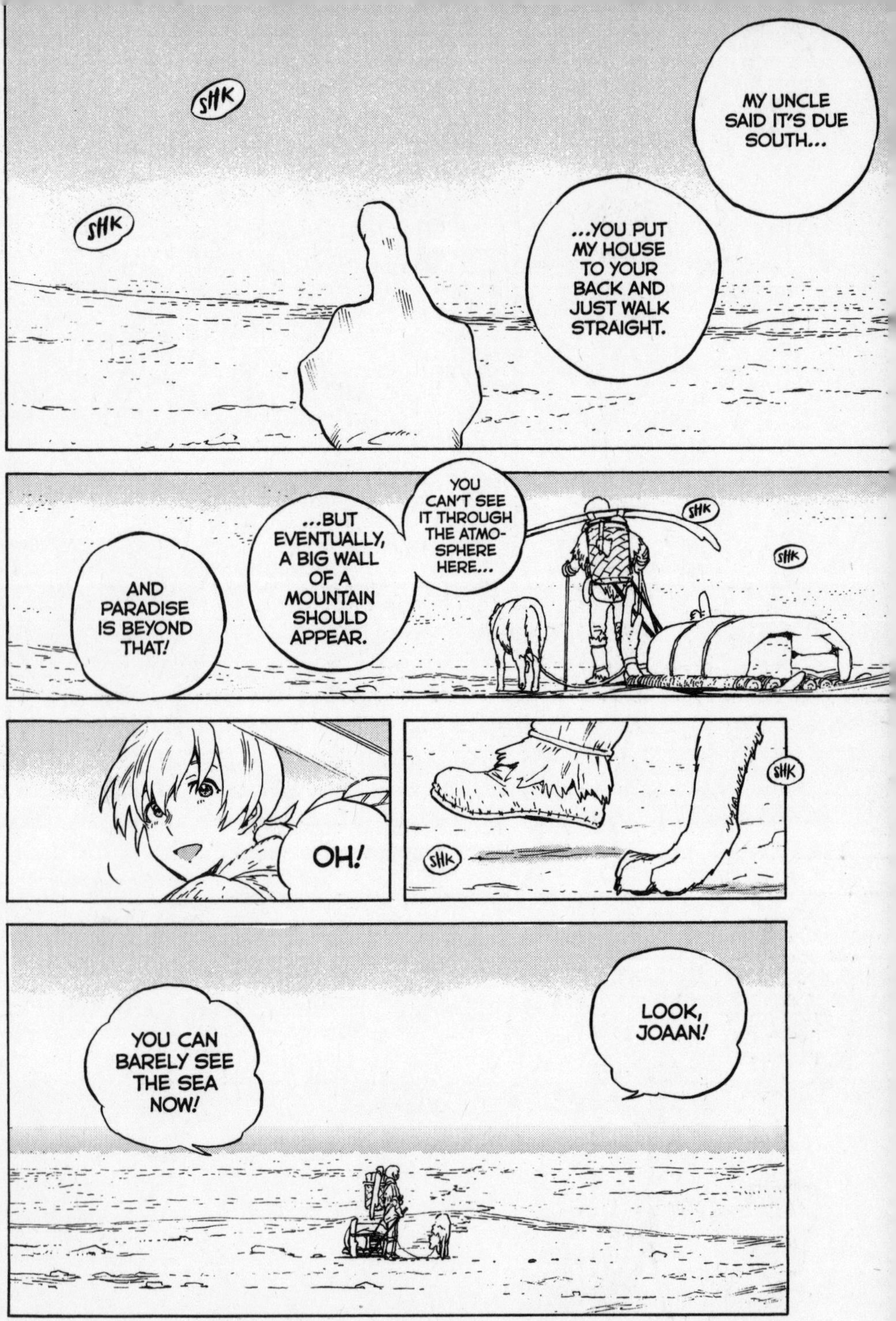
SHK
SHK
MY UNCLE SAID IT'S DUE SOUTH...
...YOU PUT MY HOUSE TO YOUR BACK AND JUST WALK STRAIGHT.
SHK
SHK
YOU CAN'T SEE IT THROUGH THE ATMOSPHERE HERE...
...BUT EVENTUALLY, A BIG WALL OF A MOUNTAIN SHOULD APPEAR.
AND PARADISE IS BEYOND THAT!
SHK
SHK
OH!
LOOK, JOAAN!
YOU CAN BARELY SEE THE SEA NOW!

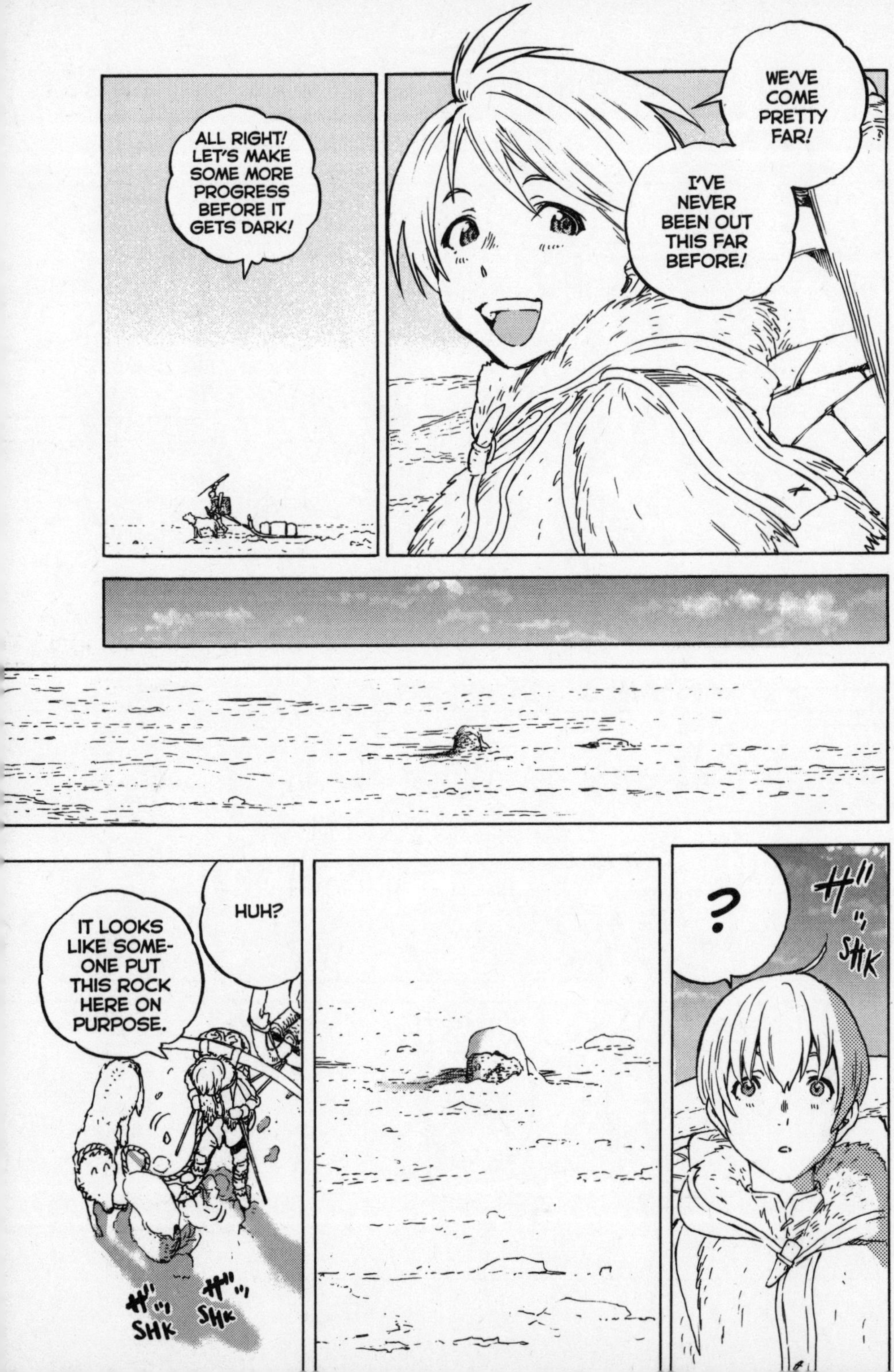
WE'VE COME PRETTY FAR!
I'VE NEVER BEEN OUT THIS FAR BEFORE!
ALL RIGHT! LET'S MAKE SOME MORE PROGRESS BEFORE IT GETS DARK!
?
ザッ SHK
HUH?
IT LOOKS LIKE SOME-ONE PUT THIS ROCK HERE ON PURPOSE.
ザッ SHK
ザッ SHK

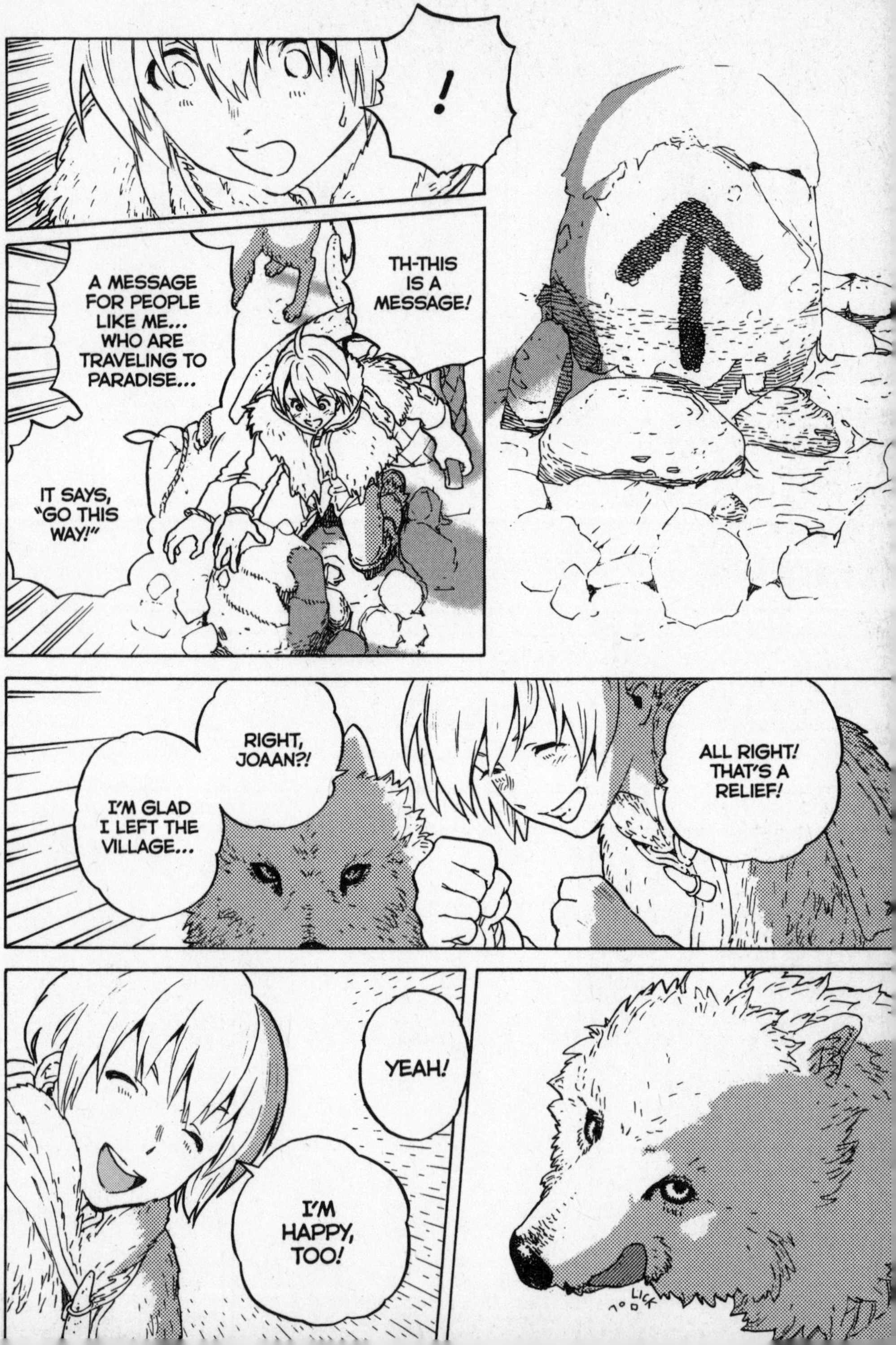
!
TH-THIS IS A MESSAGE!
A MESSAGE FOR PEOPLE LIKE ME... WHO ARE TRAVELING TO PARADISE...
IT SAYS, "GO THIS WAY!"
ALL RIGHT! THAT'S A RELIEF!
RIGHT, JOAAN?!
I'M GLAD I LEFT THE VILLAGE...
LICK
YEAH!
I'M HAPPY, TOO!

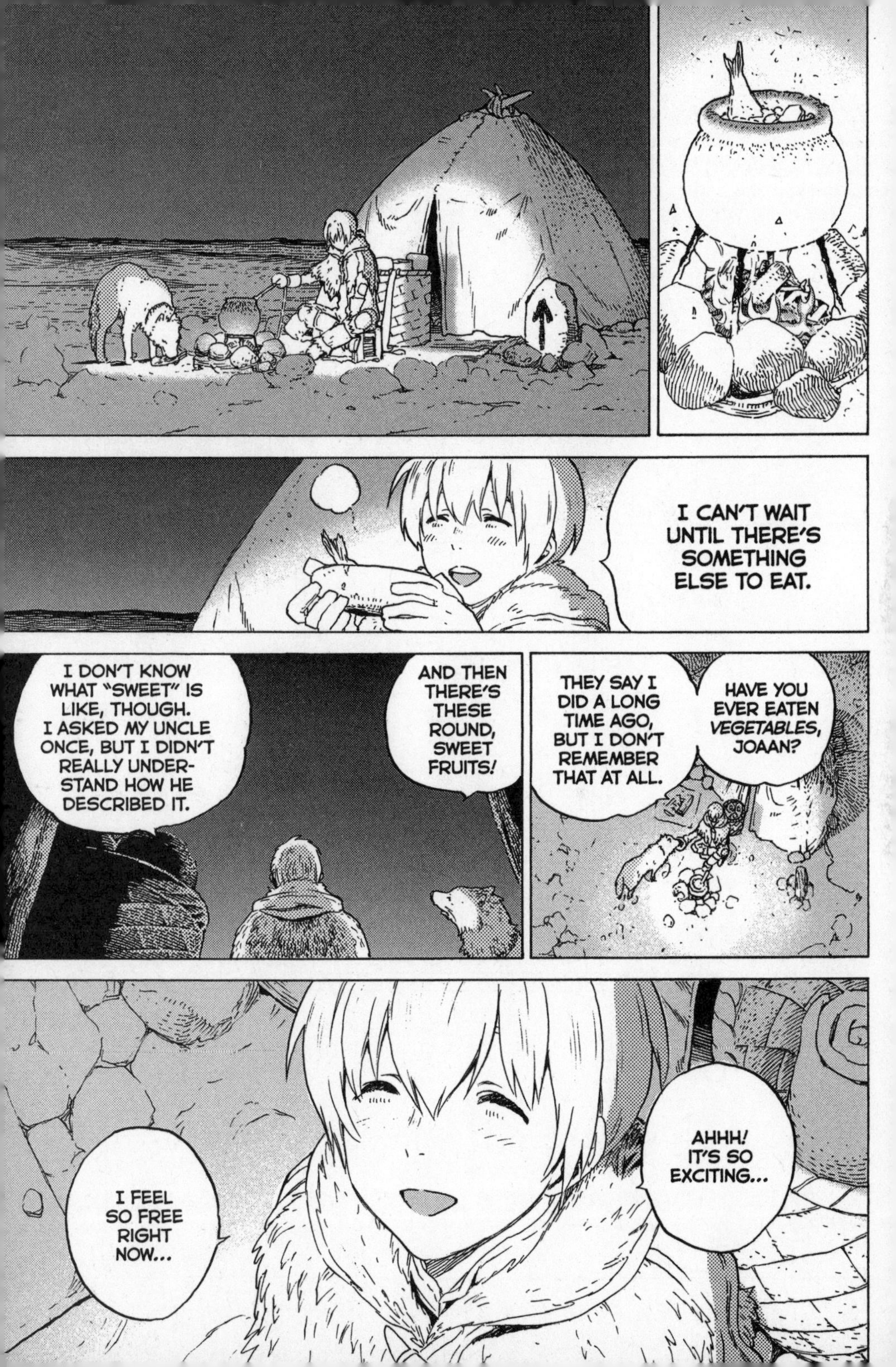
I CAN'T WAIT UNTIL THERE'S SOMETHING ELSE TO EAT.
HAVE YOU EVER EATEN *VEGETABLES*, JOAAN?
THEY SAY I DID A LONG TIME AGO, BUT I DON'T REMEMBER THAT AT ALL.
AND THEN THERE'S THESE ROUND, SWEET FRUITS!
I DON'T KNOW WHAT "SWEET" IS LIKE, THOUGH. I ASKED MY UNCLE ONCE, BUT I DIDN'T REALLY UNDER-STAND HOW HE DESCRIBED IT.
AHHH! IT'S SO EXCITING...
I FEEL SO FREE RIGHT NOW...

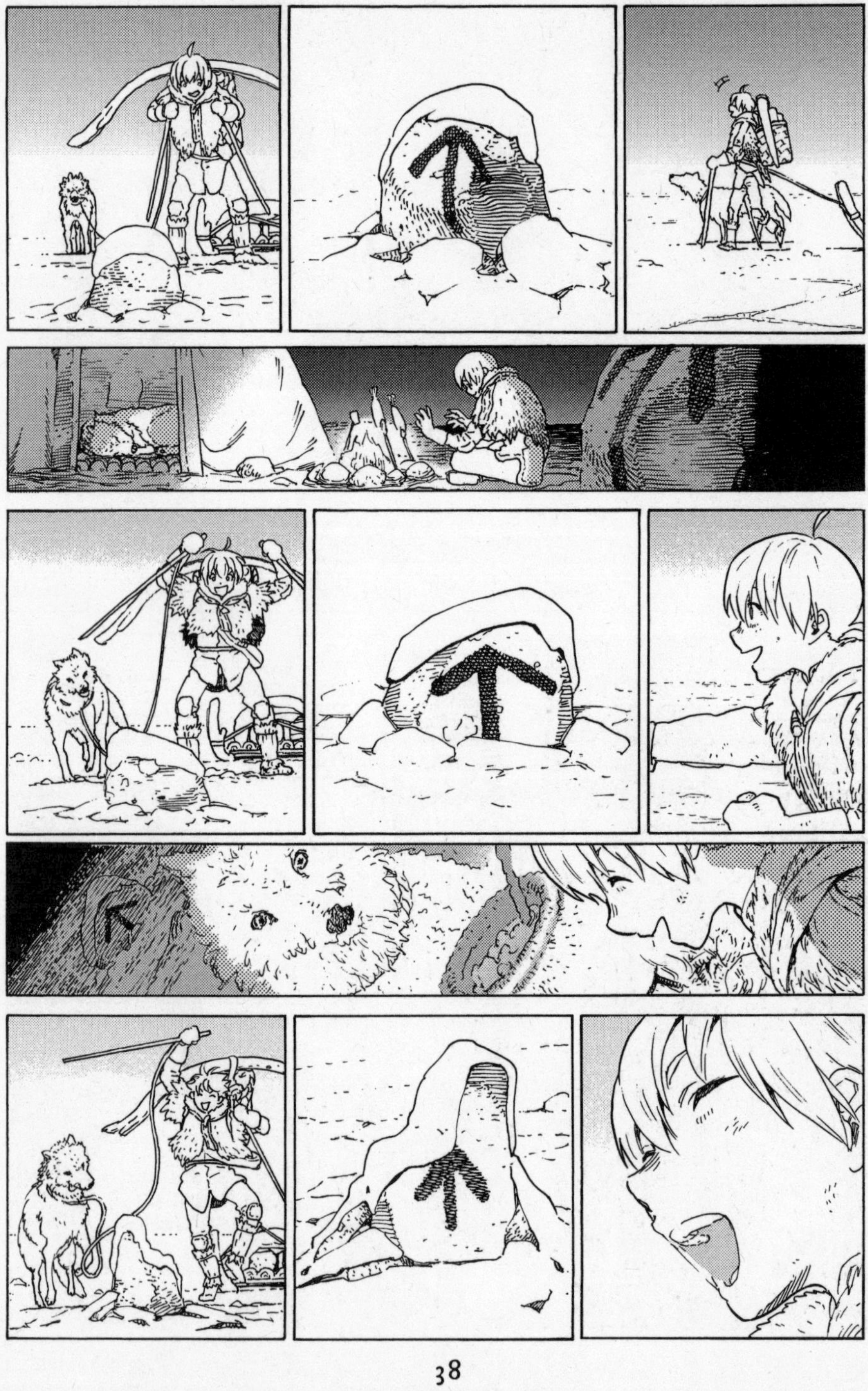

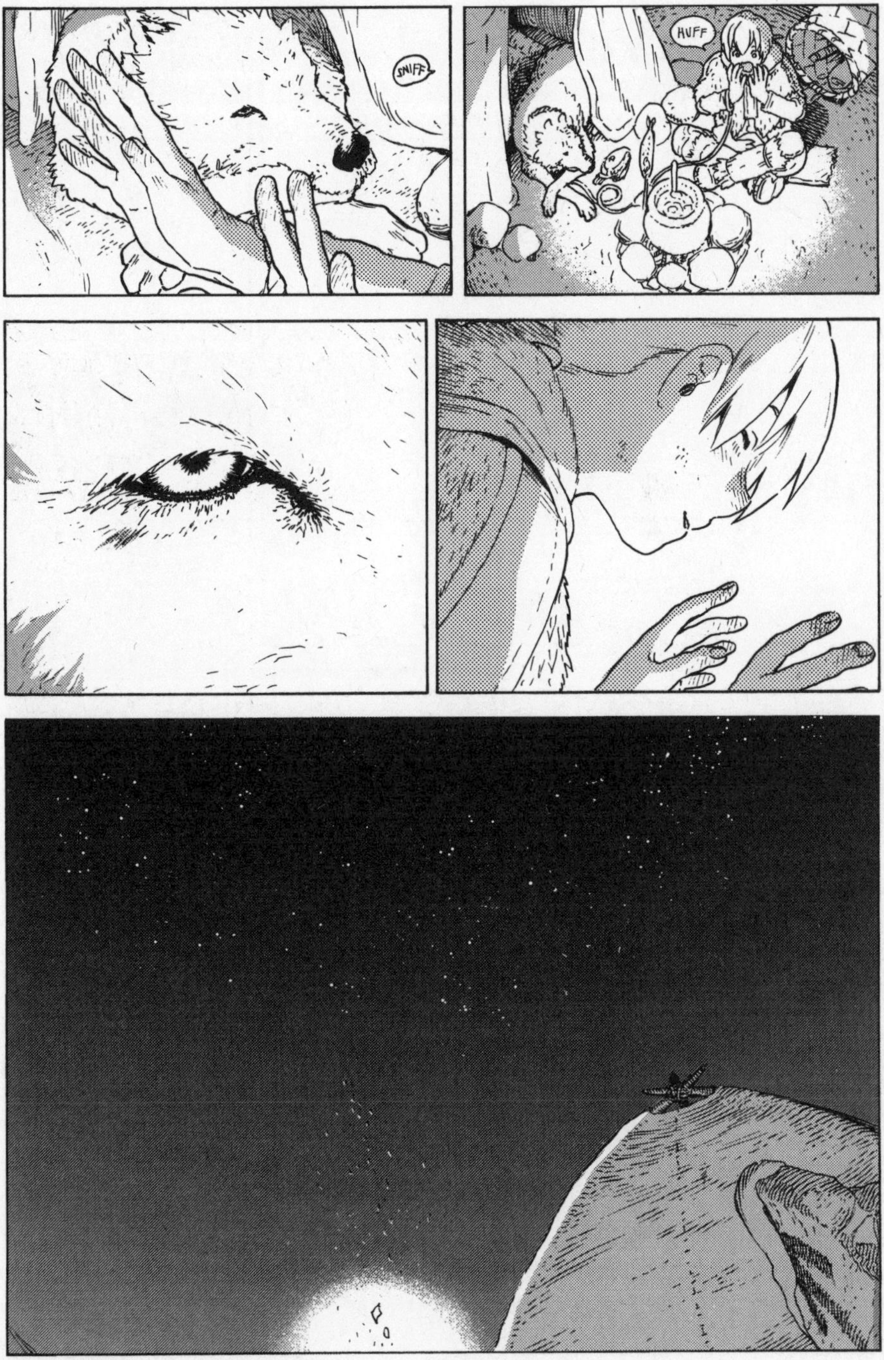
HUFF
SNIFF

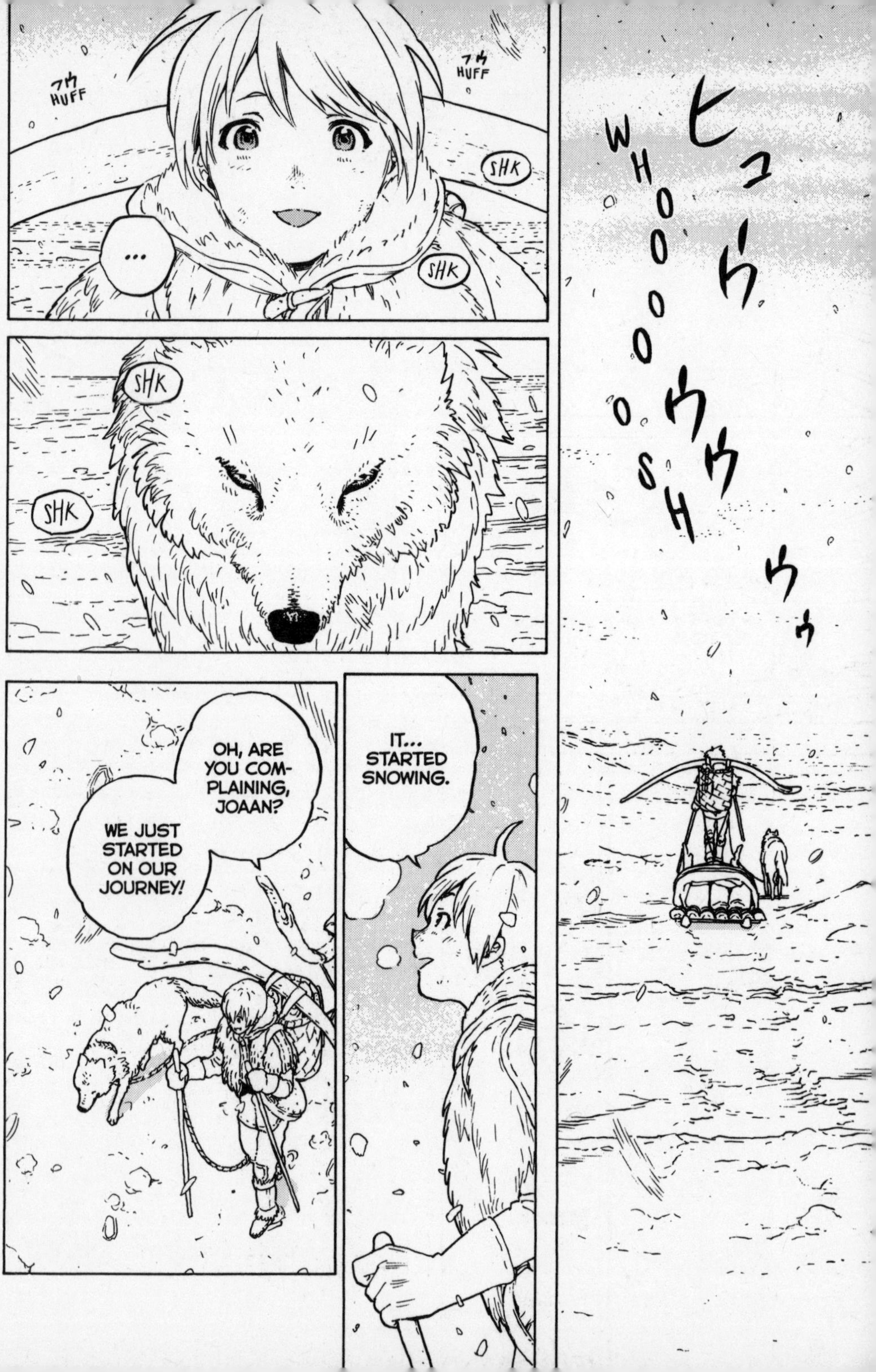

WHOOOOOOSH
フウ HUFF
フウ HUFF
SHK
SHK
...
SHK
SHK
IT... STARTED SNOWING.
OH, ARE YOU COMPLAINING, JOAAN?
WE JUST STARTED ON OUR JOURNEY!

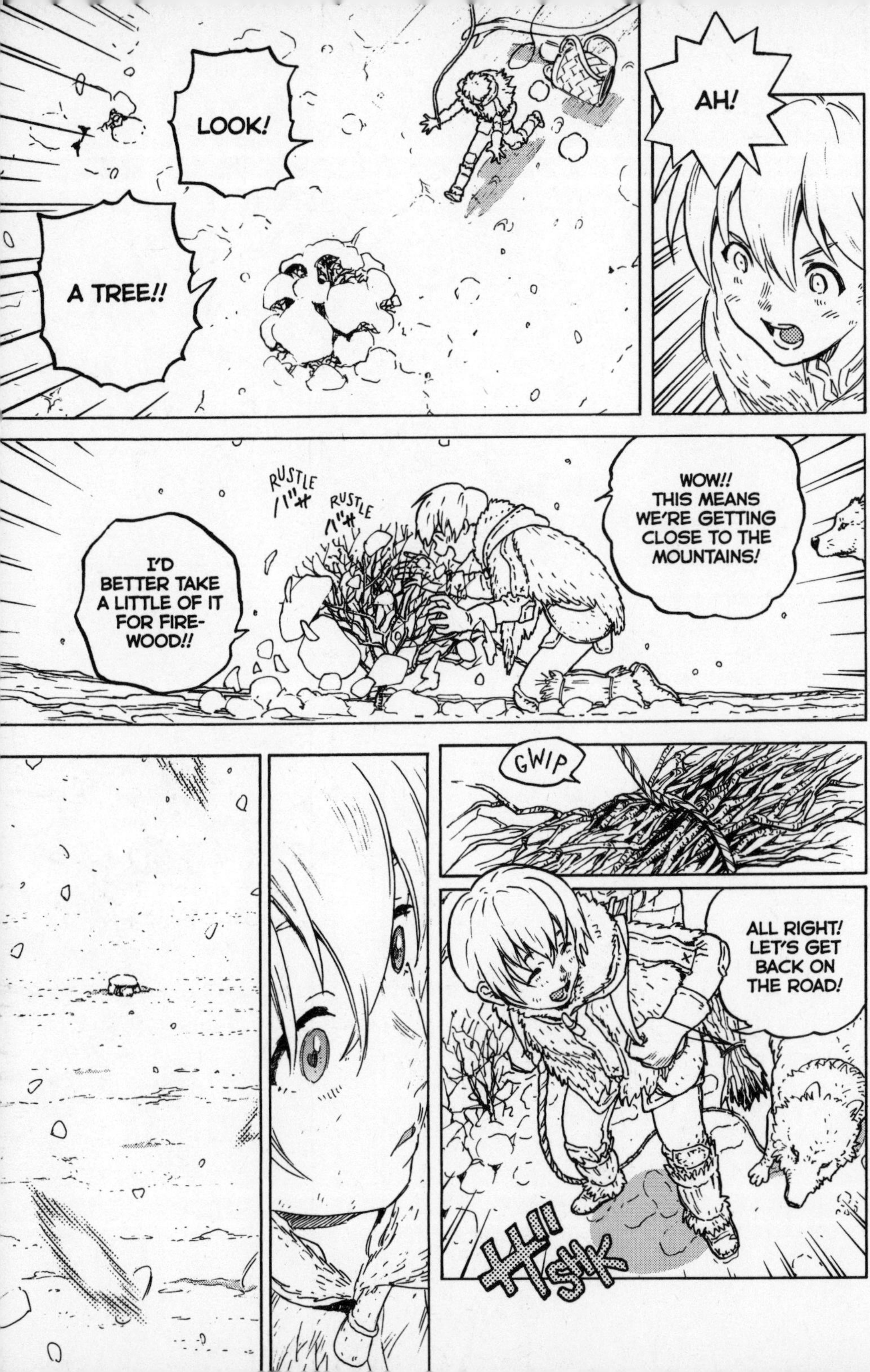
AH!
LOOK!
A TREE!!
WOW!! THIS MEANS WE'RE GETTING CLOSE TO THE MOUNTAINS!
RUSTLE
RUSTLE
I'D BETTER TAKE A LITTLE OF IT FOR FIRE-WOOD!!
GWIP
ALL RIGHT! LET'S GET BACK ON THE ROAD!
HTSK

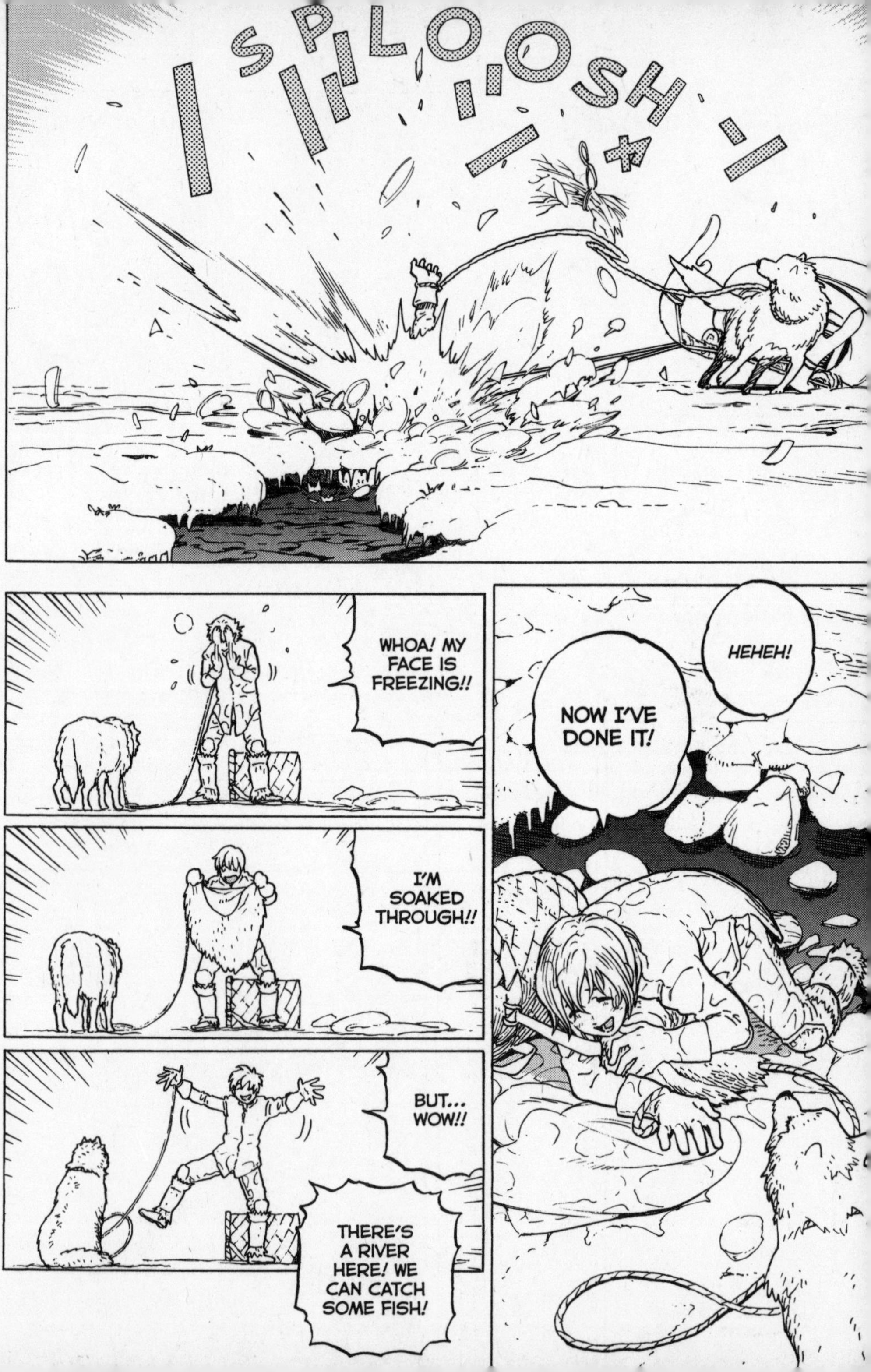
SPLOOSH
HEHEH!
NOW I'VE DONE IT!
WHOA! MY FACE IS FREEZING!!
I'M SOAKED THROUGH!!
BUT... WOW!!
THERE'S A RIVER HERE! WE CAN CATCH SOME FISH!

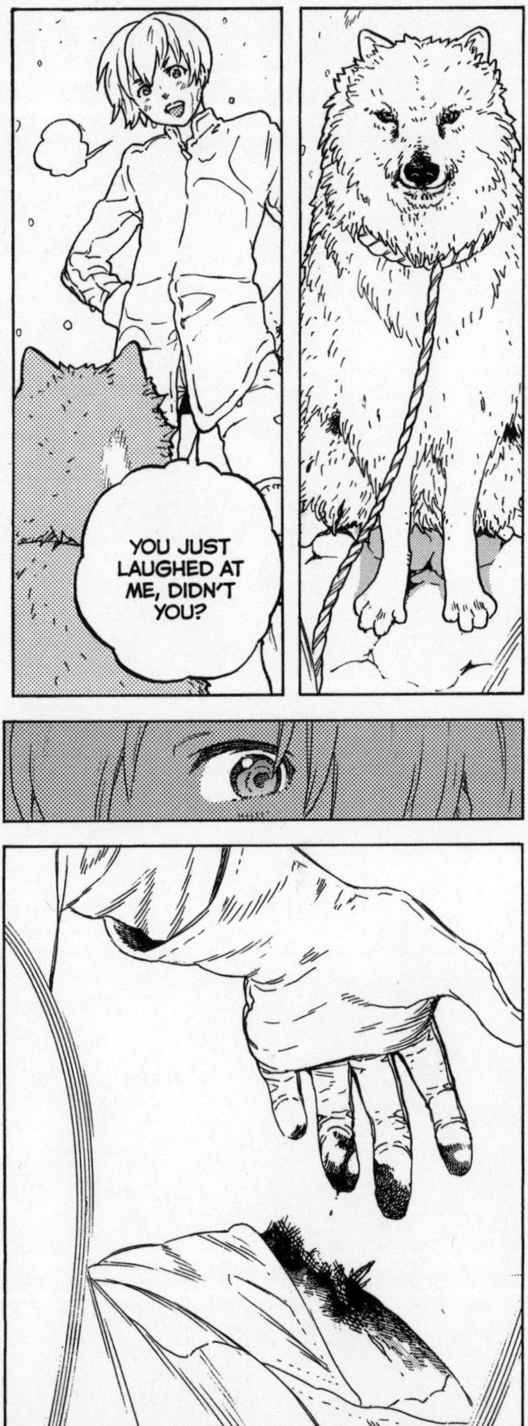
YOU JUST LAUGHED AT ME, DIDN'T YOU?

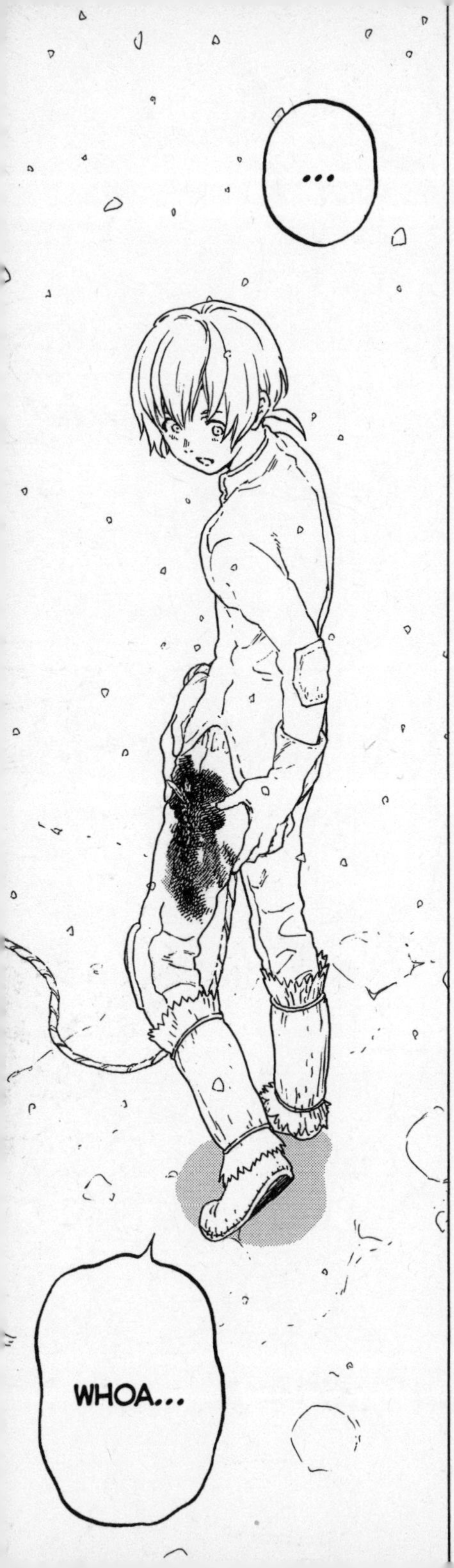
...
WHOA...

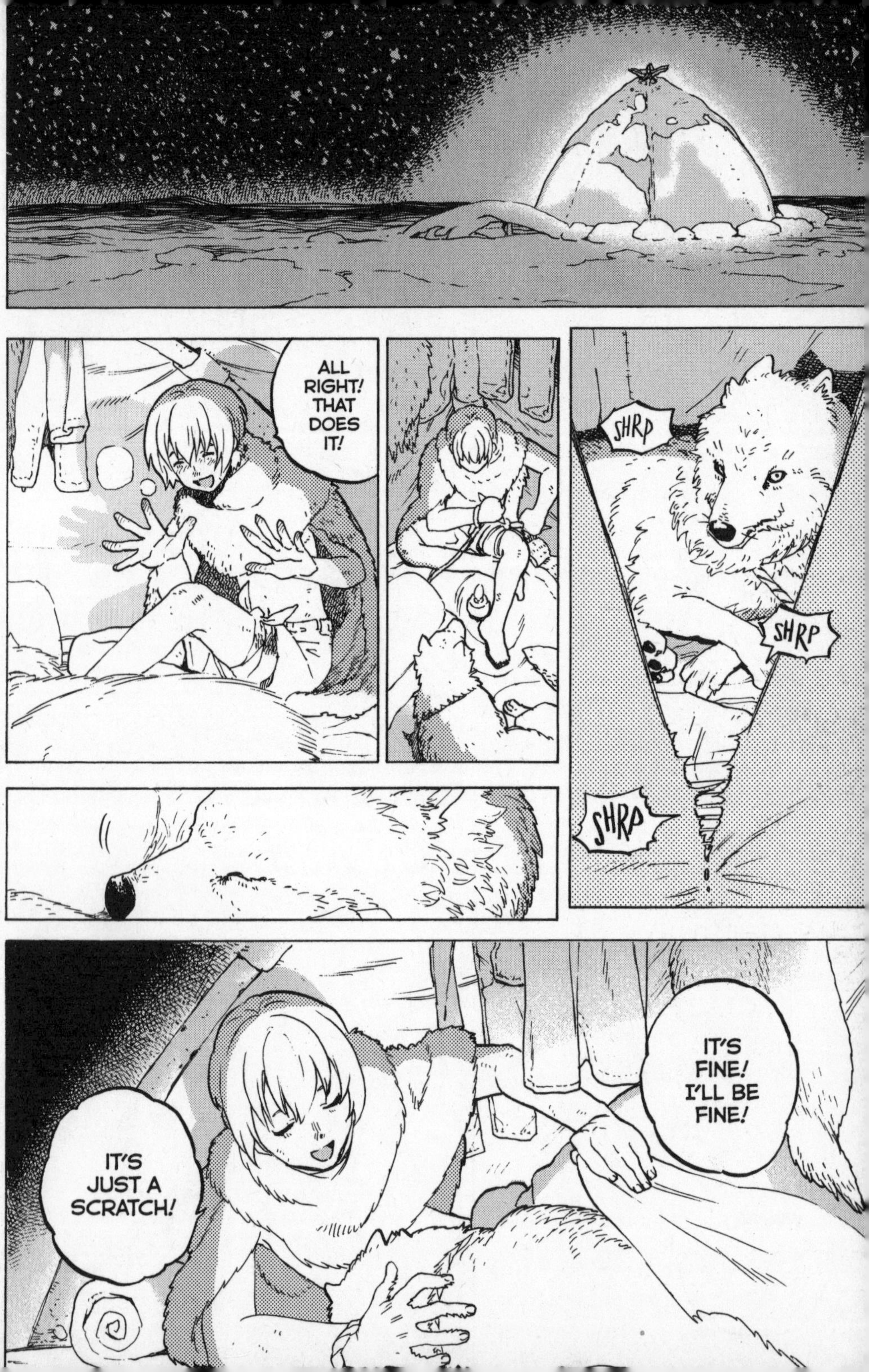
SHRP
SHRP
SHRP
ALL RIGHT! THAT DOES IT!
IT'S FINE! I'LL BE FINE!
IT'S JUST A SCRATCH!

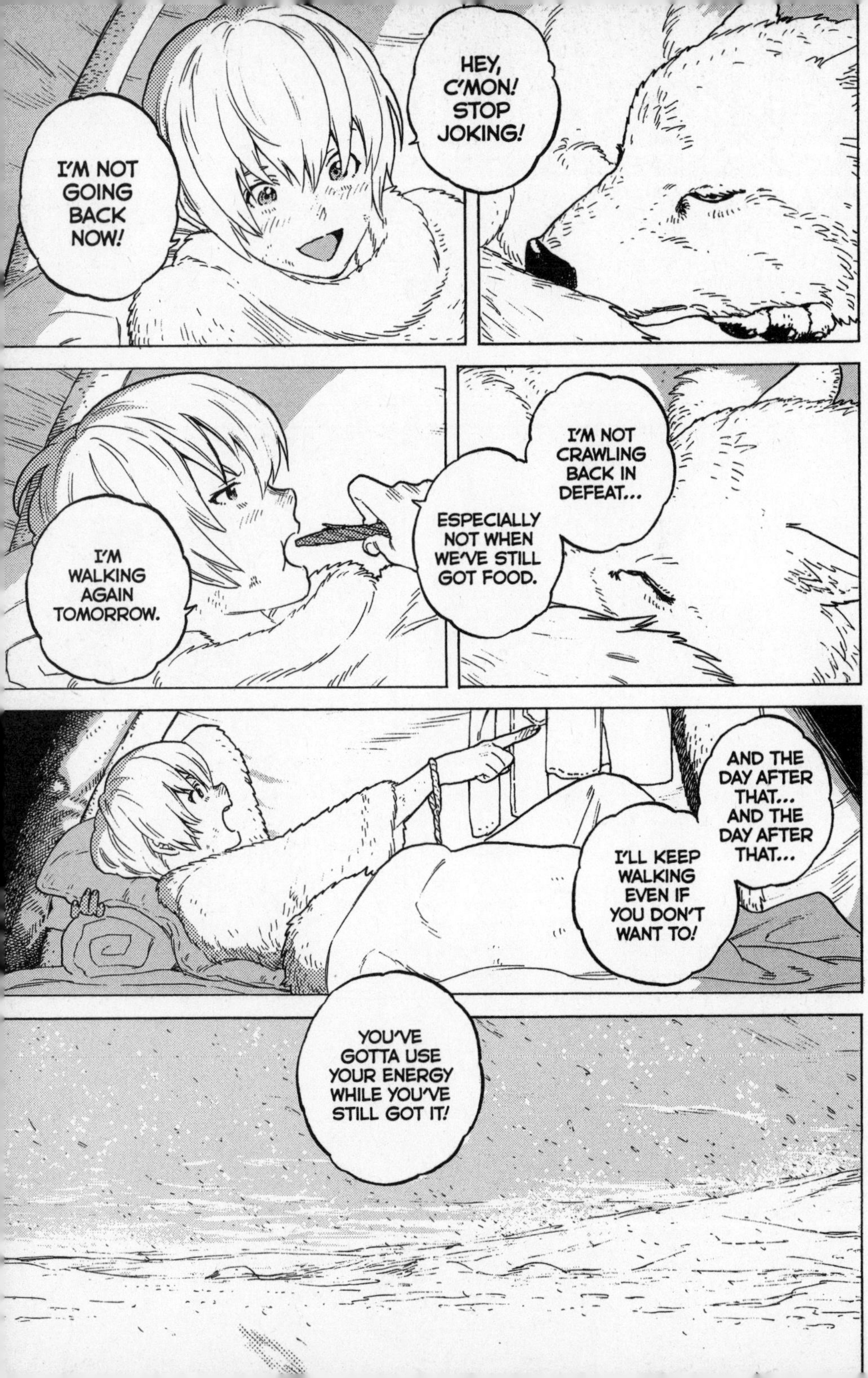
HEY, C'MON! STOP JOKING!
I'M NOT GOING BACK NOW!
I'M NOT CRAWLING BACK IN DEFEAT...
ESPECIALLY NOT WHEN WE'VE STILL GOT FOOD.
I'M WALKING AGAIN TOMORROW.
AND THE DAY AFTER THAT... AND THE DAY AFTER THAT...
I'LL KEEP WALKING EVEN IF YOU DON'T WANT TO!
YOU'VE GOTTA USE YOUR ENERGY WHILE YOU'VE STILL GOT IT!

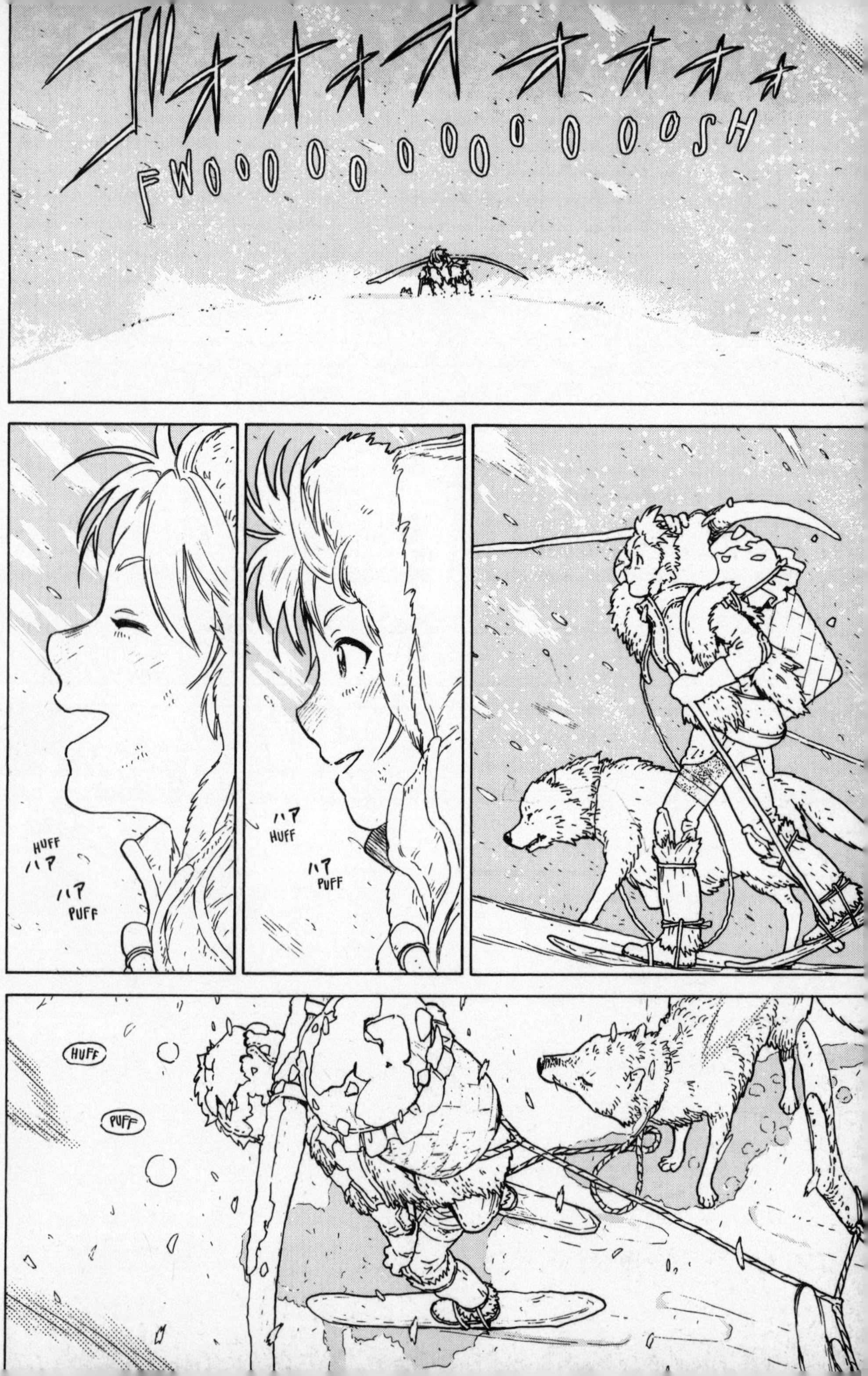

ゴォォォォオォォォォ
FWOOOOOOOOOOOSH
ハア
HUFF
ハア
PUFF
HUFF
ハア
ハア
PUFF
HUFF
PUFF

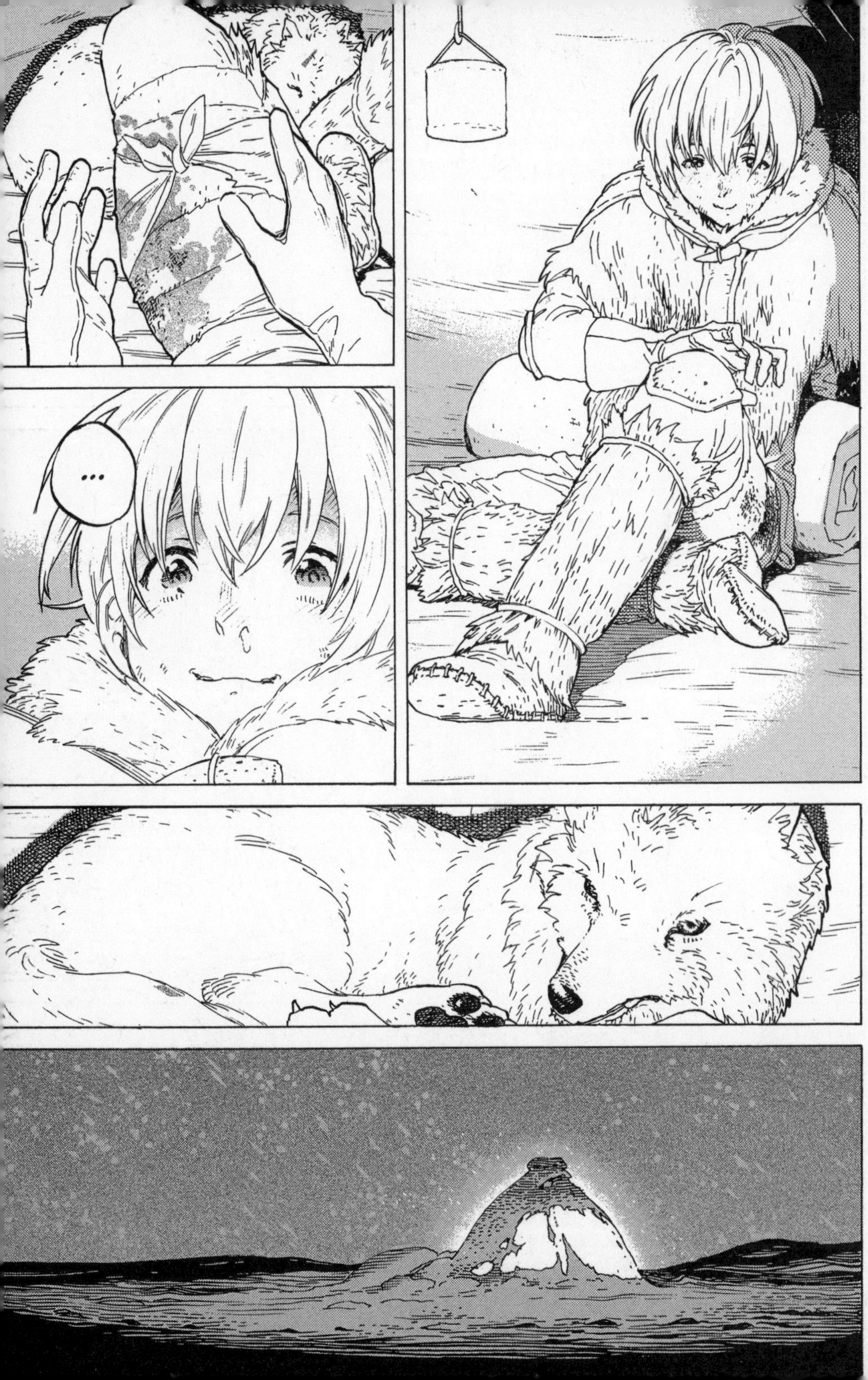
...

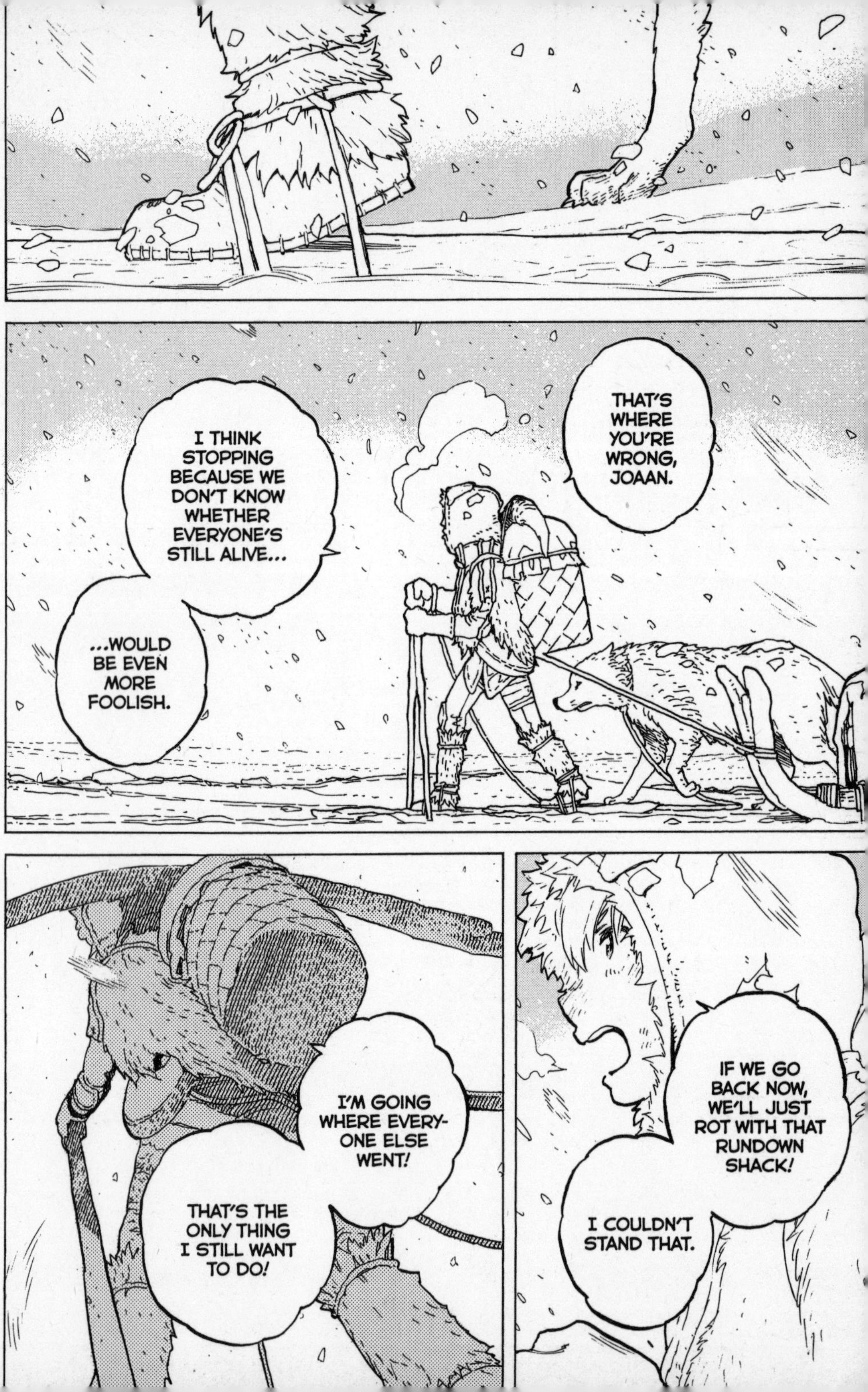
THAT'S WHERE YOU'RE WRONG, JOAAN.
I THINK STOPPING BECAUSE WE DON'T KNOW WHETHER EVERYONE'S STILL ALIVE...
...WOULD BE EVEN MORE FOOLISH.
IF WE GO BACK NOW, WE'LL JUST ROT WITH THAT RUNDOWN SHACK!
I COULDN'T STAND THAT.
I'M GOING WHERE EVERY-ONE ELSE WENT!
THAT'S THE ONLY THING I STILL WANT TO DO!

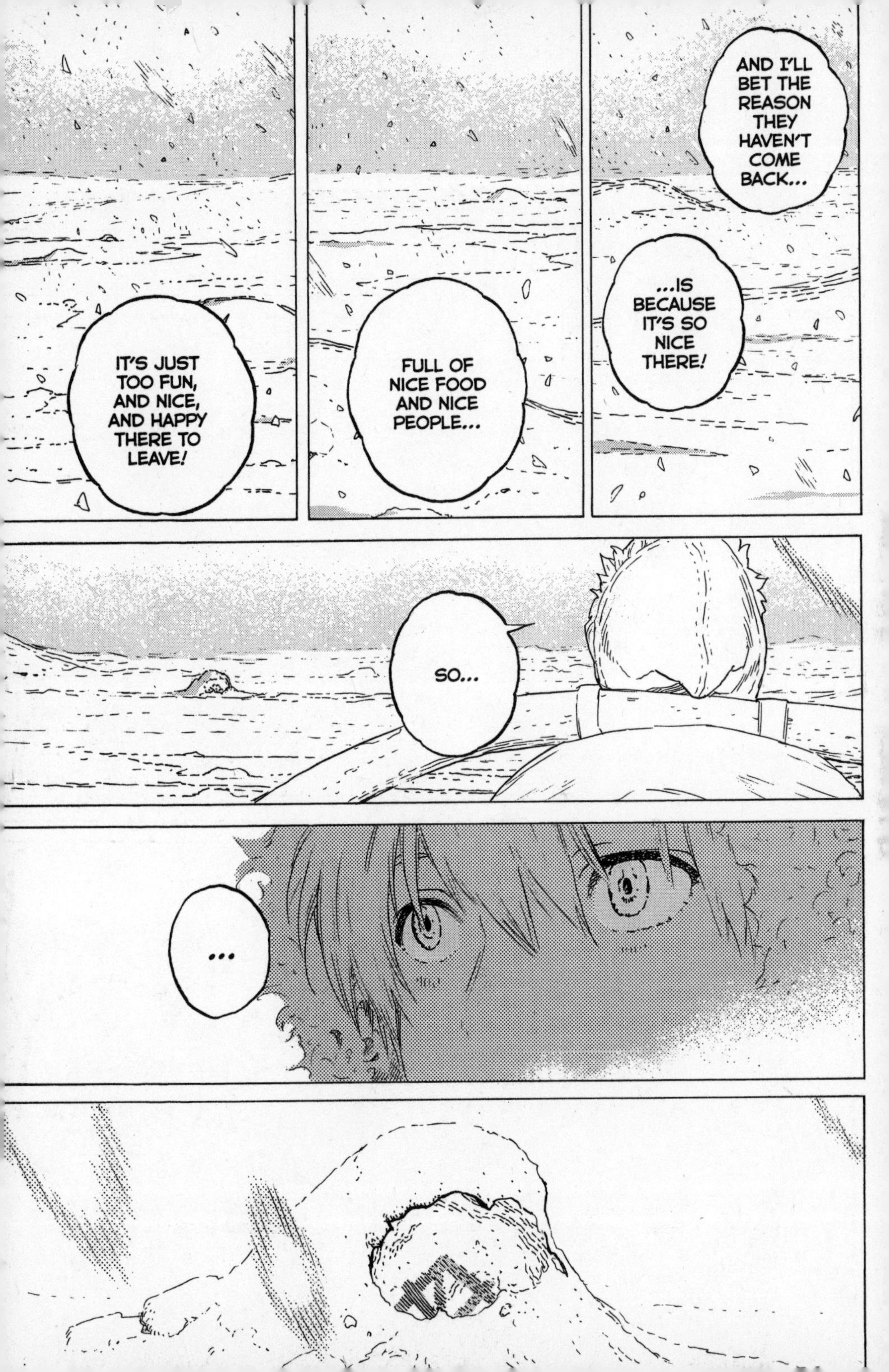
AND I'LL BET THE REASON THEY HAVEN'T COME BACK...
...IS BECAUSE IT'S SO NICE THERE!
FULL OF NICE FOOD AND NICE PEOPLE...
IT'S JUST TOO FUN, AND NICE, AND HAPPY THERE TO LEAVE!
SO...
...

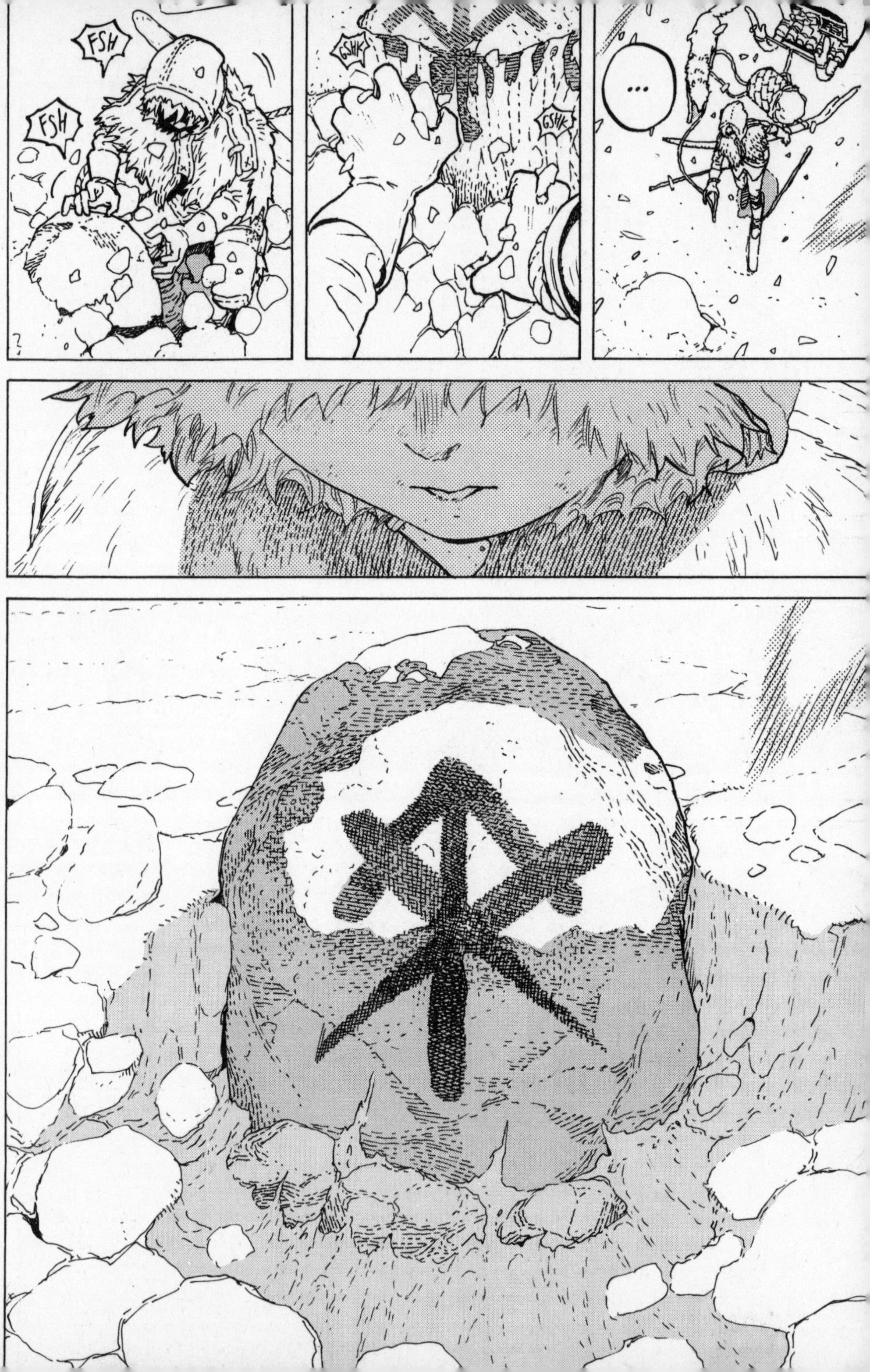
...
GSHK
GSHK
FSH
FSH

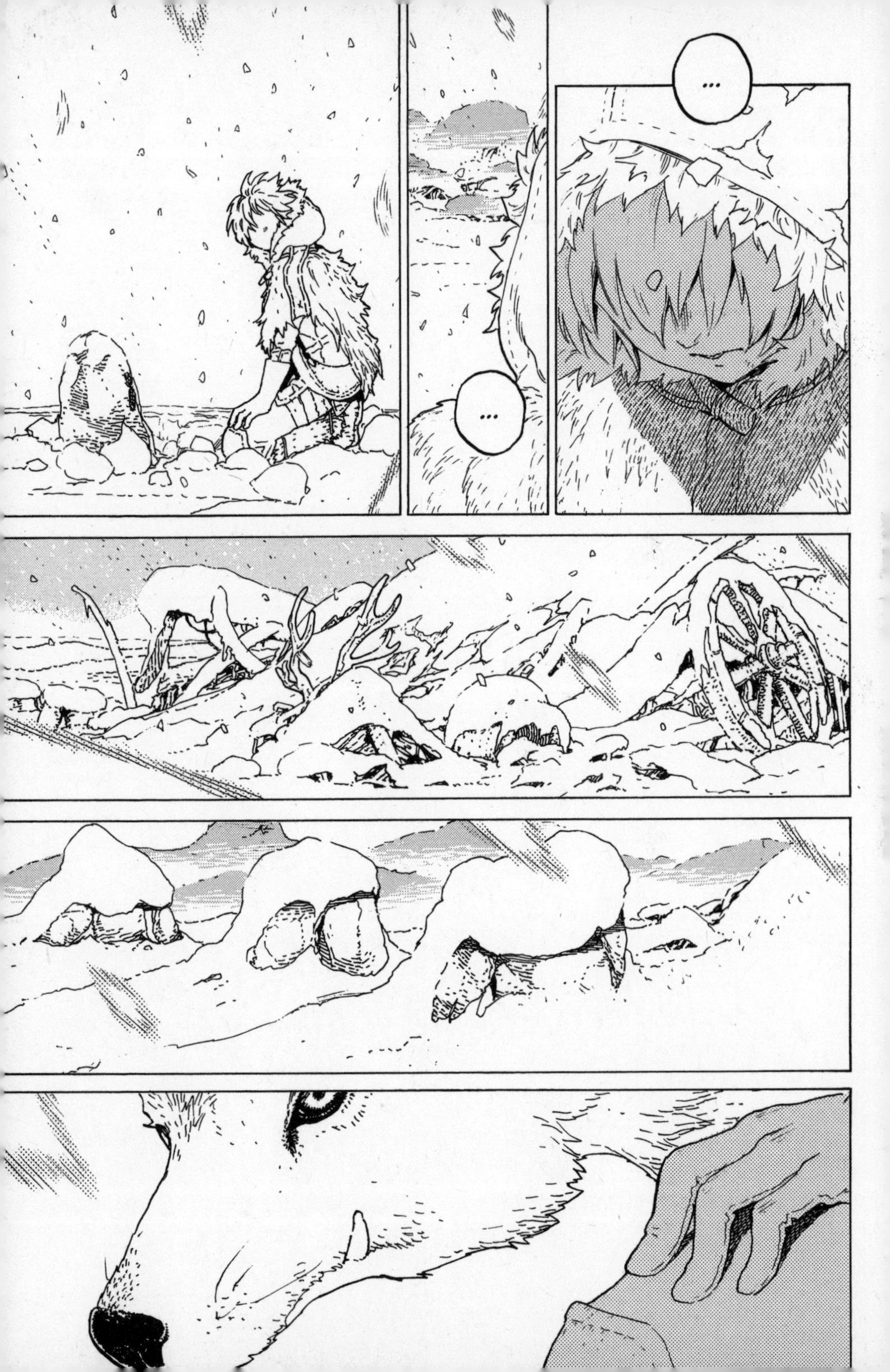
...
...

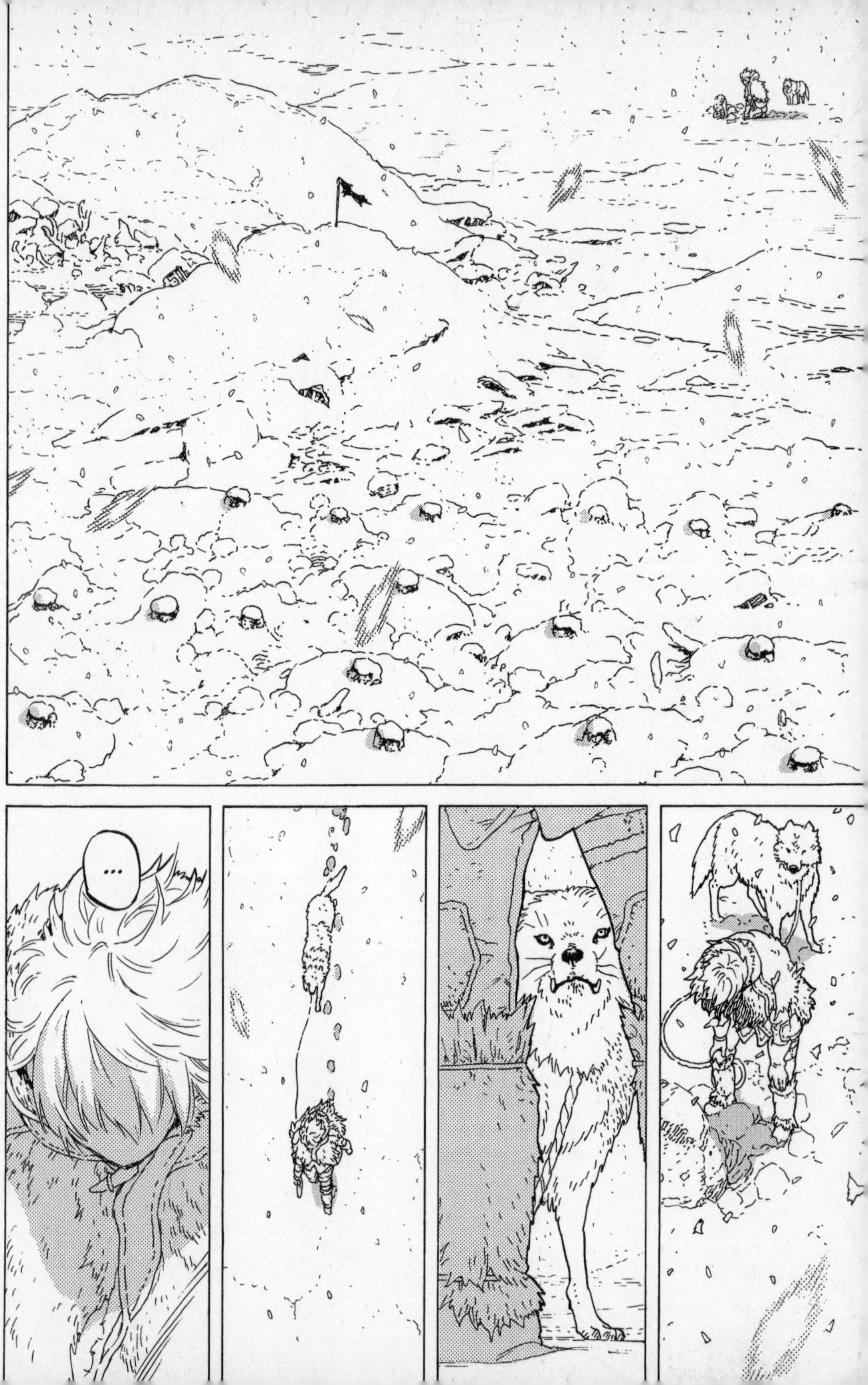
...

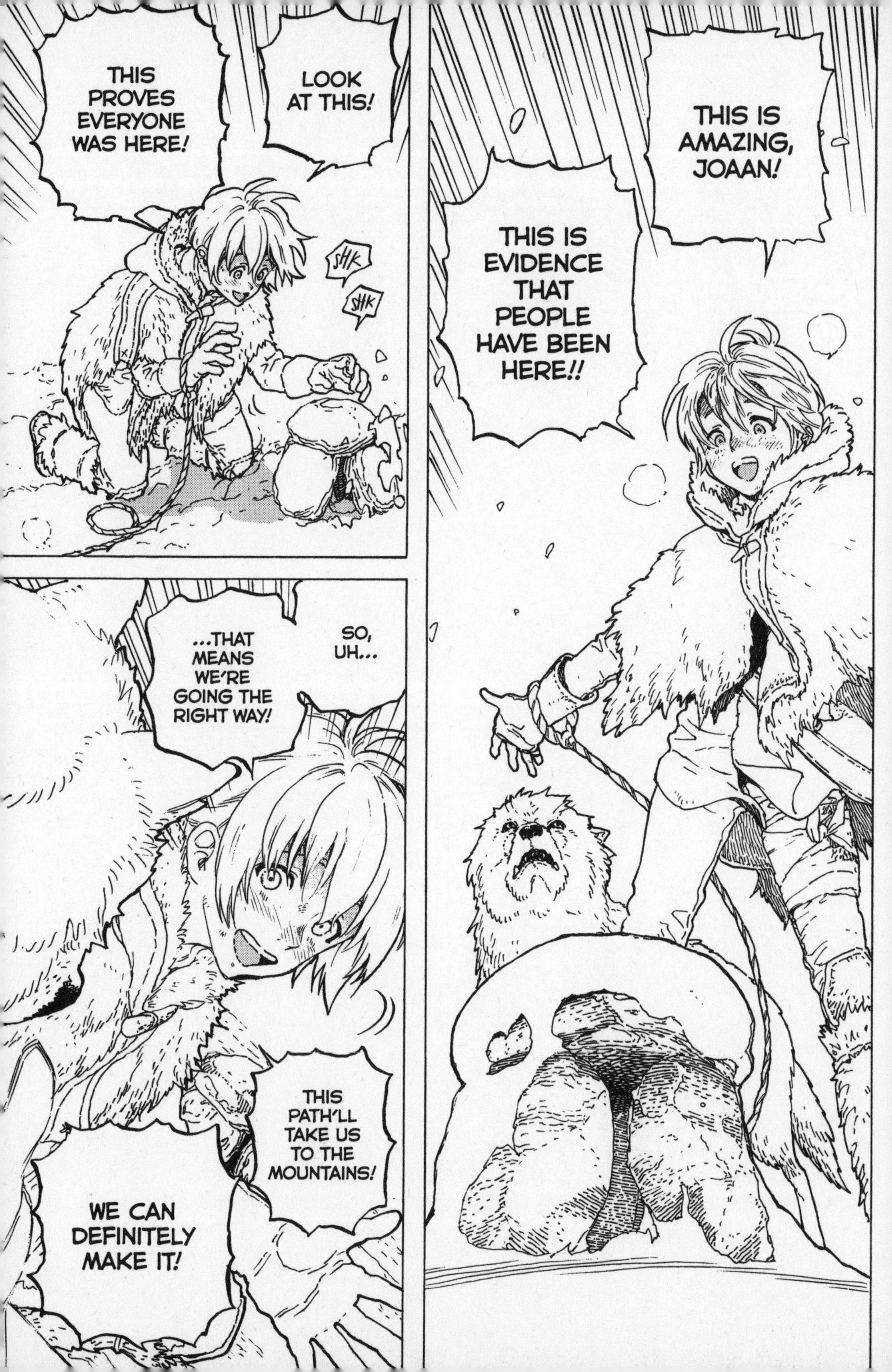
THIS IS AMAZING, JOAAN!
THIS IS EVIDENCE THAT PEOPLE HAVE BEEN HERE!!
LOOK AT THIS!
THIS PROVES EVERYONE WAS HERE!
SHK
SHK
SO, UH...
...THAT MEANS WE'RE GOING THE RIGHT WAY!
THIS PATH'LL TAKE US TO THE MOUNTAINS!
WE CAN DEFINITELY MAKE IT!

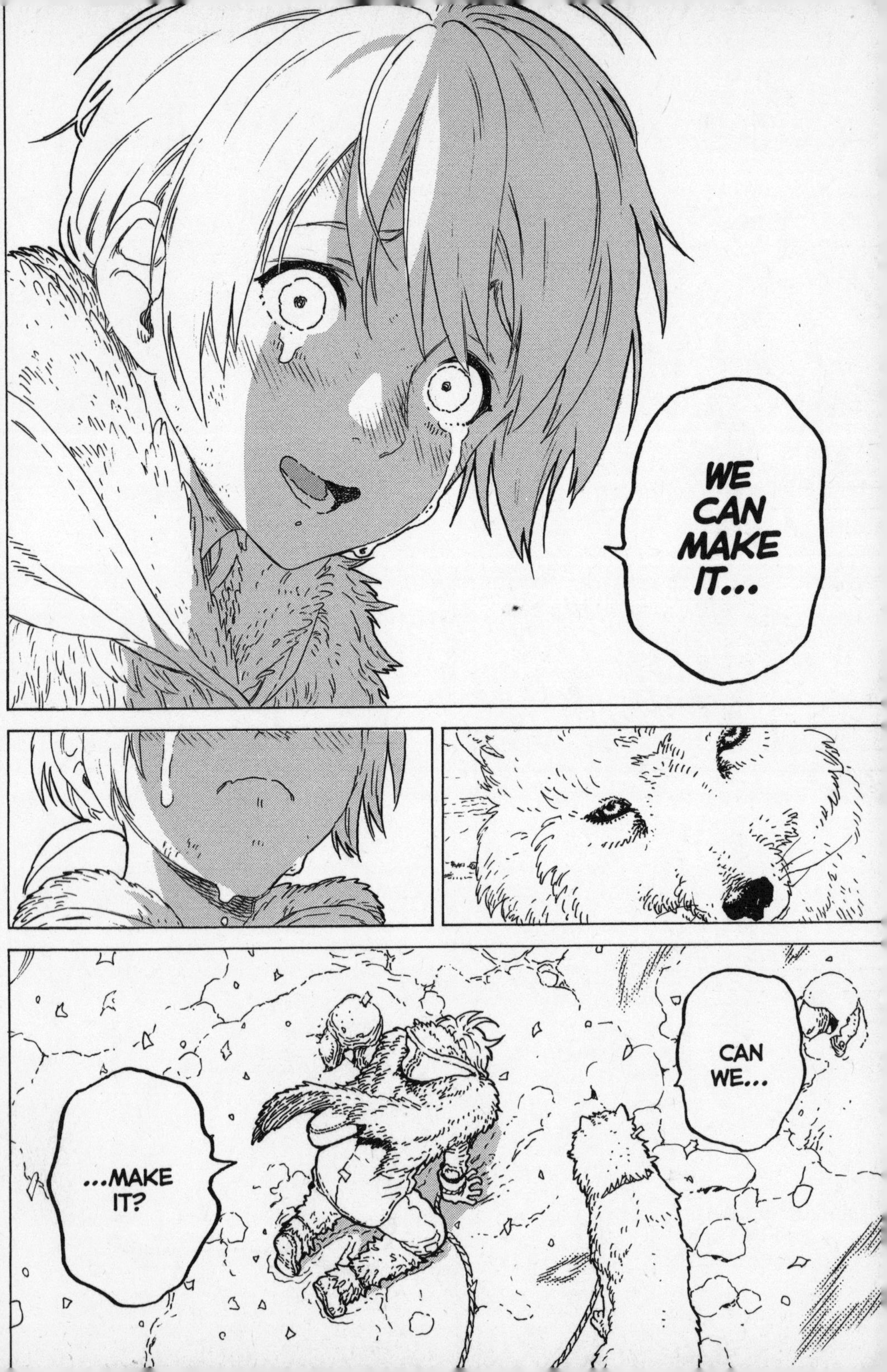
WE CAN MAKE IT...
CAN WE...
...MAKE IT?

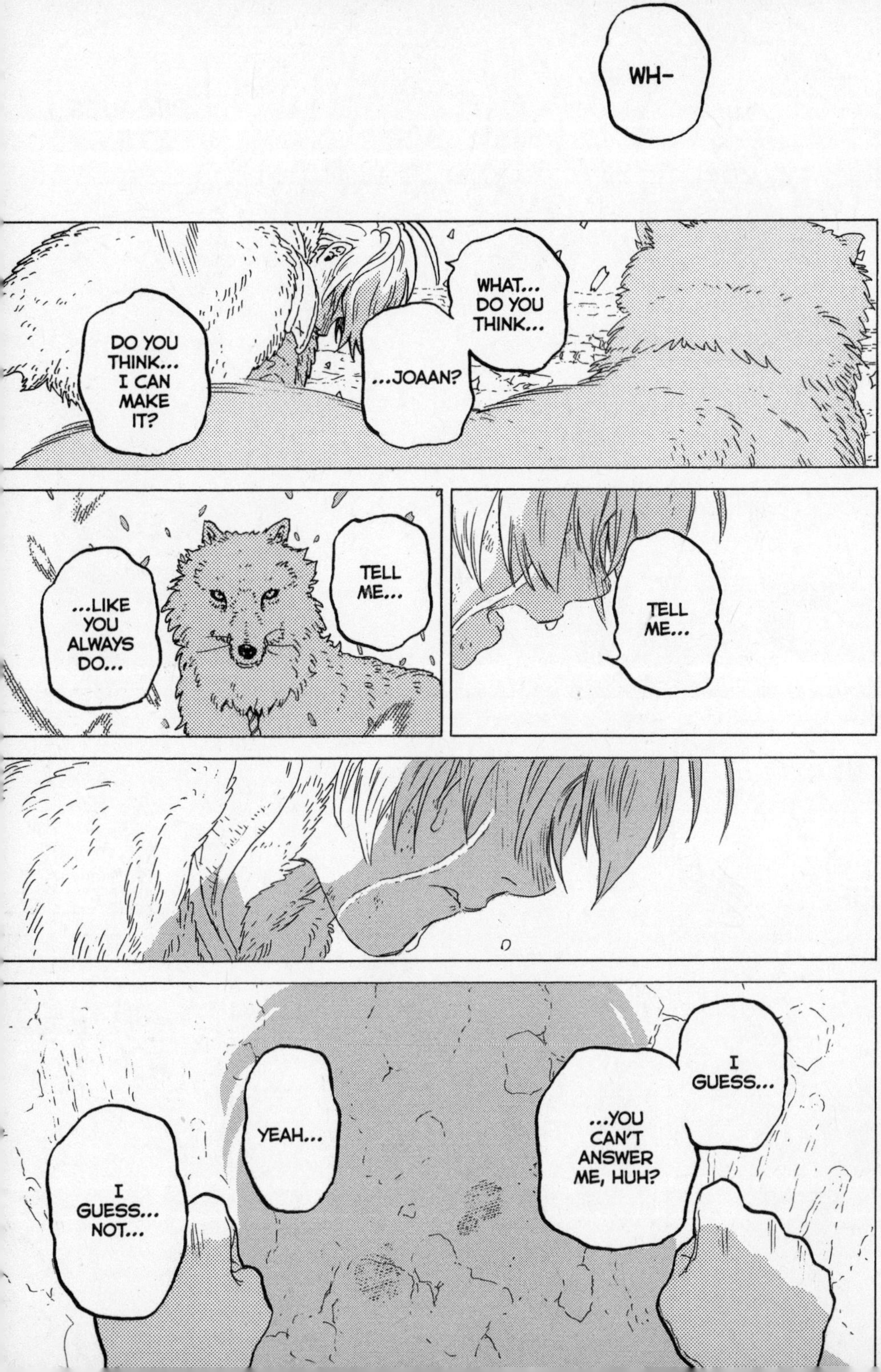
WH-
WHAT... DO YOU THINK...
...JOAAN?
DO YOU THINK... I CAN MAKE IT?
TELL ME...
TELL ME...
...LIKE YOU ALWAYS DO...
I GUESS...
...YOU CAN'T ANSWER ME, HUH?
YEAH...
I GUESS... NOT...

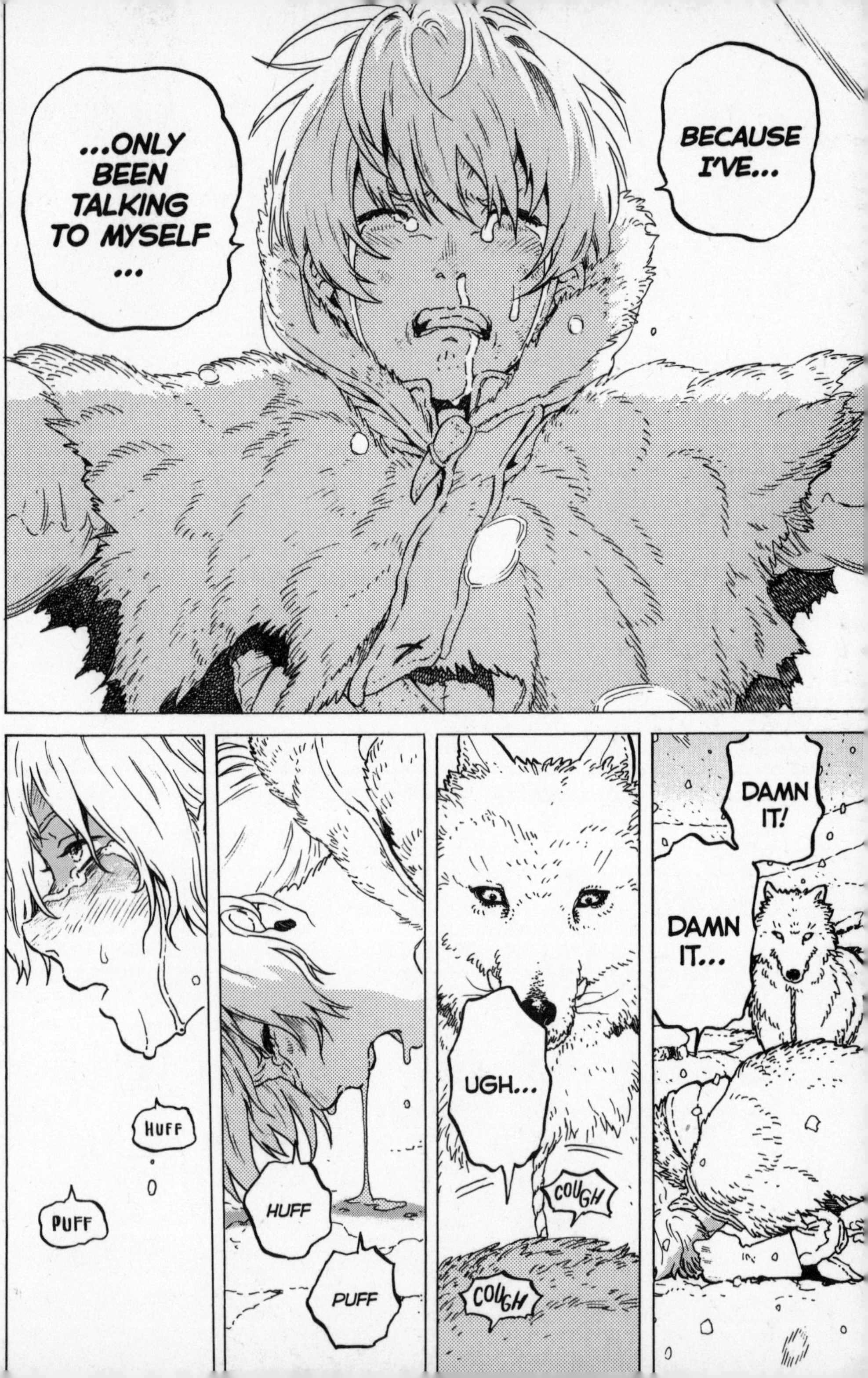
BECAUSE I'VE...
...ONLY BEEN TALKING TO MYSELF ...
DAMN IT!
DAMN IT...
UGH...
COUGH
COUGH
HUFF
PUFF
HUFF
PUFF

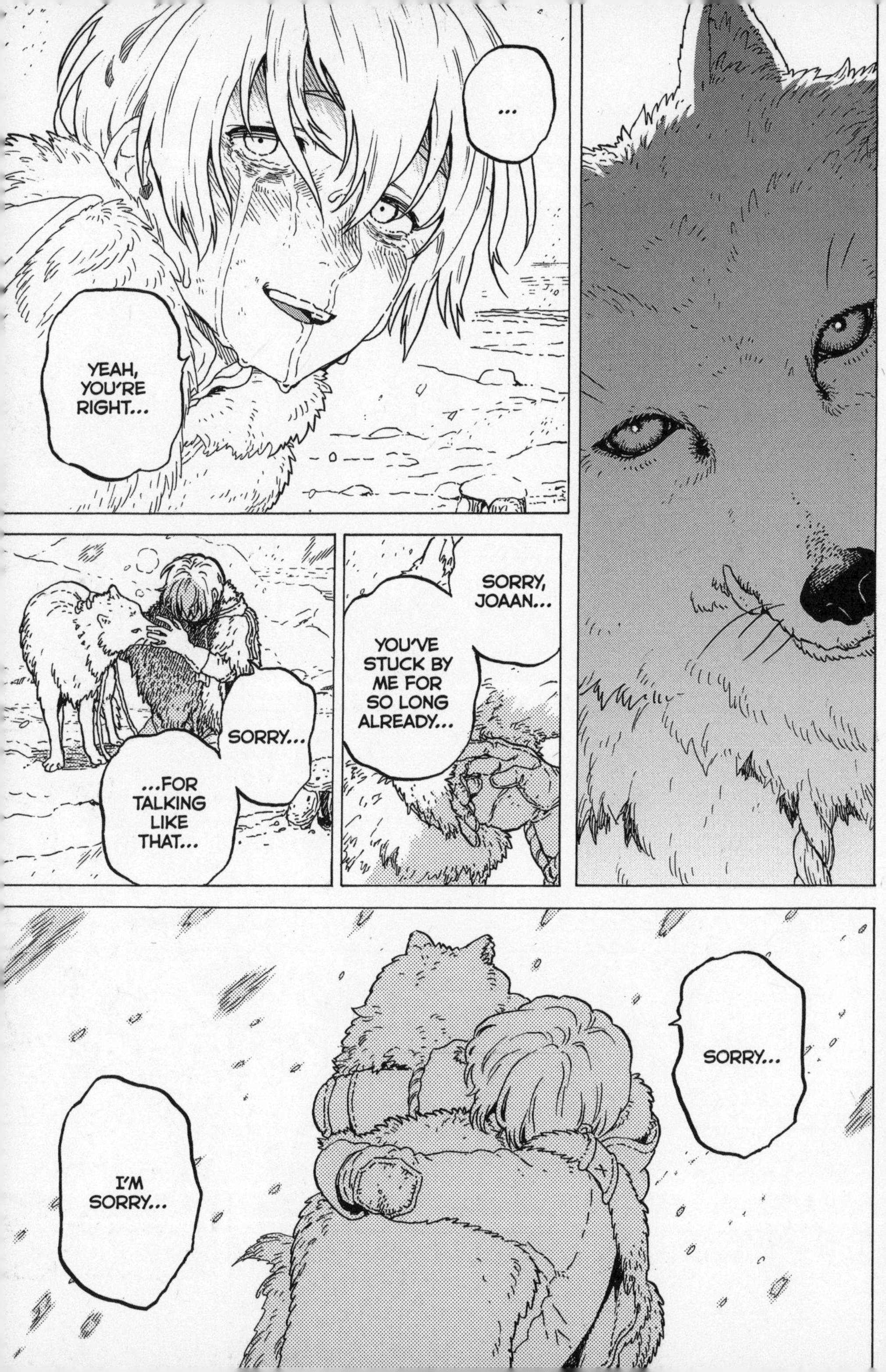
...
YEAH, YOU'RE RIGHT...
SORRY, JOAAN...
YOU'VE STUCK BY ME FOR SO LONG ALREADY...
SORRY...
...FOR TALKING LIKE THAT...
SORRY...
I'M SORRY...

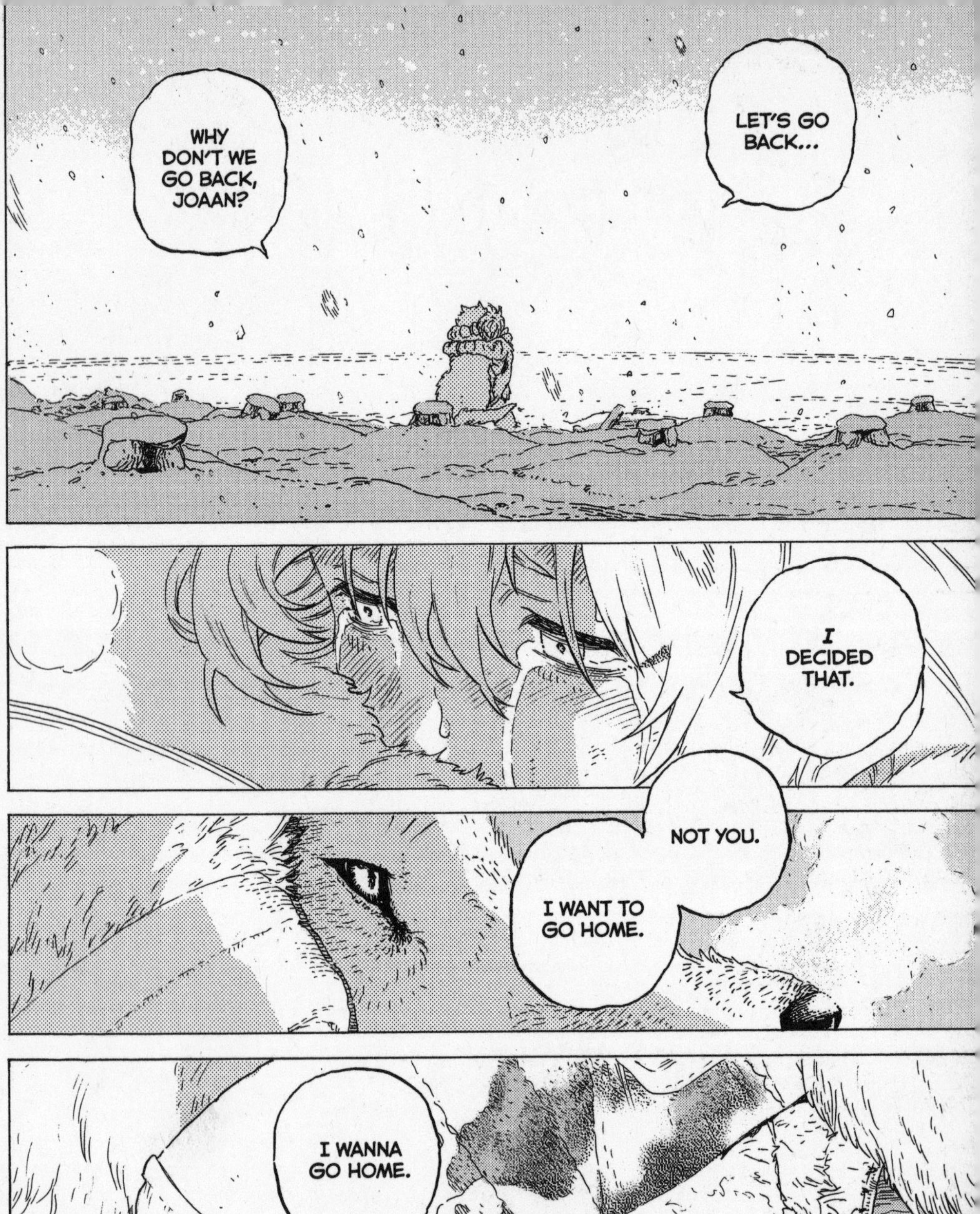
LET'S GO BACK...
WHY DON'T WE GO BACK, JOAAN?
I DECIDED THAT.
NOT YOU.
I WANT TO GO HOME.
I WANNA GO HOME.
LET'S GO BACK...

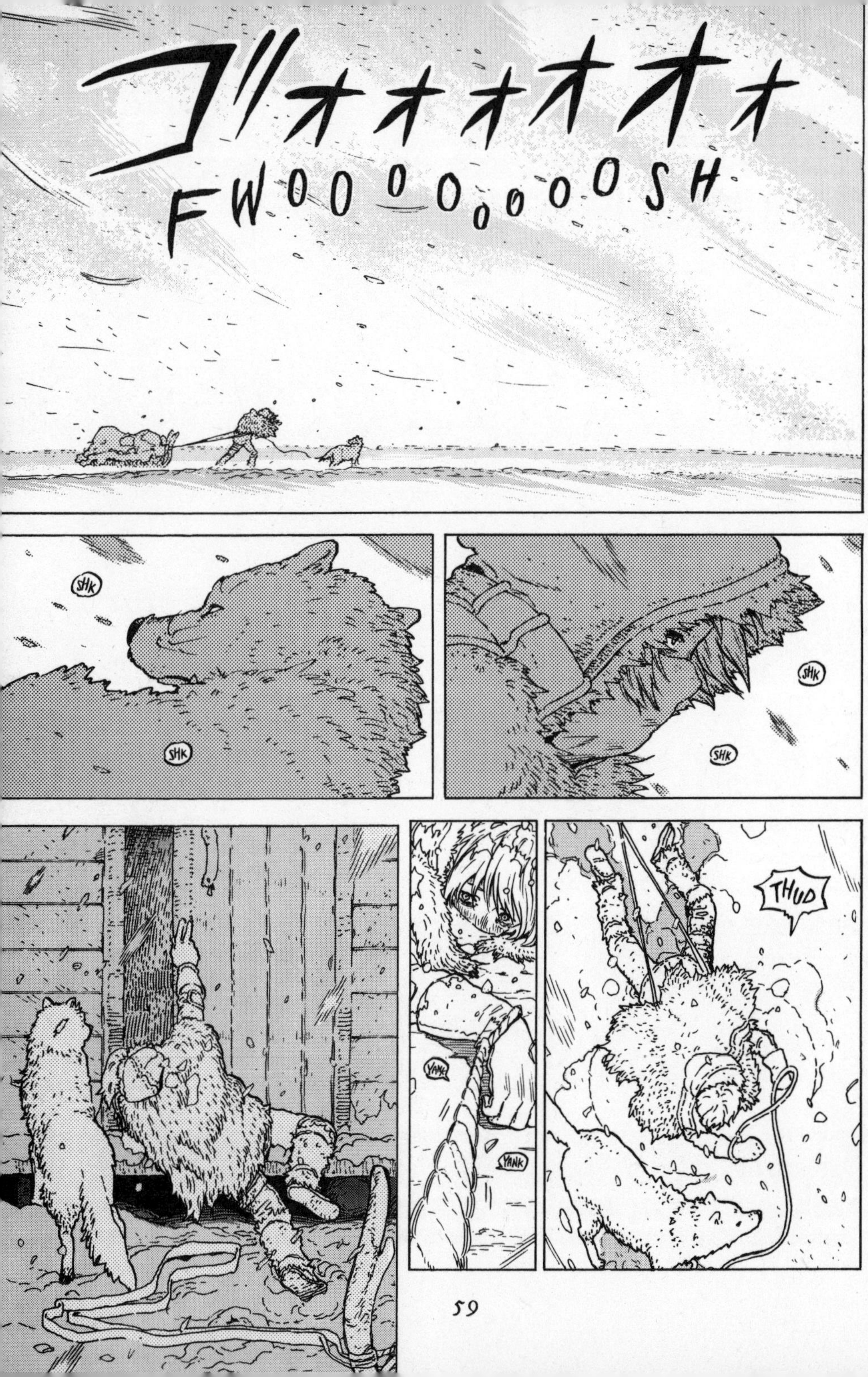
ゴオオオオオオ
FWOOOOOOOOSH
SHK
SHK
SHK
SHK
THUD
YANK
YANK

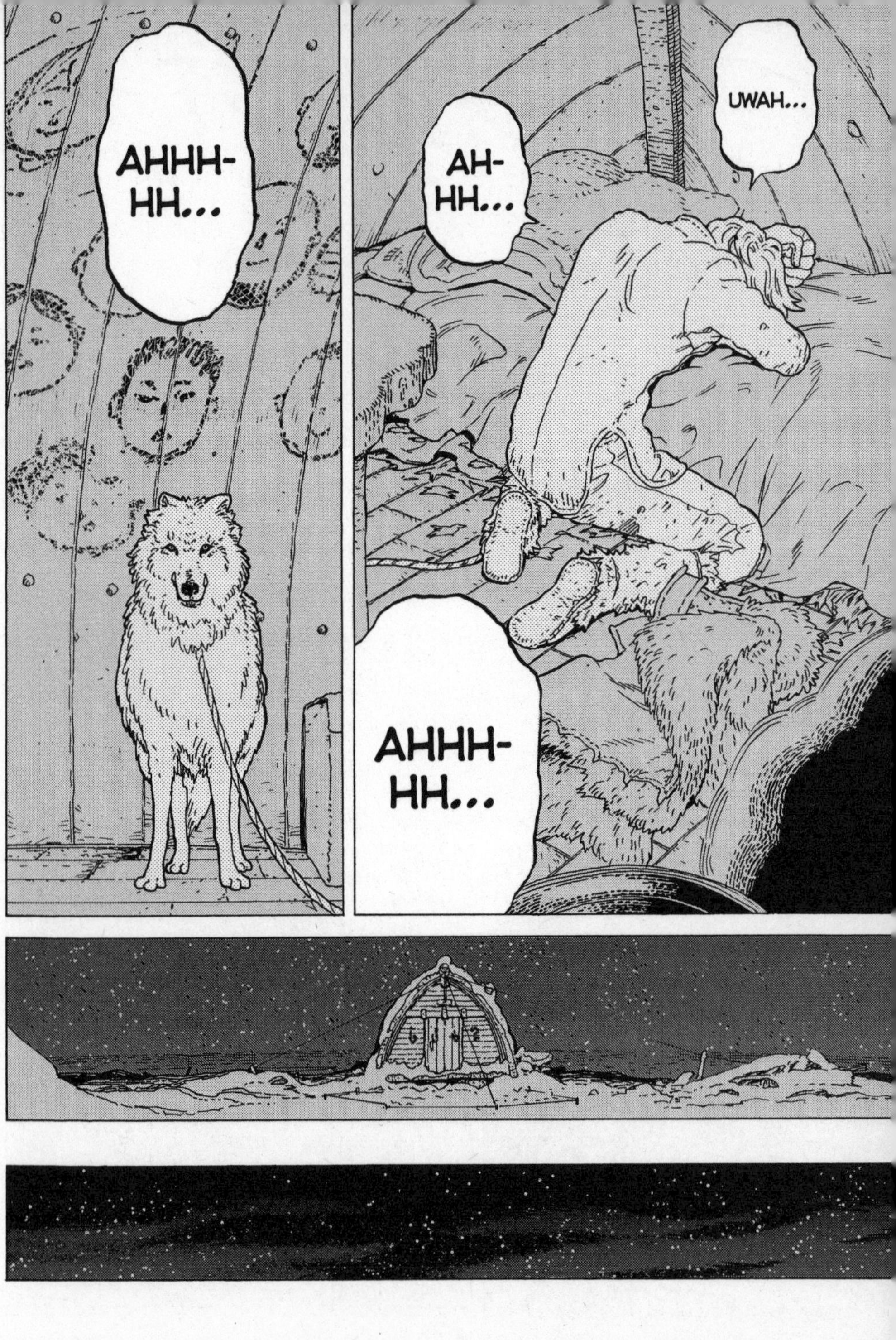
UWAH...
AH-HH...
AHHH-HH...
AHHH-HH...

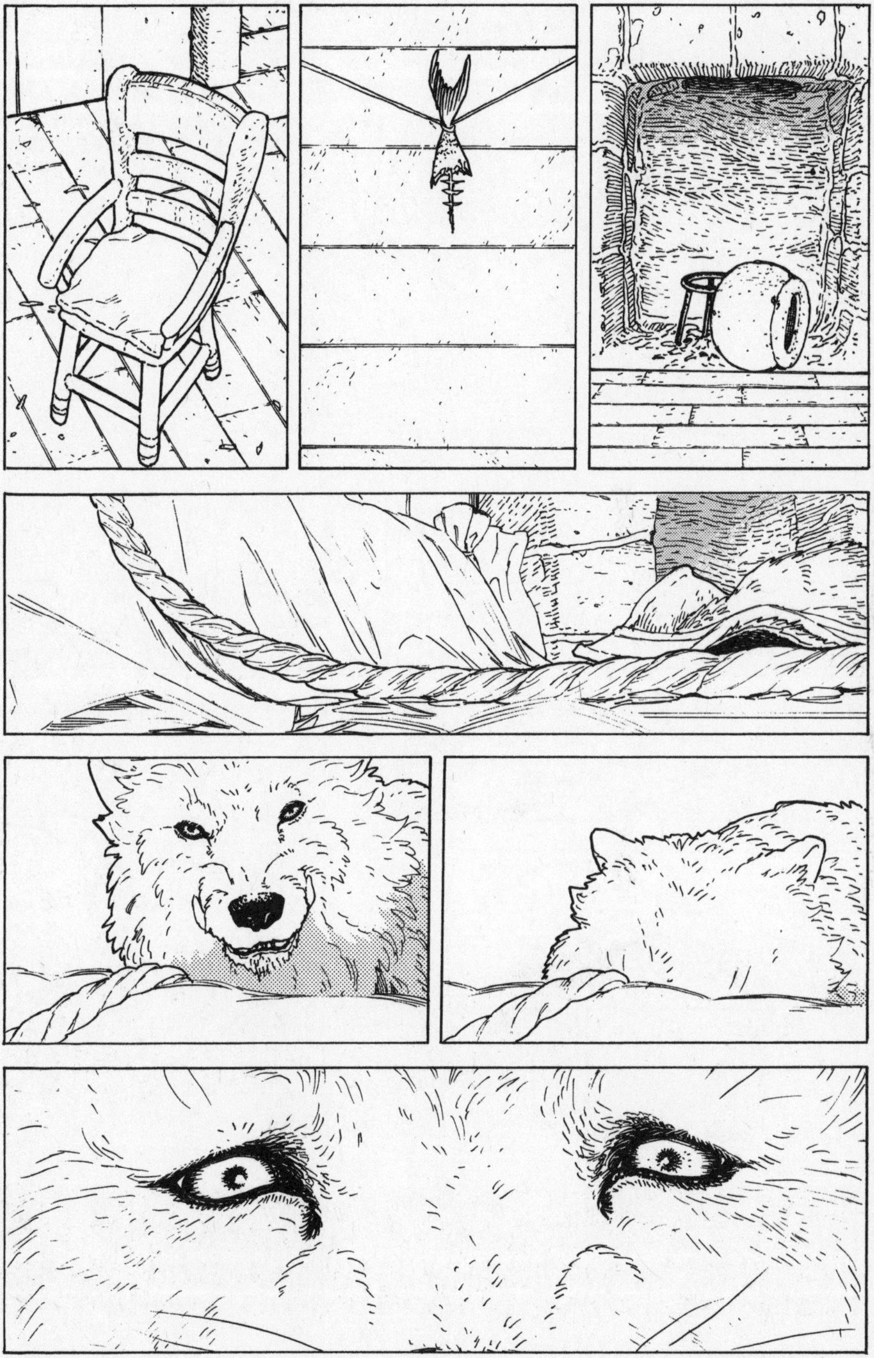

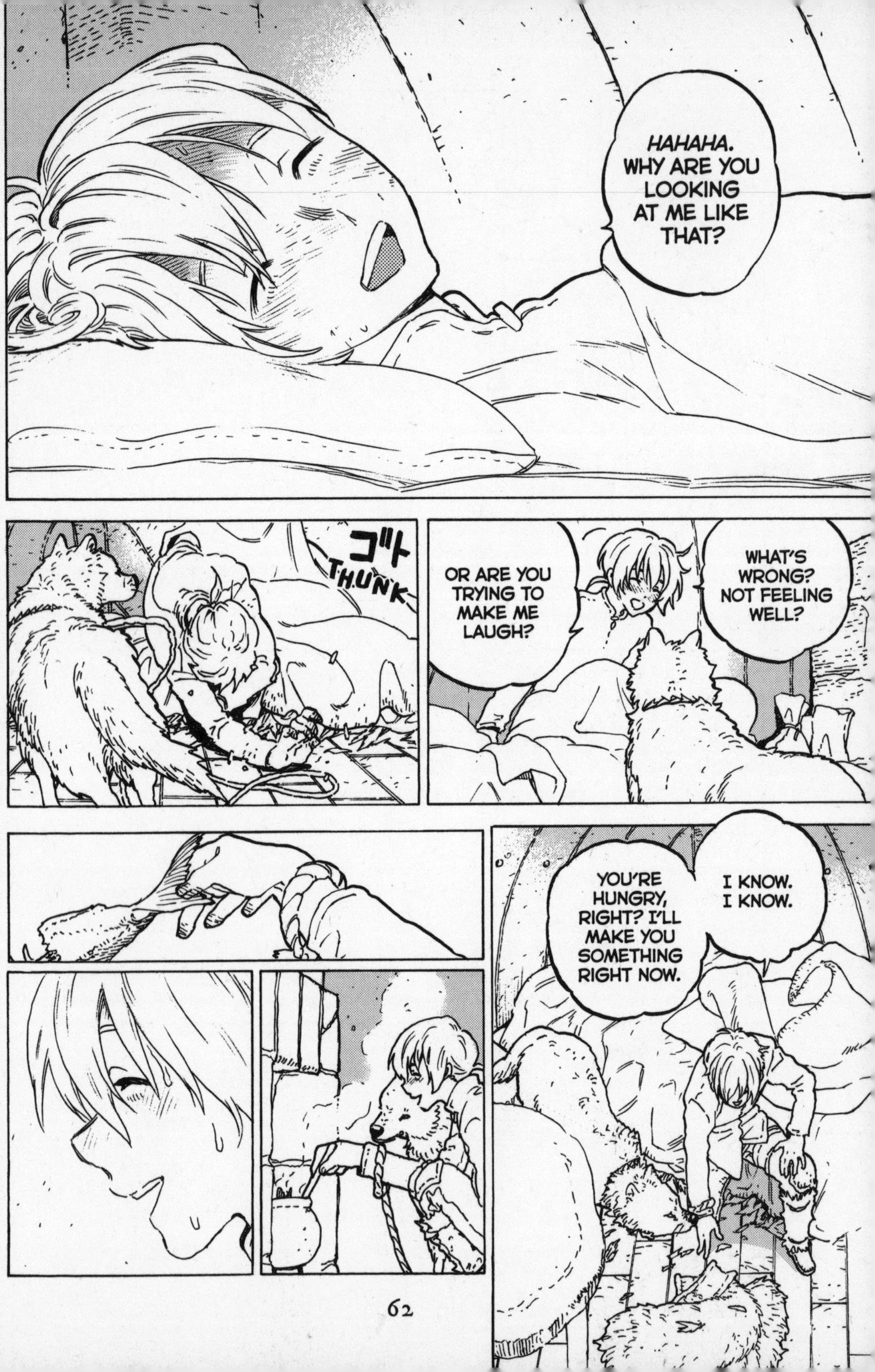
HAHAHA. WHY ARE YOU LOOKING AT ME LIKE THAT?
WHAT'S WRONG? NOT FEELING WELL?
OR ARE YOU TRYING TO MAKE ME LAUGH?
ゴト
THUNK
I KNOW. I KNOW.
YOU'RE HUNGRY, RIGHT? I'LL MAKE YOU SOMETHING RIGHT NOW.

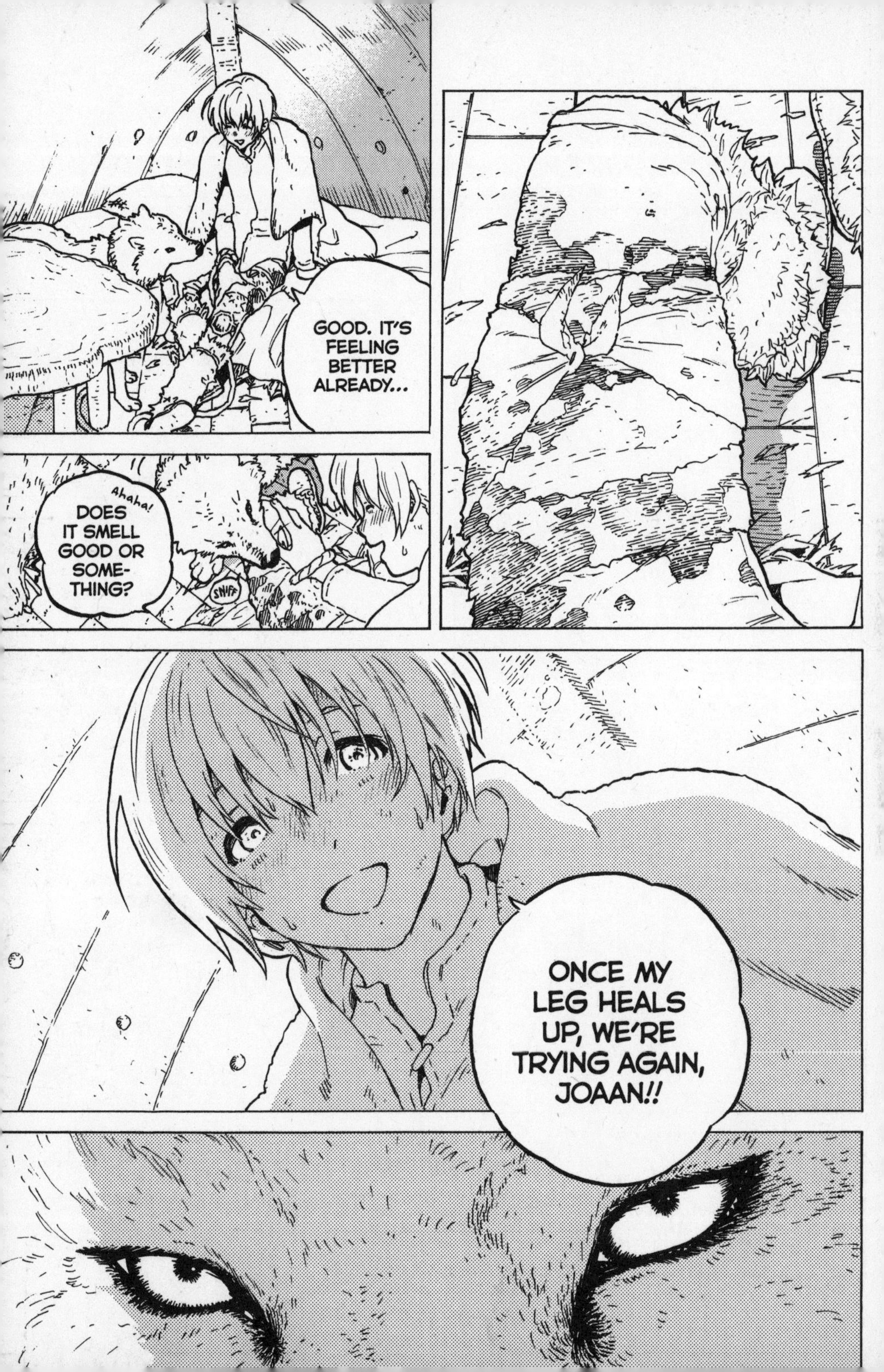
GOOD. IT'S FEELING BETTER ALREADY...
Ahaha!
DOES IT SMELL GOOD OR SOME-THING?
SNIFF
ONCE MY LEG HEALS UP, WE'RE TRYING AGAIN, JOAAN!!

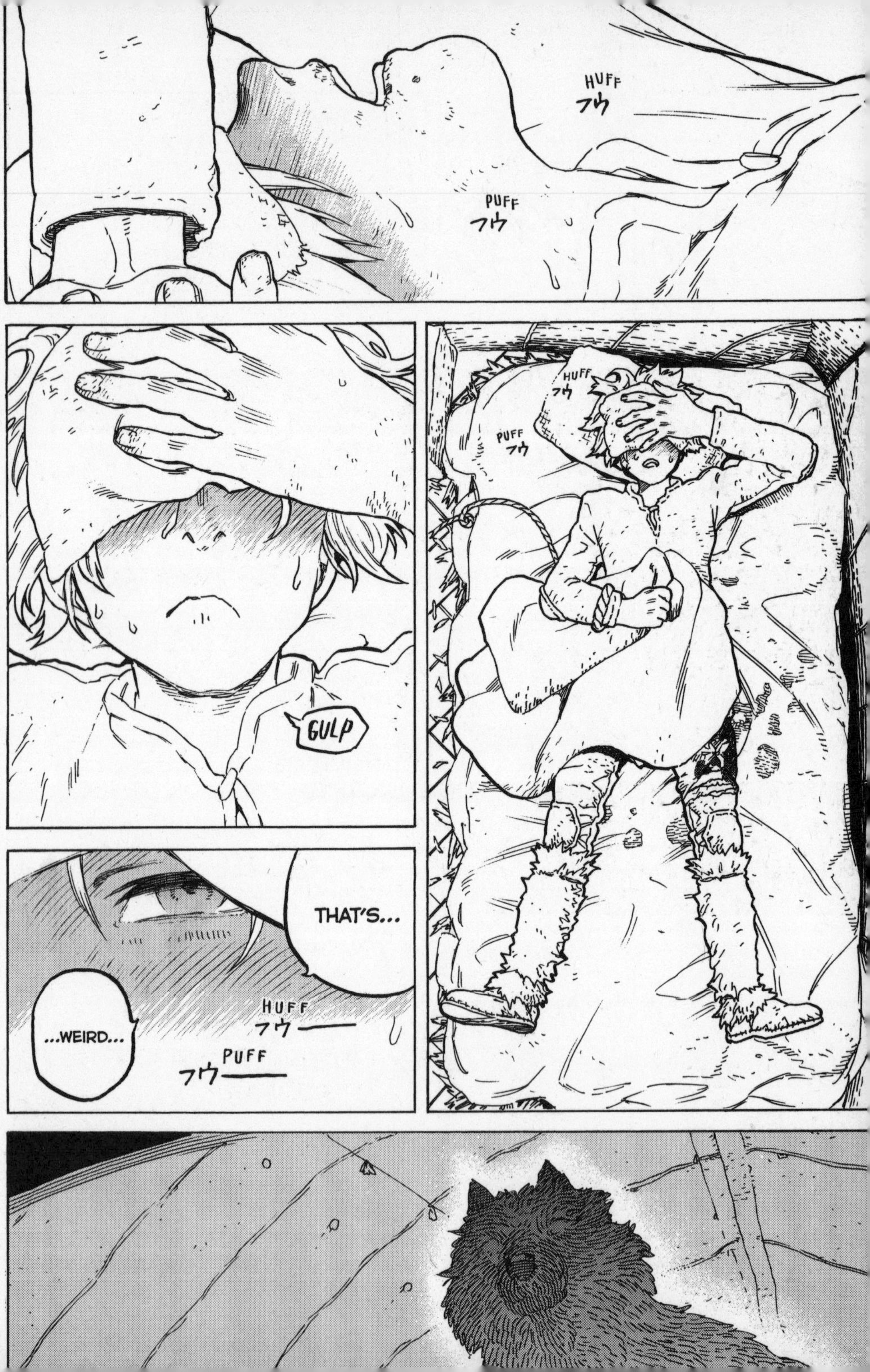
HUFF
フウ
PUFF
フウ
HUFF
フウ
PUFF
フウ
GULP
THAT'S...
...WEIRD...
HUFF
フウ——
PUFF
フウ——

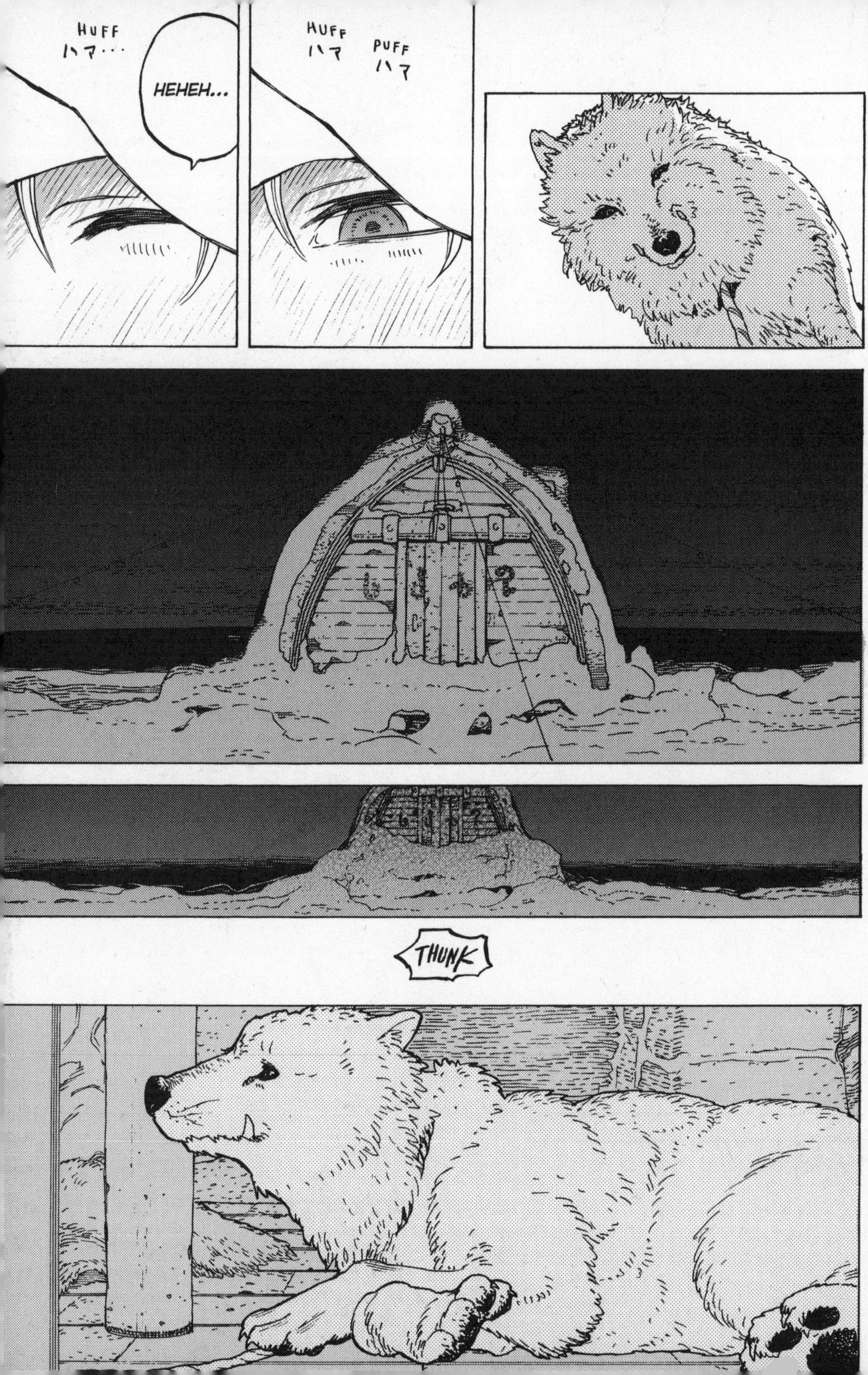
HUFF ハァ
PUFF ハァ
HUFF ハァ…
HEHEH...
THUNK

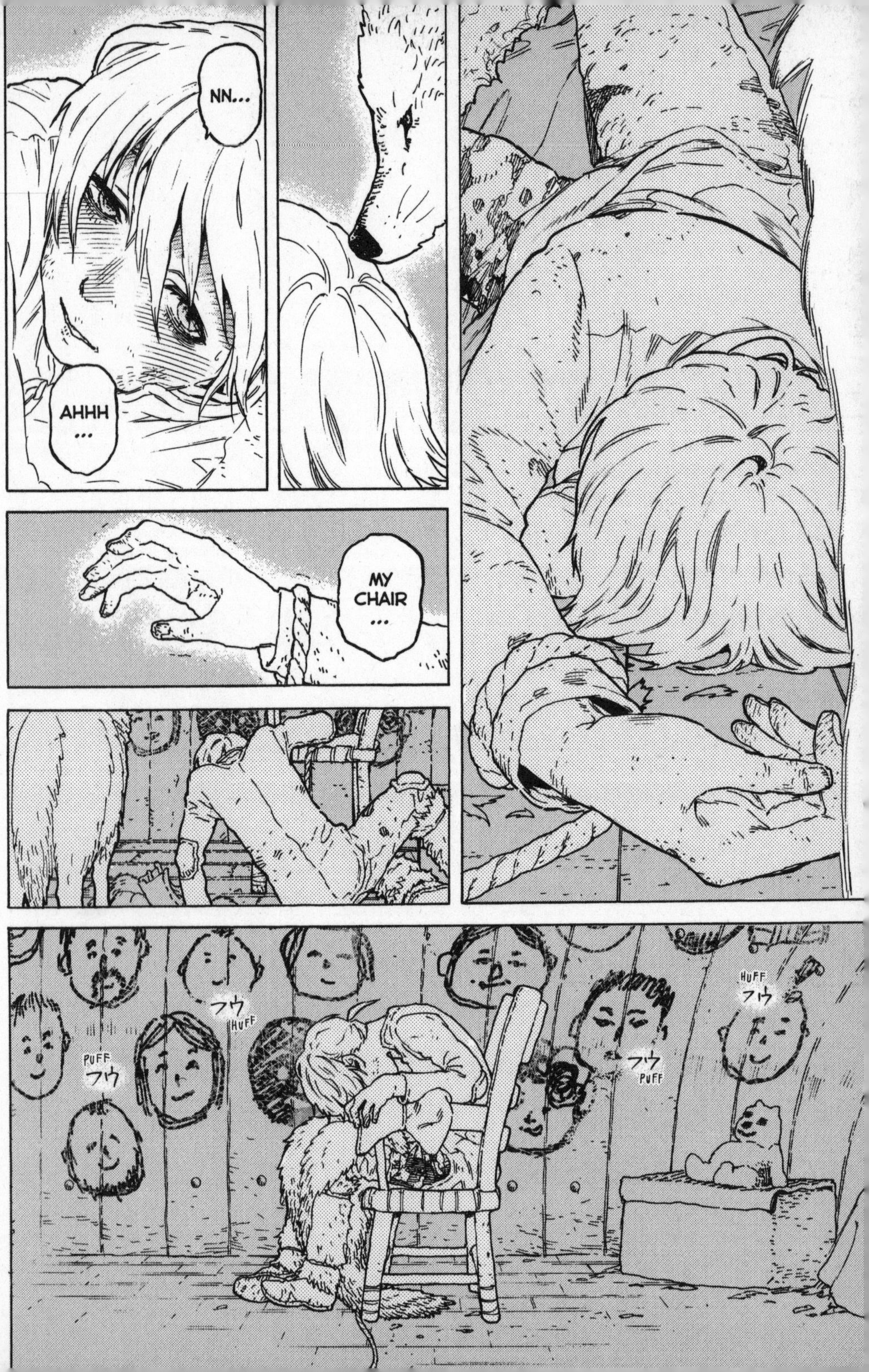
NN...
AHHH ...
MY CHAIR ...
HUFF フウ
フウ PUFF
フウ HUFF
PUFF フウ

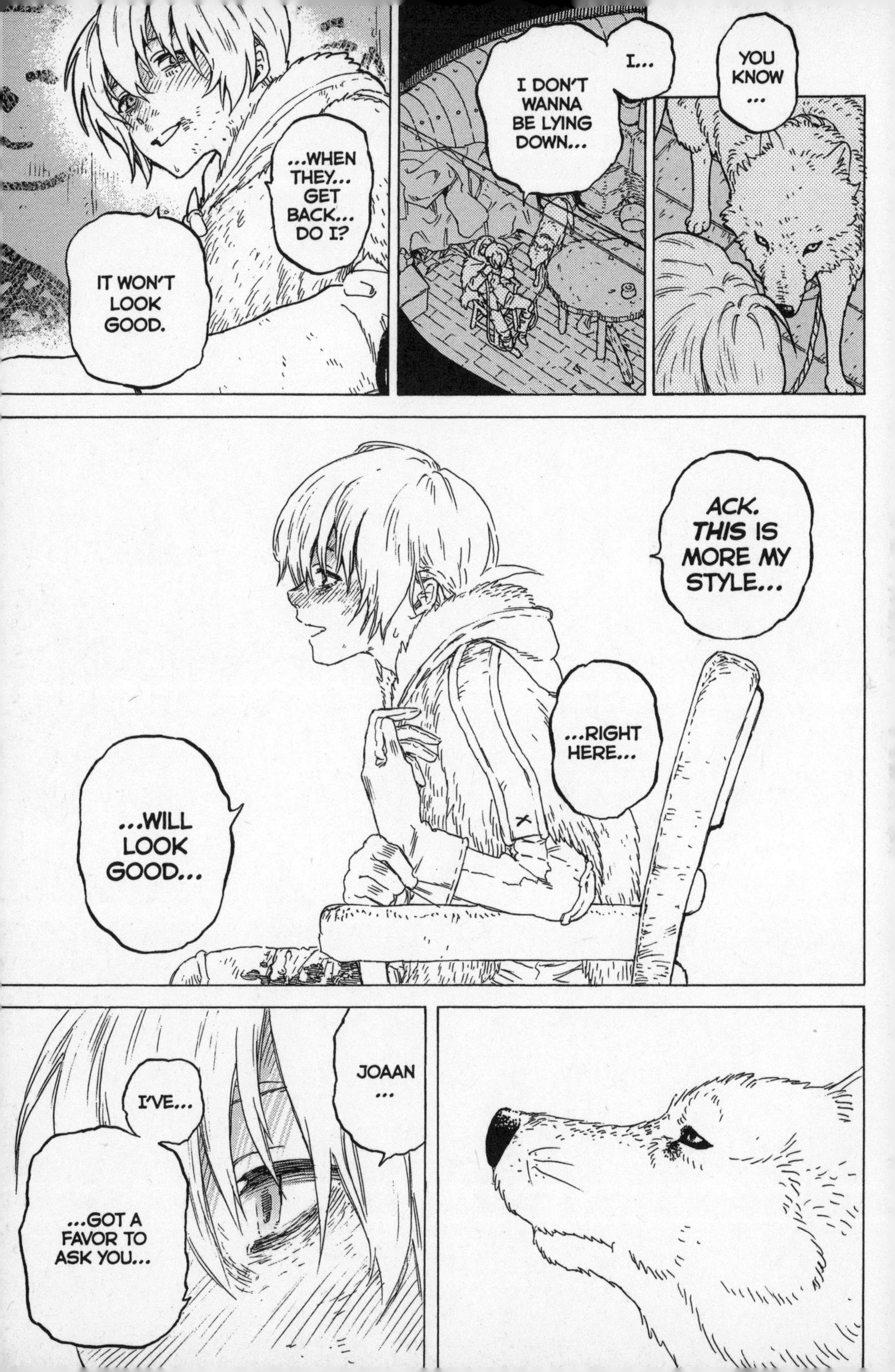
YOU KNOW ...
I...
I DON'T WANNA BE LYING DOWN...
...WHEN THEY... GET BACK... DO I?
IT WON'T LOOK GOOD.
ACK. *THIS* IS MORE MY STYLE...
...RIGHT HERE...
...WILL LOOK GOOD...
JOAAN ...
I'VE...
...GOT A FAVOR TO ASK YOU...

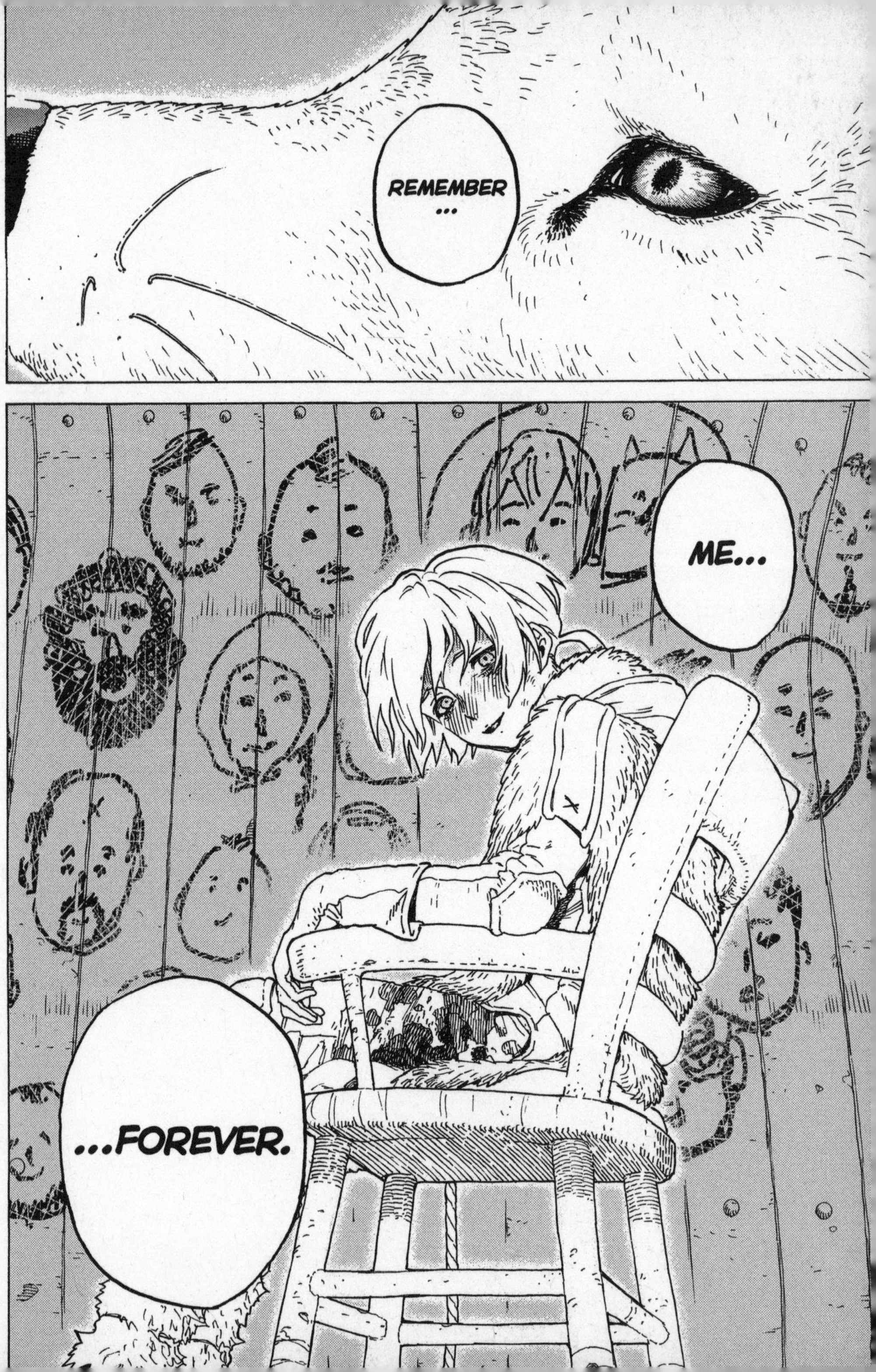
REMEMBER ...
ME...
...FOREVER.

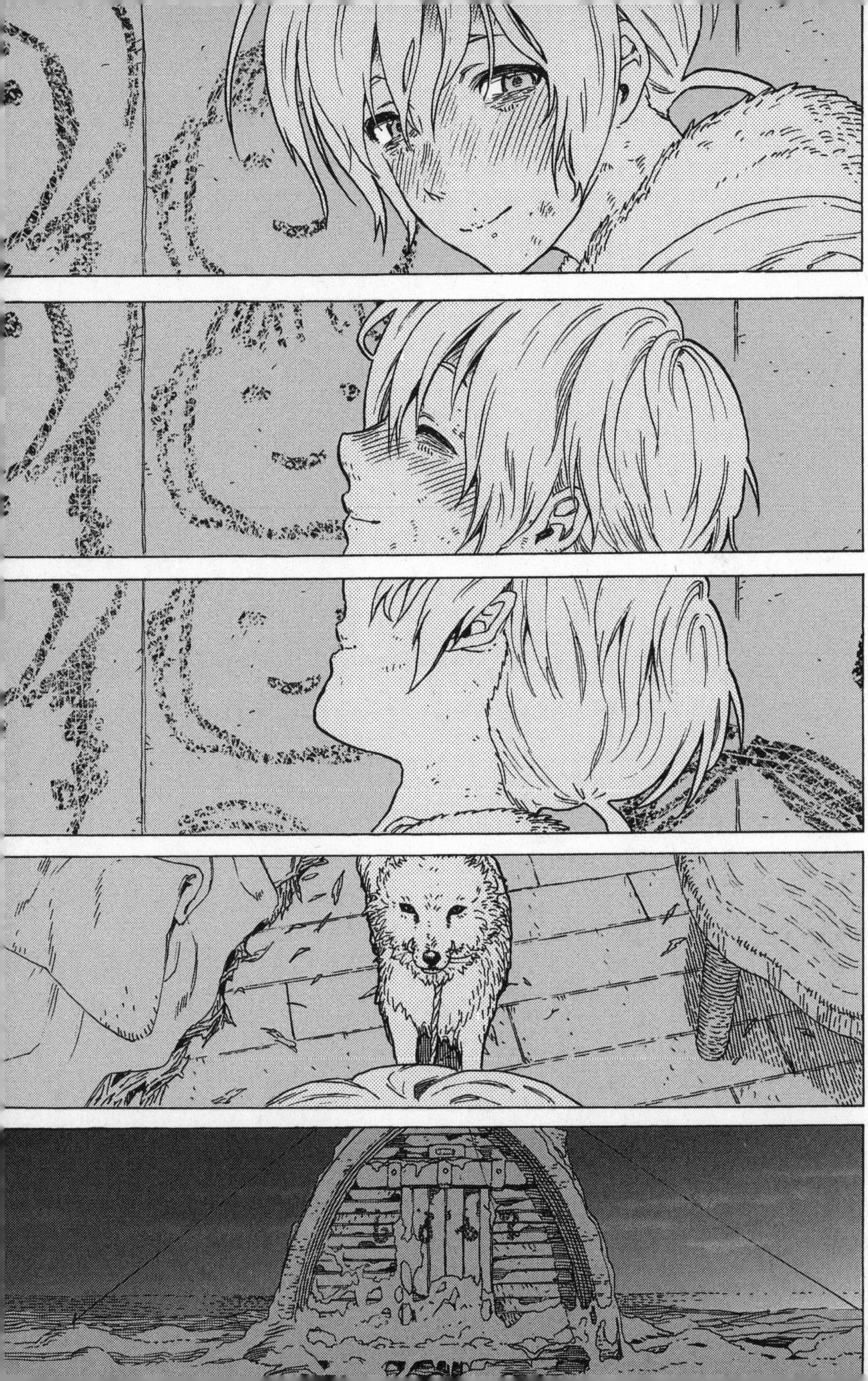

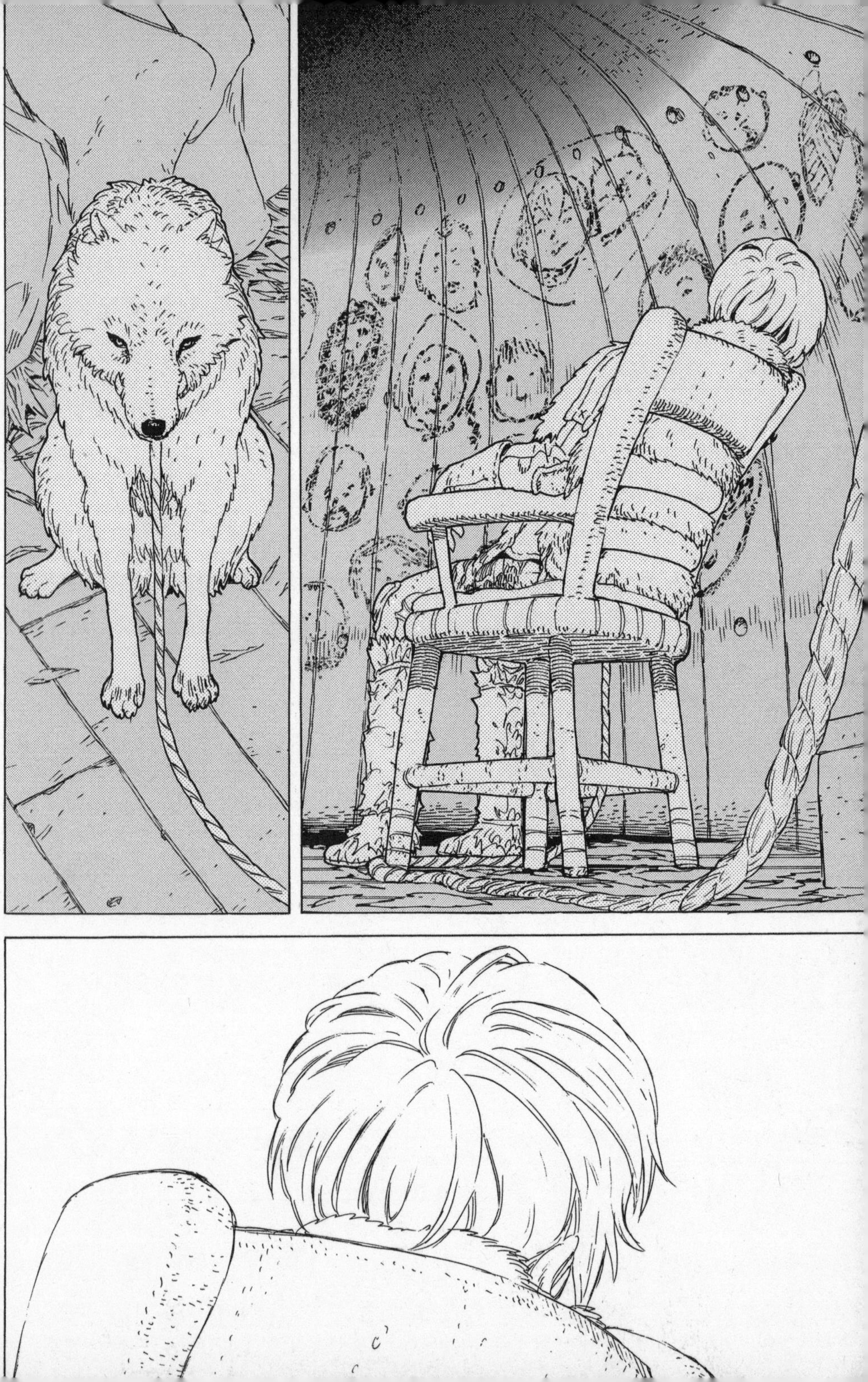

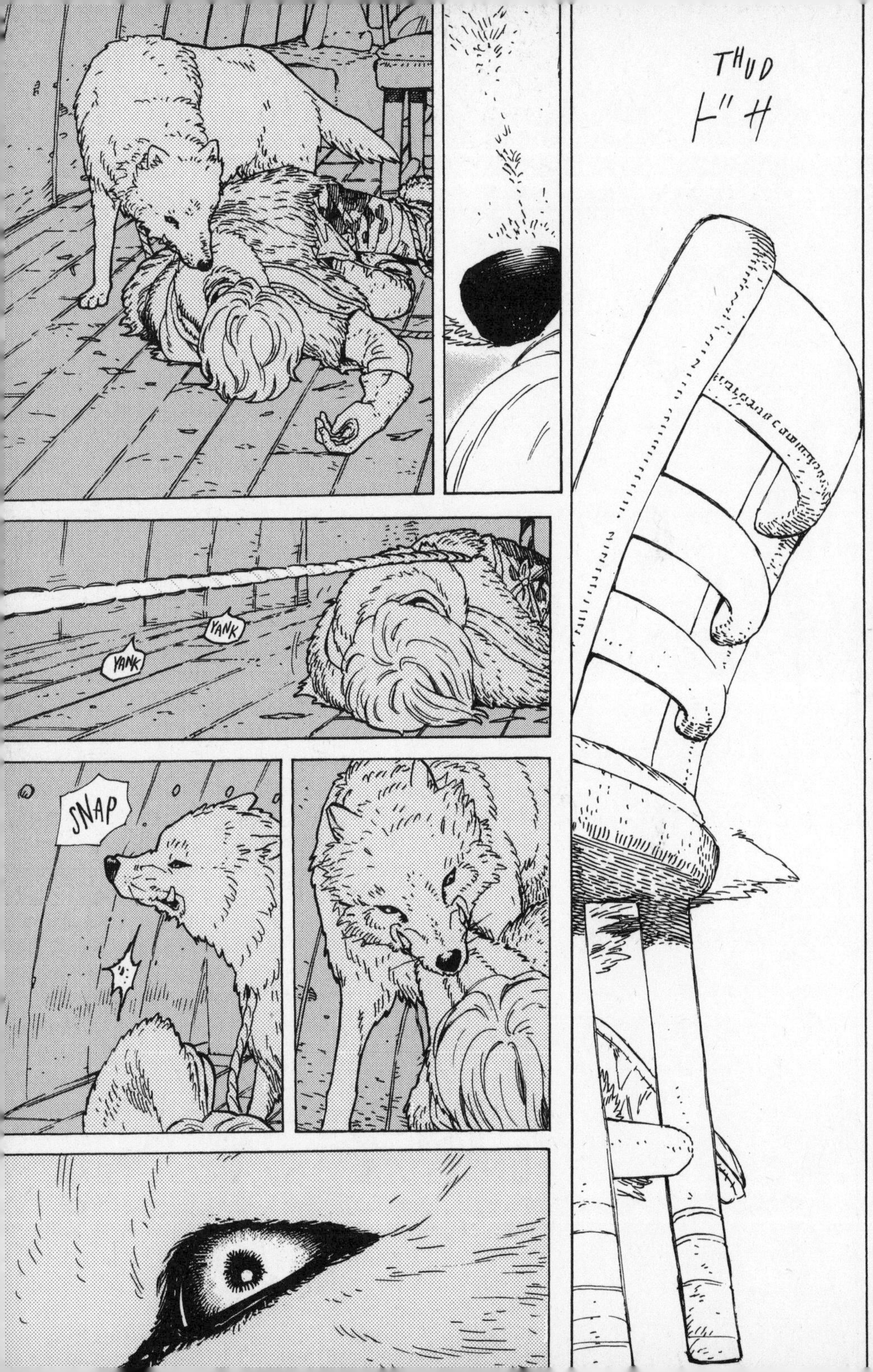
THUD
ドサ
YANK
YANK
SNAP

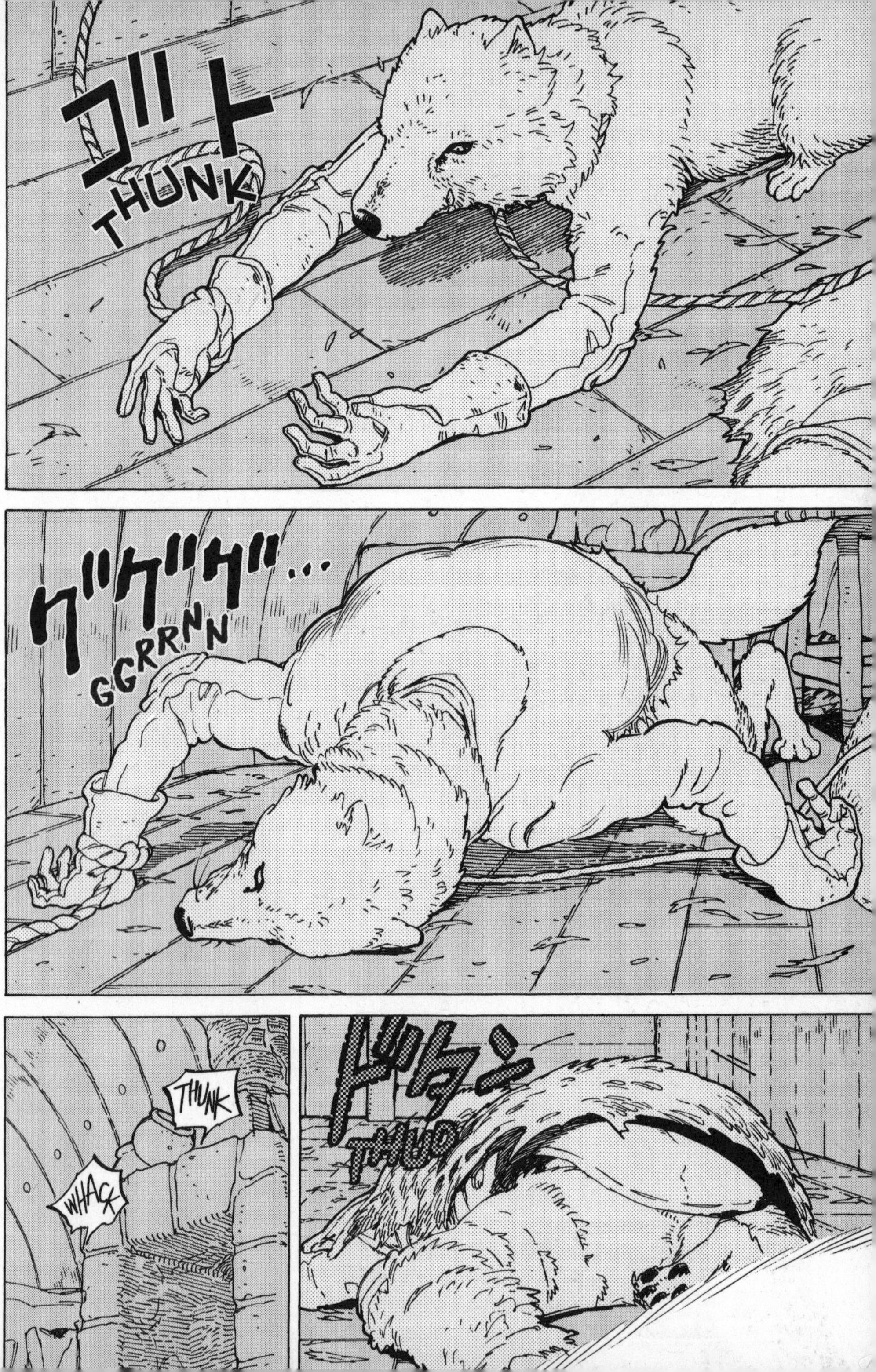
ゴト
THUNK
グググ…
GGRRNN
ドサッ
THUD
THUNK
WHACK

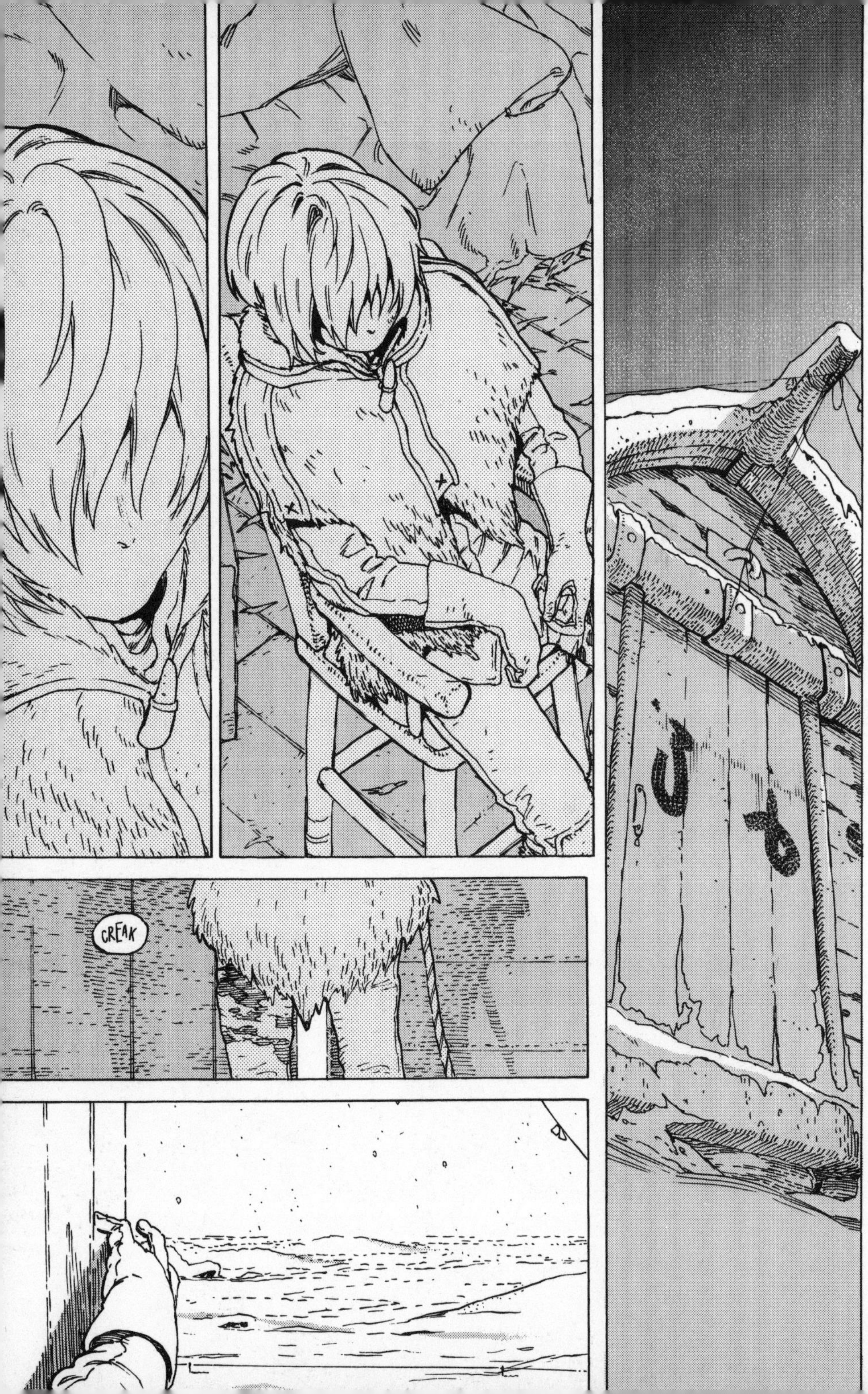
CREAK

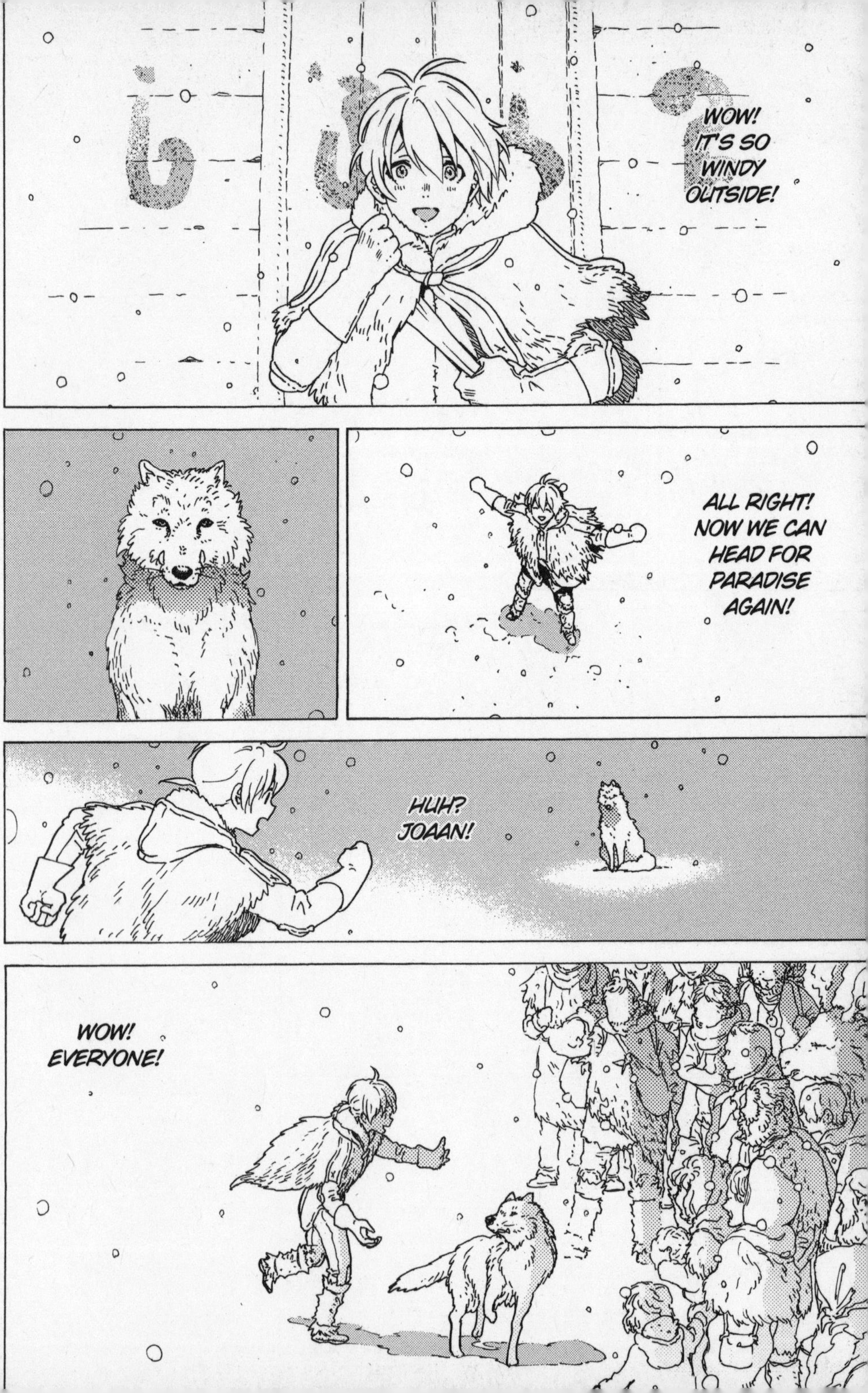
WOW! IT'S SO WINDY OUTSIDE!
ALL RIGHT! NOW WE CAN HEAD FOR PARADISE AGAIN!
HUH? JOAAN!
WOW! EVERYONE!

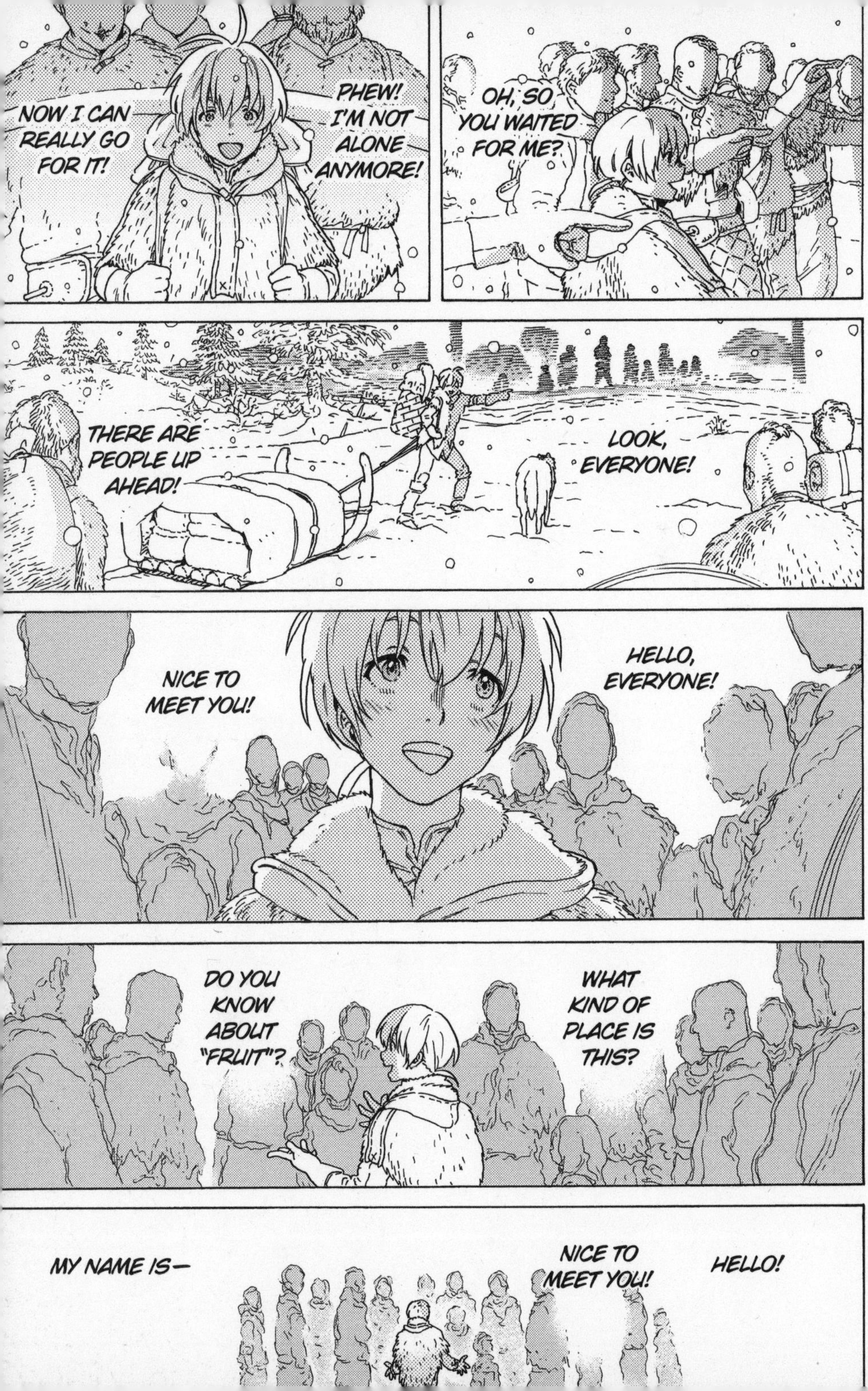
OH, SO YOU WAITED FOR ME?
PHEW! I'M NOT ALONE ANYMORE!
NOW I CAN REALLY GO FOR IT!
LOOK, EVERYONE!
THERE ARE PEOPLE UP AHEAD!
HELLO, EVERYONE!
NICE TO MEET YOU!
WHAT KIND OF PLACE IS THIS?
DO YOU KNOW ABOUT "FRUIT"?
HELLO!
NICE TO MEET YOU!
MY NAME IS—

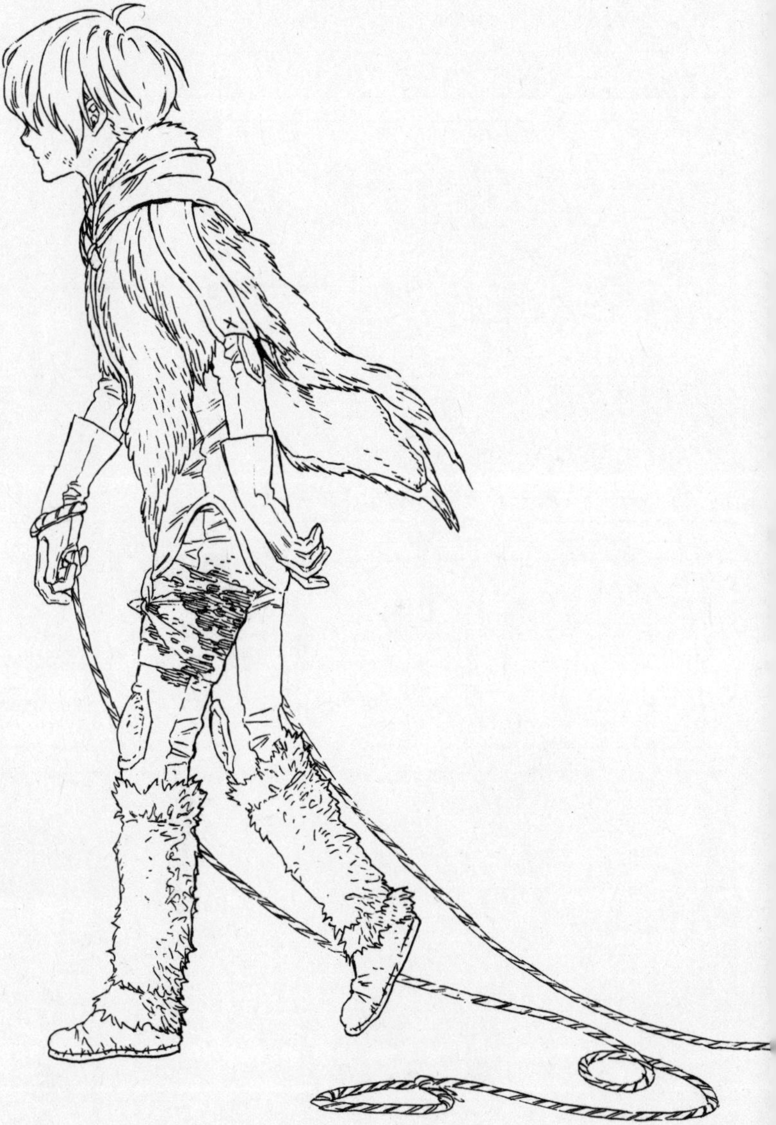

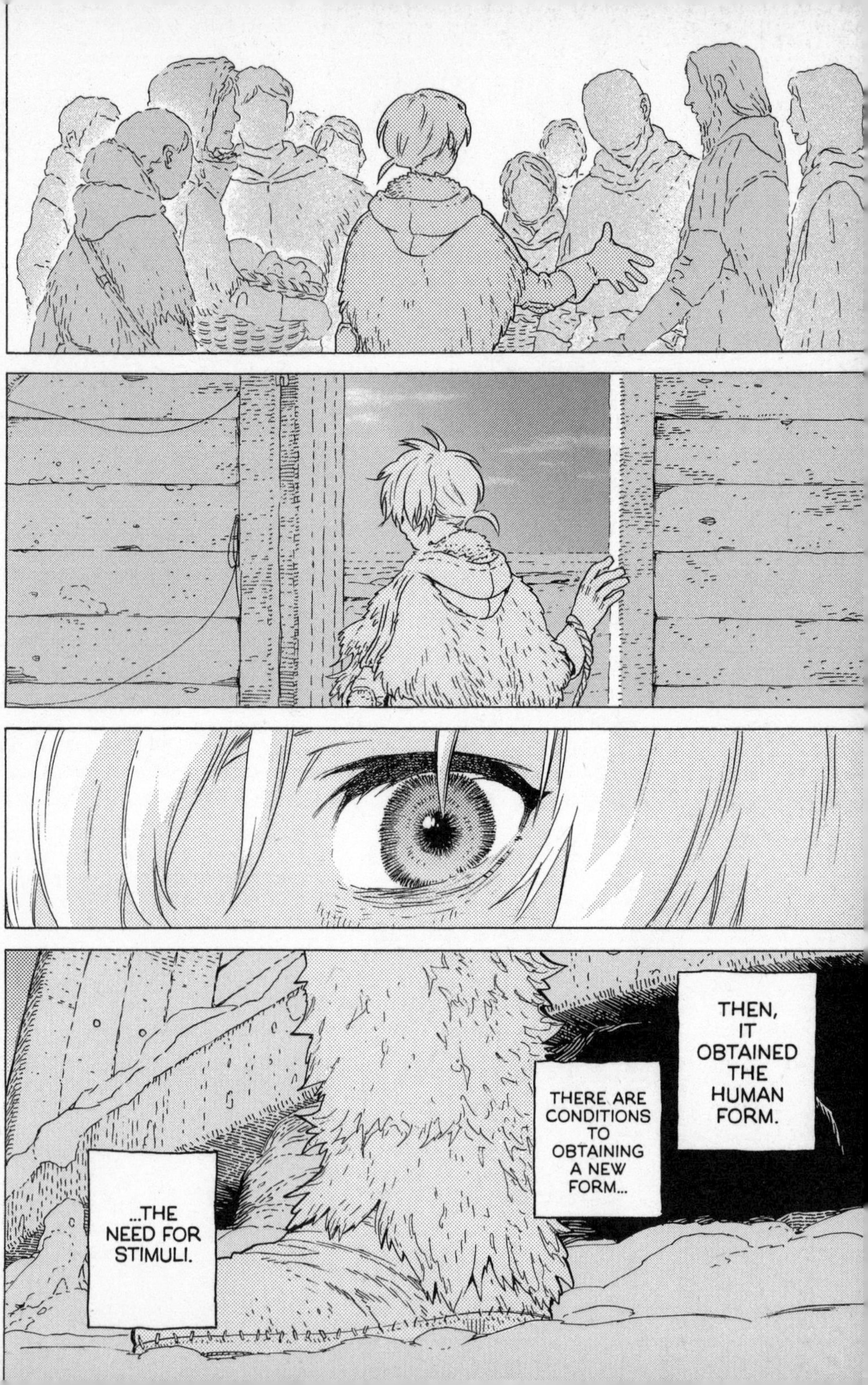
THEN, IT OBTAINED THE HUMAN FORM.
THERE ARE CONDITIONS TO OBTAINING A NEW FORM...
...THE NEED FOR STIMULI.

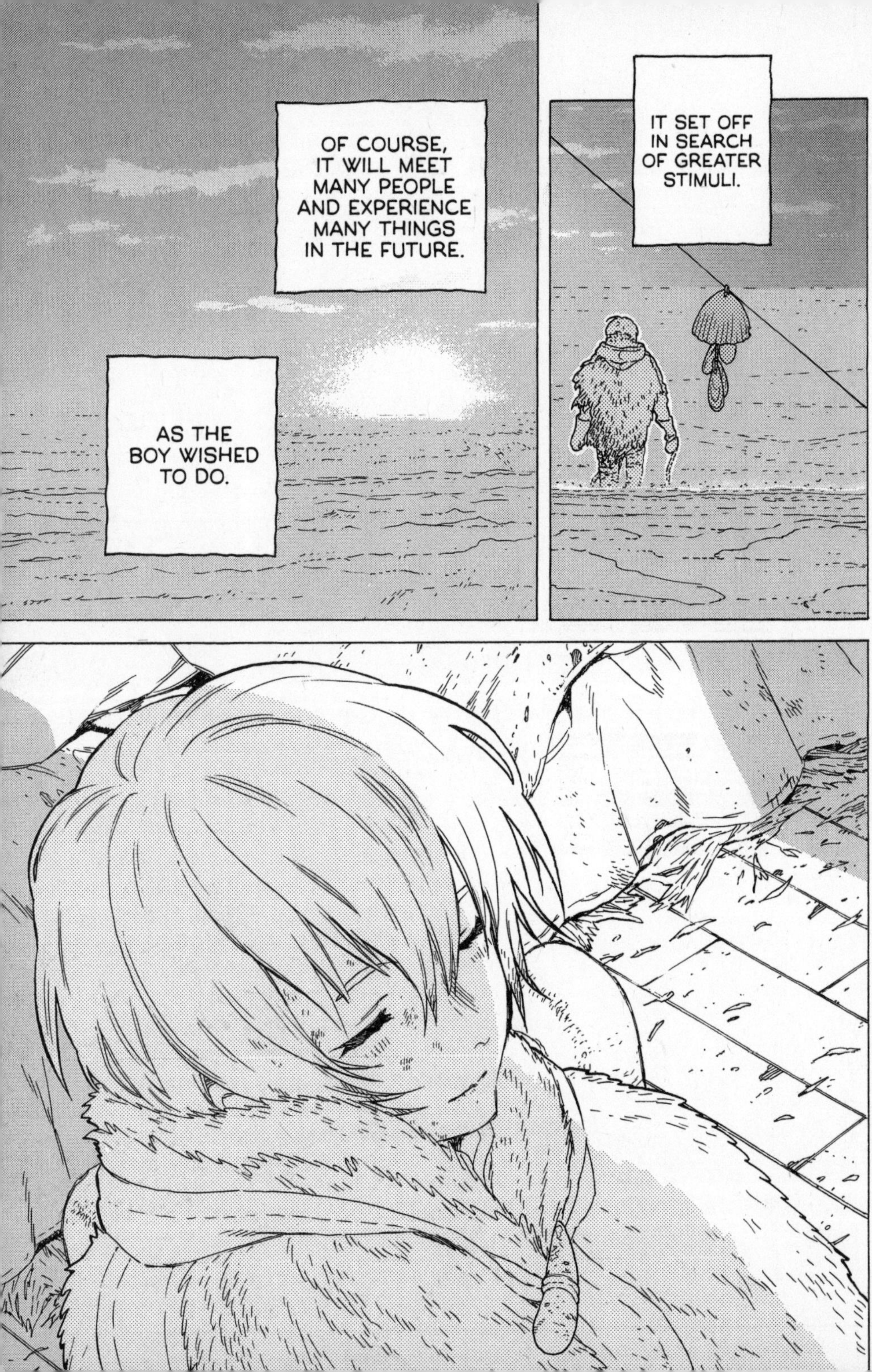
IT SET OFF IN SEARCH OF GREATER STIMULI.
OF COURSE, IT WILL MEET MANY PEOPLE AND EXPERIENCE MANY THINGS IN THE FUTURE.
AS THE BOY WISHED TO DO.

ز-ڒزٜ۲

ONIGUMA AND THE MAIDEN OF NINANNAH

Long ago, we descended upon this land.

This plentiful earth brought about
an abundance of fish, grains, and fruit.

All of these riches, however, belonged to
the god of the mountains, Oniguma.

Oniguma soon became enraged,
and devoured humans to satisfy its hunger.

Then, one day, a maiden from the land of Ninannah
stood up and offered herself to Oniguma.

Oniguma's hunger was quelled, and it took her in as a wife.

THE HISTORIAN OF YANOME
THE LEGEND OF THE FOUR SYMBOLS

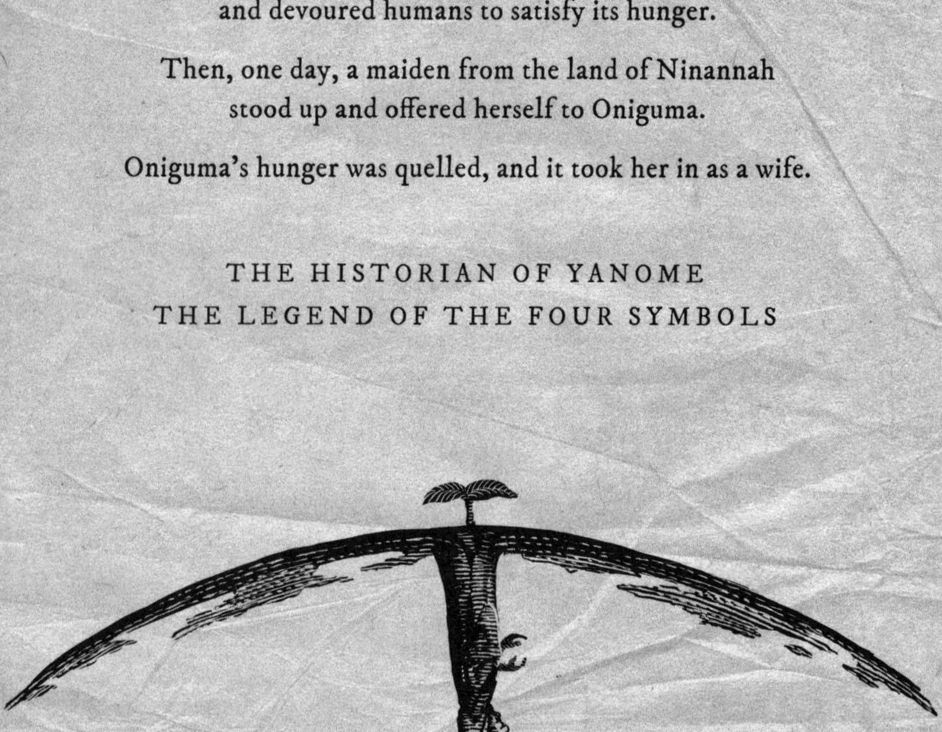

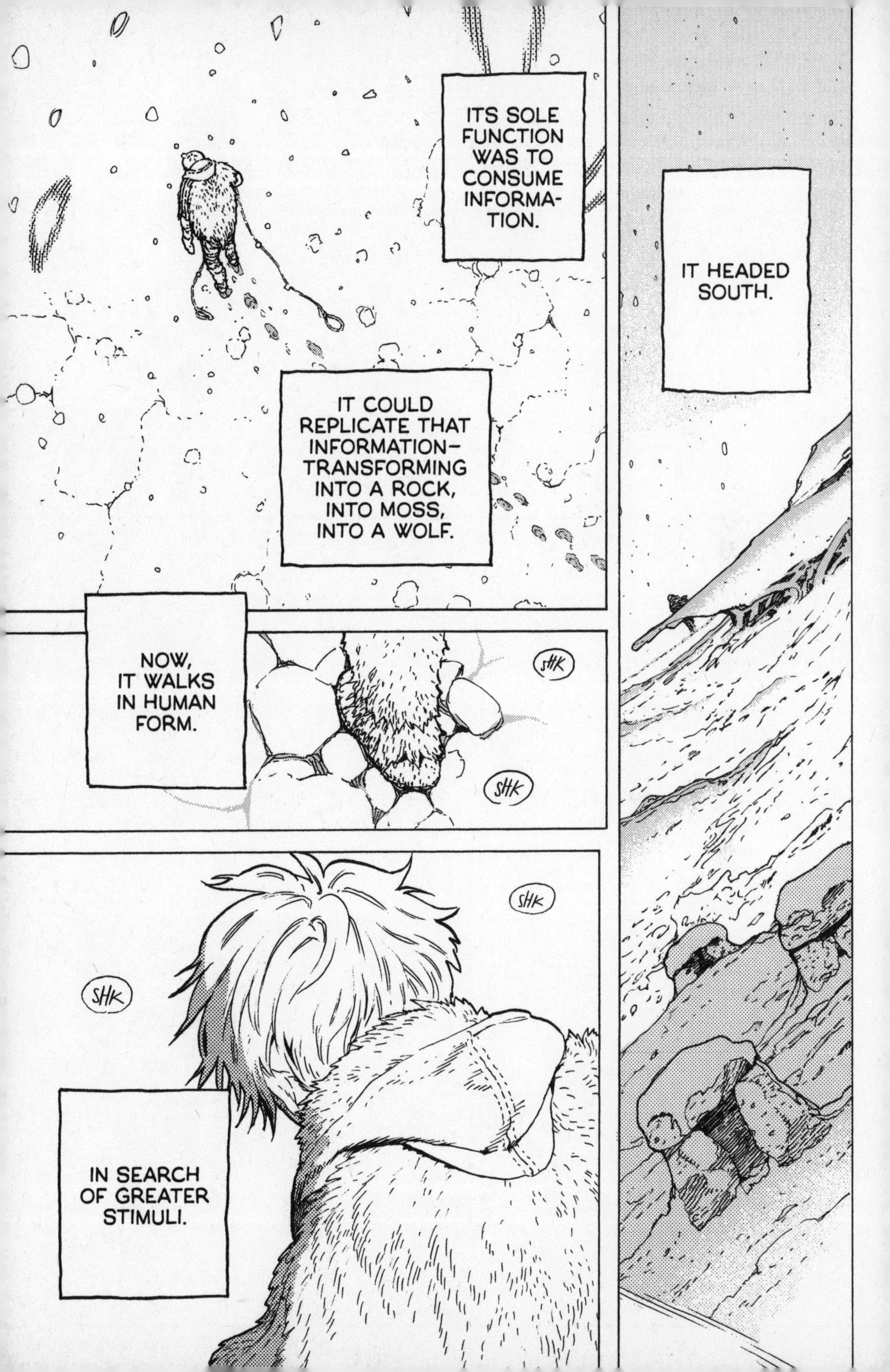
IT HEADED SOUTH.
ITS SOLE FUNCTION WAS TO CONSUME INFORMATION.
IT COULD REPLICATE THAT INFORMATION— TRANSFORMING INTO A ROCK, INTO MOSS, INTO A WOLF.
SHK
NOW, IT WALKS IN HUMAN FORM.
SHK
SHK
SHK
IN SEARCH OF GREATER STIMULI.

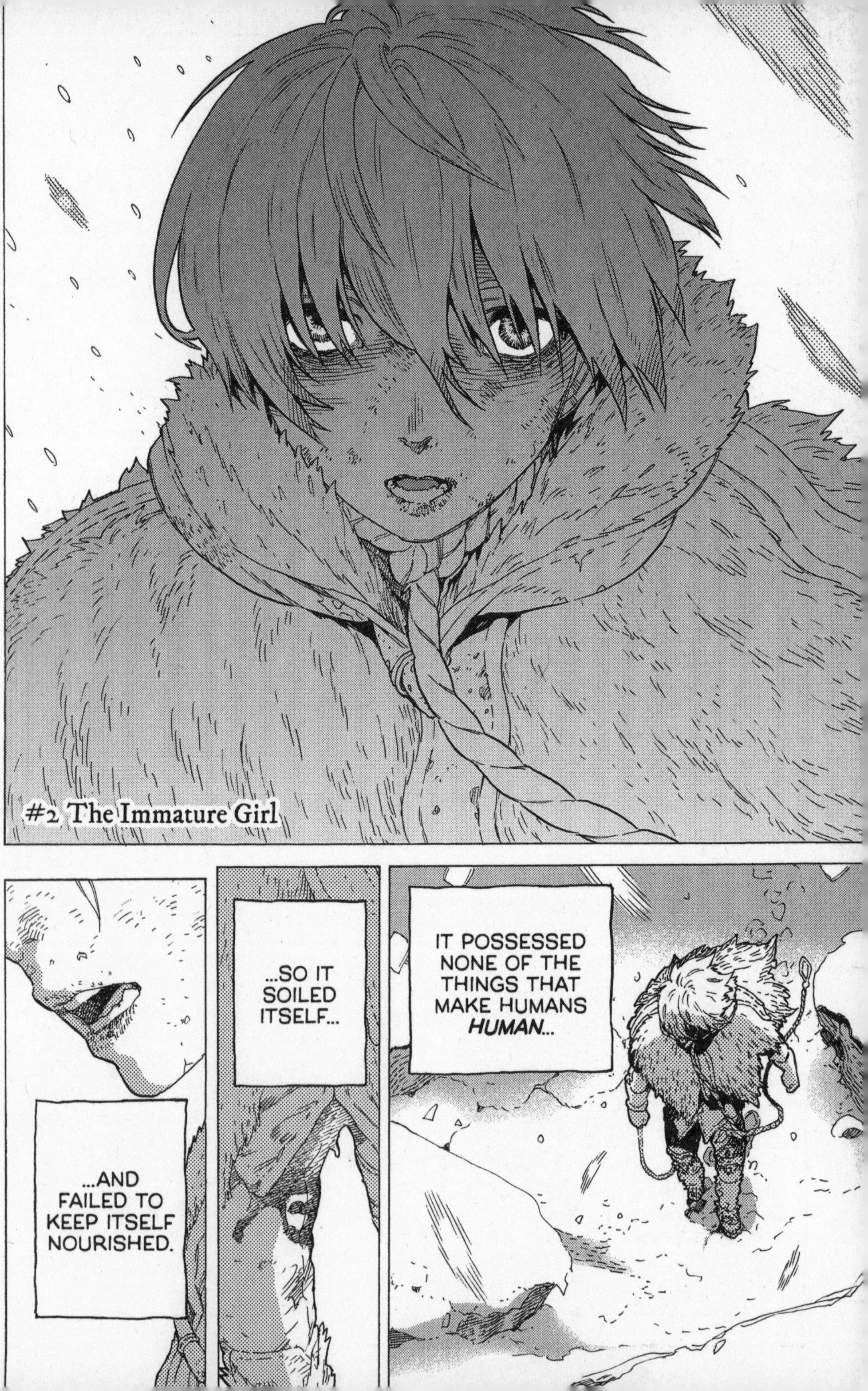
#2 The Immature Girl
IT POSSESSED NONE OF THE THINGS THAT MAKE HUMANS *HUMAN*...
...SO IT SOILED ITSELF...
...AND FAILED TO KEEP ITSELF NOURISHED.

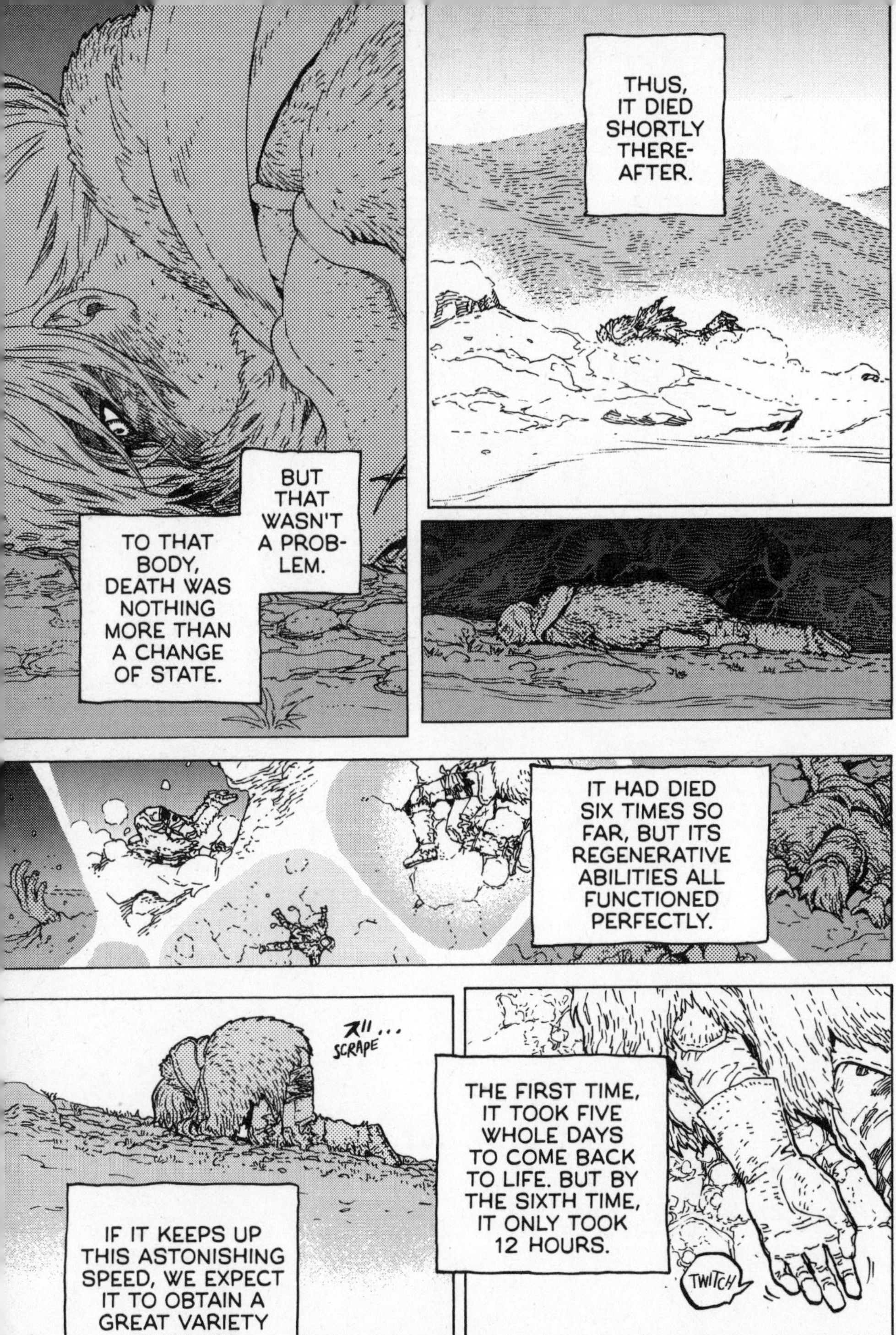
THUS, IT DIED SHORTLY THERE-AFTER.
BUT THAT WASN'T A PROB-LEM.
TO THAT BODY, DEATH WAS NOTHING MORE THAN A CHANGE OF STATE.
IT HAD DIED SIX TIMES SO FAR, BUT ITS REGENERATIVE ABILITIES ALL FUNCTIONED PERFECTLY.
THE FIRST TIME, IT TOOK FIVE WHOLE DAYS TO COME BACK TO LIFE. BUT BY THE SIXTH TIME, IT ONLY TOOK 12 HOURS.
TWITCH
ズリ...
SCRAPE
IF IT KEEPS UP THIS ASTONISHING SPEED, WE EXPECT IT TO OBTAIN A GREAT VARIETY OF THINGS.

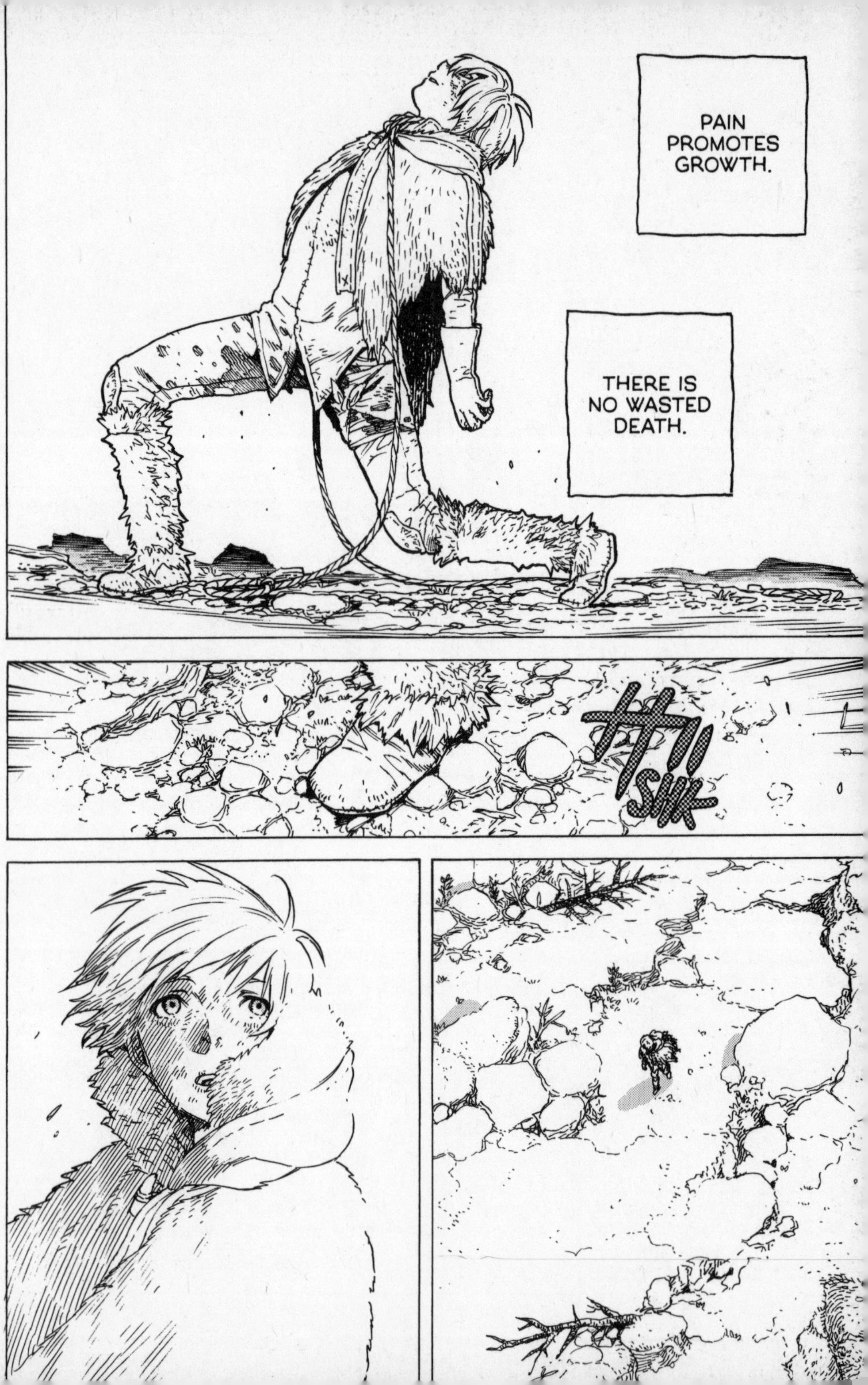
PAIN PROMOTES GROWTH.
THERE IS NO WASTED DEATH.
SHK

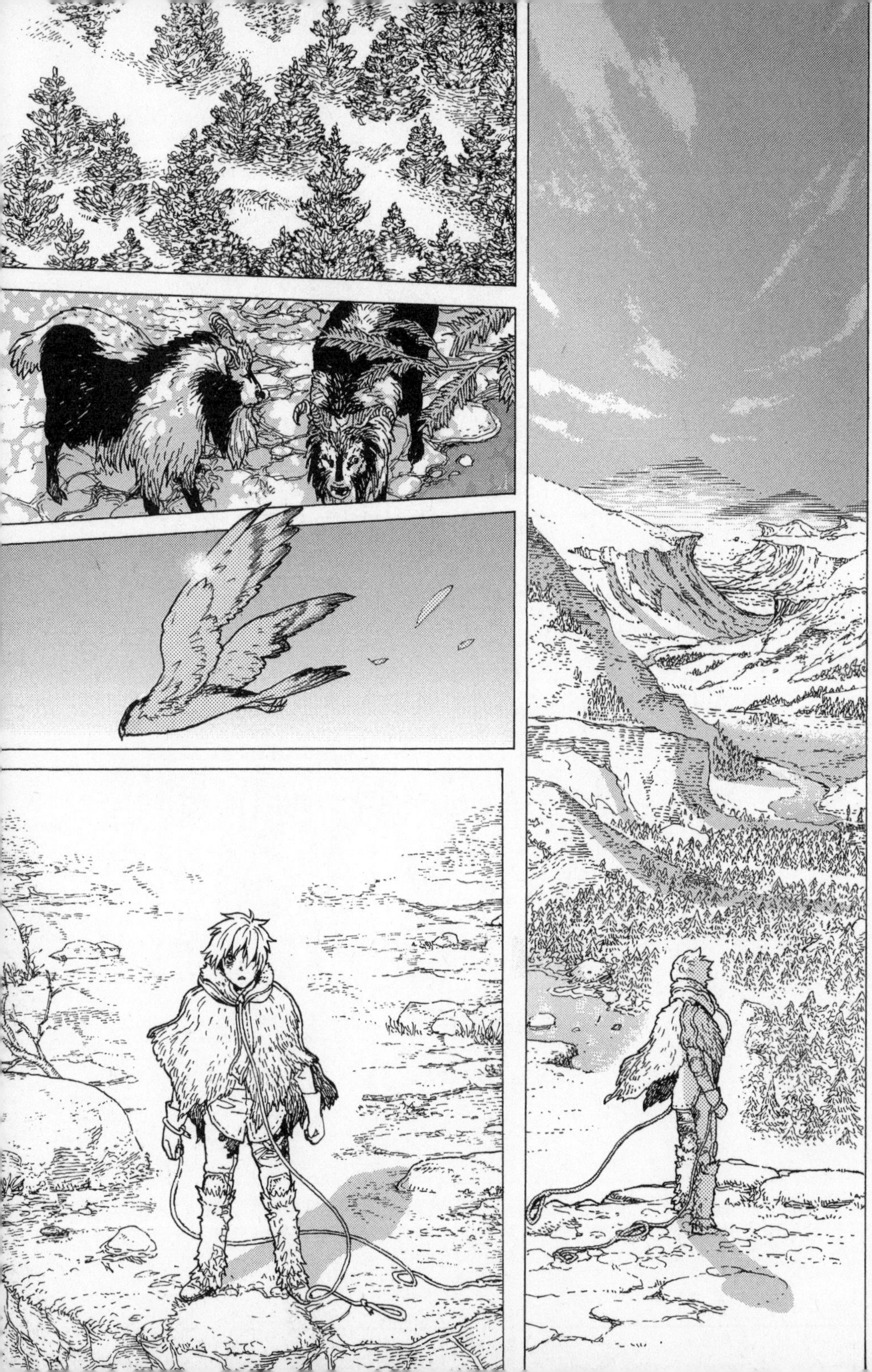

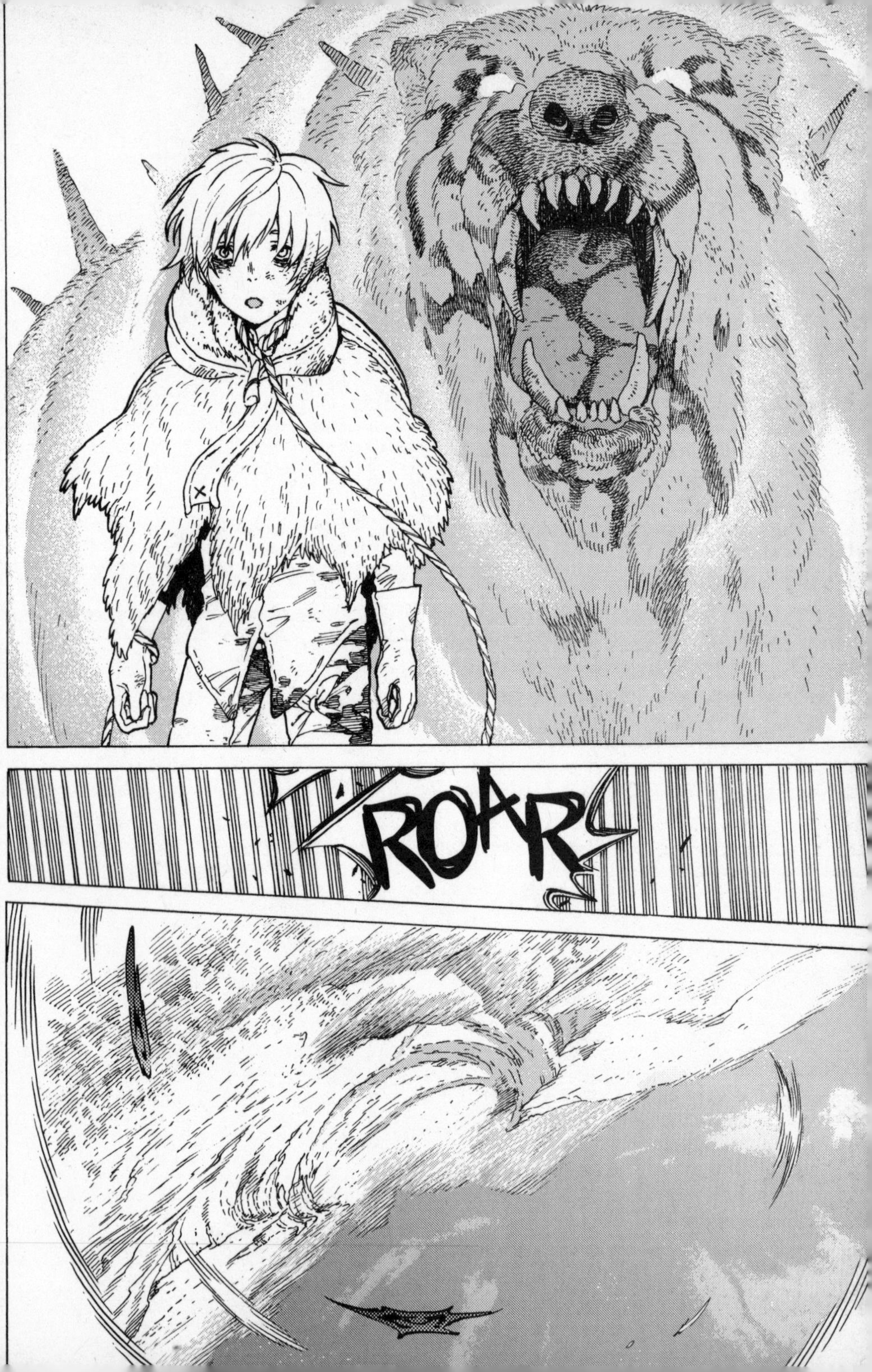
ROAR

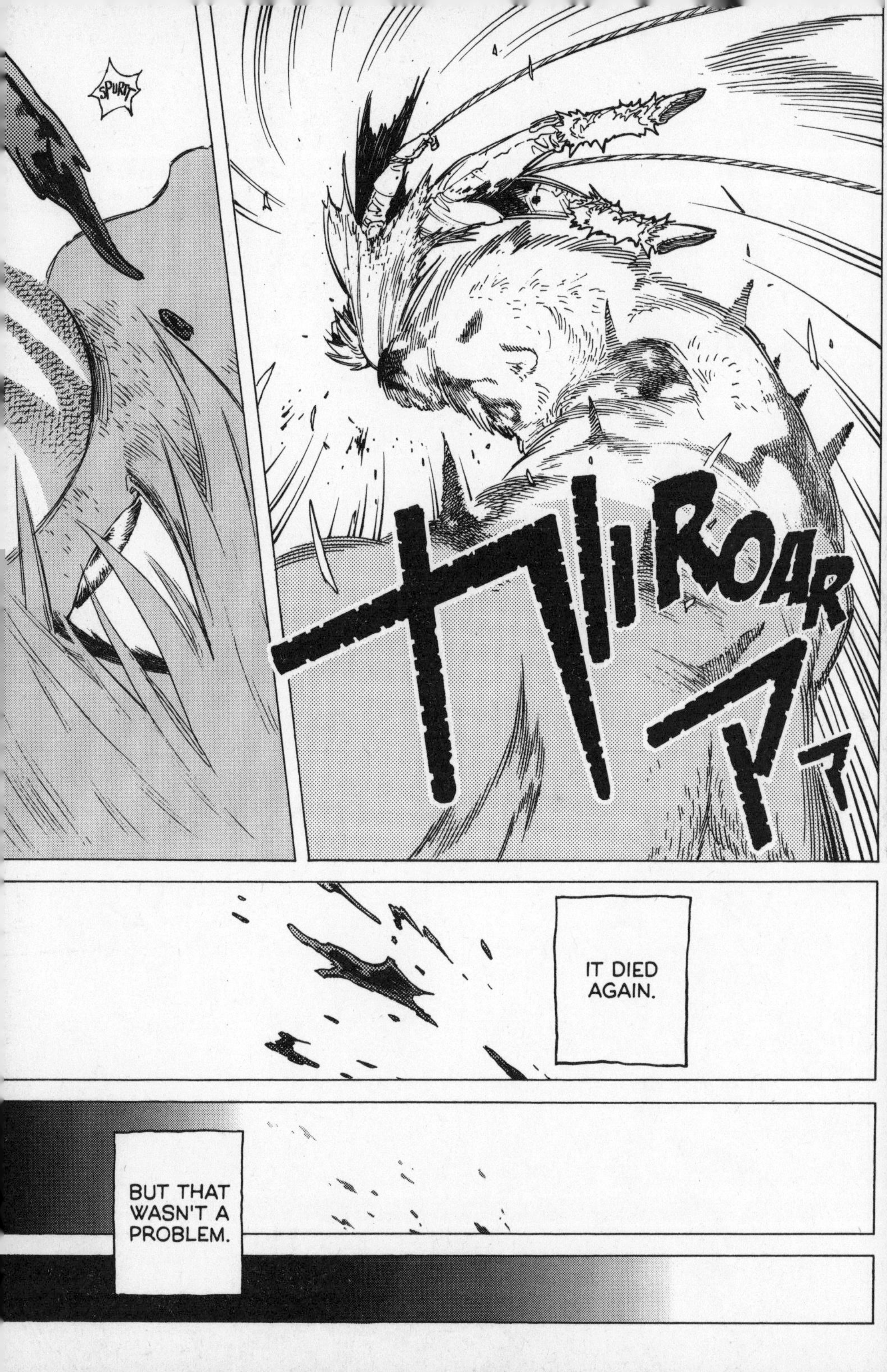
ROAR
SPURT
IT DIED AGAIN.
BUT THAT WASN'T A PROBLEM.

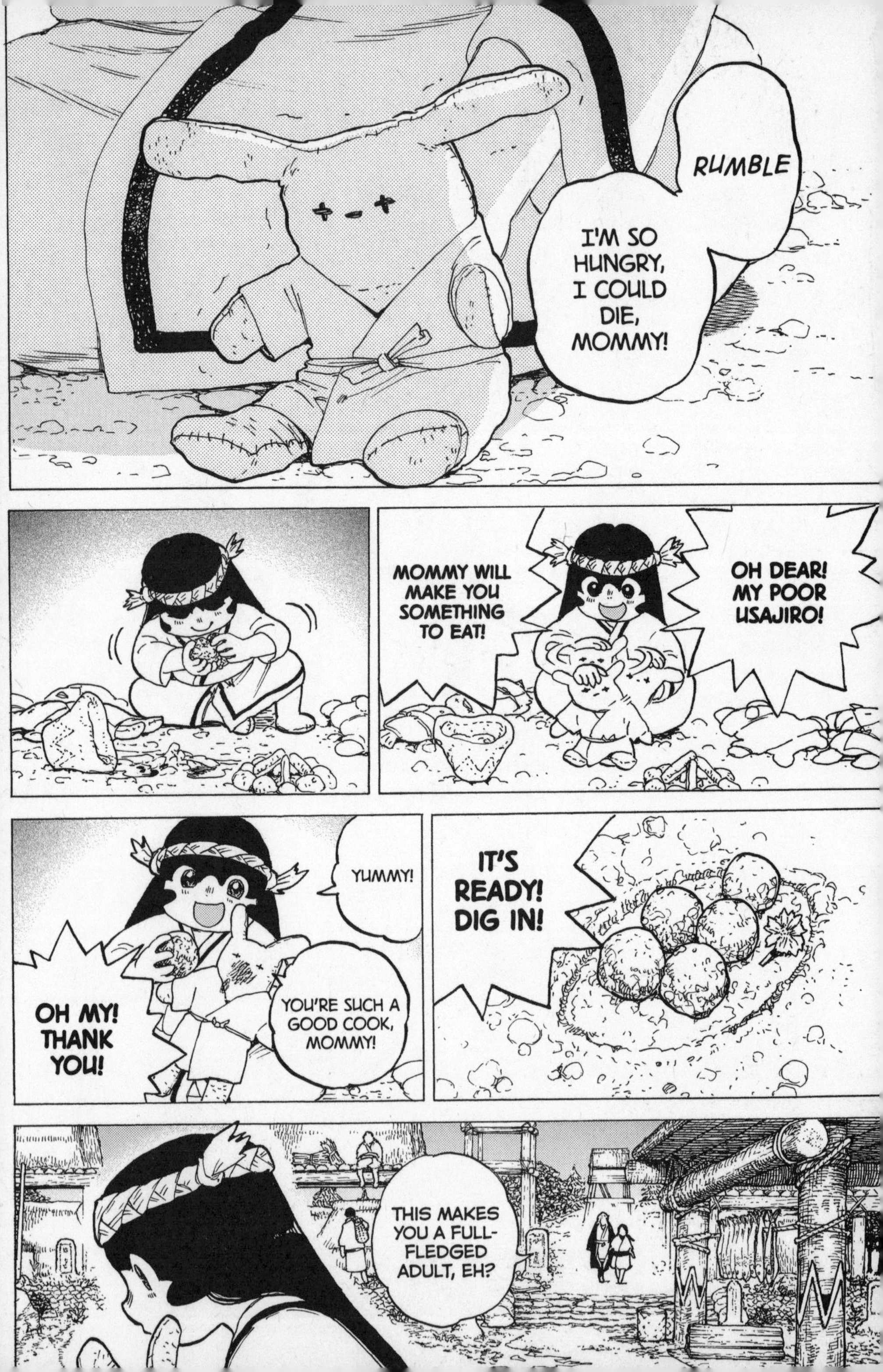
RUMBLE
I'M SO HUNGRY, I COULD DIE, MOMMY!
OH DEAR! MY POOR USAJIRO!
MOMMY WILL MAKE YOU SOMETHING TO EAT!
IT'S READY! DIG IN!
YUMMY!
YOU'RE SUCH A GOOD COOK, MOMMY!
OH MY! THANK YOU!
THIS MAKES YOU A FULL-FLEDGED ADULT, EH?

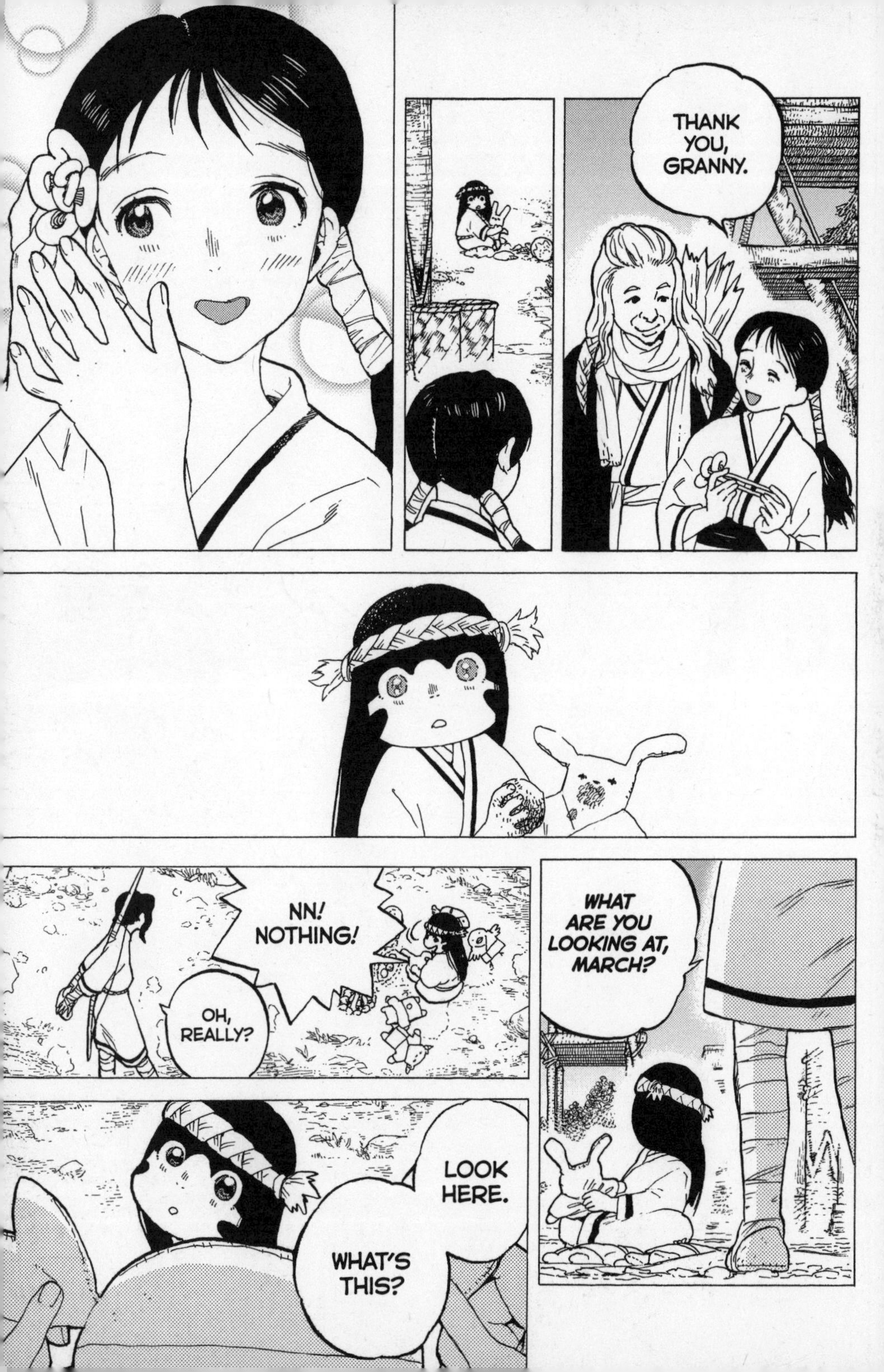
THANK YOU, GRANNY.
WHAT ARE YOU LOOKING AT, MARCH?
NN! NOTHING!
OH, REALLY?
LOOK HERE.
WHAT'S THIS?

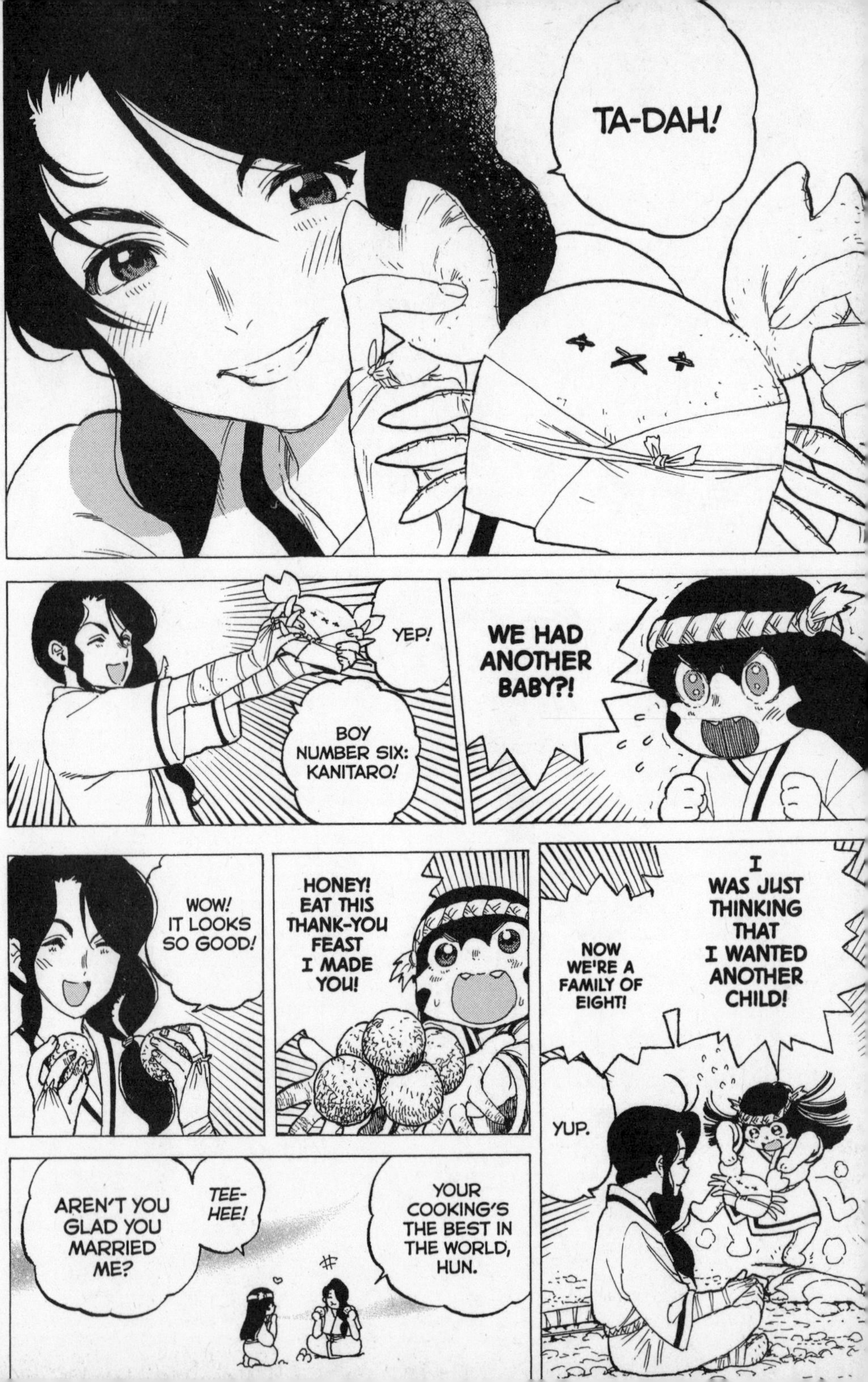
TA-DAH!
WE HAD ANOTHER BABY?!
YEP!
BOY NUMBER SIX: KANITARO!
I WAS JUST THINKING THAT I WANTED ANOTHER CHILD!
NOW WE'RE A FAMILY OF EIGHT!
YUP.
HONEY! EAT THIS THANK-YOU FEAST I MADE YOU!
WOW! IT LOOKS SO GOOD!
YOUR COOKING'S THE BEST IN THE WORLD, HUN.
TEE-HEE!
AREN'T YOU GLAD YOU MARRIED ME?

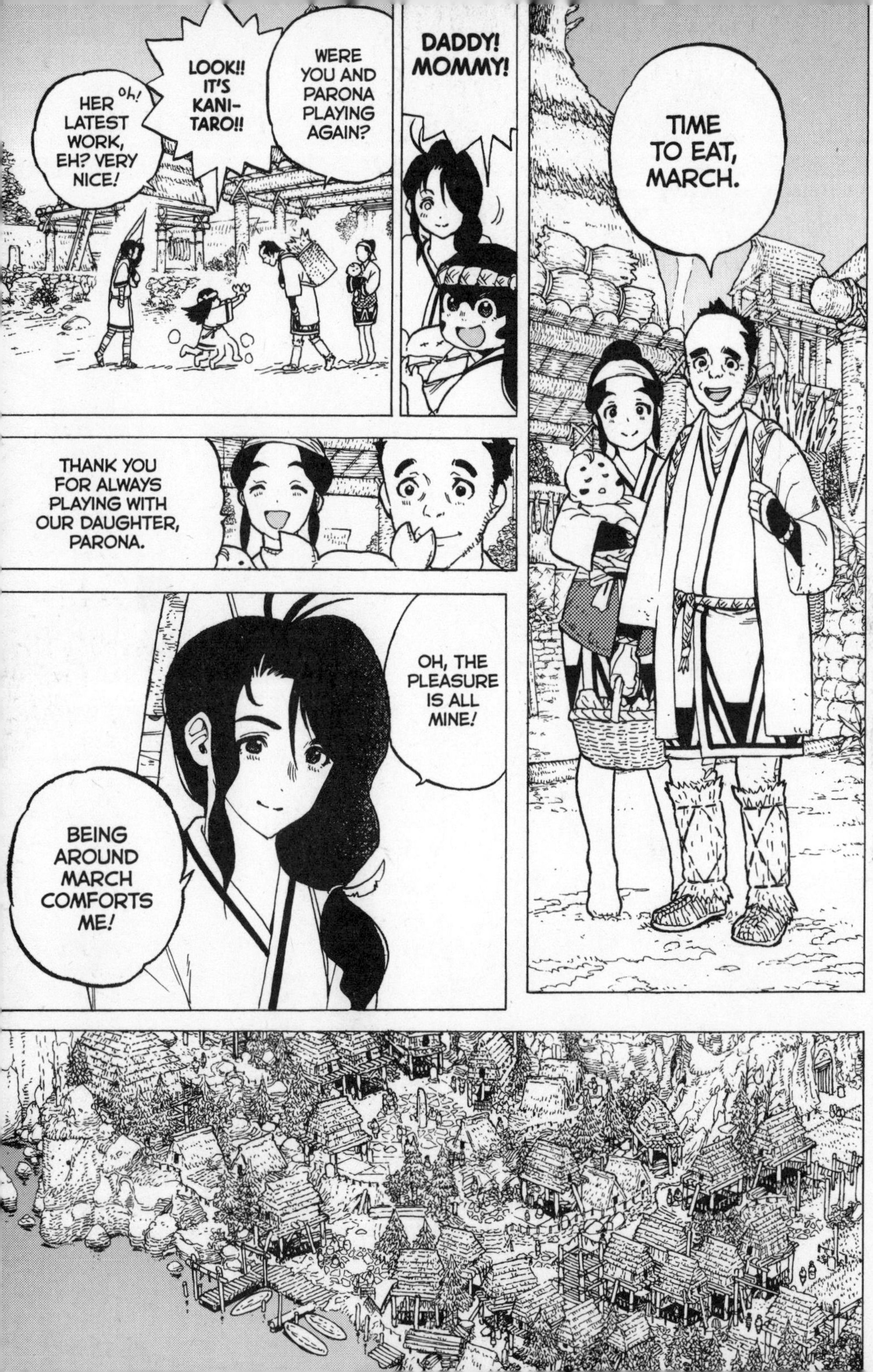
TIME TO EAT, MARCH.
DADDY! MOMMY!
WERE YOU AND PARONA PLAYING AGAIN?
LOOK!! IT'S KANI-TARO!!
oh!
HER LATEST WORK, EH? VERY NICE!
THANK YOU FOR ALWAYS PLAYING WITH OUR DAUGHTER, PARONA.
OH, THE PLEASURE IS ALL MINE!
BEING AROUND MARCH COMFORTS ME!

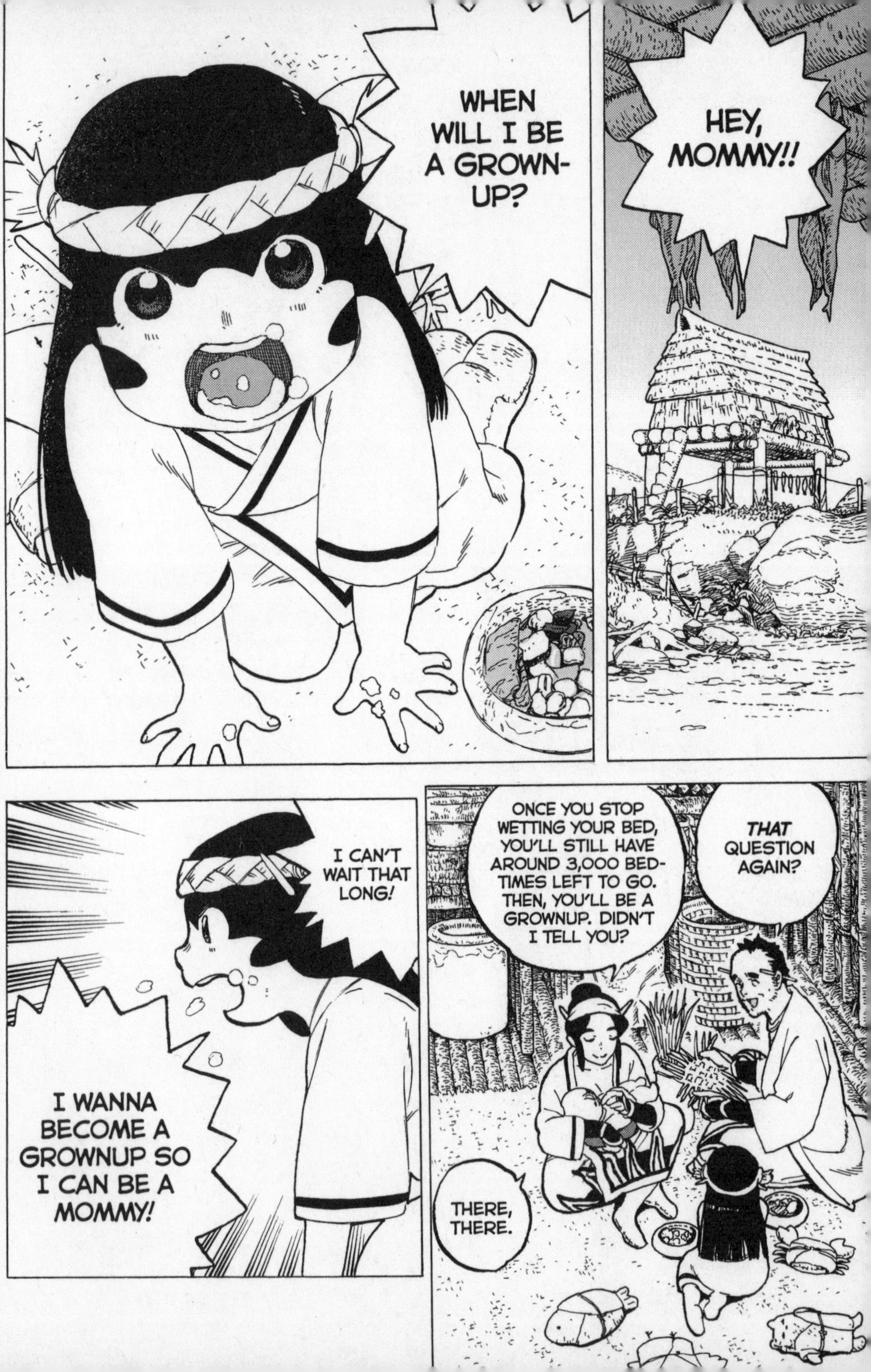
HEY, MOMMY!!
WHEN WILL I BE A GROWN-UP?
THAT QUESTION AGAIN?
ONCE YOU STOP WETTING YOUR BED, YOU'LL STILL HAVE AROUND 3,000 BED-TIMES LEFT TO GO. THEN, YOU'LL BE A GROWNUP. DIDN'T I TELL YOU?
THERE, THERE.
I CAN'T WAIT THAT LONG!
I WANNA BECOME A GROWNUP SO I CAN BE A MOMMY!

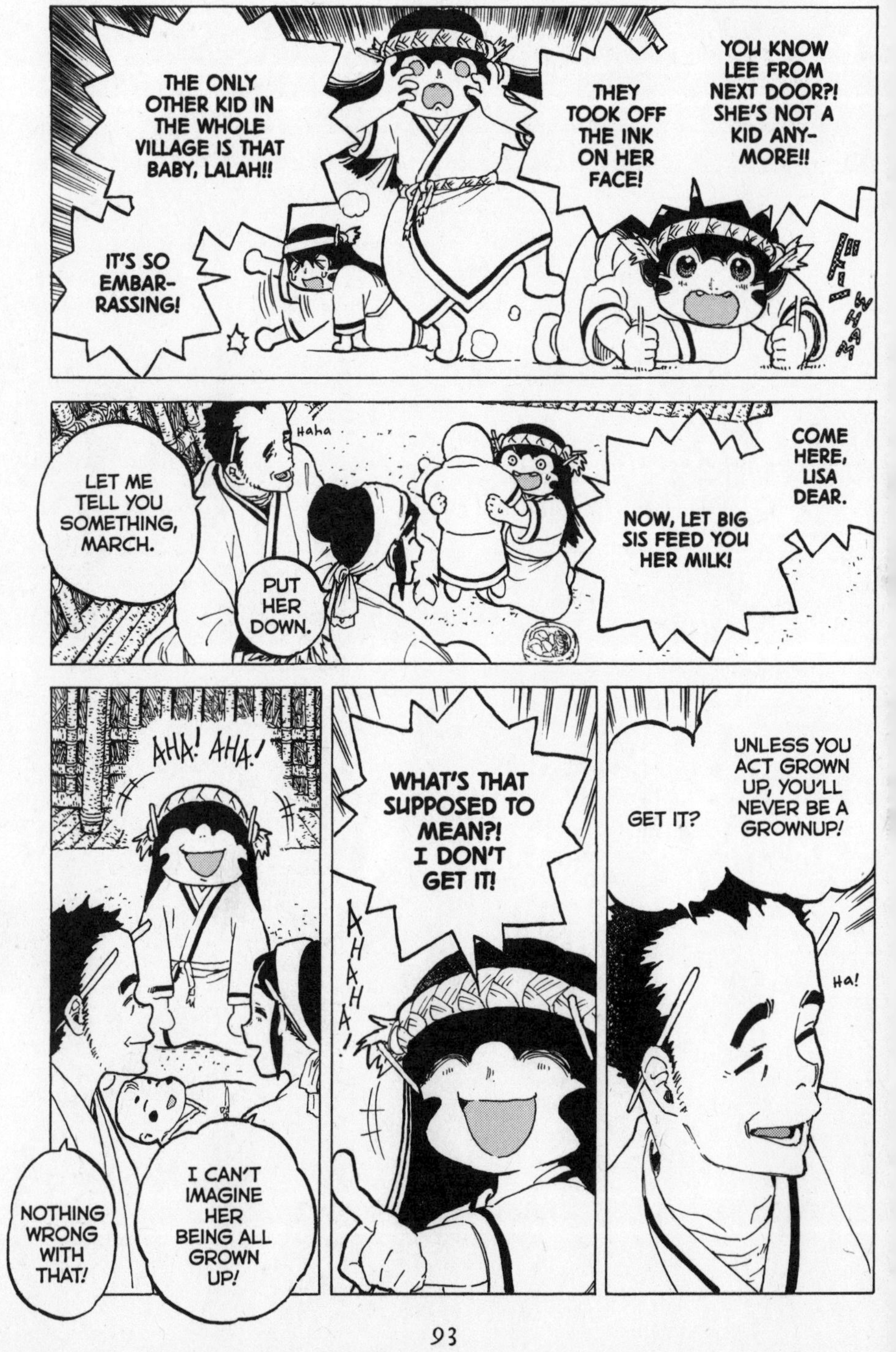
YOU KNOW LEE FROM NEXT DOOR?! SHE'S NOT A KID ANY-MORE!!
THEY TOOK OFF THE INK ON HER FACE!
THE ONLY OTHER KID IN THE WHOLE VILLAGE IS THAT BABY, LALAH!!
IT'S SO EMBAR-RASSING!
COME HERE, LISA DEAR.
NOW, LET BIG SIS FEED YOU HER MILK!
Haha
LET ME TELL YOU SOMETHING, MARCH.
PUT HER DOWN.
UNLESS YOU ACT GROWN UP, YOU'LL NEVER BE A GROWNUP!
GET IT?
Ha!
WHAT'S THAT SUPPOSED TO MEAN?! I DON'T GET IT!
AHAHA!
AHA! AHA!
I CAN'T IMAGINE HER BEING ALL GROWN UP!
NOTHING WRONG WITH THAT!

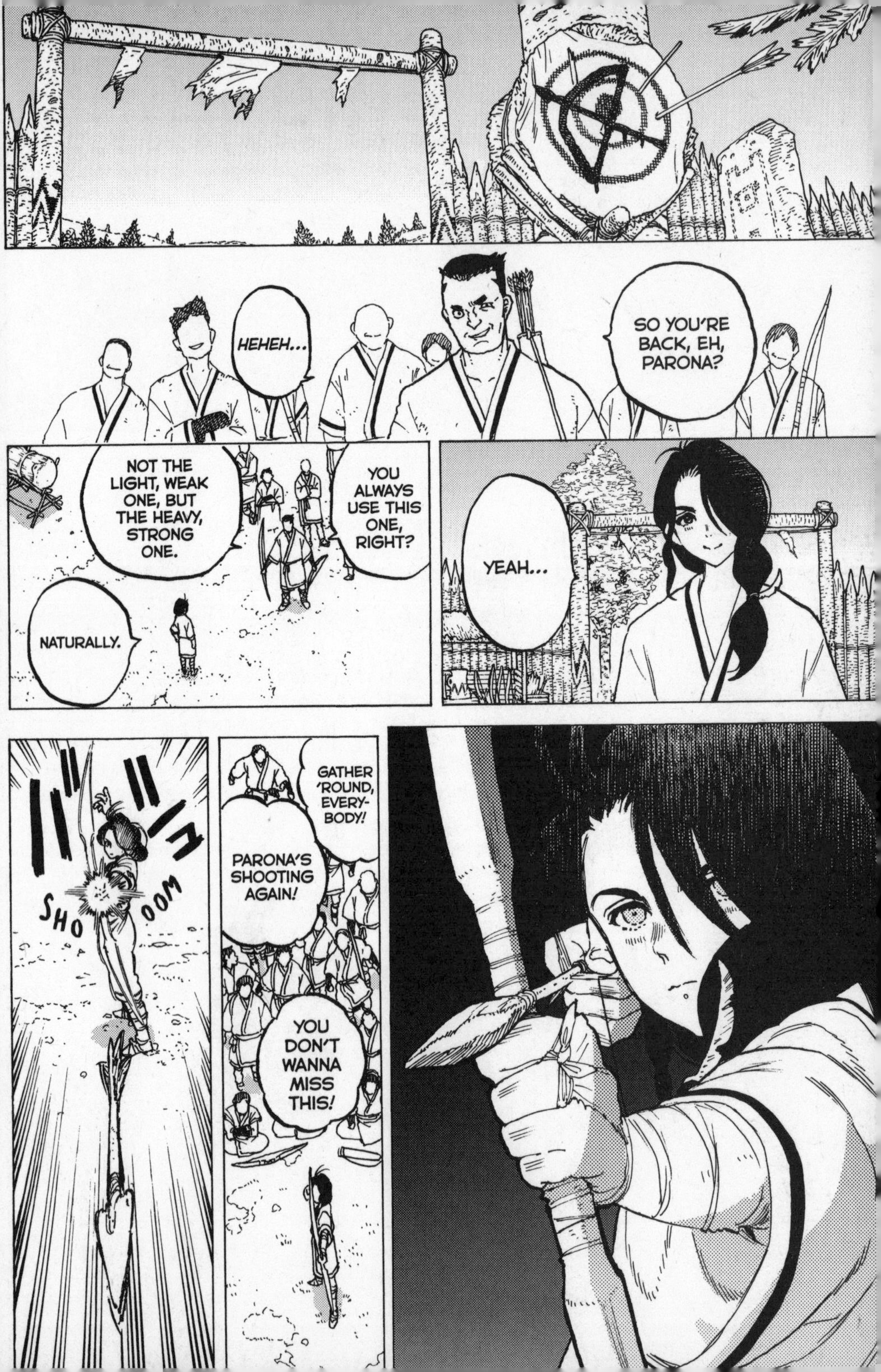
SO YOU'RE BACK, EH, PARONA?
HEHEH...
YEAH...
YOU ALWAYS USE THIS ONE, RIGHT?
NOT THE LIGHT, WEAK ONE, BUT THE HEAVY, STRONG ONE.
NATURALLY.
GATHER 'ROUND, EVERYBODY!
PARONA'S SHOOTING AGAIN!
YOU DON'T WANNA MISS THIS!
SHOOOM

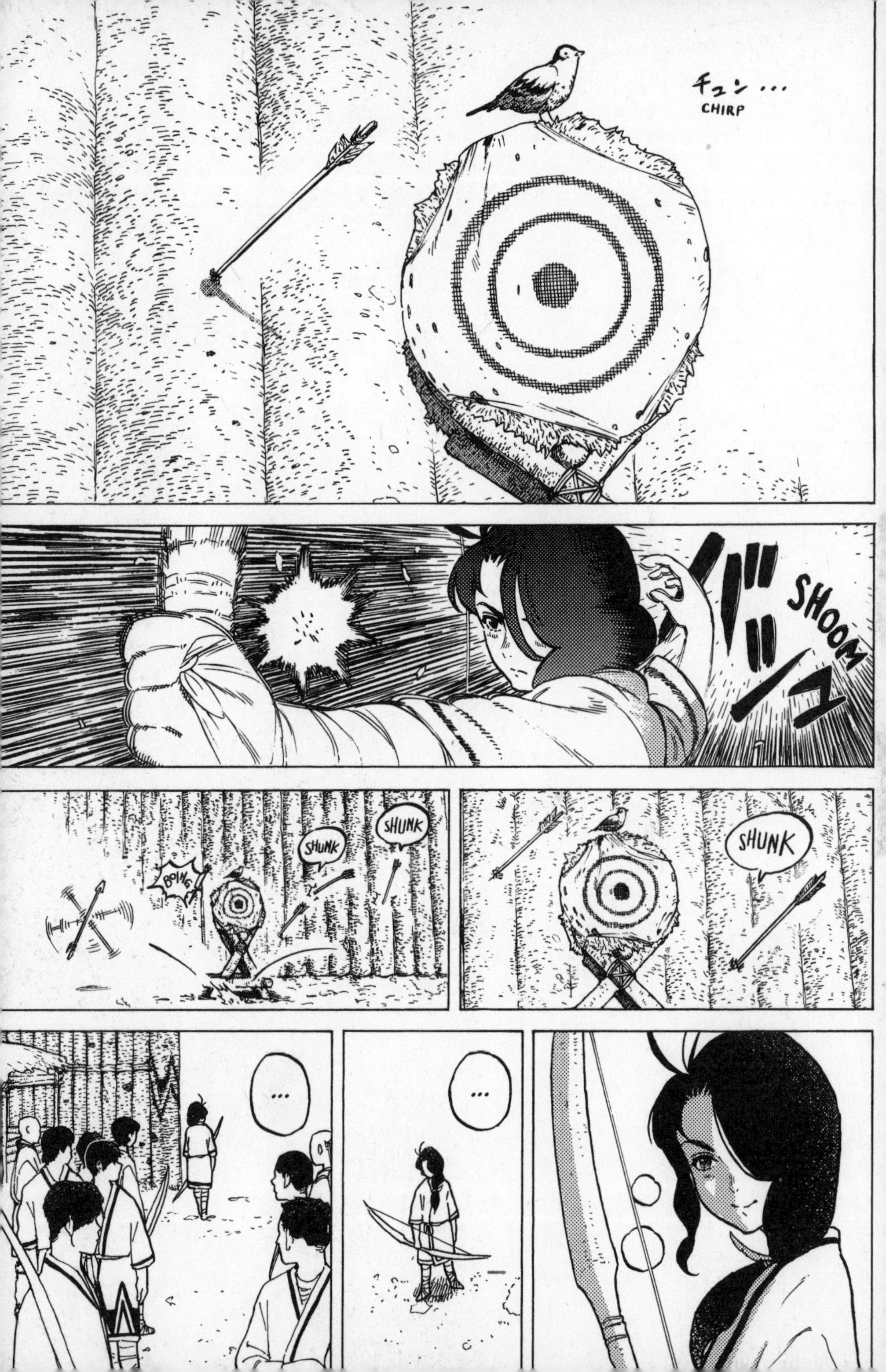
チュン…
CHIRP
ジュ
SHOOM
SHUNK
SHUNK
SHUNK
BOING
...
...

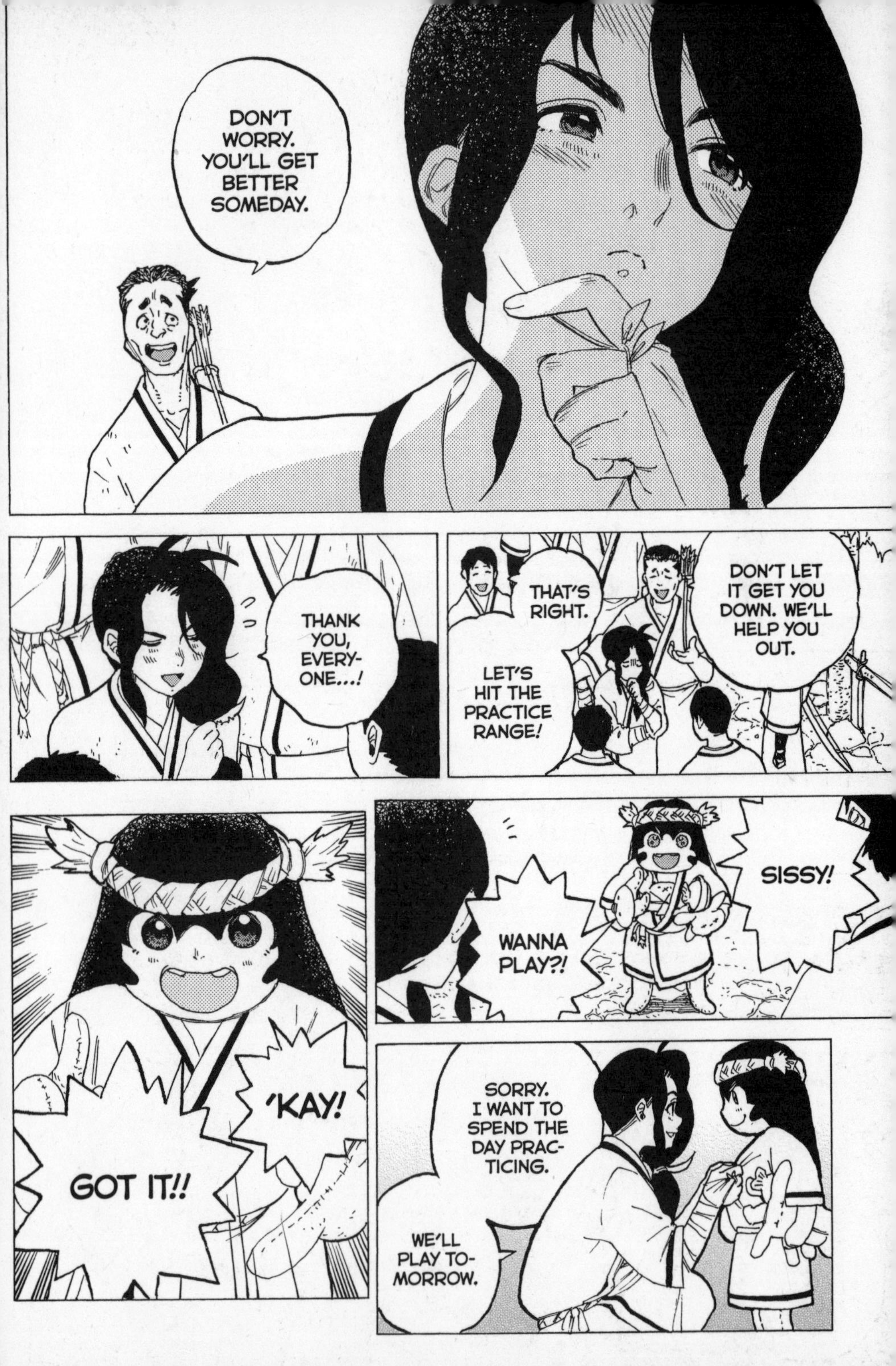
DON'T WORRY. YOU'LL GET BETTER SOMEDAY.
DON'T LET IT GET YOU DOWN. WE'LL HELP YOU OUT.
THAT'S RIGHT.
LET'S HIT THE PRACTICE RANGE!
THANK YOU, EVERY-ONE...!
SISSY!
WANNA PLAY?!
SORRY. I WANT TO SPEND THE DAY PRAC-TICING.
WE'LL PLAY TO-MORROW.
'KAY!
GOT IT!!

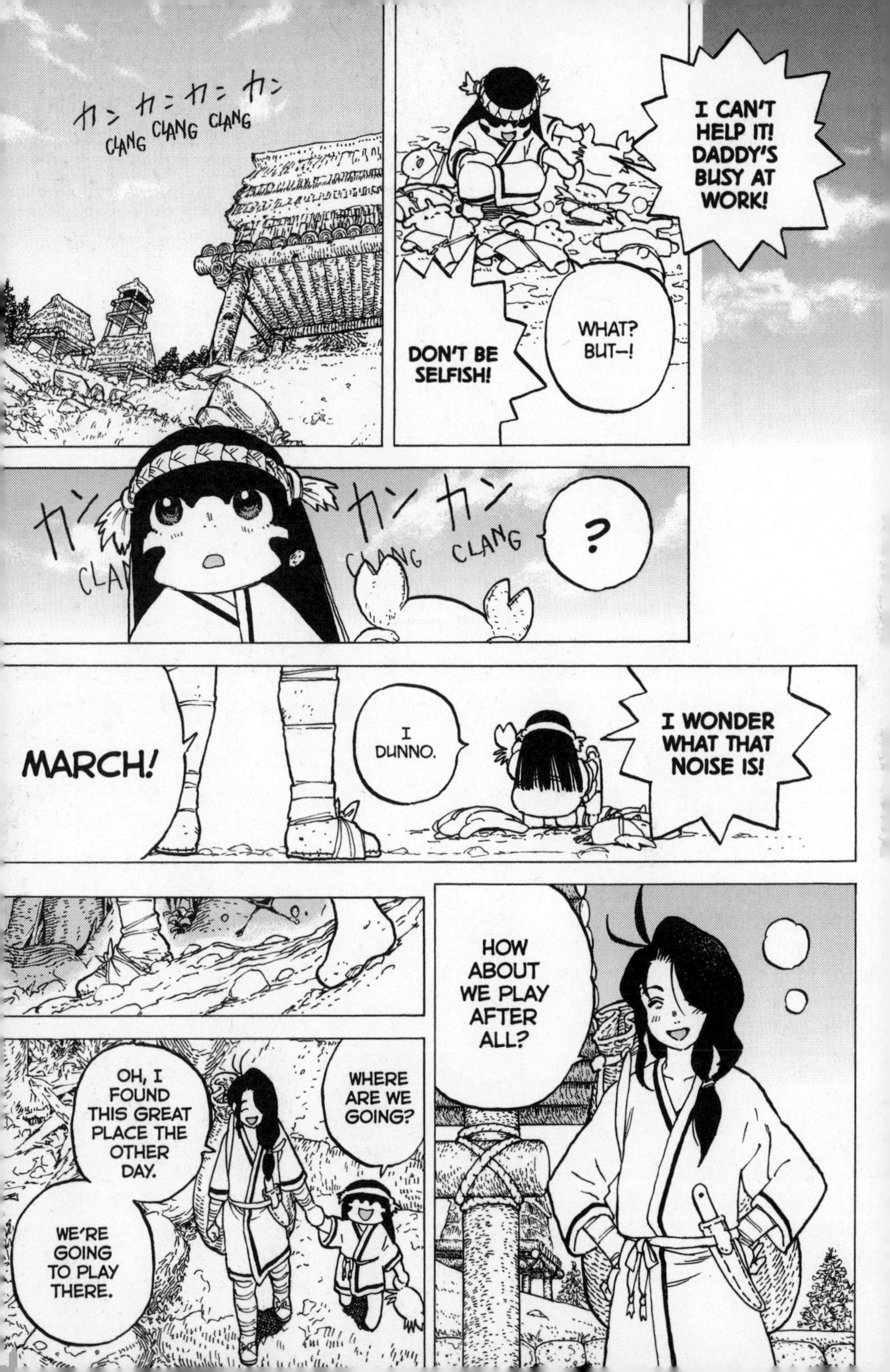
I CAN'T HELP IT! DADDY'S BUSY AT WORK!
WHAT? BUT–!
DON'T BE SELFISH!
カンカンカンカン
CLANG CLANG CLANG
カンカンカン
CLANG CLANG
?
I WONDER WHAT THAT NOISE IS!
I DUNNO.
MARCH!
HOW ABOUT WE PLAY AFTER ALL?
WHERE ARE WE GOING?
OH, I FOUND THIS GREAT PLACE THE OTHER DAY.
WE'RE GOING TO PLAY THERE.

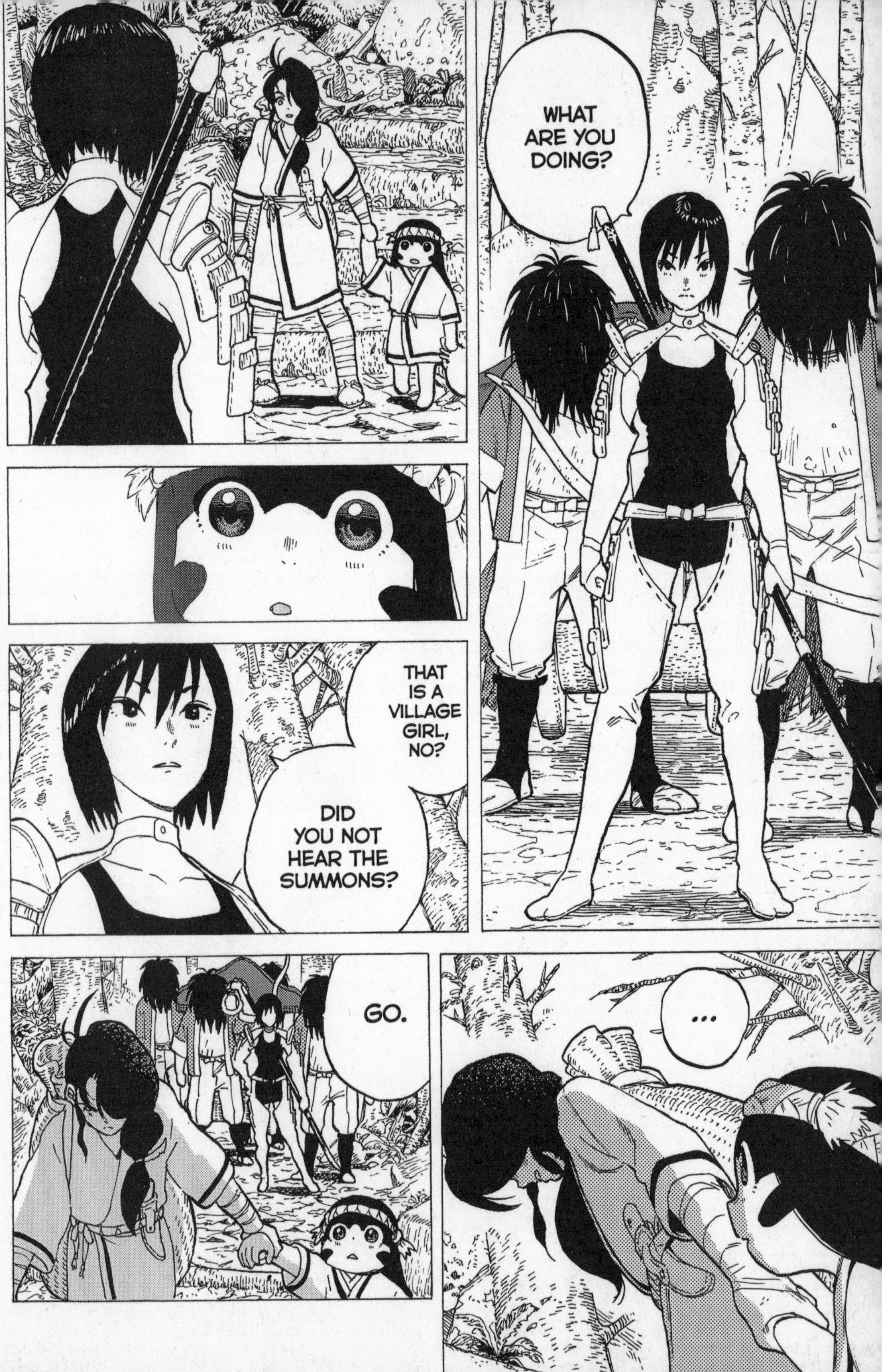
WHAT ARE YOU DOING?
THAT IS A VILLAGE GIRL, NO?
DID YOU NOT HEAR THE SUMMONS?
...
GO.

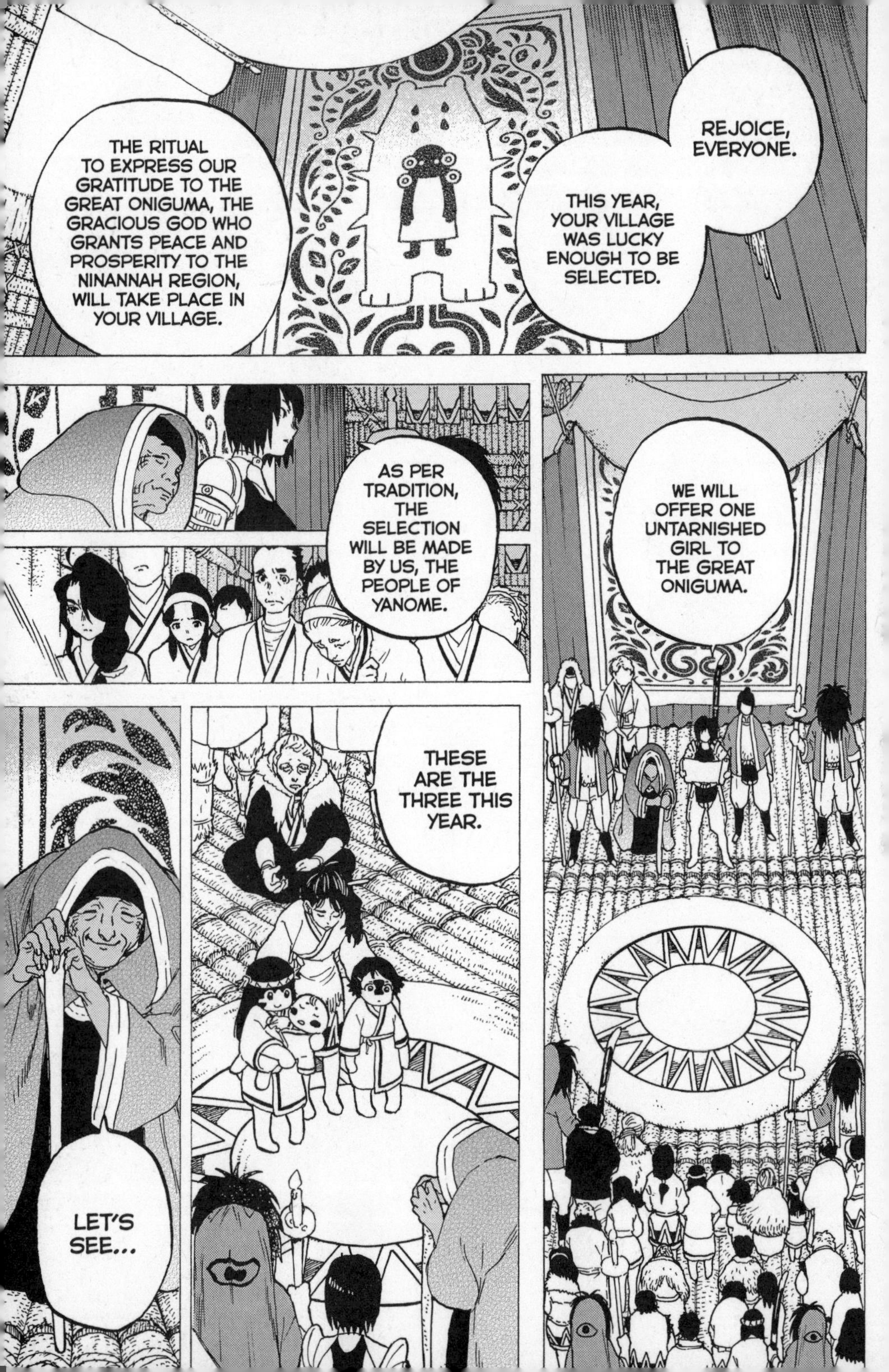
REJOICE, EVERYONE.
THIS YEAR, YOUR VILLAGE WAS LUCKY ENOUGH TO BE SELECTED.
THE RITUAL TO EXPRESS OUR GRATITUDE TO THE GREAT ONIGUMA, THE GRACIOUS GOD WHO GRANTS PEACE AND PROSPERITY TO THE NINANNAH REGION, WILL TAKE PLACE IN YOUR VILLAGE.
WE WILL OFFER ONE UNTARNISHED GIRL TO THE GREAT ONIGUMA.
AS PER TRADITION, THE SELECTION WILL BE MADE BY US, THE PEOPLE OF YANOME.
THESE ARE THE THREE THIS YEAR.
LET'S SEE...

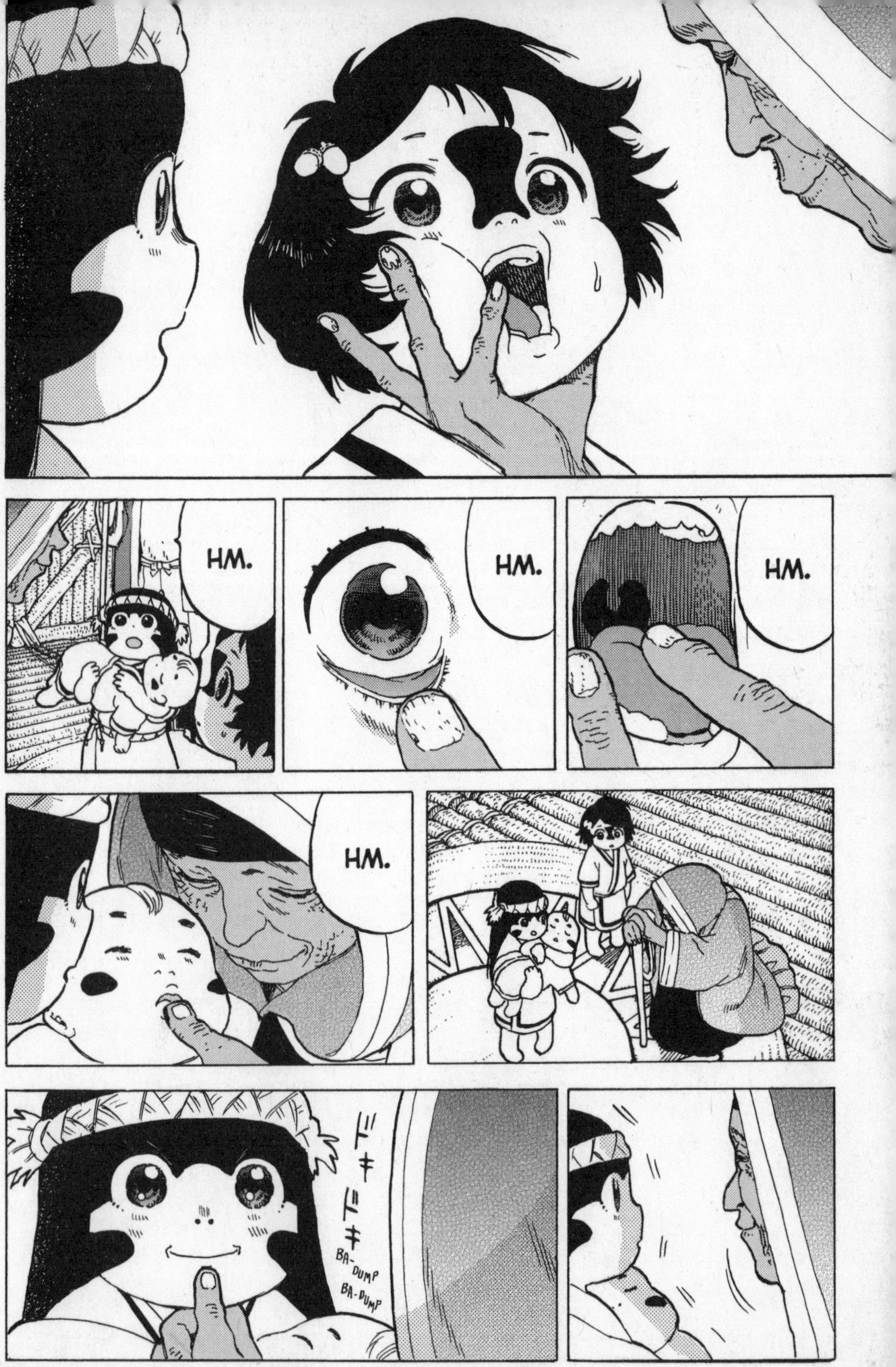
HM.
HM.
HM.
HM.
ドキドキ
BA-DUMP BA-DUMP

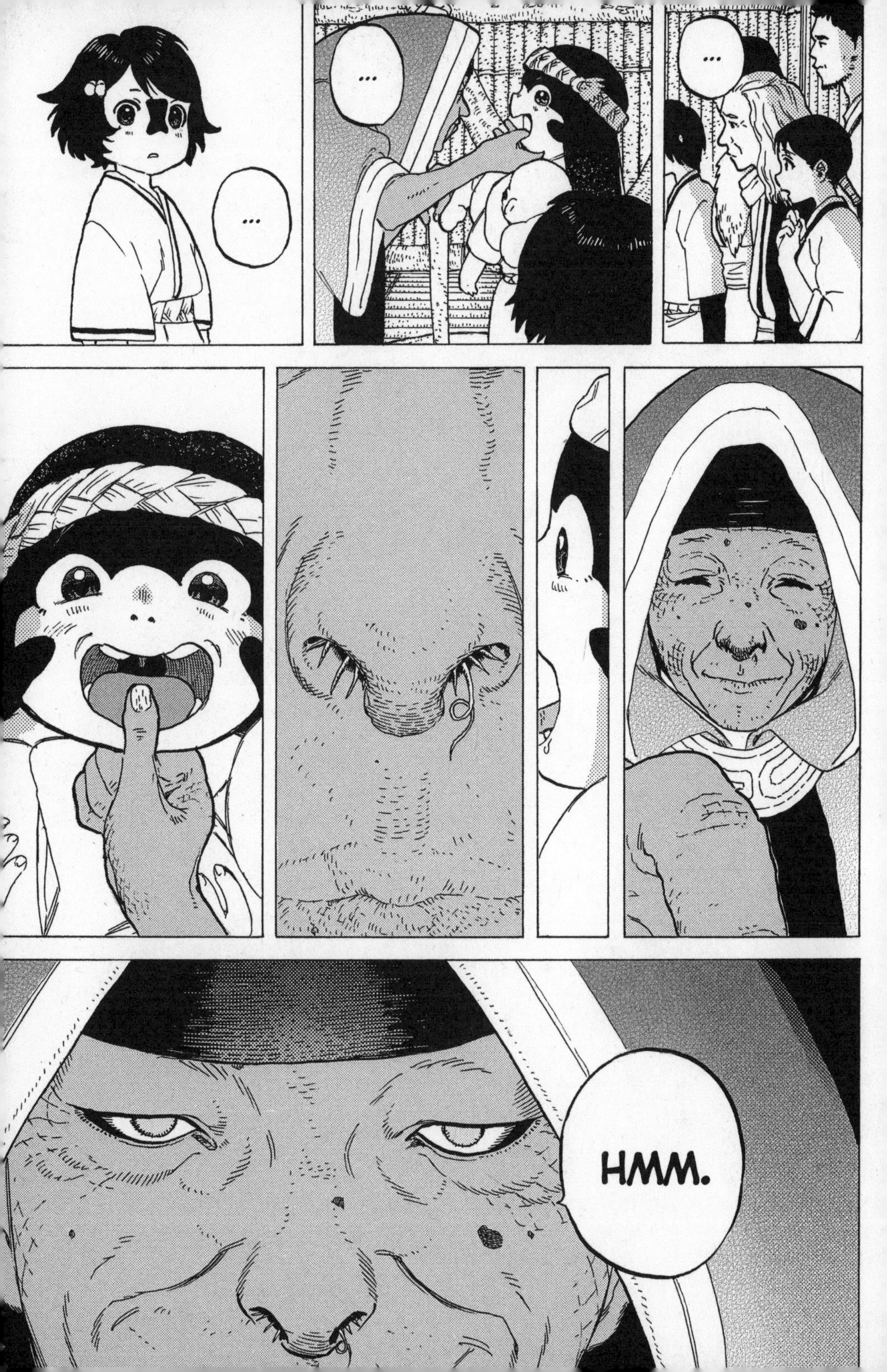
...
...
...
HMM.

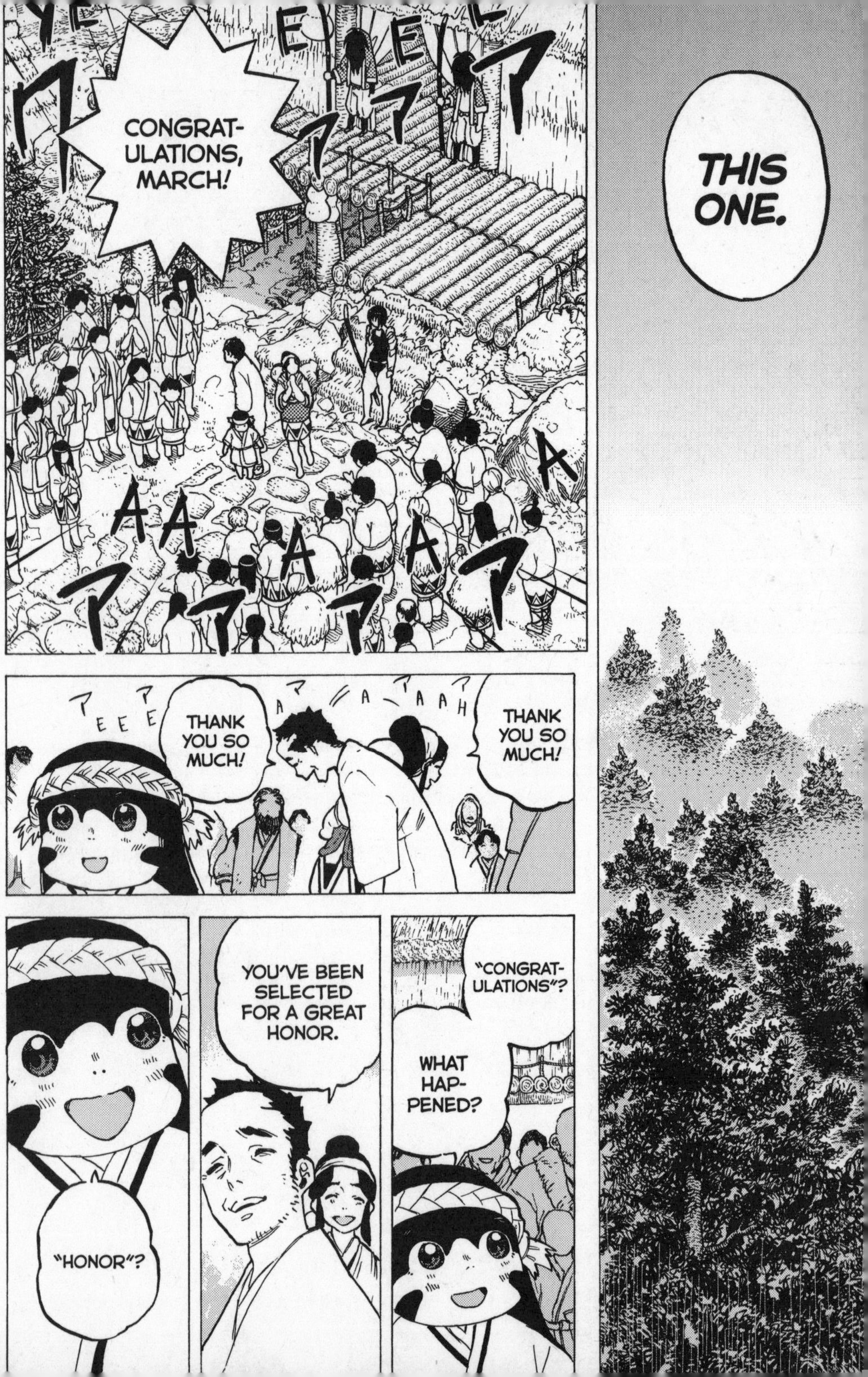
THIS ONE.
CONGRAT-ULATIONS, MARCH!
THANK YOU SO MUCH!
THANK YOU SO MUCH!
"CONGRAT-ULATIONS"?
WHAT HAP-PENED?
YOU'VE BEEN SELECTED FOR A GREAT HONOR.
"HONOR"?

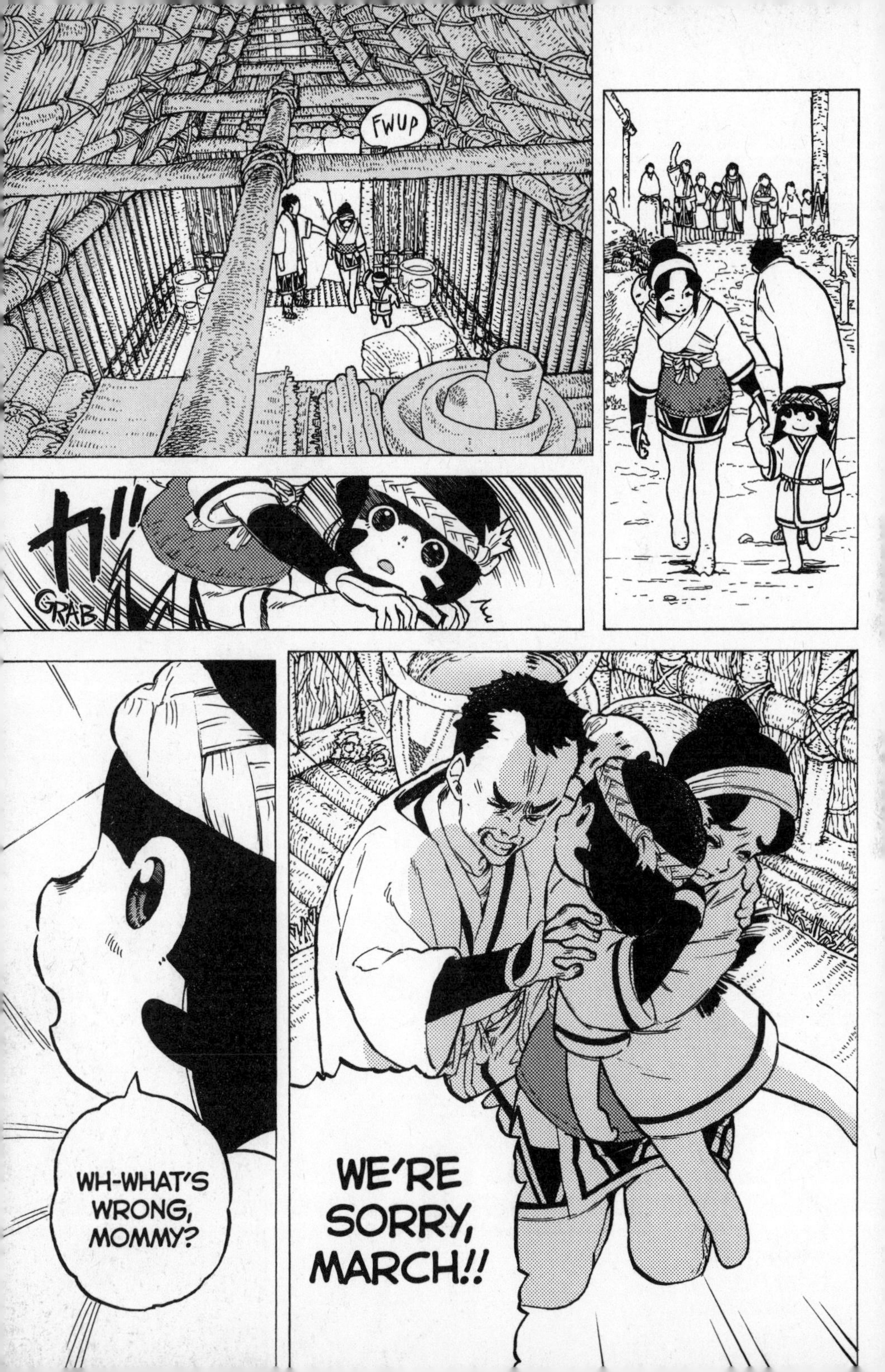
FWUP
ガ
GRAB
WE'RE SORRY, MARCH!!
WH-WHAT'S WRONG, MOMMY?

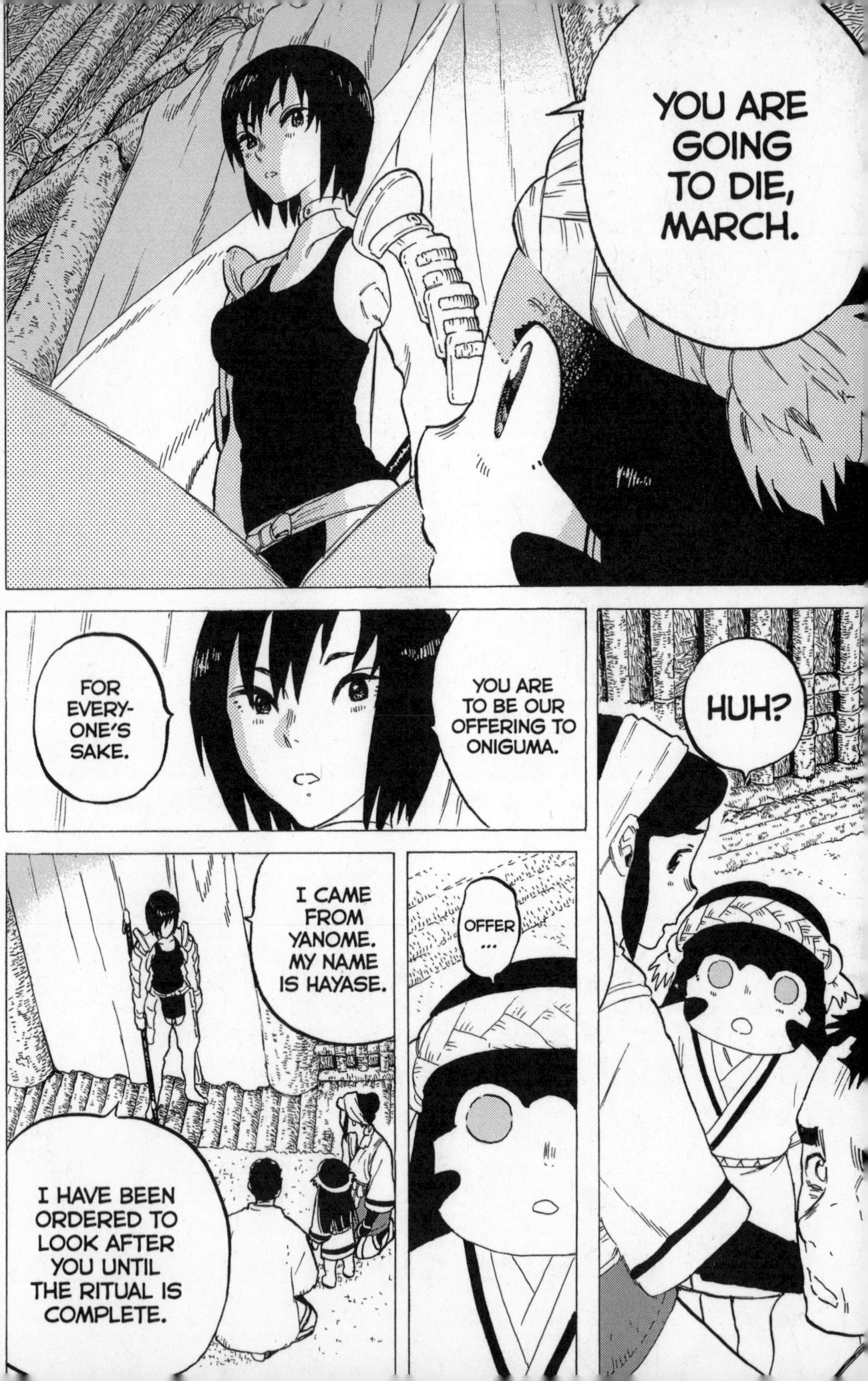
YOU ARE GOING TO DIE, MARCH.
HUH?
YOU ARE TO BE OUR OFFERING TO ONIGUMA.
FOR EVERY-ONE'S SAKE.
OFFER...
I CAME FROM YANOME. MY NAME IS HAYASE.
I HAVE BEEN ORDERED TO LOOK AFTER YOU UNTIL THE RITUAL IS COMPLETE.

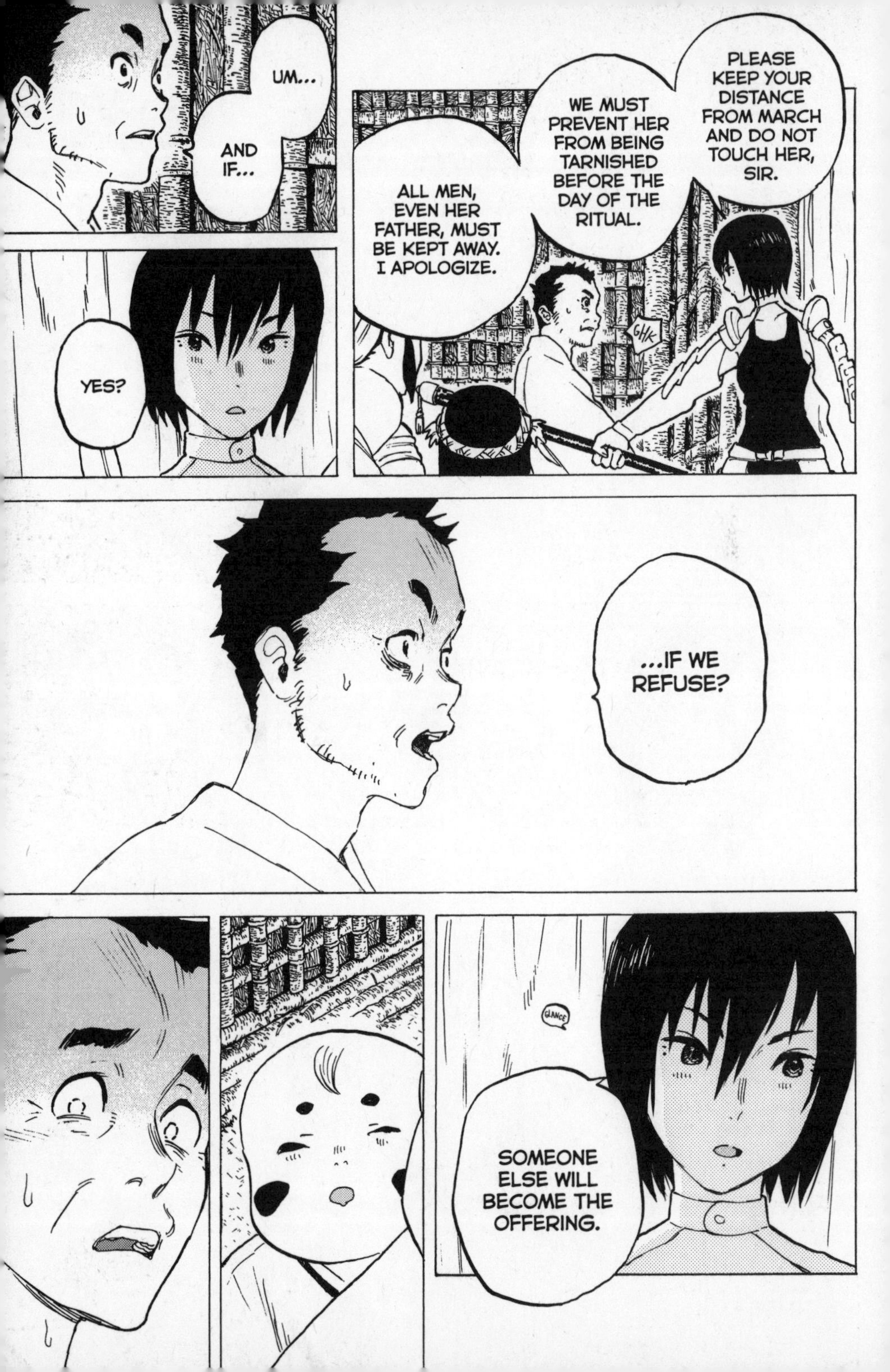
PLEASE KEEP YOUR DISTANCE FROM MARCH AND DO NOT TOUCH HER, SIR.
WE MUST PREVENT HER FROM BEING TARNISHED BEFORE THE DAY OF THE RITUAL.
ALL MEN, EVEN HER FATHER, MUST BE KEPT AWAY. I APOLOGIZE.
GHK
UM...
AND IF...
YES?
...IF WE REFUSE?
GLANCE
SOMEONE ELSE WILL BECOME THE OFFERING.

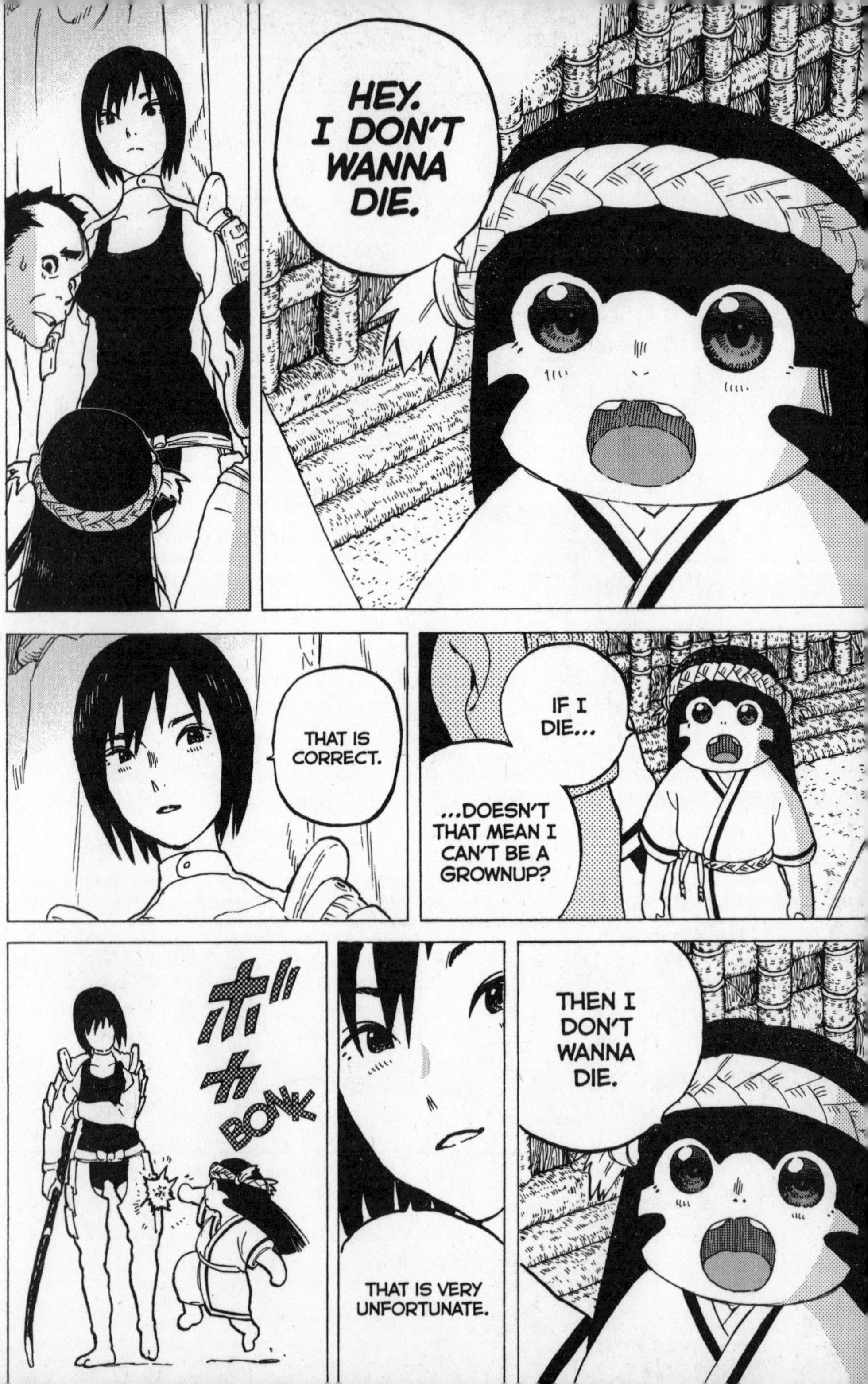
HEY. I DON'T WANNA DIE.
IF I DIE...
...DOESN'T THAT MEAN I CAN'T BE A GROWNUP?
THAT IS CORRECT.
THEN I DON'T WANNA DIE.
THAT IS VERY UNFORTUNATE.
ボカ
BONK

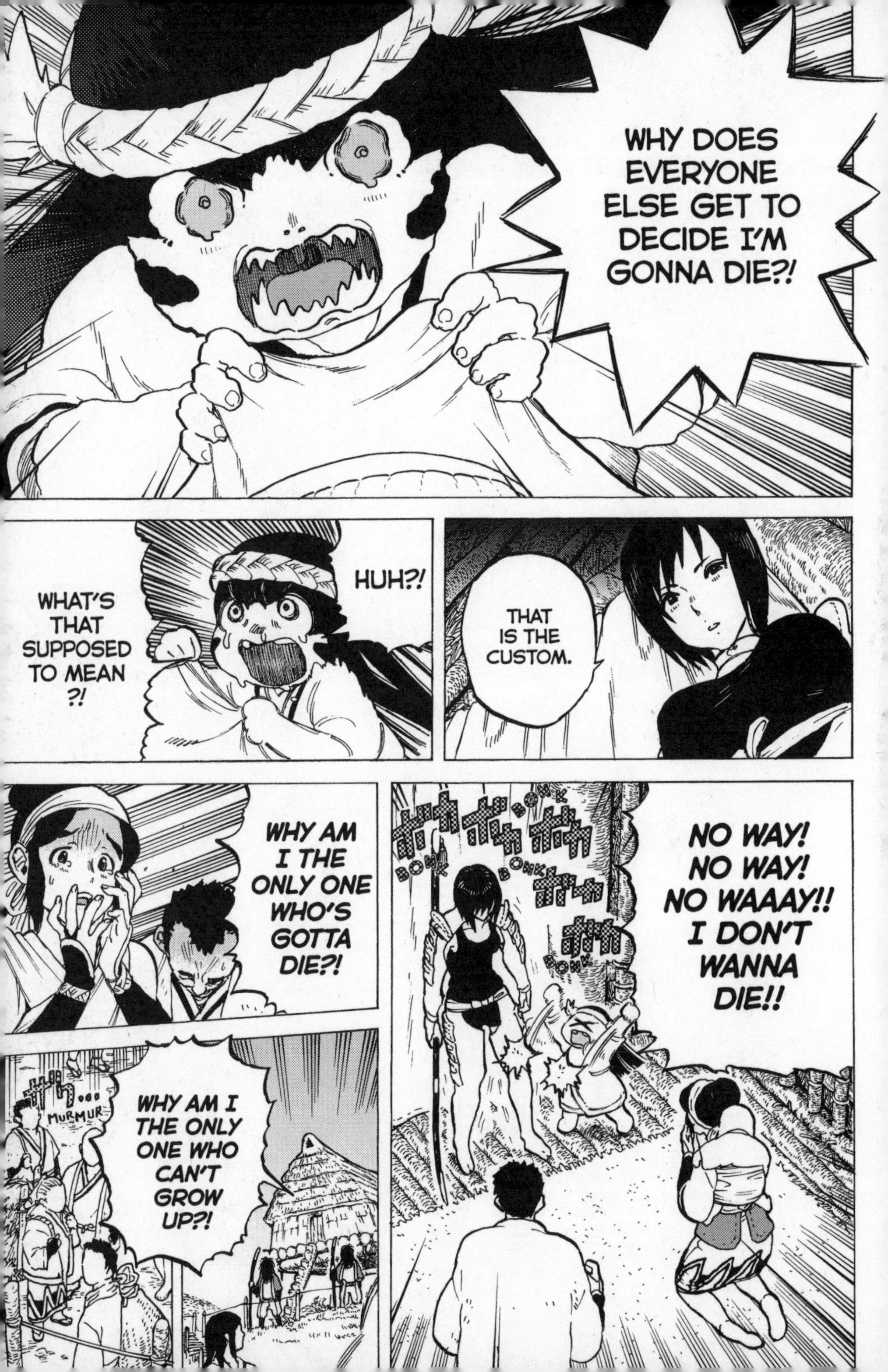
WHY DOES EVERYONE ELSE GET TO DECIDE I'M GONNA DIE?!
THAT IS THE CUSTOM.
HUH?!
WHAT'S THAT SUPPOSED TO MEAN ?!
NO WAY! NO WAY! NO WAAAY!! I DON'T WANNA DIE!!
BONK BONK BONK BONK
WHY AM I THE ONLY ONE WHO'S GOTTA DIE?!
MURMUR
WHY AM I THE ONLY ONE WHO CAN'T GROW UP?!

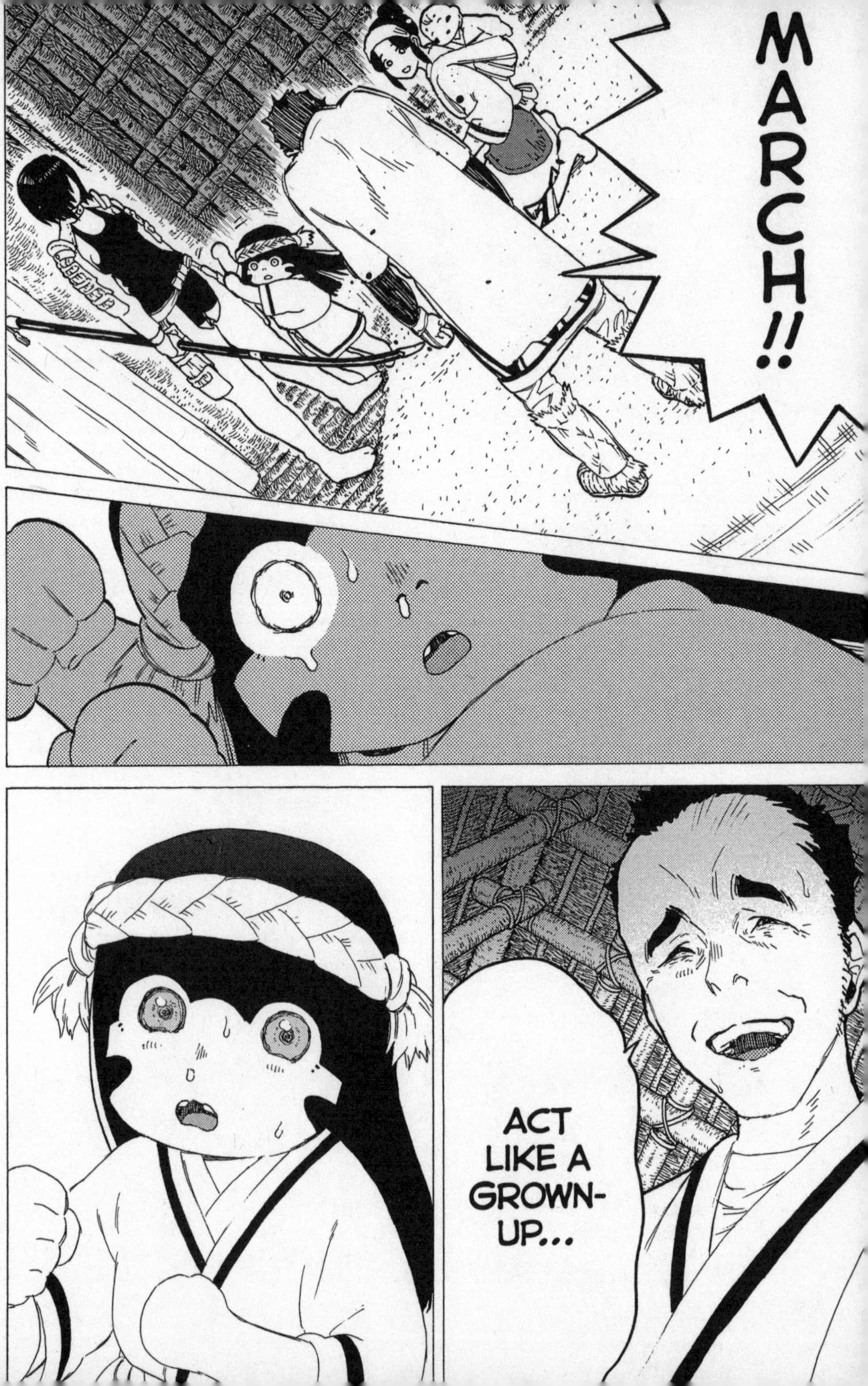
MARCH!!
ACT LIKE A GROWN-UP...

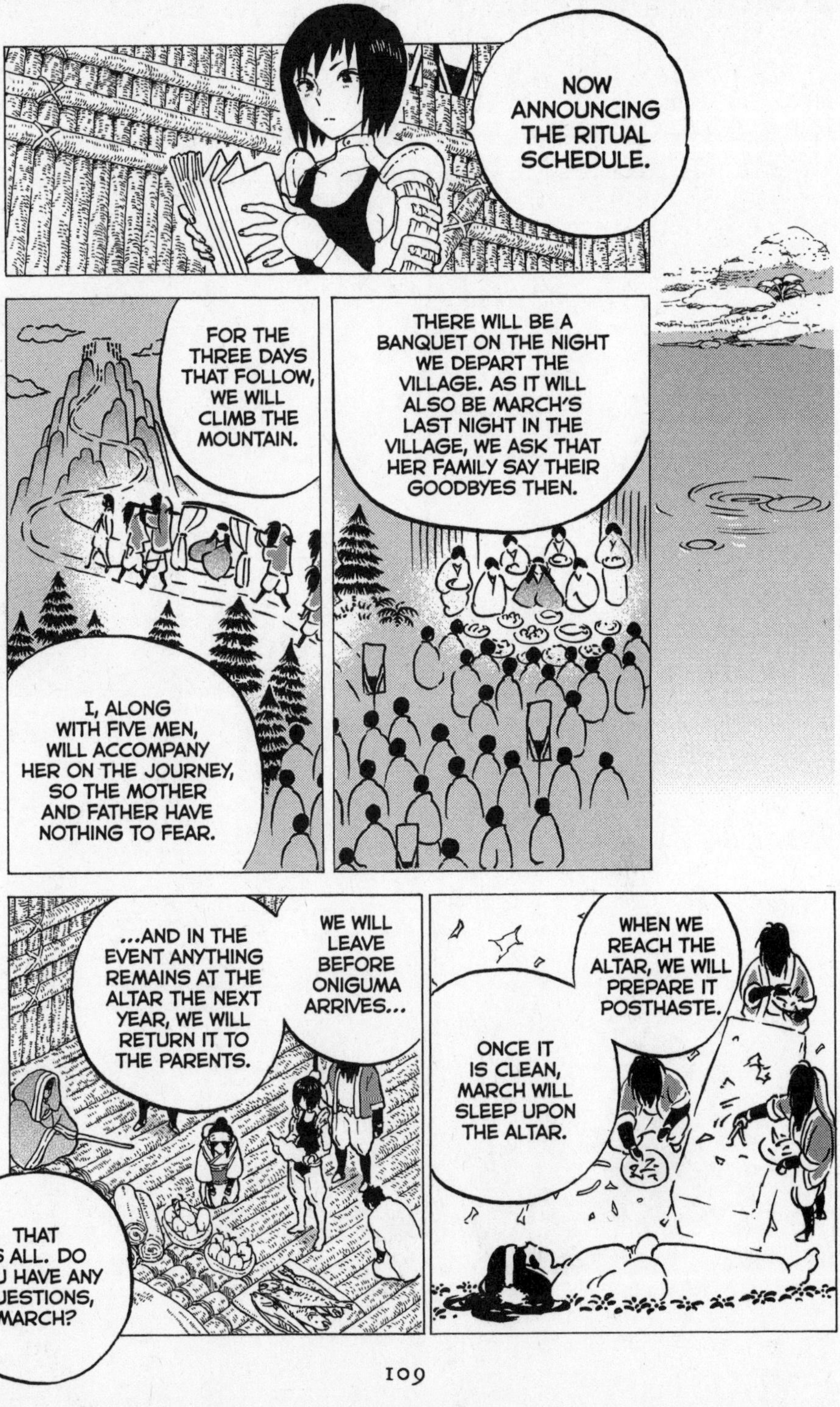
NOW ANNOUNCING THE RITUAL SCHEDULE.
THERE WILL BE A BANQUET ON THE NIGHT WE DEPART THE VILLAGE. AS IT WILL ALSO BE MARCH'S LAST NIGHT IN THE VILLAGE, WE ASK THAT HER FAMILY SAY THEIR GOODBYES THEN.
FOR THE THREE DAYS THAT FOLLOW, WE WILL CLIMB THE MOUNTAIN.
I, ALONG WITH FIVE MEN, WILL ACCOMPANY HER ON THE JOURNEY, SO THE MOTHER AND FATHER HAVE NOTHING TO FEAR.
WHEN WE REACH THE ALTAR, WE WILL PREPARE IT POSTHASTE.
ONCE IT IS CLEAN, MARCH WILL SLEEP UPON THE ALTAR.
WE WILL LEAVE BEFORE ONIGUMA ARRIVES...
...AND IN THE EVENT ANYTHING REMAINS AT THE ALTAR THE NEXT YEAR, WE WILL RETURN IT TO THE PARENTS.
THAT IS ALL. DO YOU HAVE ANY QUESTIONS, MARCH?

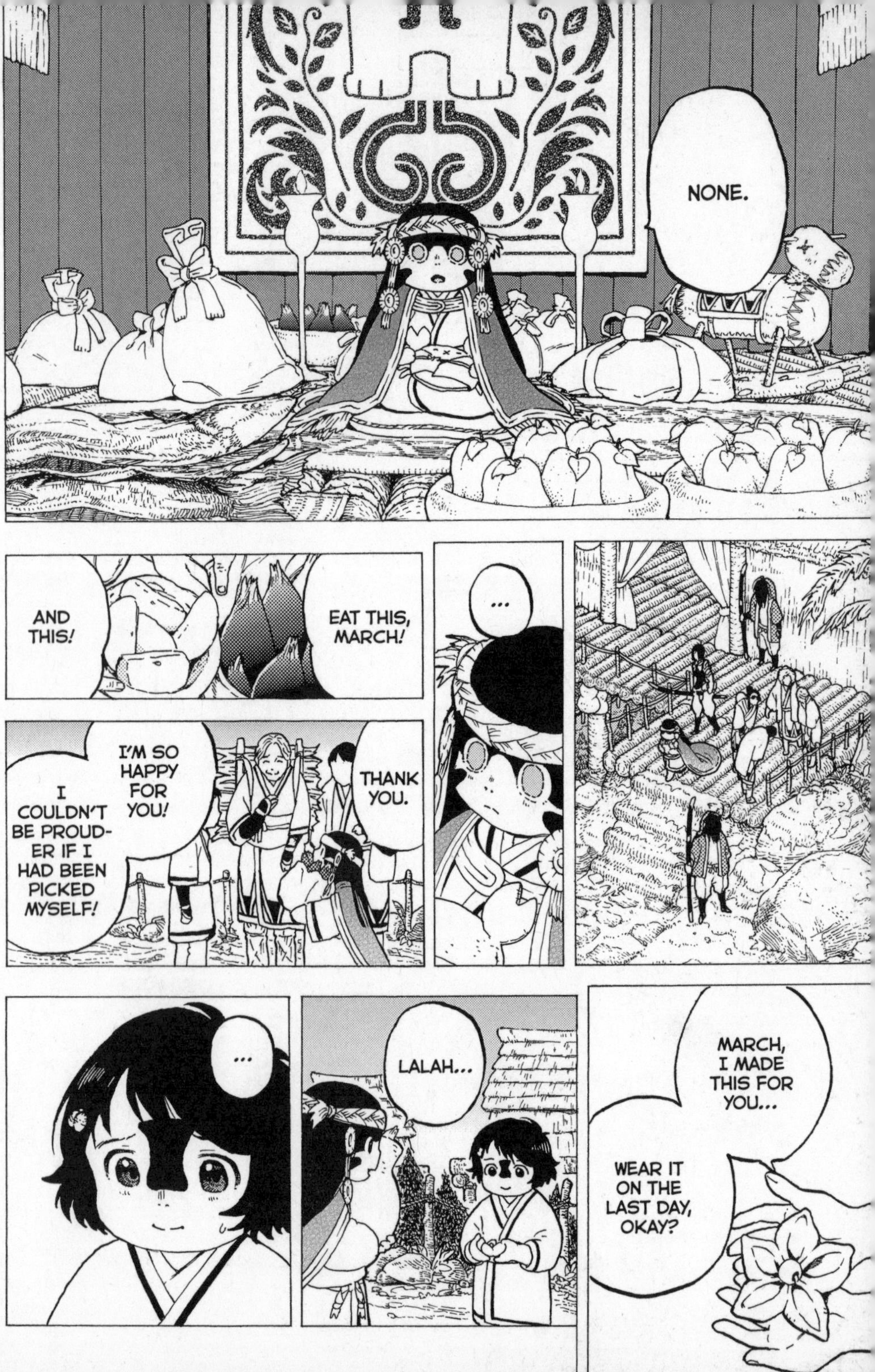
NONE.
...
EAT THIS, MARCH!
AND THIS!
THANK YOU.
I'M SO HAPPY FOR YOU!
I COULDN'T BE PROUDER IF I HAD BEEN PICKED MYSELF!
MARCH, I MADE THIS FOR YOU...
WEAR IT ON THE LAST DAY, OKAY?
LALAH...
...

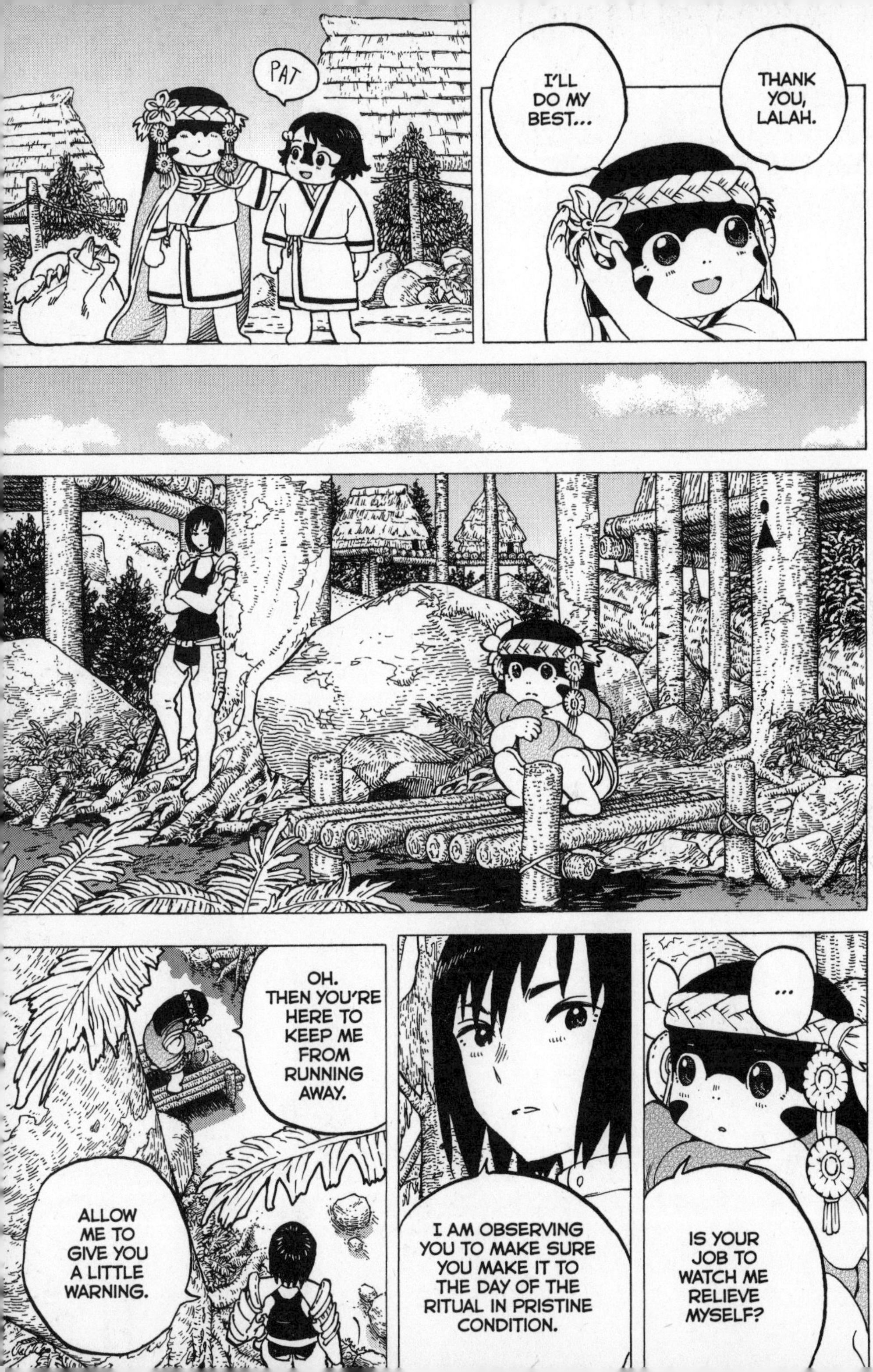
THANK YOU, LALAH.
I'LL DO MY BEST...
PAT
...
IS YOUR JOB TO WATCH ME RELIEVE MYSELF?
I AM OBSERVING YOU TO MAKE SURE YOU MAKE IT TO THE DAY OF THE RITUAL IN PRISTINE CONDITION.
OH. THEN YOU'RE HERE TO KEEP ME FROM RUNNING AWAY.
ALLOW ME TO GIVE YOU A LITTLE WARNING.

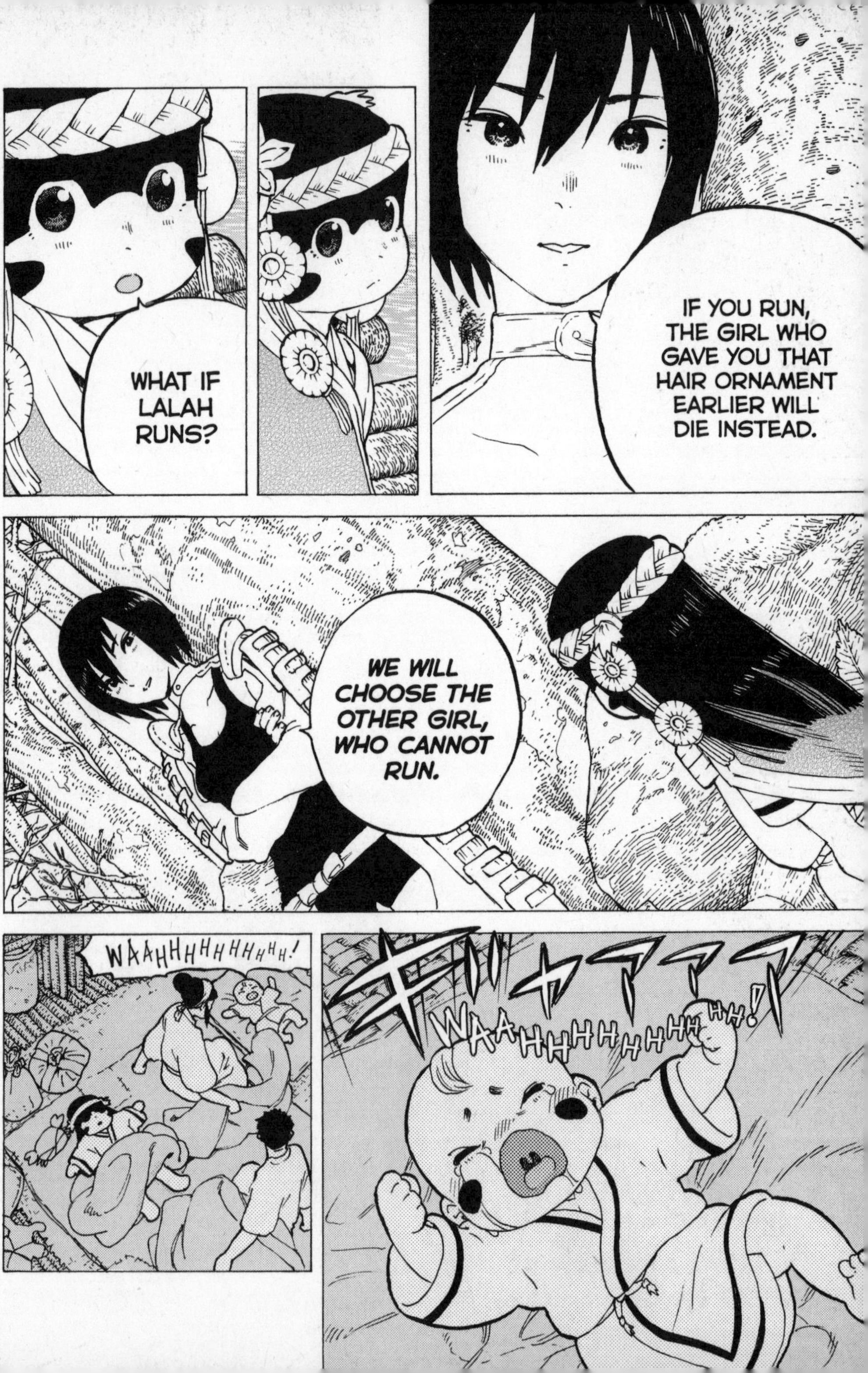
IF YOU RUN, THE GIRL WHO GAVE YOU THAT HAIR ORNAMENT EARLIER WILL DIE INSTEAD.
WHAT IF LALAH RUNS?
WE WILL CHOOSE THE OTHER GIRL, WHO CANNOT RUN.
WAAHHHHHHHHHH!
WAAHHHHHHHH!

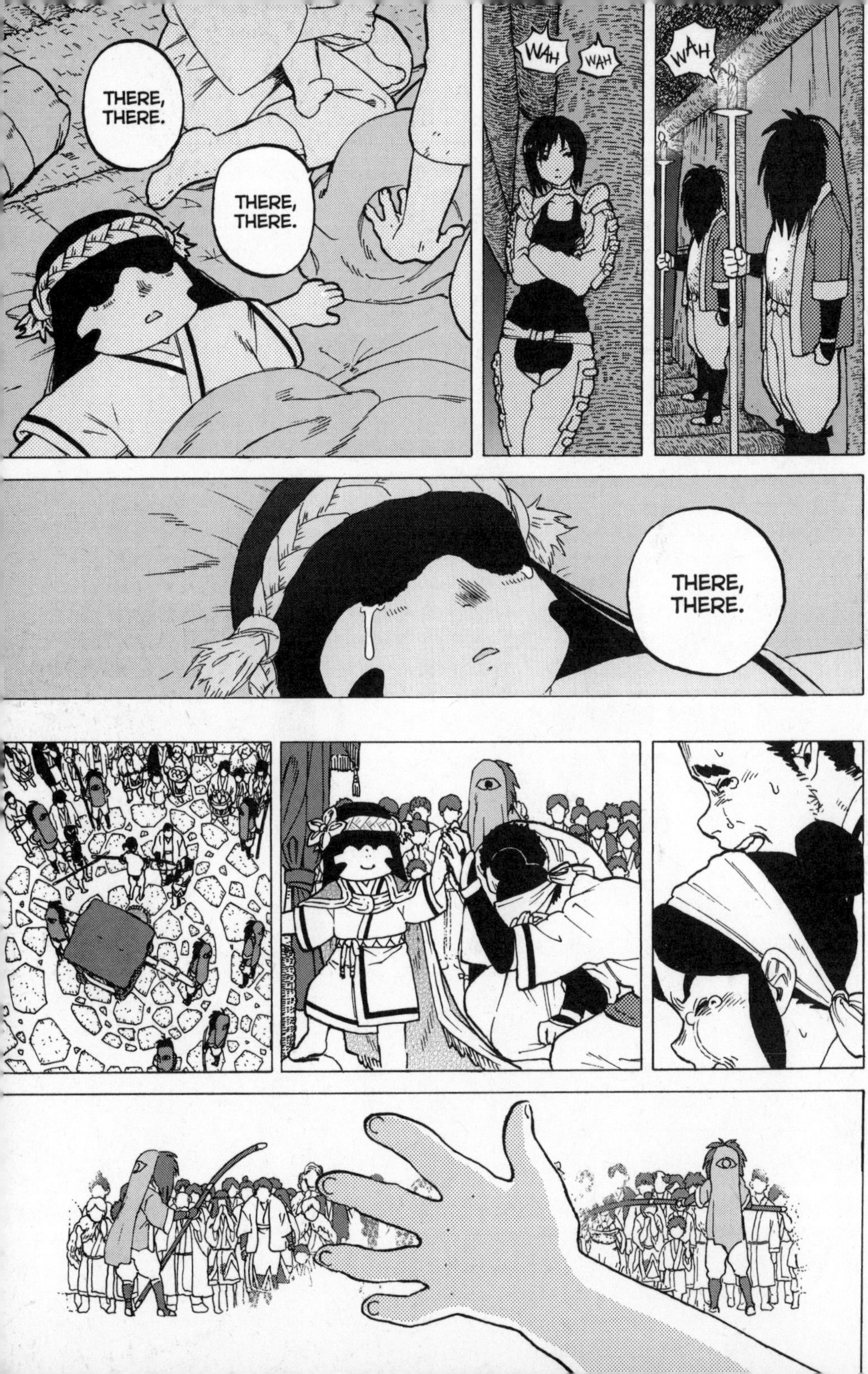
WAH
WAH
WAH
THERE, THERE.
THERE, THERE.
THERE, THERE.

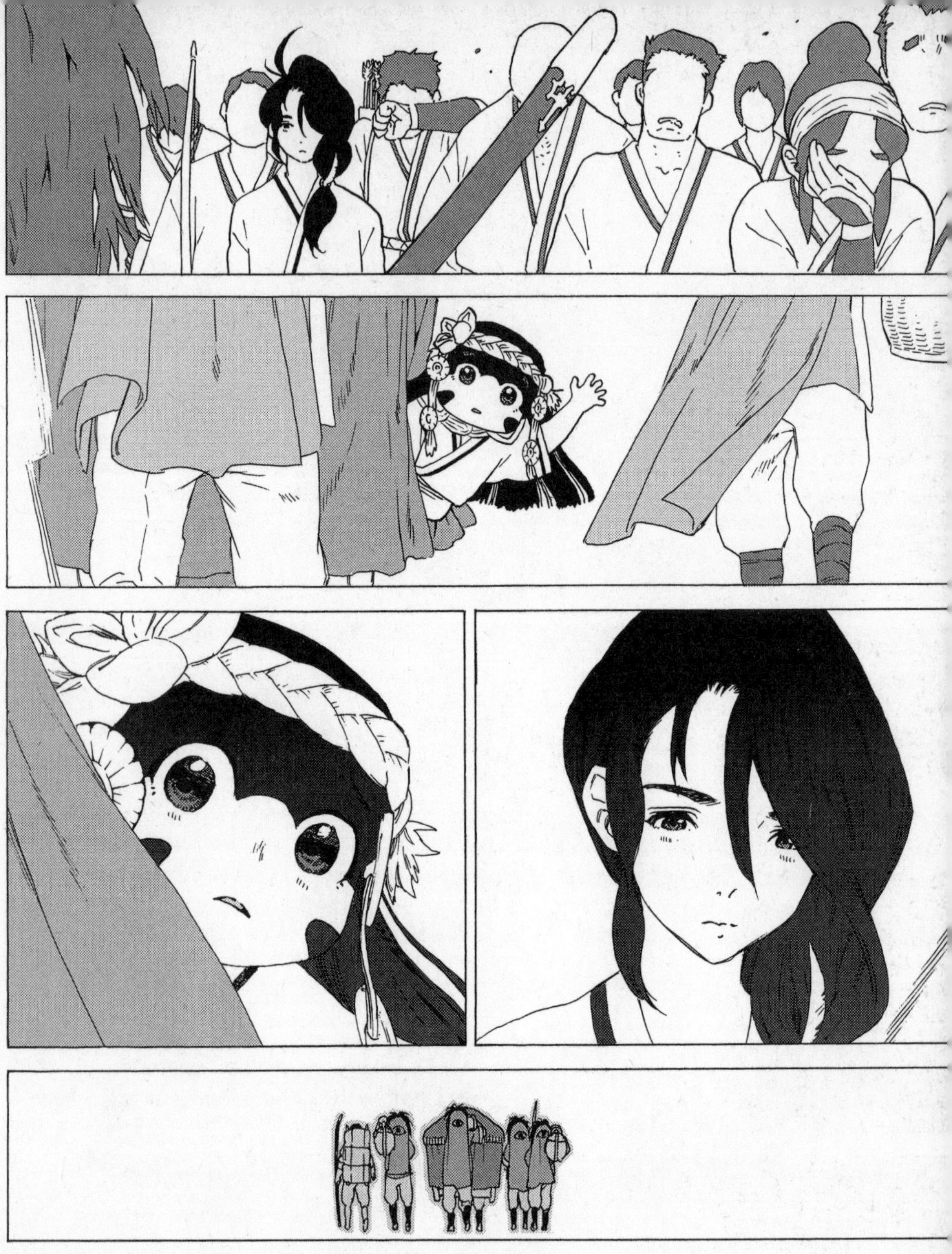

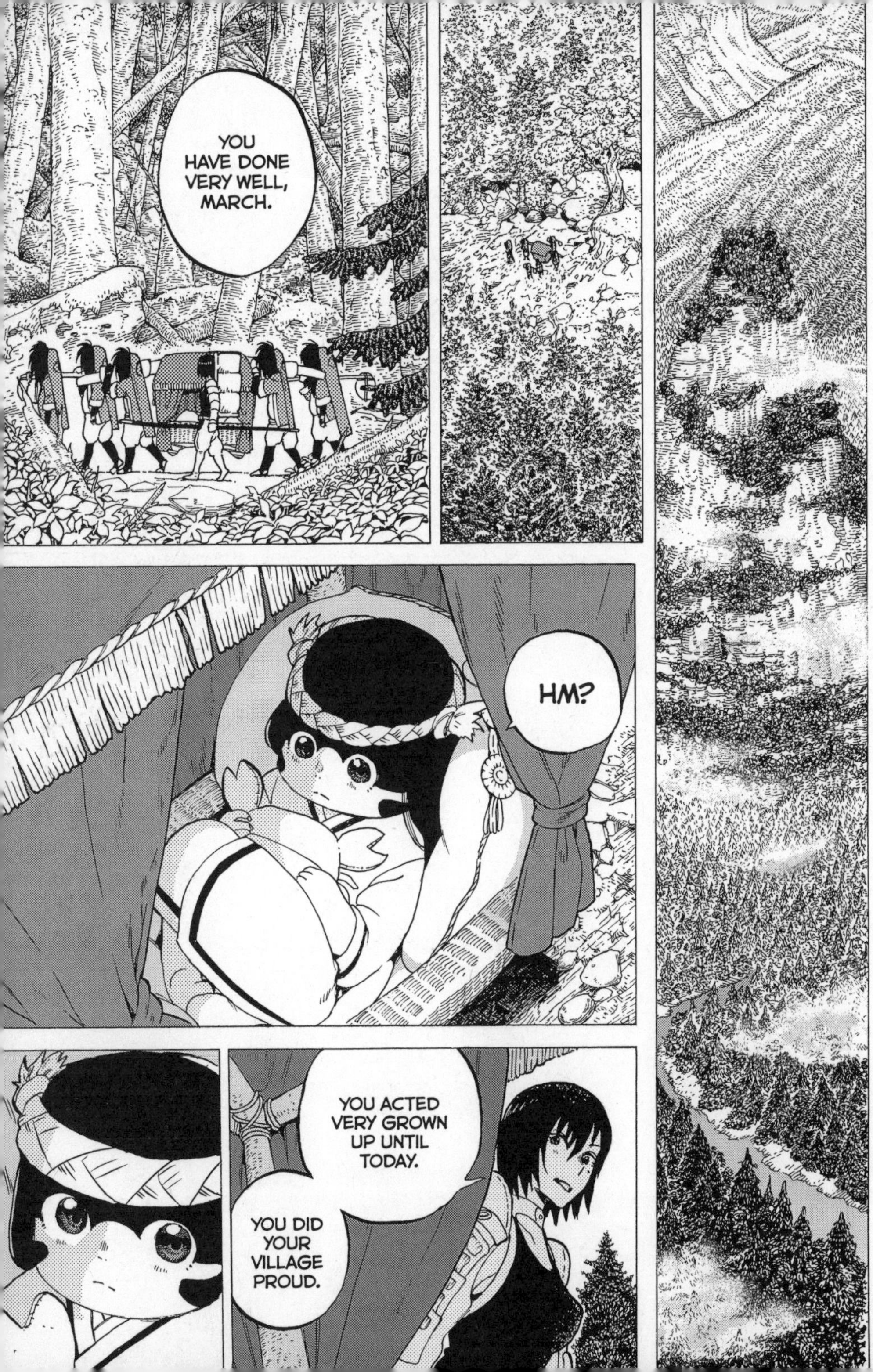

YOU HAVE DONE VERY WELL, MARCH.
HM?
YOU ACTED VERY GROWN UP UNTIL TODAY.
YOU DID YOUR VILLAGE PROUD.

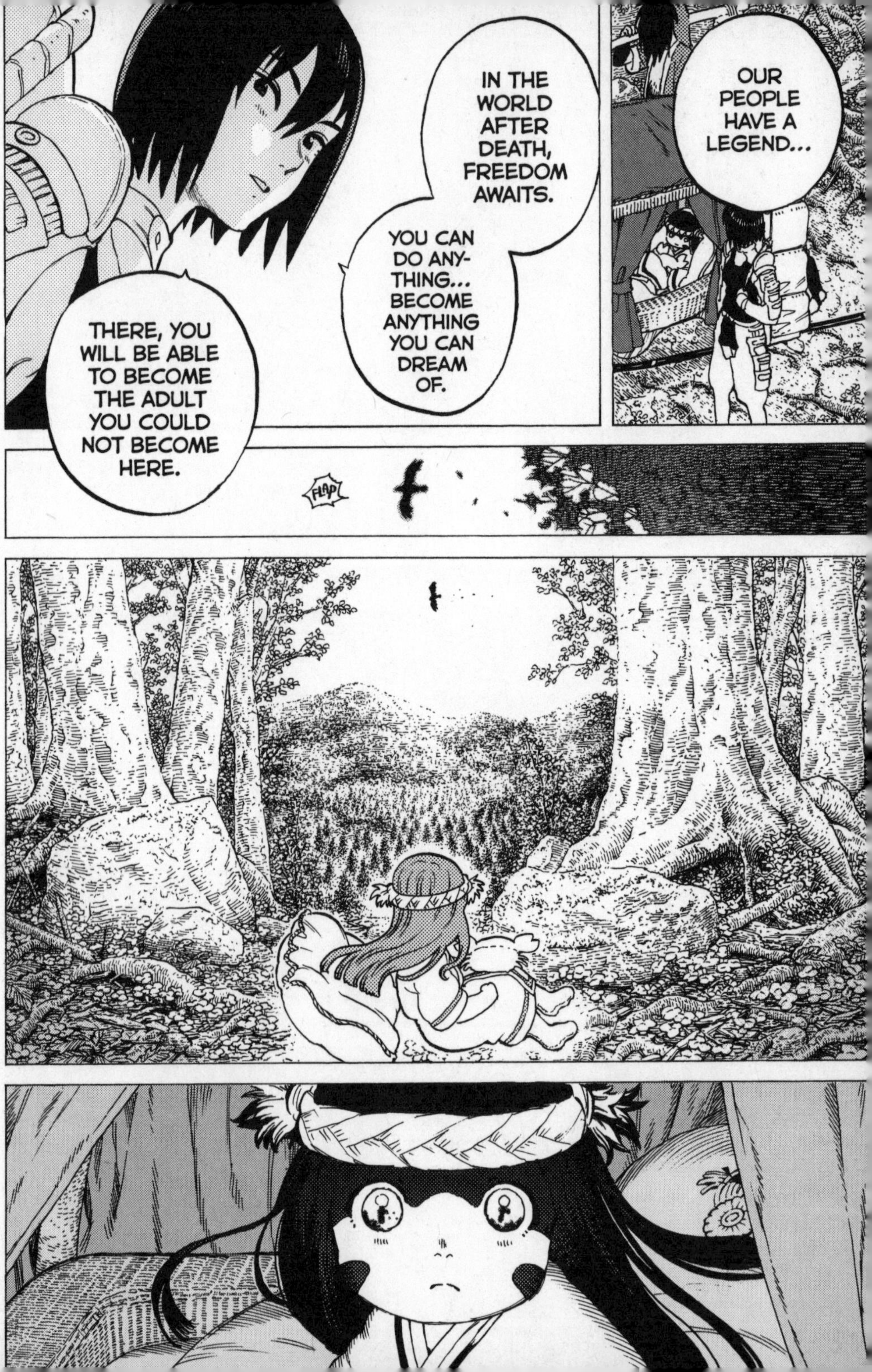
OUR PEOPLE HAVE A LEGEND...
IN THE WORLD AFTER DEATH, FREEDOM AWAITS.
YOU CAN DO ANY-THING... BECOME ANYTHING YOU CAN DREAM OF.
THERE, YOU WILL BE ABLE TO BECOME THE ADULT YOU COULD NOT BECOME HERE.
FLAP

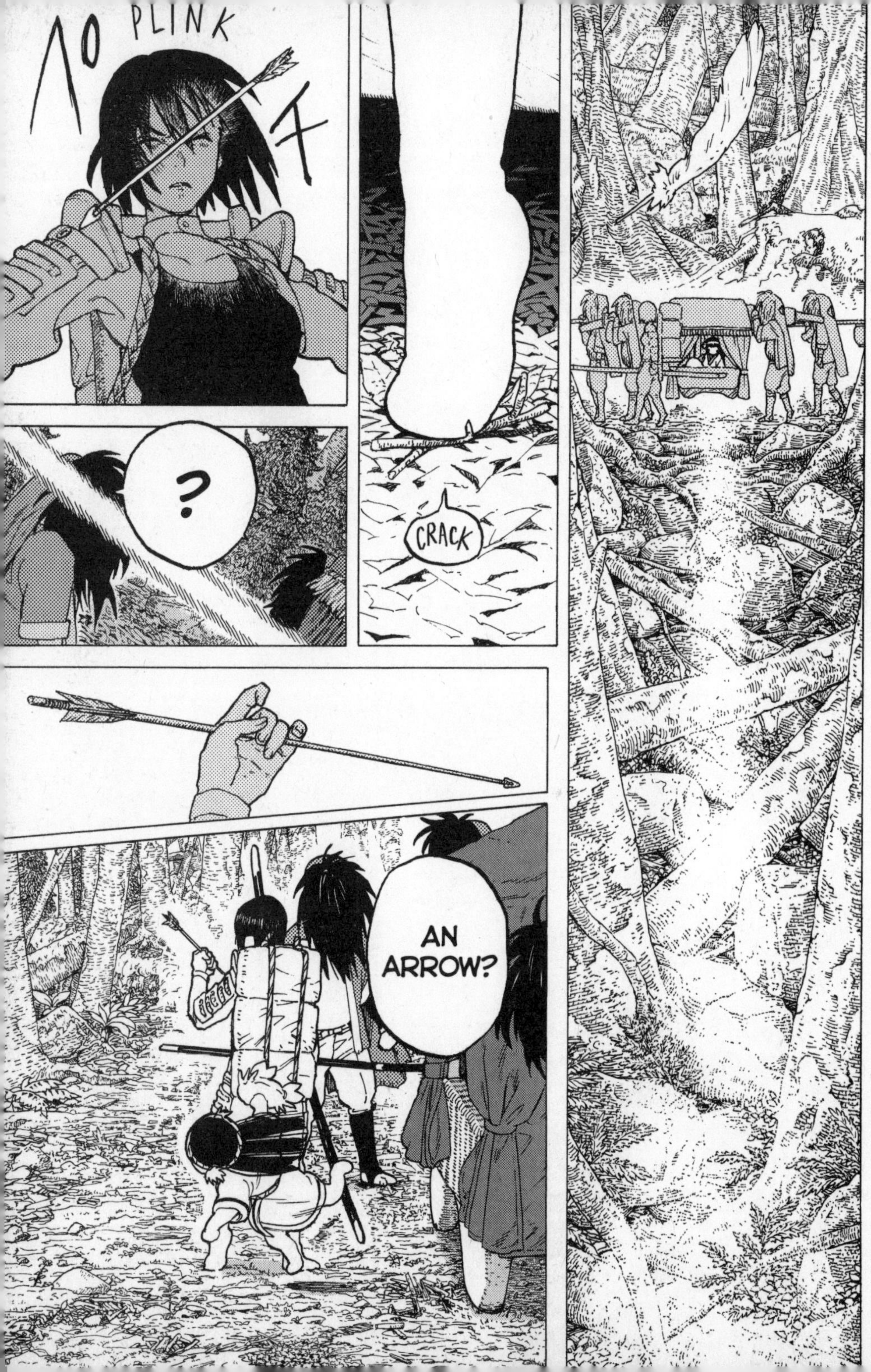
CRACK
PLINK
?
AN ARROW?

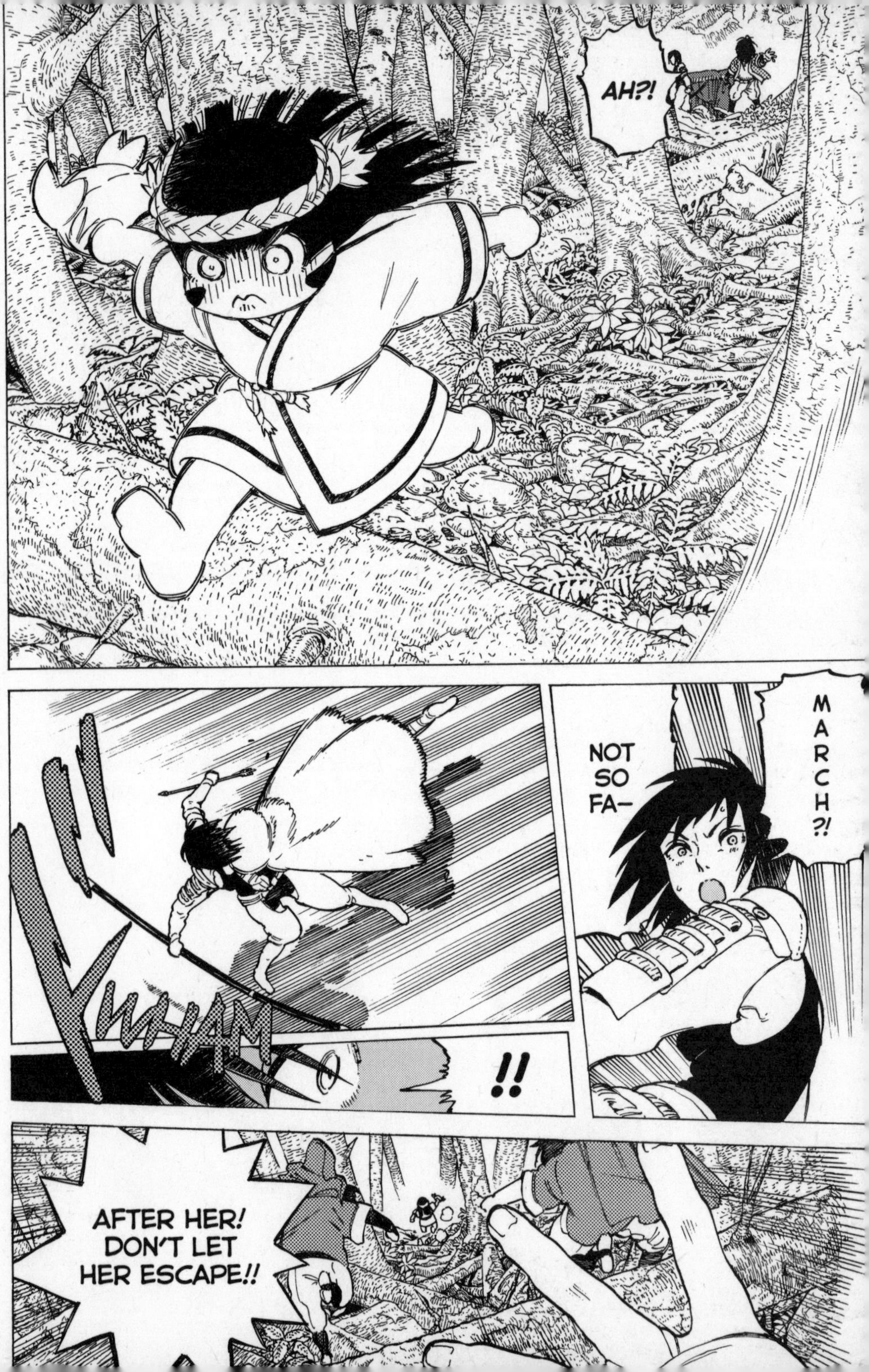
AH?!
MARCH?!
NOT SO FA—
WHAM
!!
AFTER HER! DON'T LET HER ESCAPE!!

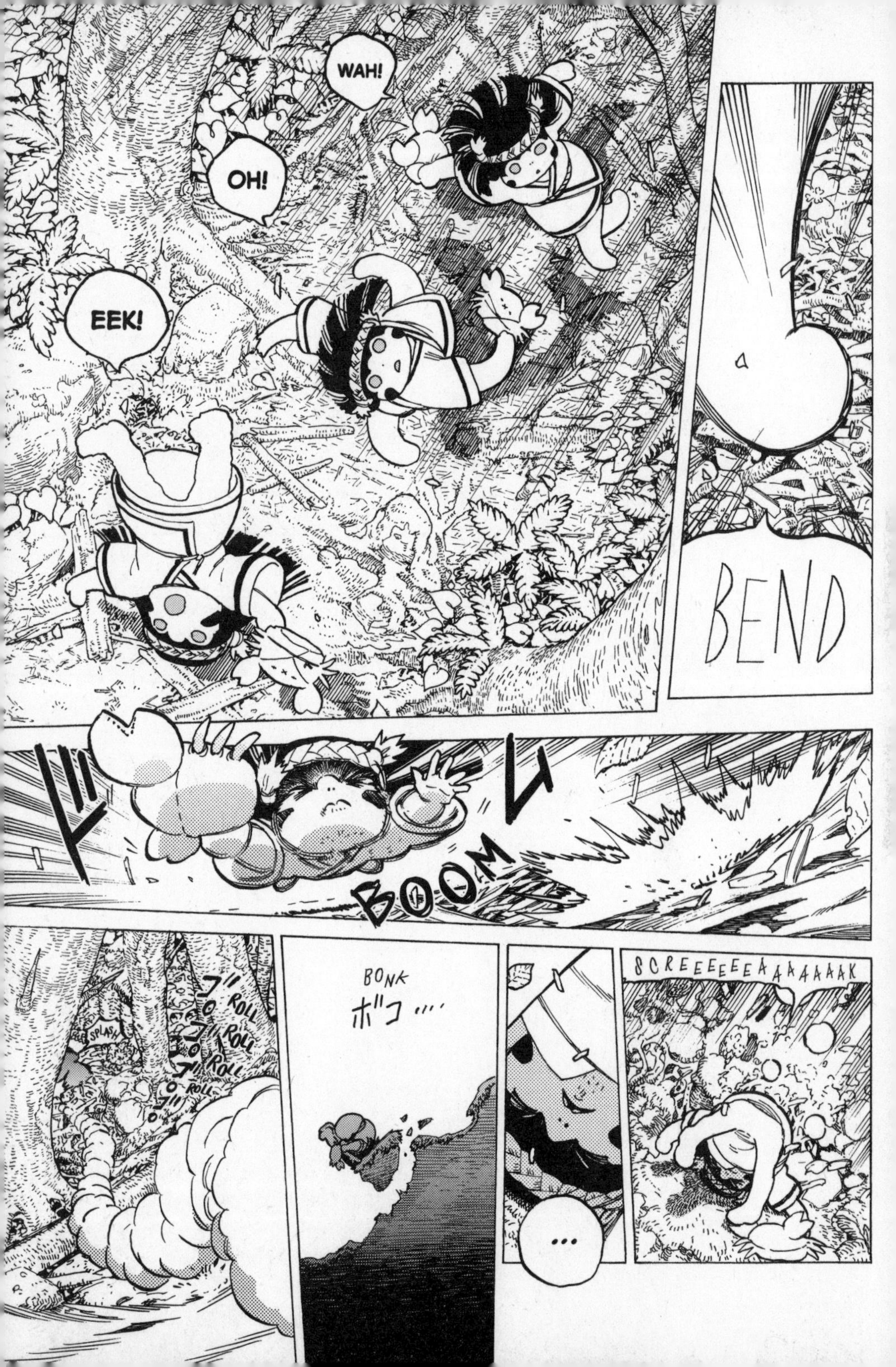
BEND
WAH!
OH!
EEK!
BOOM
SCREEEEEEAAAAAAAK
...
BONK
ボコ…
ROLL
ROLL
ROLL
ROLL
SPLASH

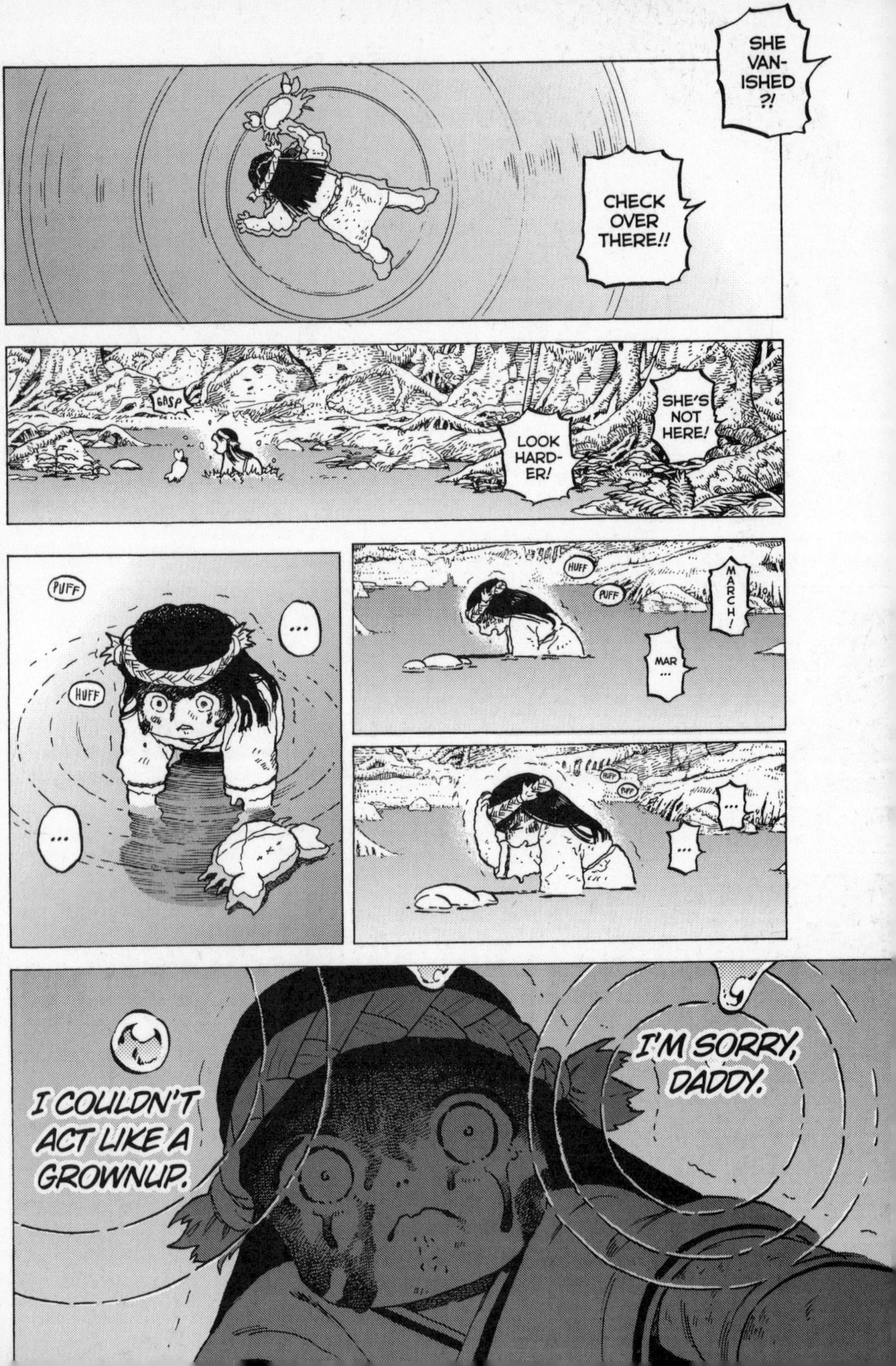
SHE VAN-ISHED?!
CHECK OVER THERE!!
SHE'S NOT HERE!
LOOK HARDER!
GASP
MARCH!
MAR...
HUFF
PUFF
...
...
PUFF
HUFF
...
...
HUFF
PUFF
I'M SORRY, DADDY.
I COULDN'T ACT LIKE A GROWNUP.

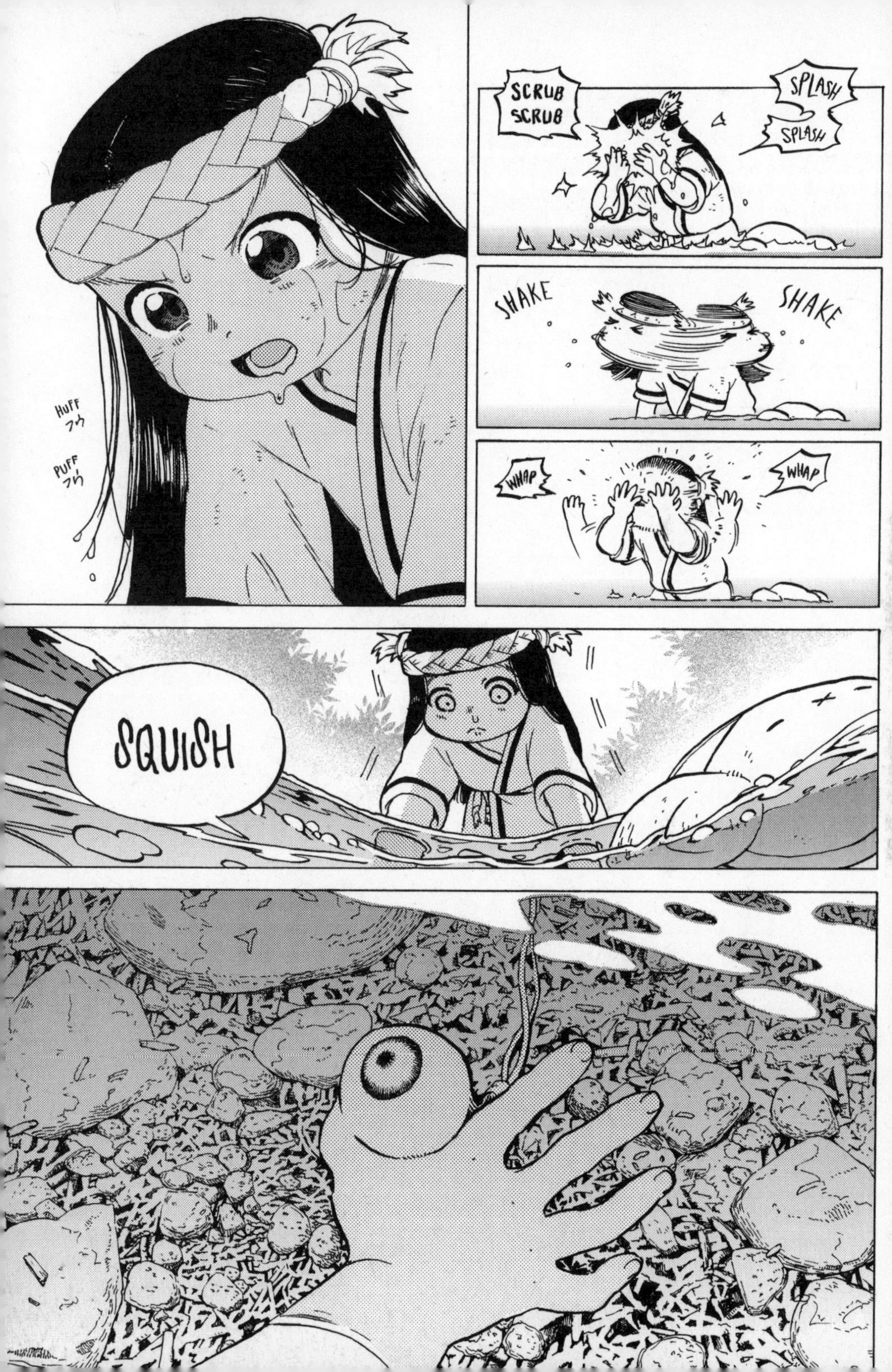
SPLASH
SPLASH
SCRUB SCRUB
SHAKE
SHAKE
WHAP
WHAP
HUFF フゥ
PUFF フゥ
SQUISH

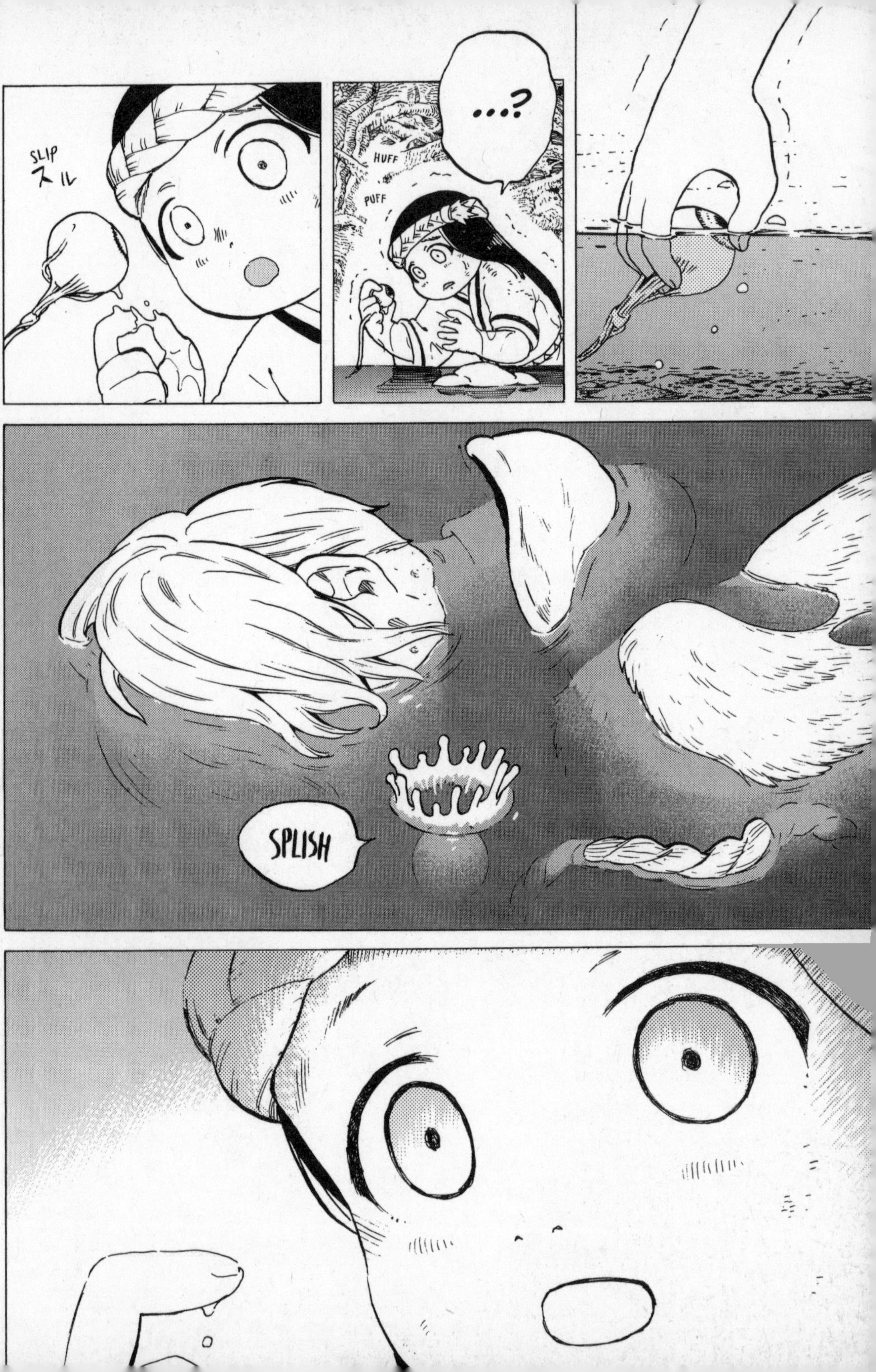
...?
HUFF
PUFF
SLIP
スル
SPLISH

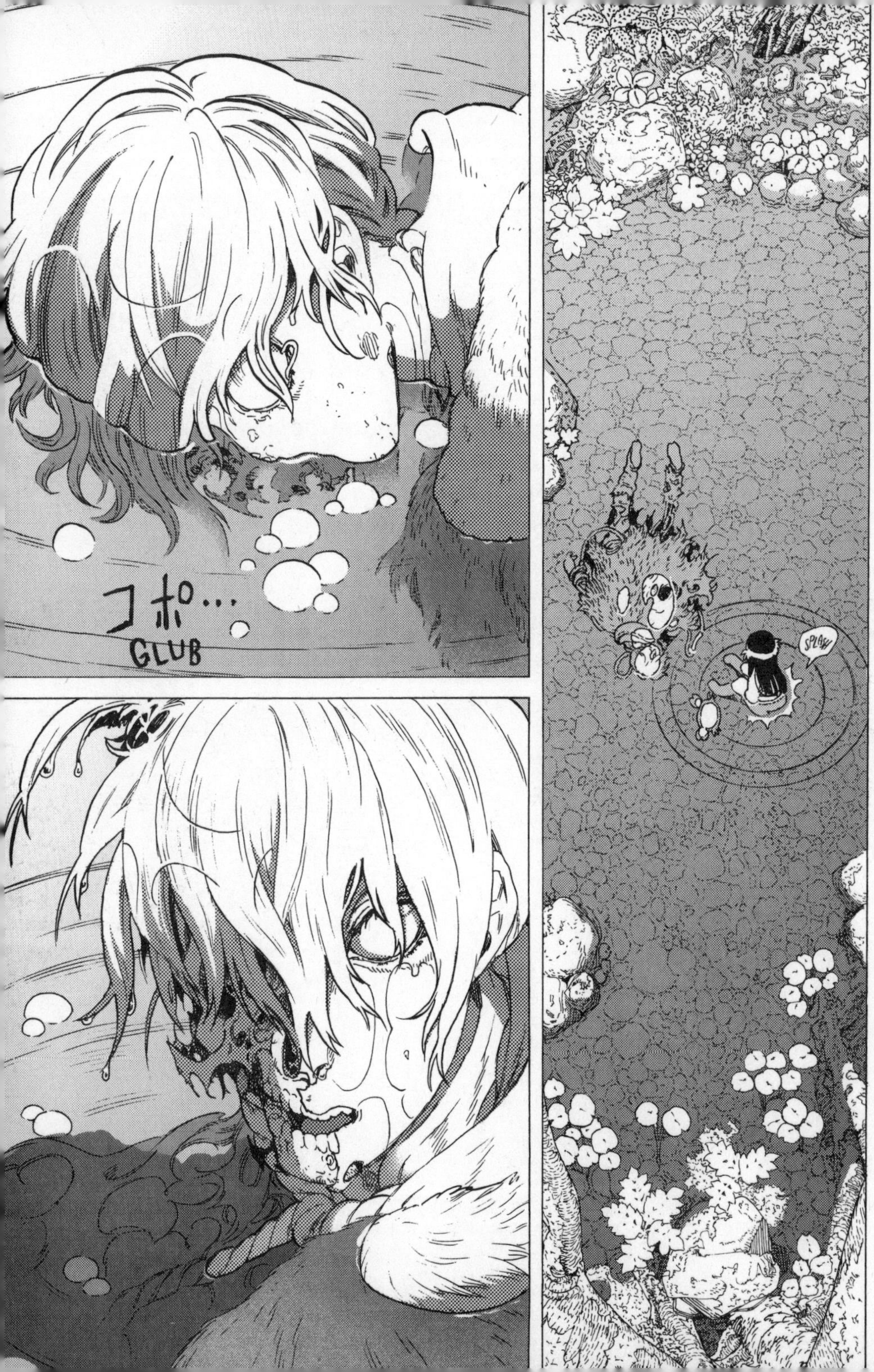
SPLASH
コポ…
GLUB

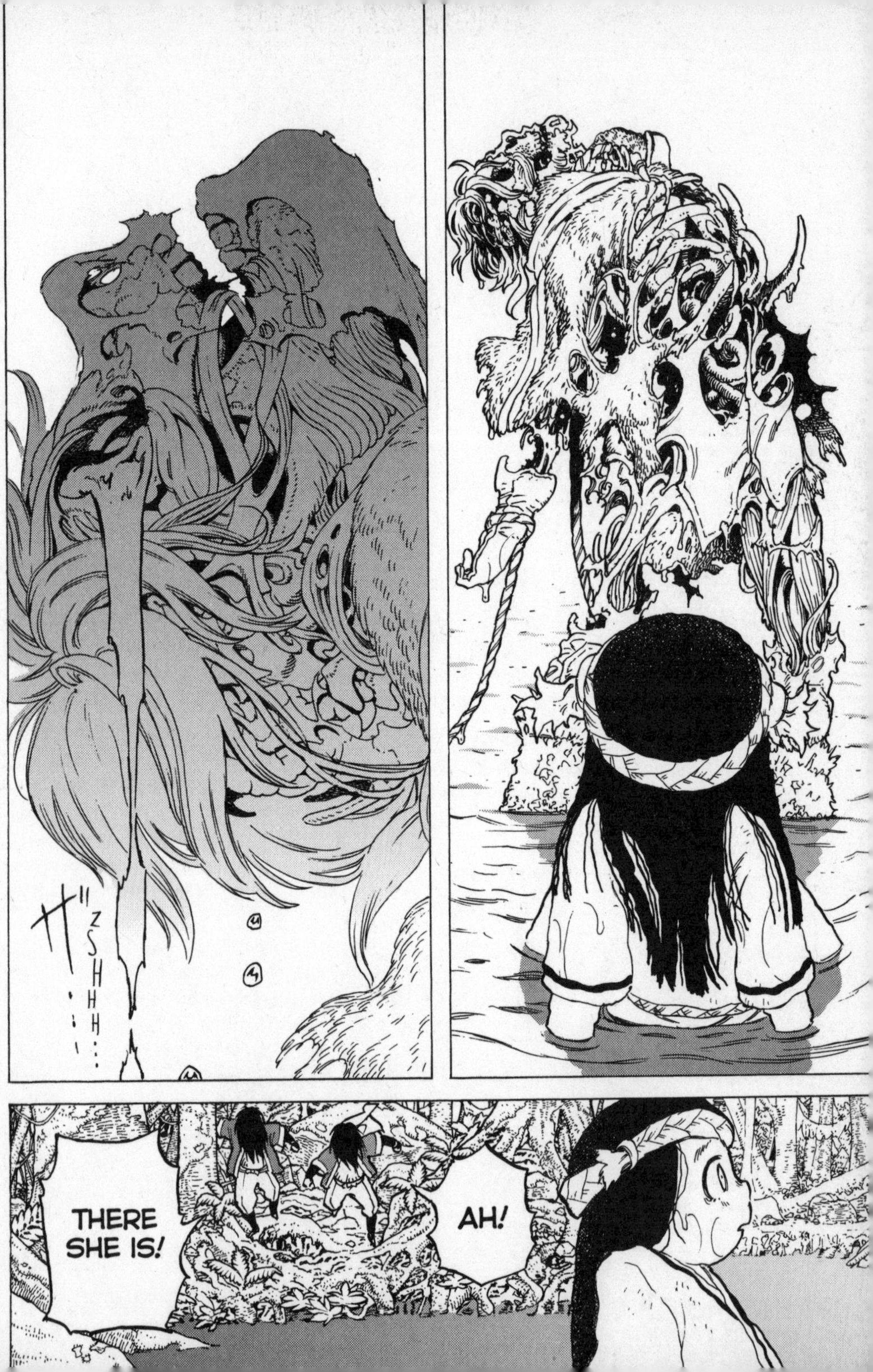
ZSHHH...
AH!
THERE SHE IS!

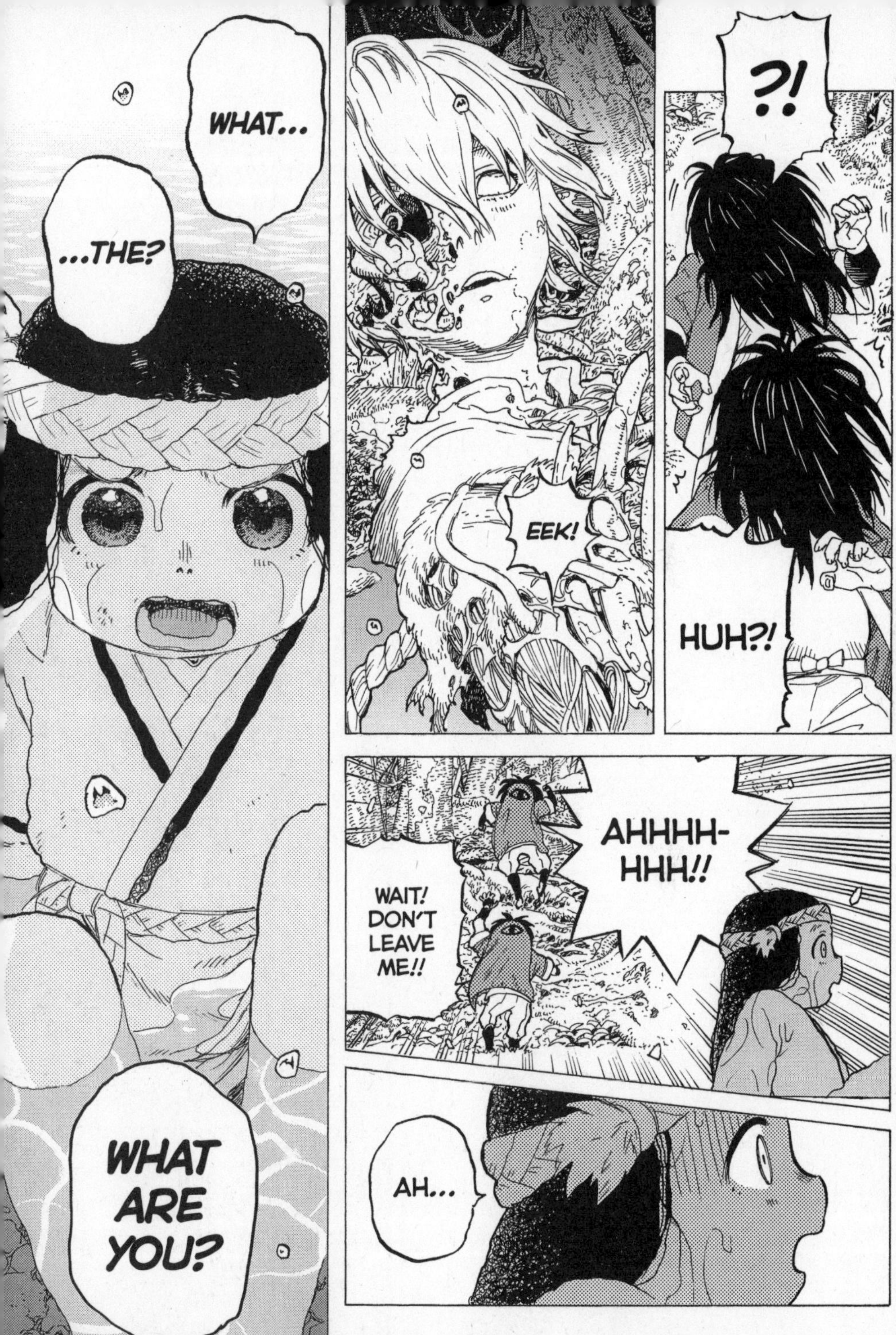
?!
HUH?!
EEK!
AHHHH-HHH!!
WAIT! DON'T LEAVE ME!!
AH...
WHAT...
...THE?
WHAT ARE YOU?

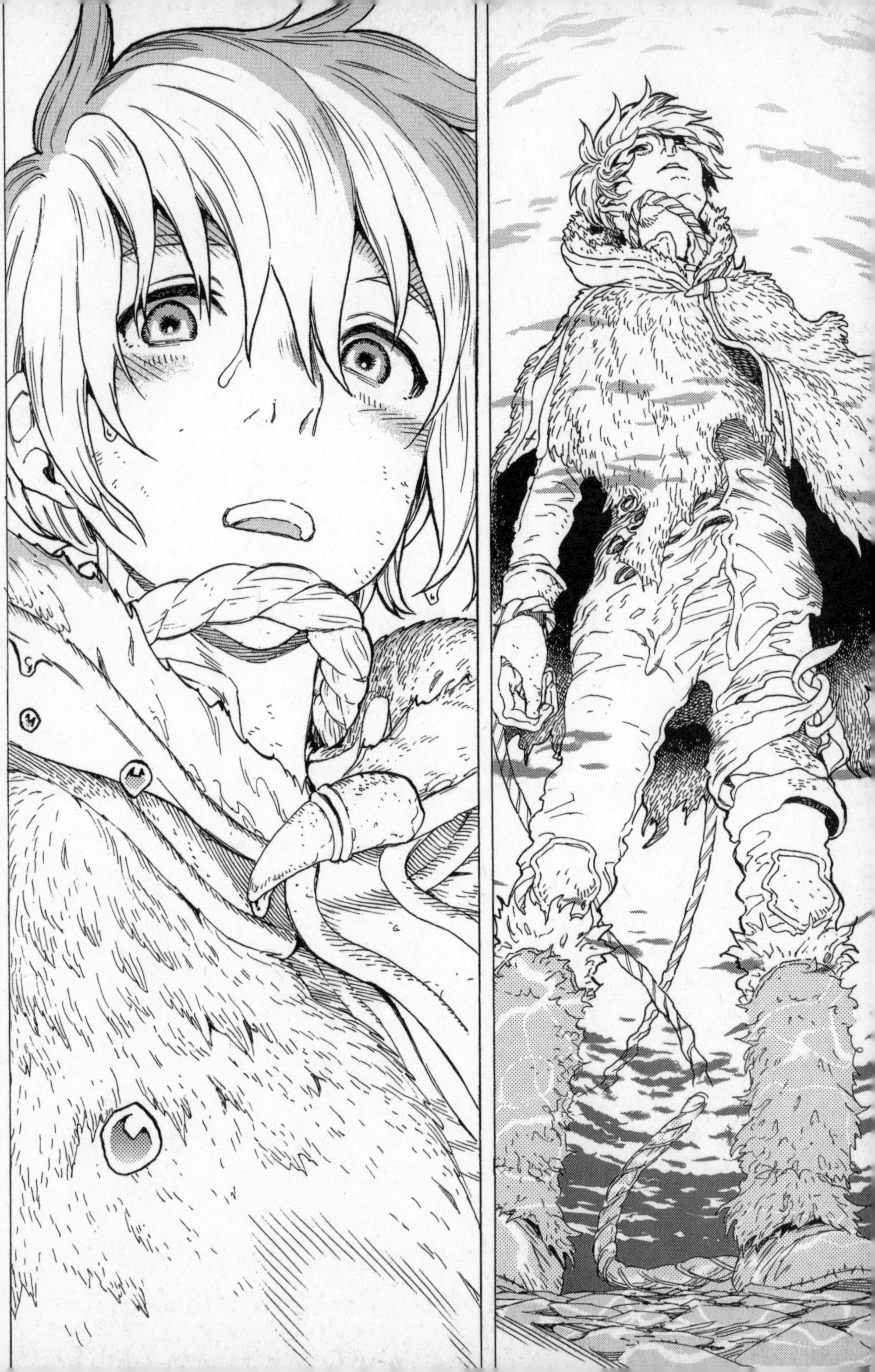

#3 Playing House

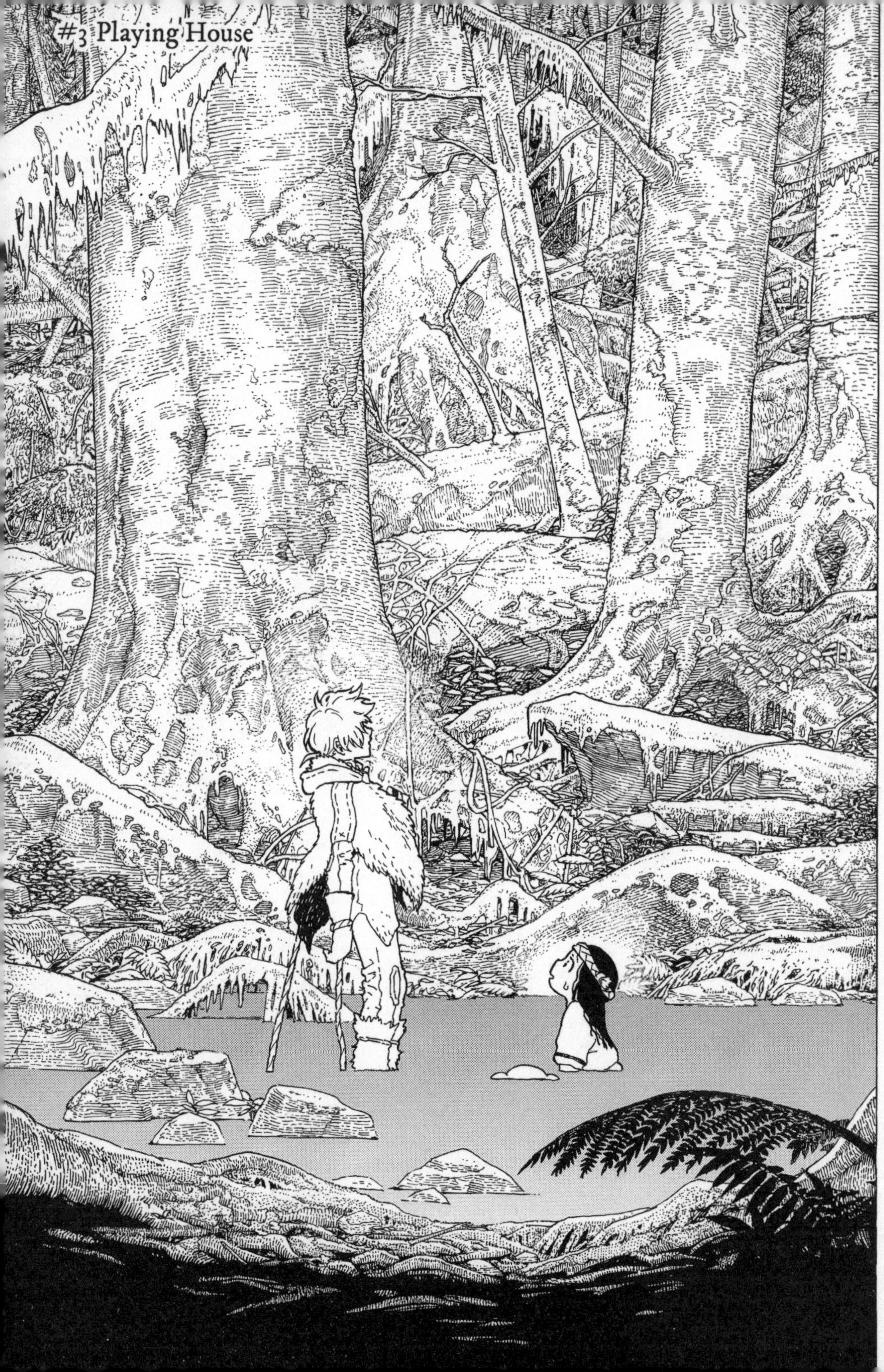

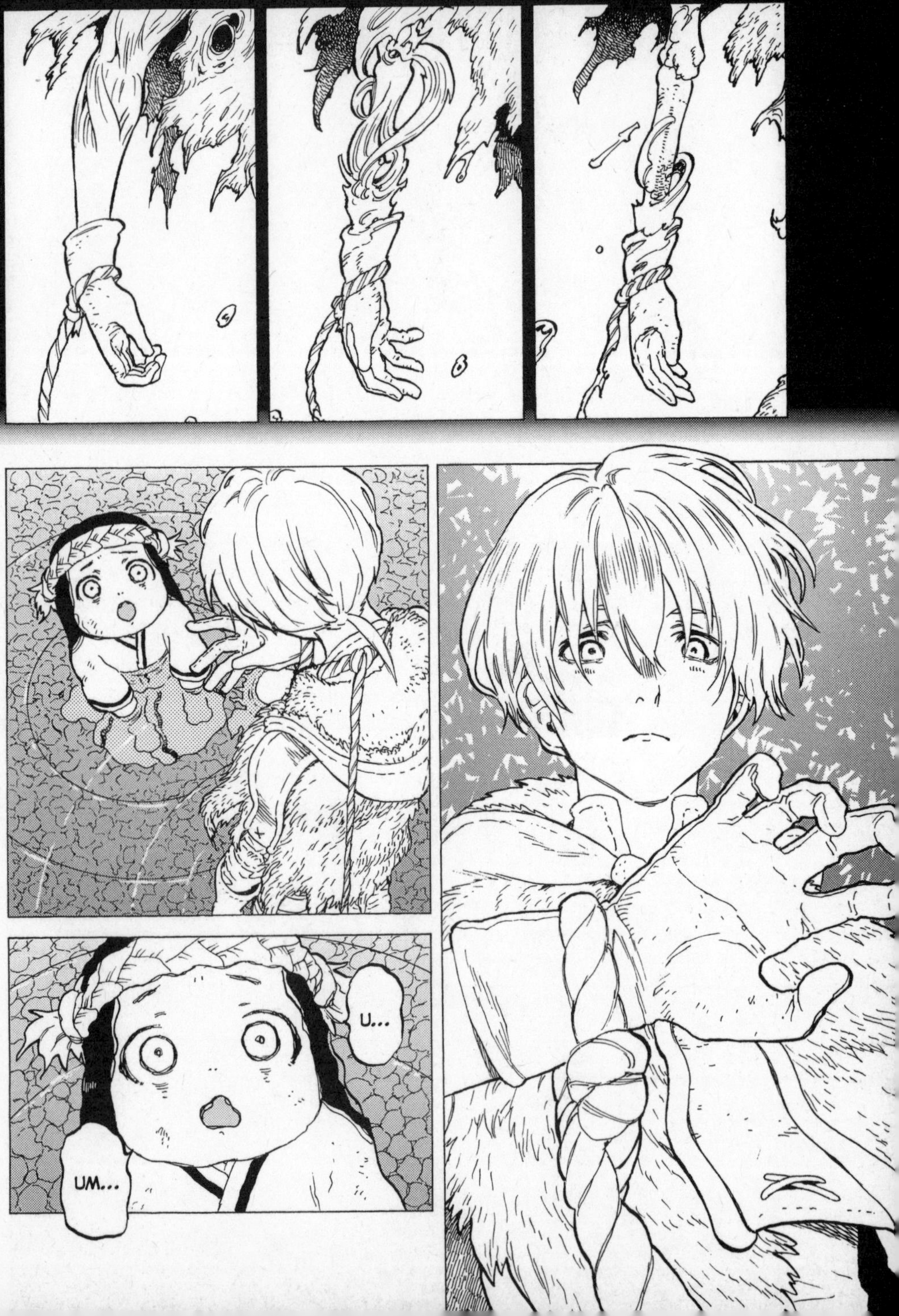
U...
UM...

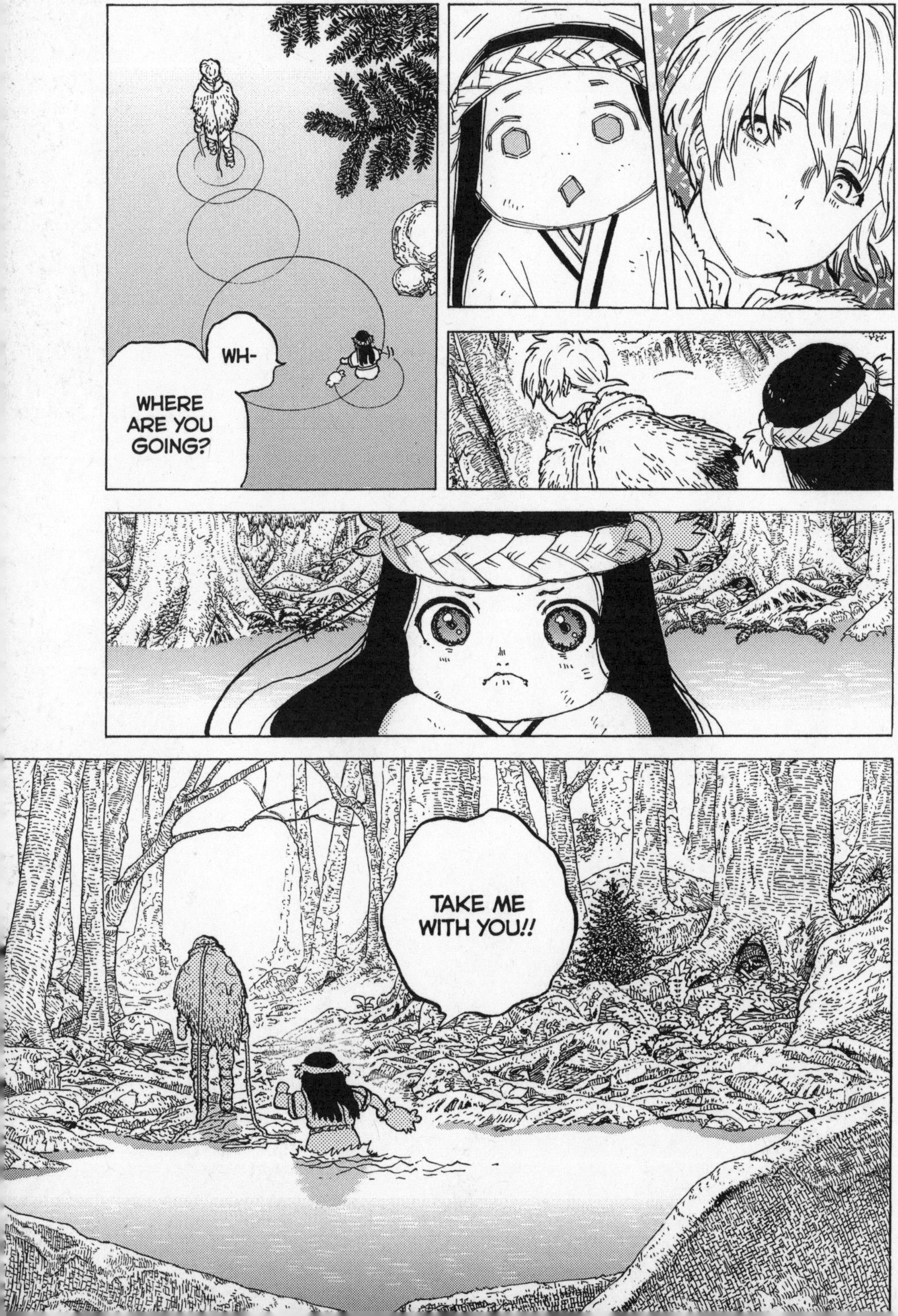
WH-
WHERE ARE YOU GOING?
TAKE ME WITH YOU!!

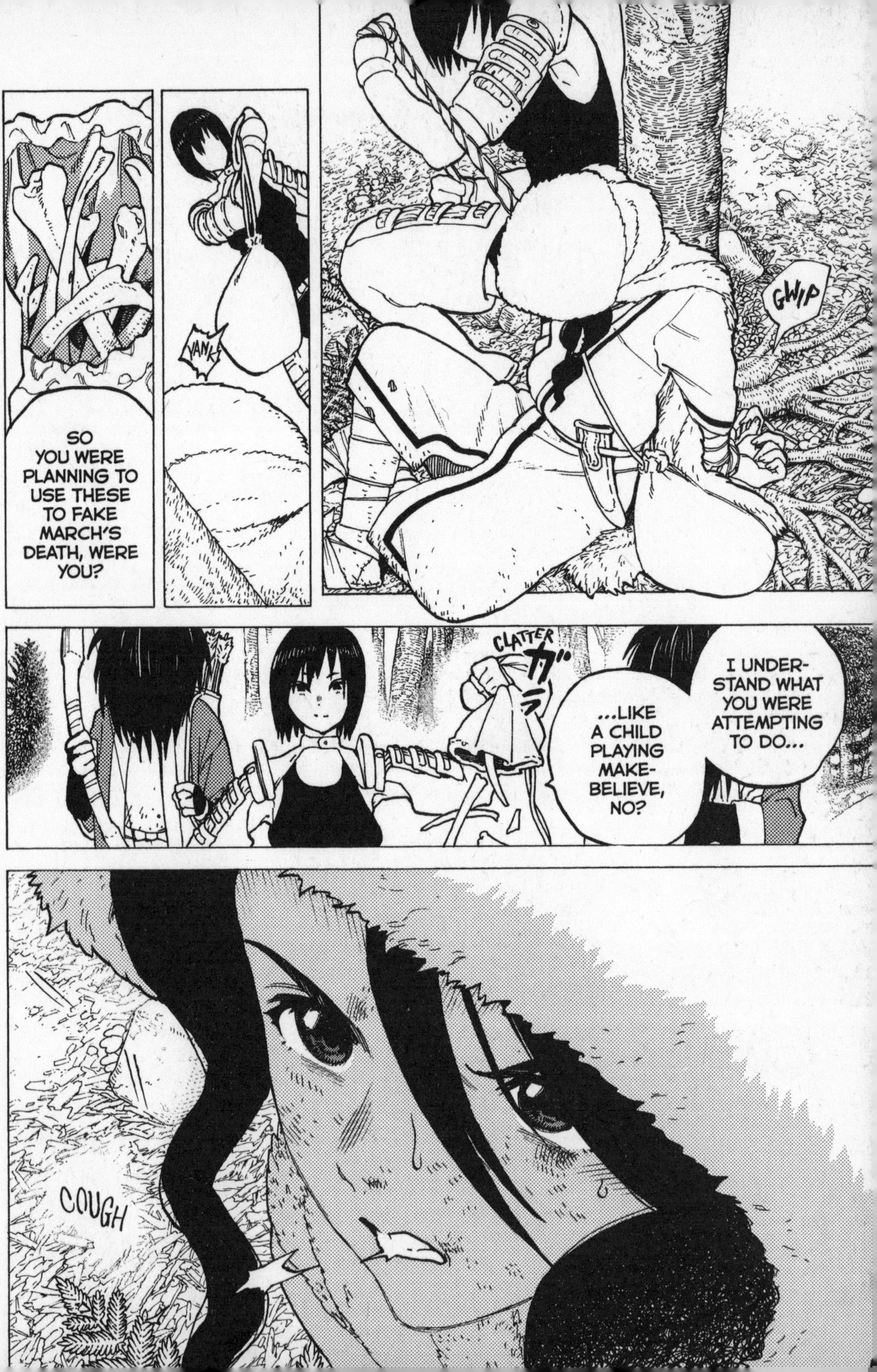
GWIP
YANK
SO YOU WERE PLANNING TO USE THESE TO FAKE MARCH'S DEATH, WERE YOU?
I UNDER-STAND WHAT YOU WERE ATTEMPTING TO DO...
...LIKE A CHILD PLAYING MAKE-BELIEVE, NO?
CLATTER
ガラ
COUGH

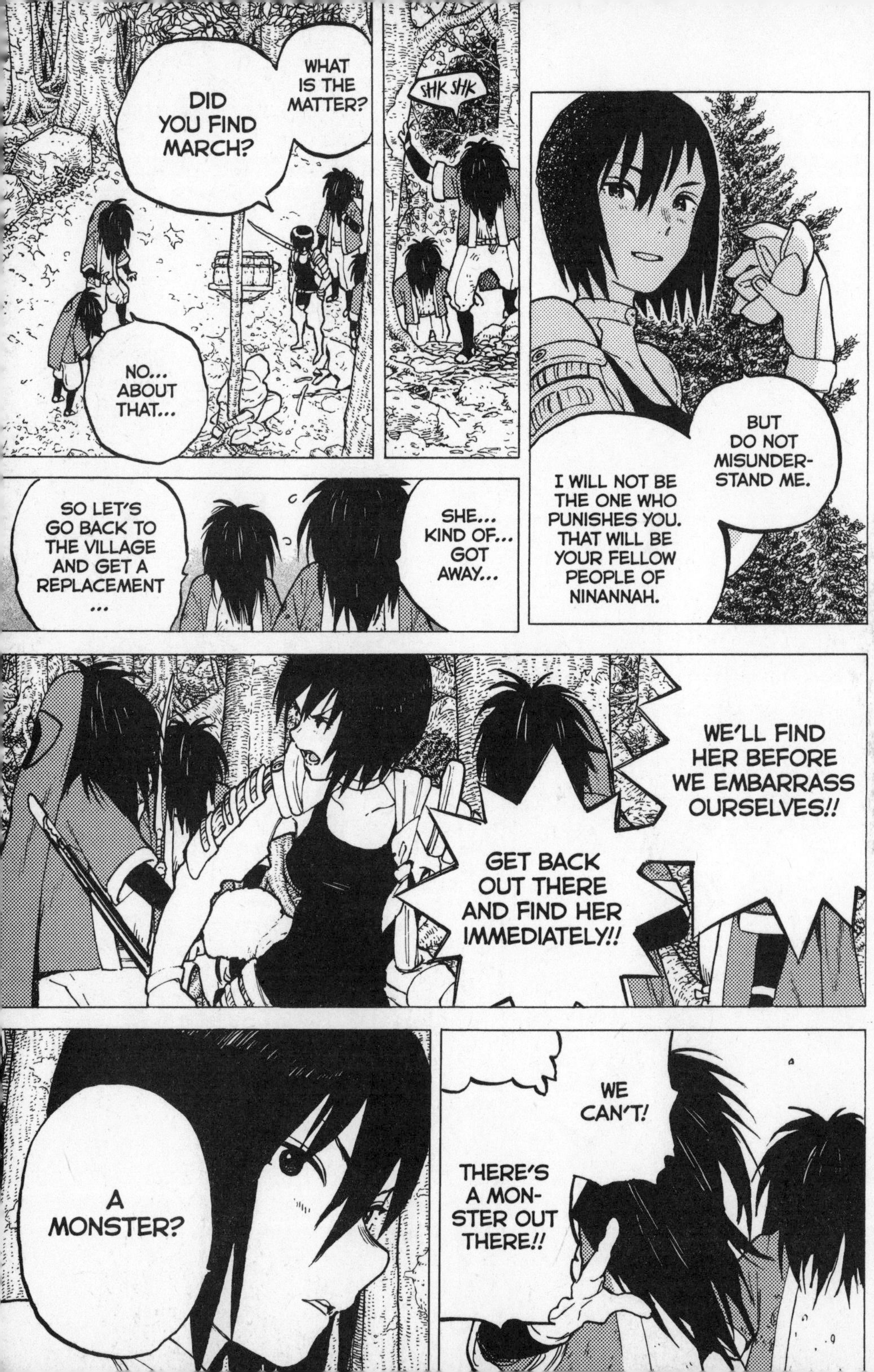

BUT DO NOT MISUNDERSTAND ME.
I WILL NOT BE THE ONE WHO PUNISHES YOU. THAT WILL BE YOUR FELLOW PEOPLE OF NINANNAH.
SHK SHK
WHAT IS THE MATTER?
DID YOU FIND MARCH?
NO... ABOUT THAT...
SHE... KIND OF... GOT AWAY...
SO LET'S GO BACK TO THE VILLAGE AND GET A REPLACEMENT ...
WE'LL FIND HER BEFORE WE EMBARRASS OURSELVES!!
GET BACK OUT THERE AND FIND HER IMMEDIATELY!!
WE CAN'T!
THERE'S A MON-STER OUT THERE!!
A MONSTER?

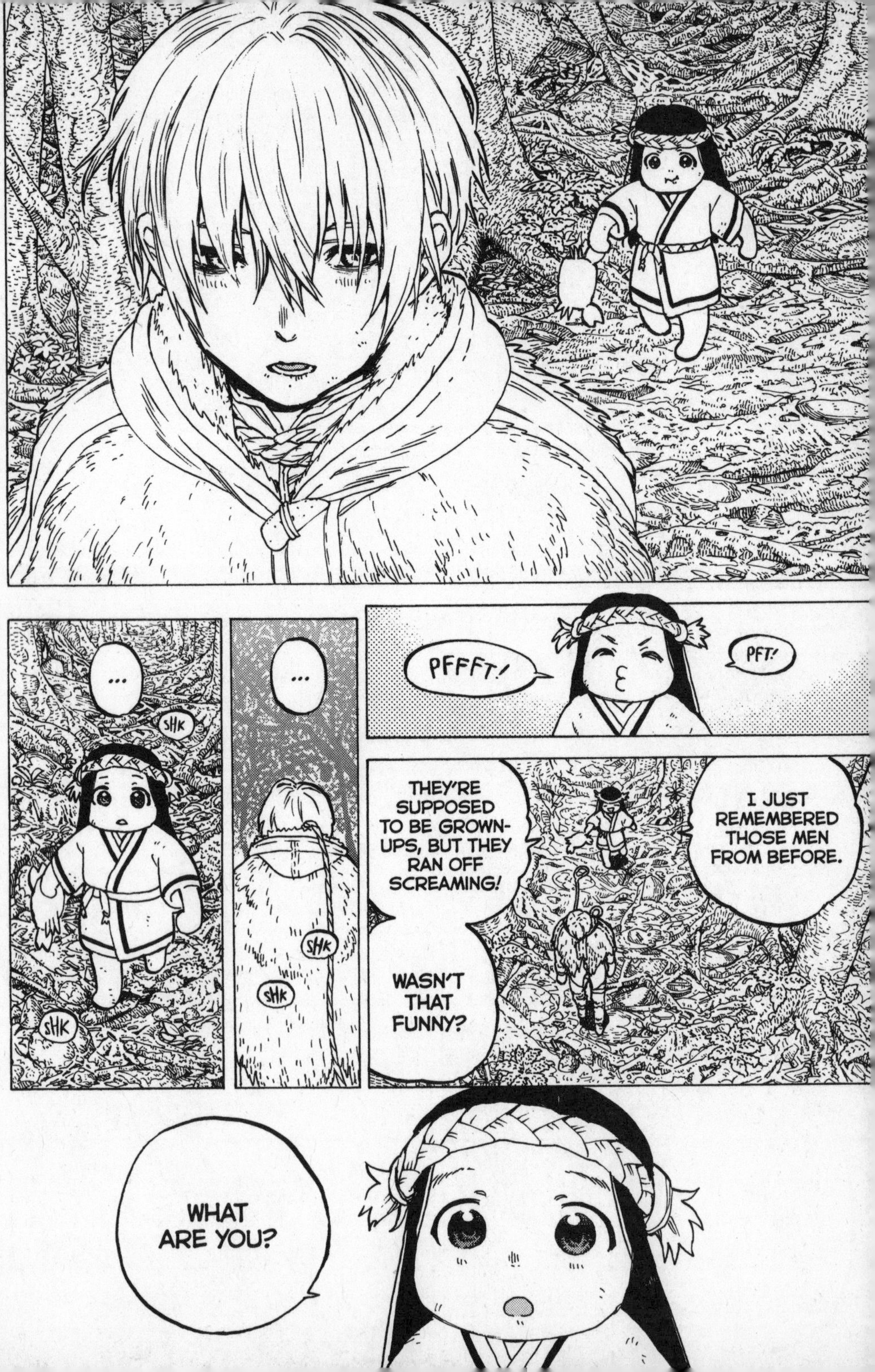
PFT!
PFFFT!
I JUST REMEMBERED THOSE MEN FROM BEFORE.
THEY'RE SUPPOSED TO BE GROWN-UPS, BUT THEY RAN OFF SCREAMING!
WASN'T THAT FUNNY?
...
SHK
SHK
...
SHK
SHK
WHAT ARE YOU?

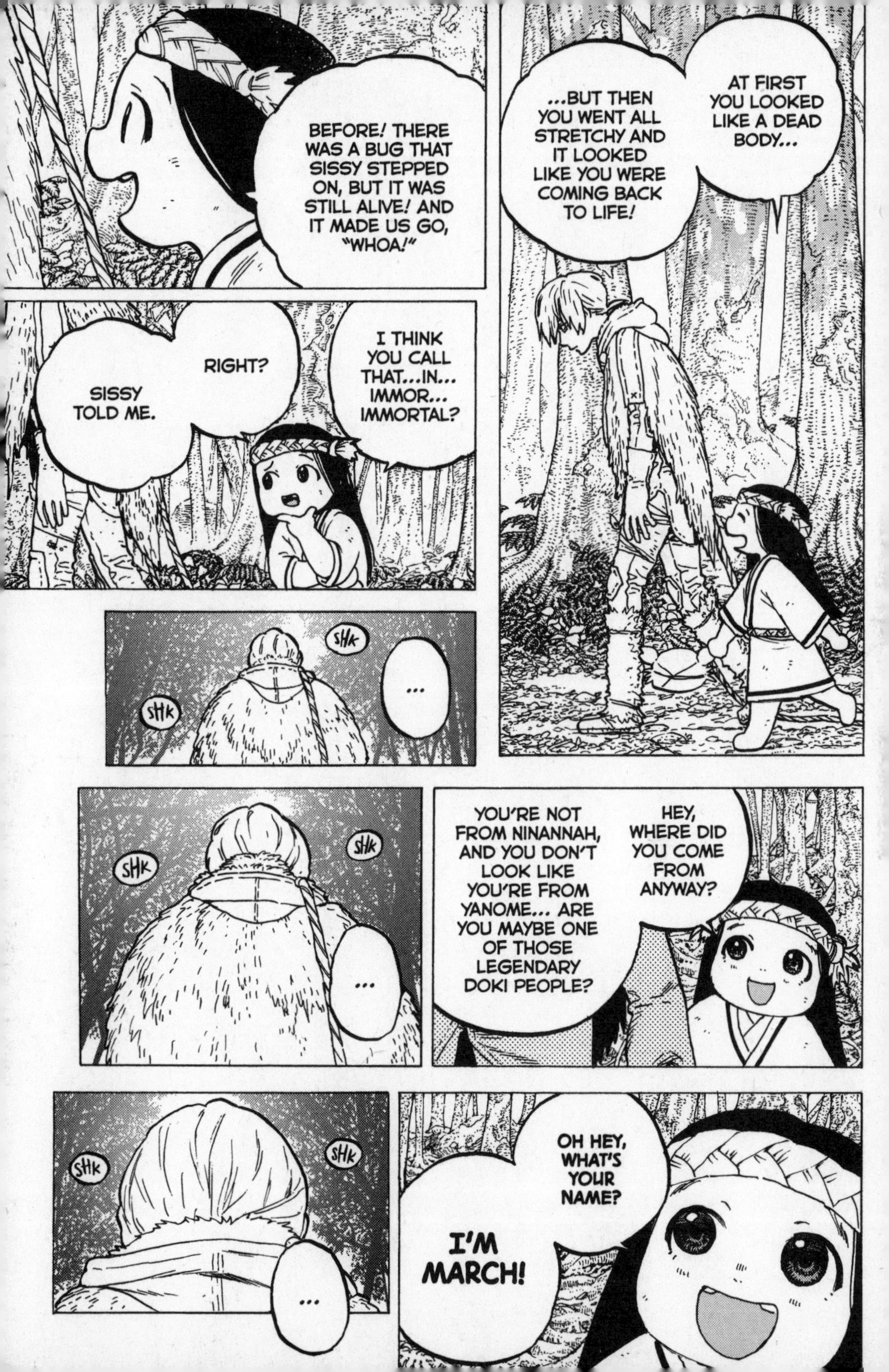
AT FIRST YOU LOOKED LIKE A DEAD BODY...
...BUT THEN YOU WENT ALL STRETCHY AND IT LOOKED LIKE YOU WERE COMING BACK TO LIFE!
BEFORE! THERE WAS A BUG THAT SISSY STEPPED ON, BUT IT WAS STILL ALIVE! AND IT MADE US GO, "WHOA!"
I THINK YOU CALL THAT...IN... IMMOR... IMMORTAL?
RIGHT?
SISSY TOLD ME.
SHK
...
SHK
HEY, WHERE DID YOU COME FROM ANYWAY?
YOU'RE NOT FROM NINANNAH, AND YOU DON'T LOOK LIKE YOU'RE FROM YANOME... ARE YOU MAYBE ONE OF THOSE LEGENDARY DOKI PEOPLE?
SHK
SHK
...
OH HEY, WHAT'S YOUR NAME?
I'M MARCH!
SHK
SHK
...

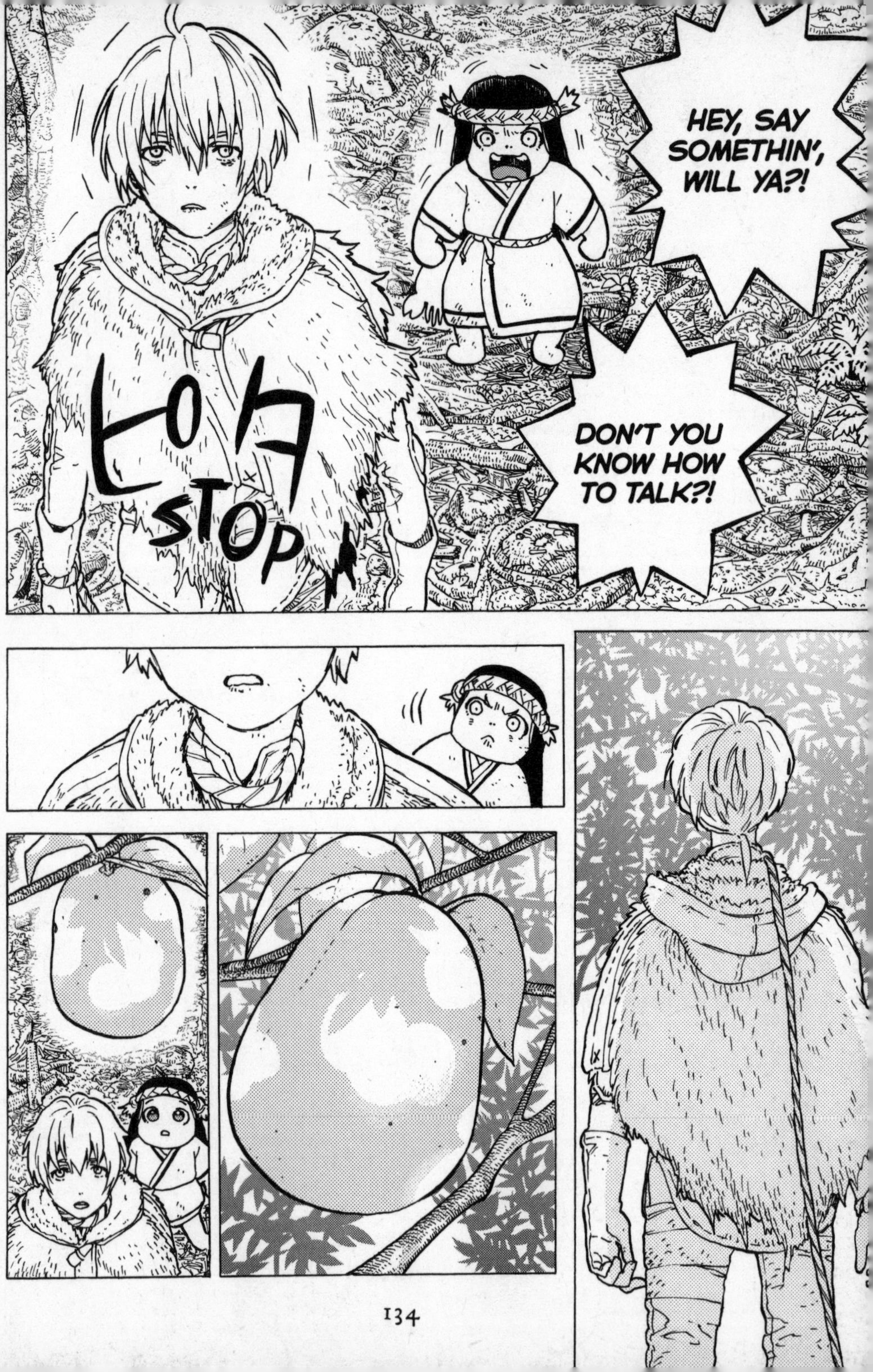
HEY, SAY SOMETHIN', WILL YA?!
DON'T YOU KNOW HOW TO TALK?!
ピタ
STOP

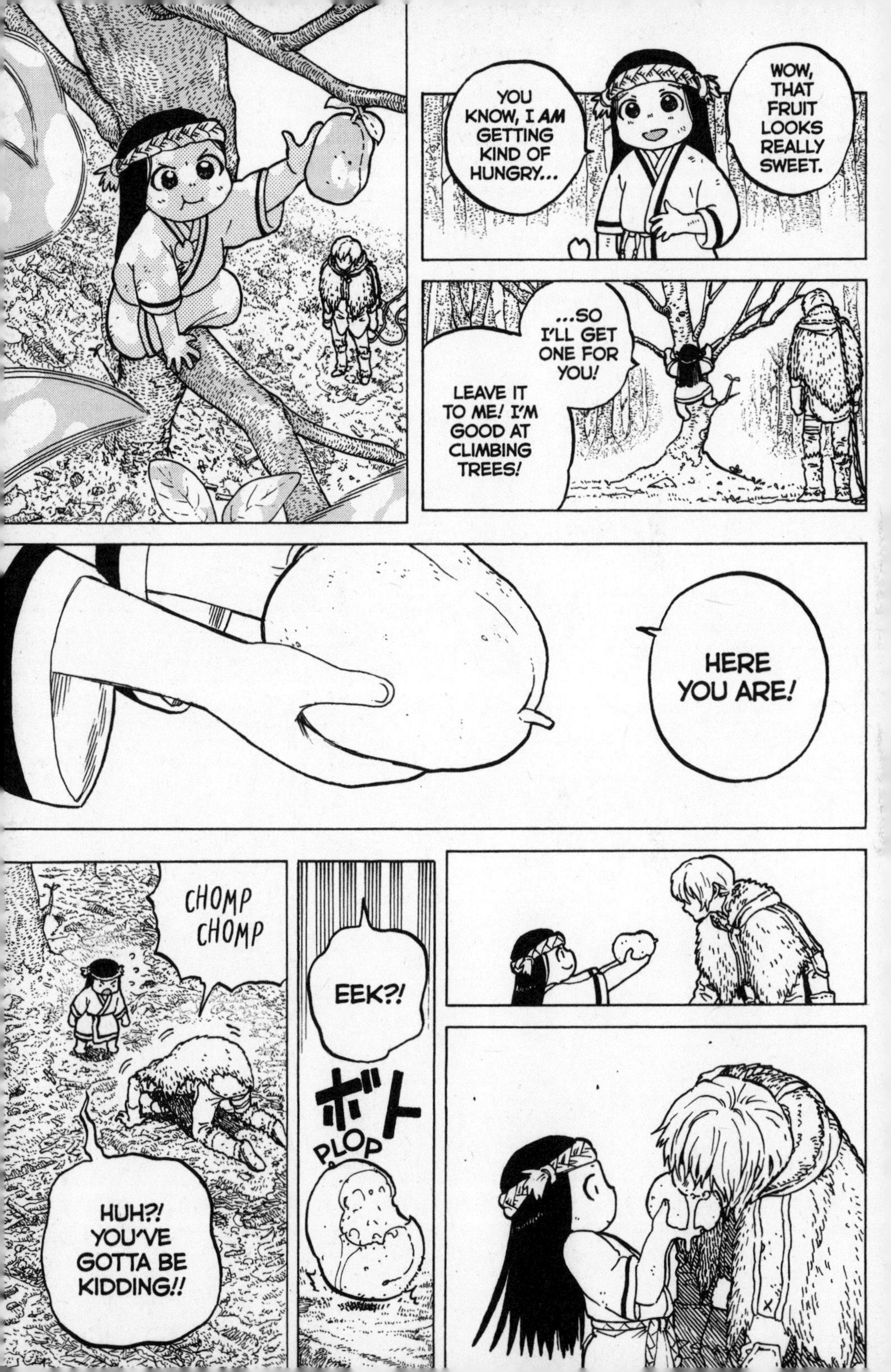
WOW, THAT FRUIT LOOKS REALLY SWEET.
YOU KNOW, I *AM* GETTING KIND OF HUNGRY...
...SO I'LL GET ONE FOR YOU!
LEAVE IT TO ME! I'M GOOD AT CLIMBING TREES!
HERE YOU ARE!
EEK?!
ボト
PLOP
CHOMP CHOMP
HUH?! YOU'VE GOTTA BE KIDDING!!

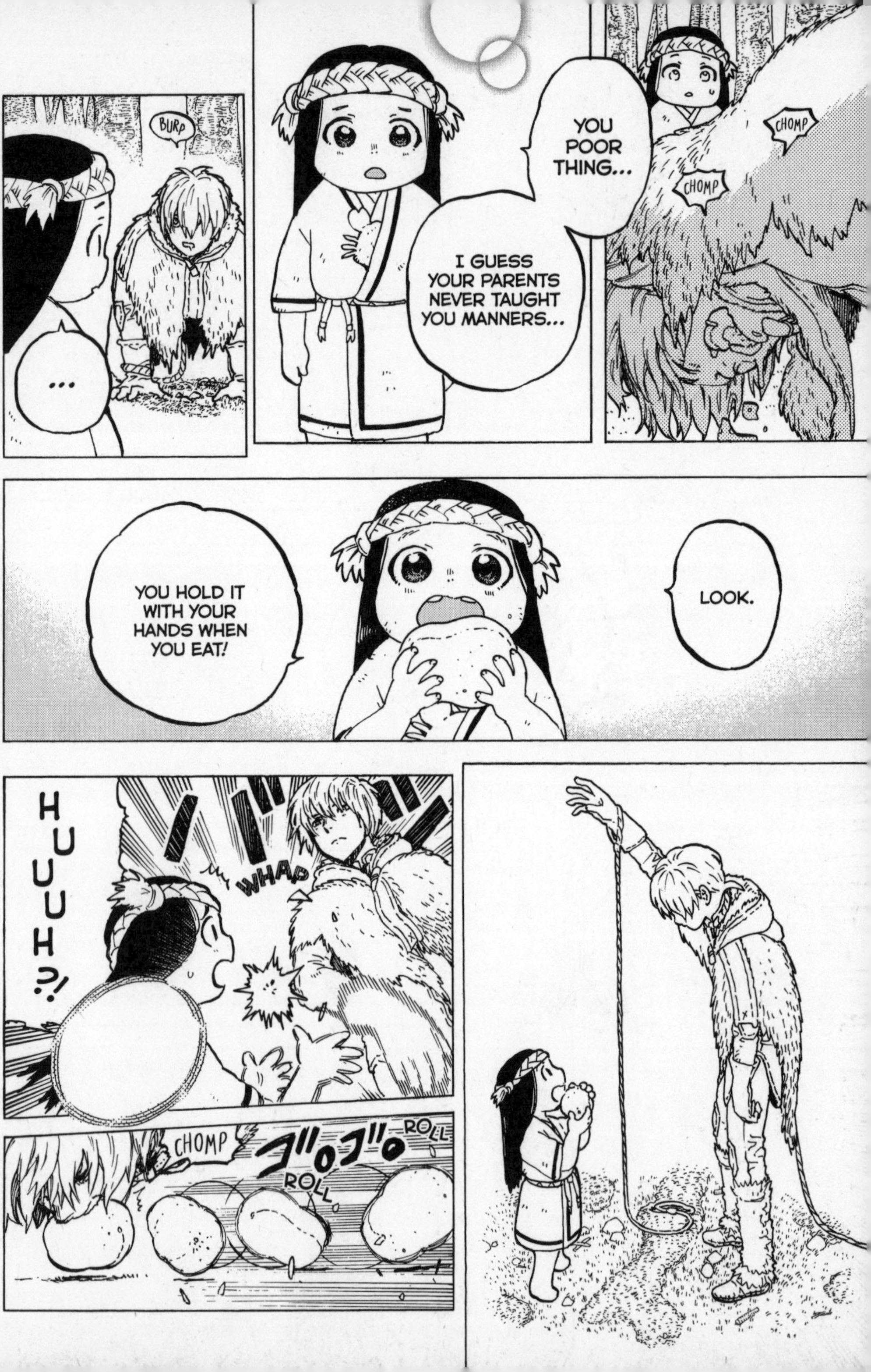
CHOMP
CHOMP
YOU POOR THING...
I GUESS YOUR PARENTS NEVER TAUGHT YOU MANNERS...
BURP
...
LOOK.
YOU HOLD IT WITH YOUR HANDS WHEN YOU EAT!
WHAP
HUUUH?!
ROLL
ゴロゴロ
ROLL
CHOMP

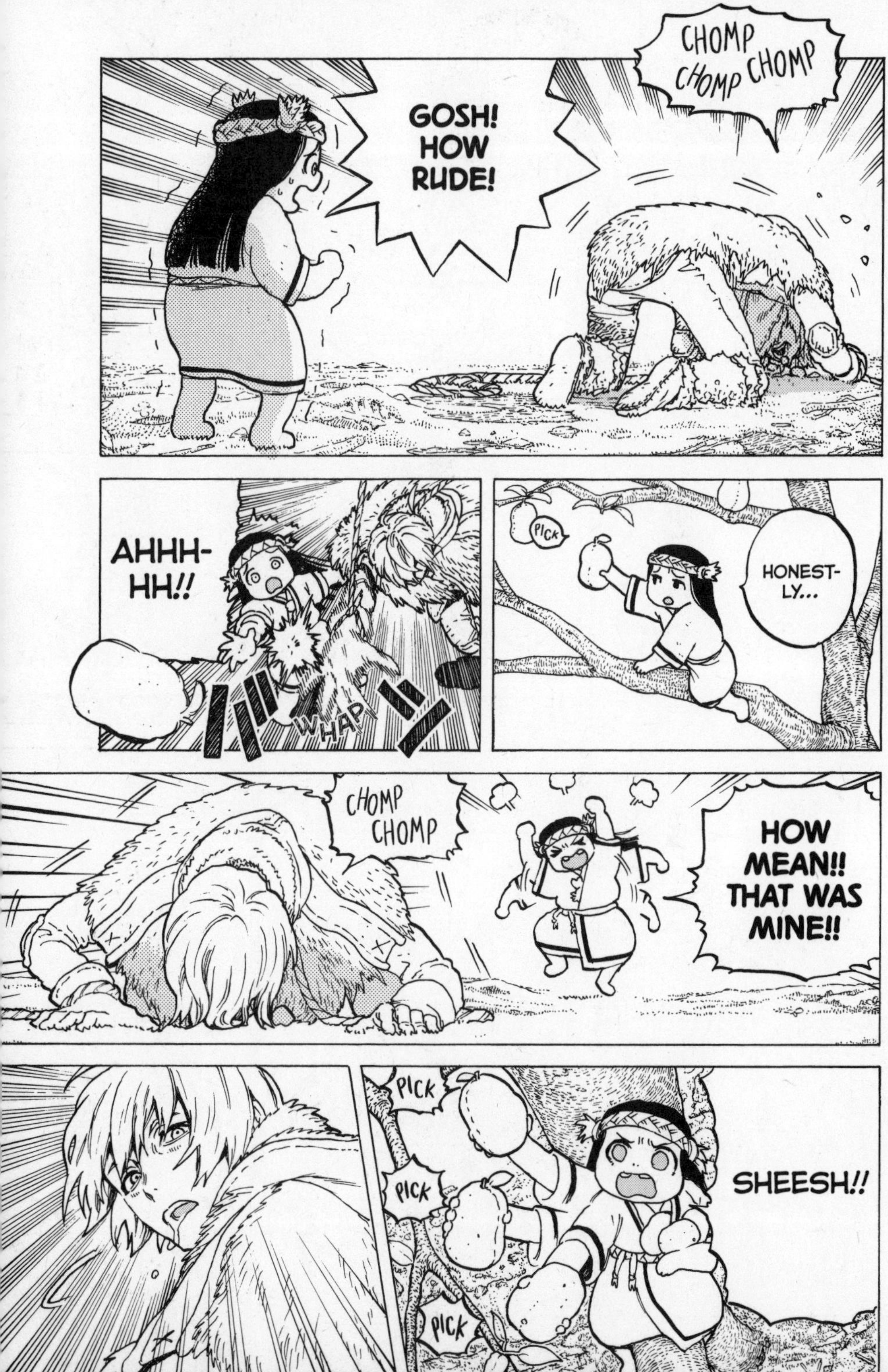
CHOMP CHOMP CHOMP
GOSH! HOW RUDE!
PICK
HONEST-LY...
AHHHH-HH!!
WHAP
HOW MEAN!! THAT WAS MINE!!
CHOMP CHOMP
PICK
SHEESH!!
PICK
PICK

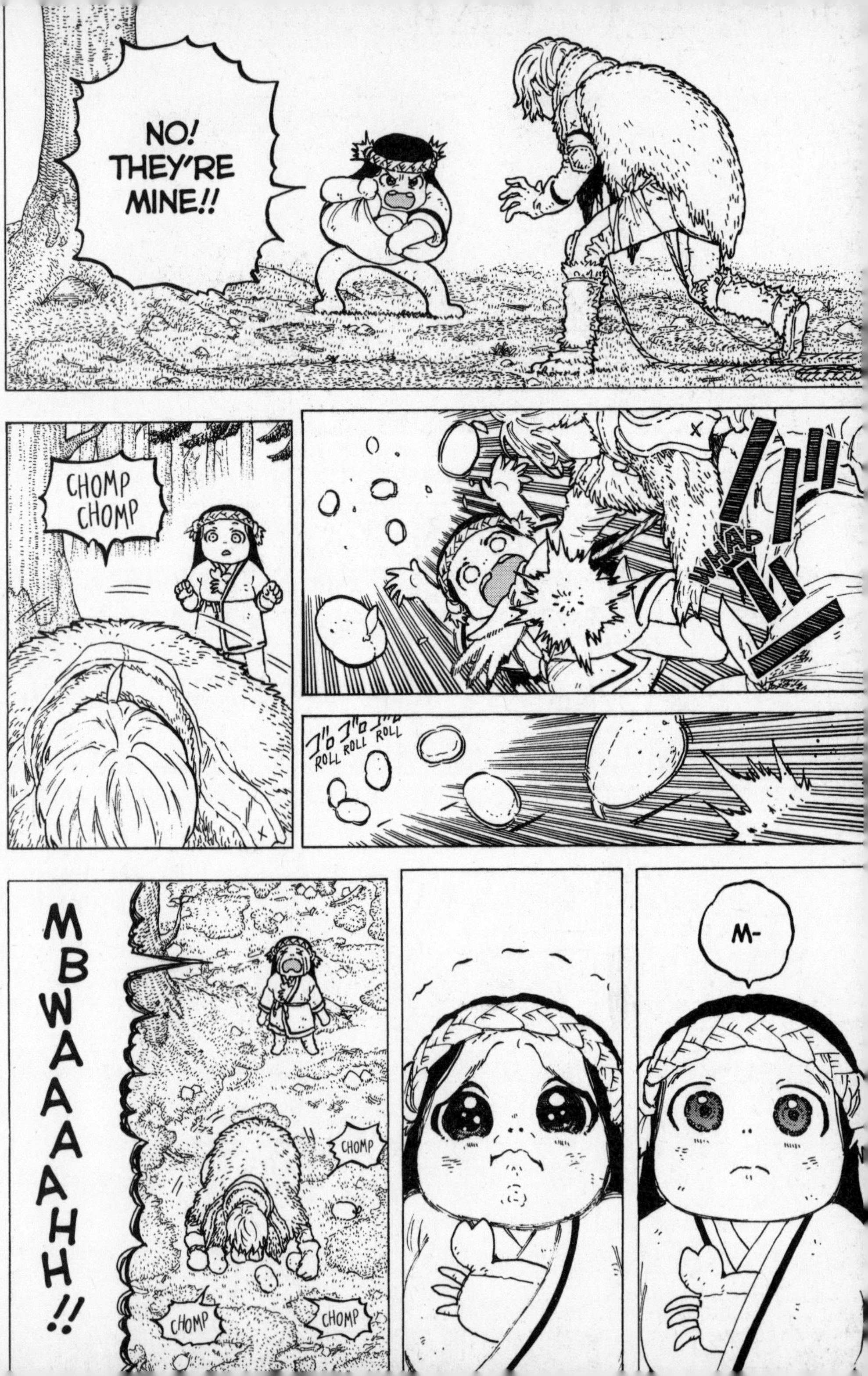
NO! THEY'RE MINE!!
WHAP
ゴロゴロゴロ ROLL ROLL ROLL
CHOMP CHOMP
M-
MBWAAAAAHH!!
CHOMP
CHOMP
CHOMP

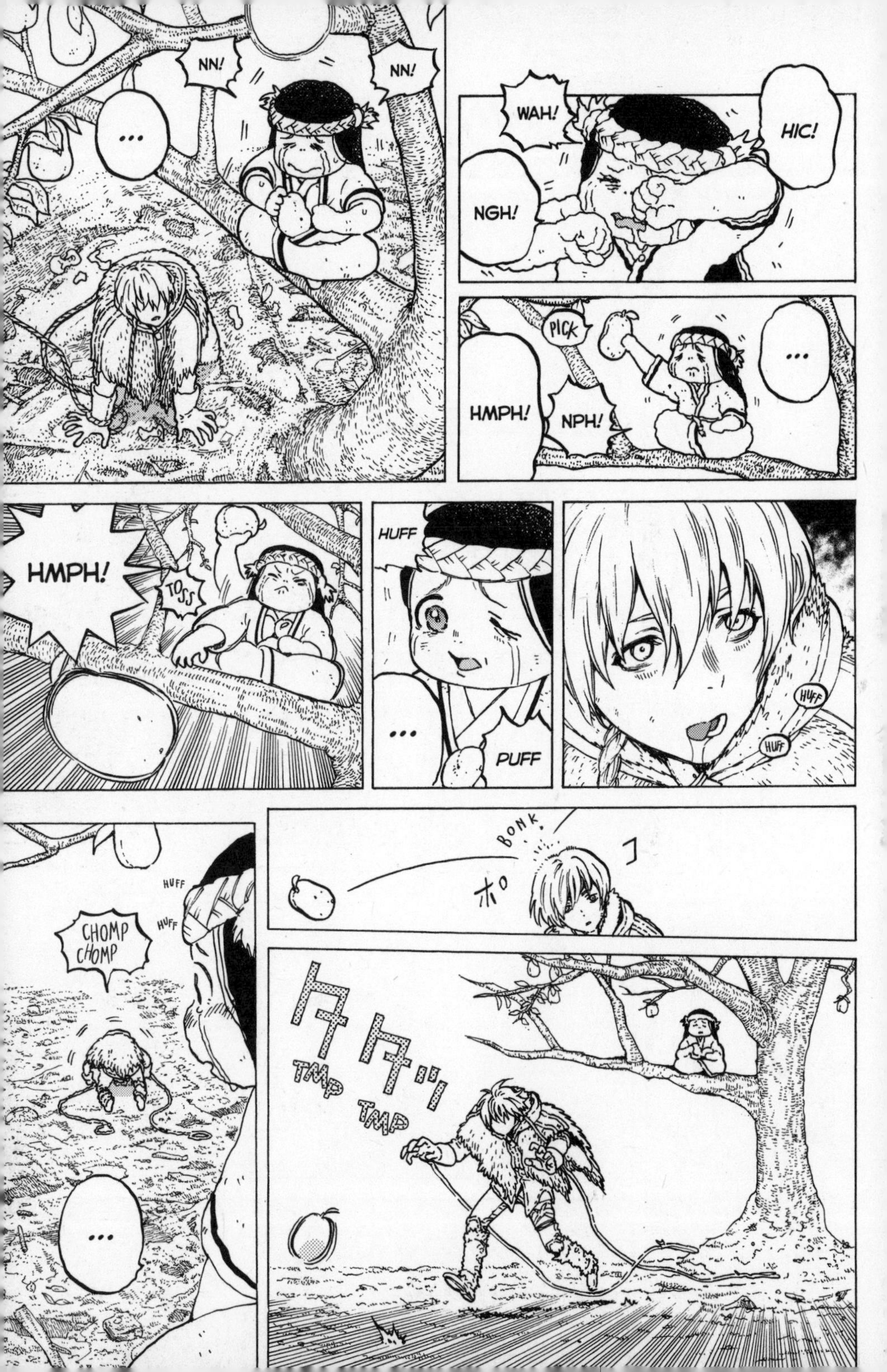
HIC!
WAH!
NGH!
...
PICK
NPH!
HMPH!
NN!
NN!
...
HUFF
HUFF
HUFF
...
PUFF
HMPH!
TOSS
コ
BONK
ホ°
タタッ
TMP
TMP
HUFF
HUFF
CHOMP CHOMP
...

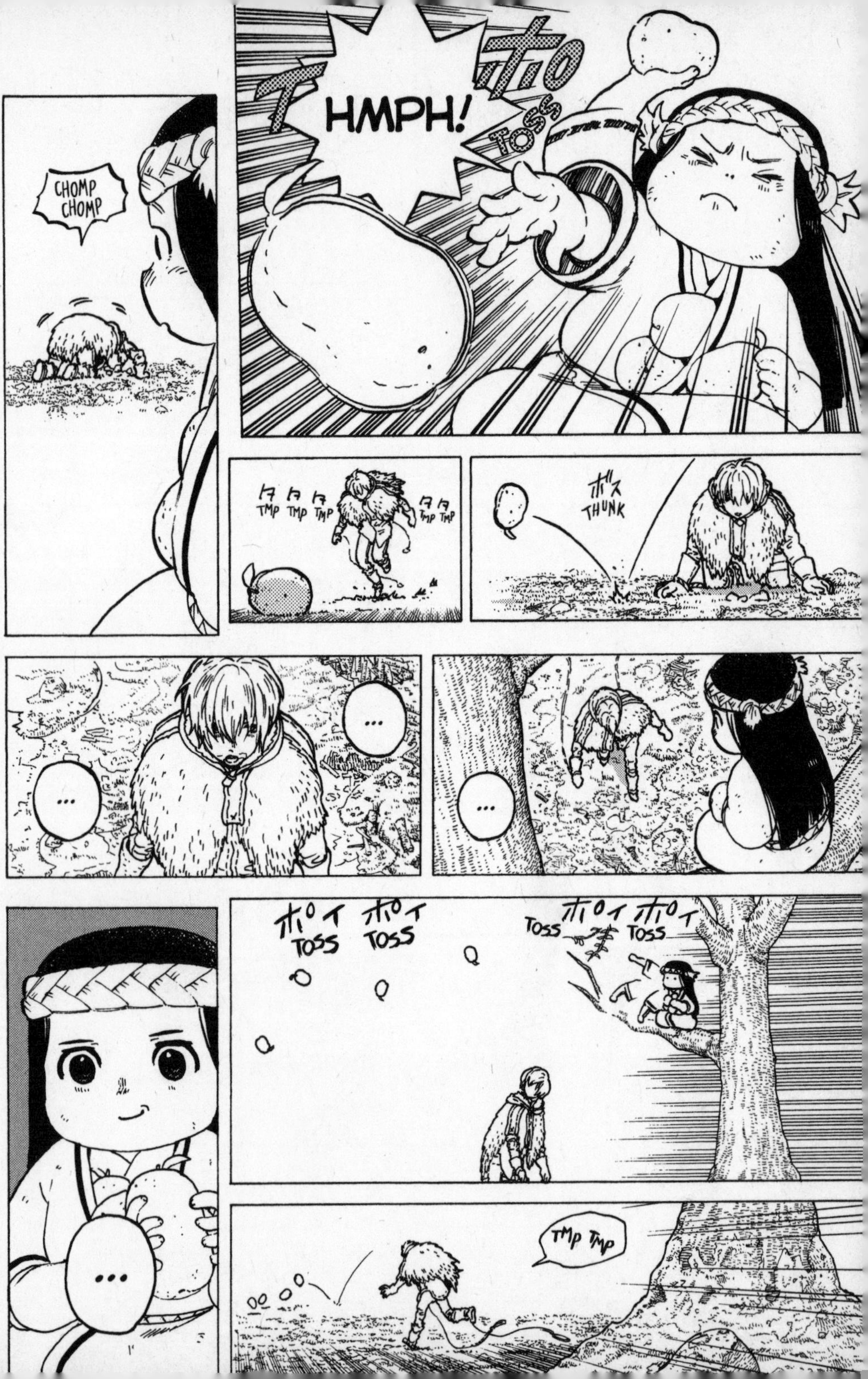HMPH!
ポイ
TOSS
ボス
THUNK
タ タ タ
TMP TMP TMP
タタ
TMP TMP
CHOMP CHOMP
...
...
...
ポイ ポイ
TOSS TOSS
ポイ ポイ
TOSS TOSS
TMP TMP
...

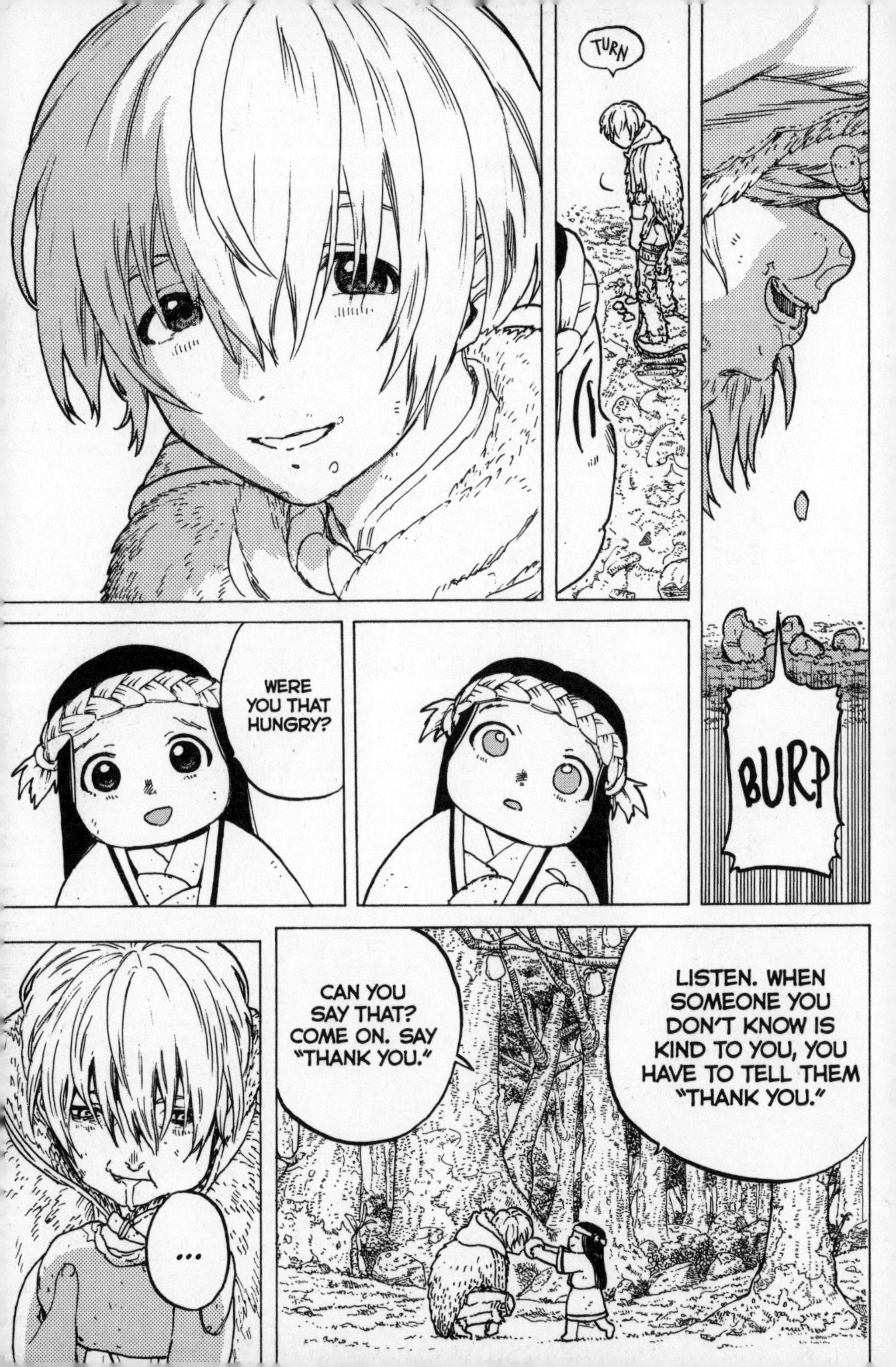
TURN
BURP
WERE YOU THAT HUNGRY?
LISTEN. WHEN SOMEONE YOU DON'T KNOW IS KIND TO YOU, YOU HAVE TO TELL THEM "THANK YOU."
CAN YOU SAY THAT? COME ON. SAY "THANK YOU."
...

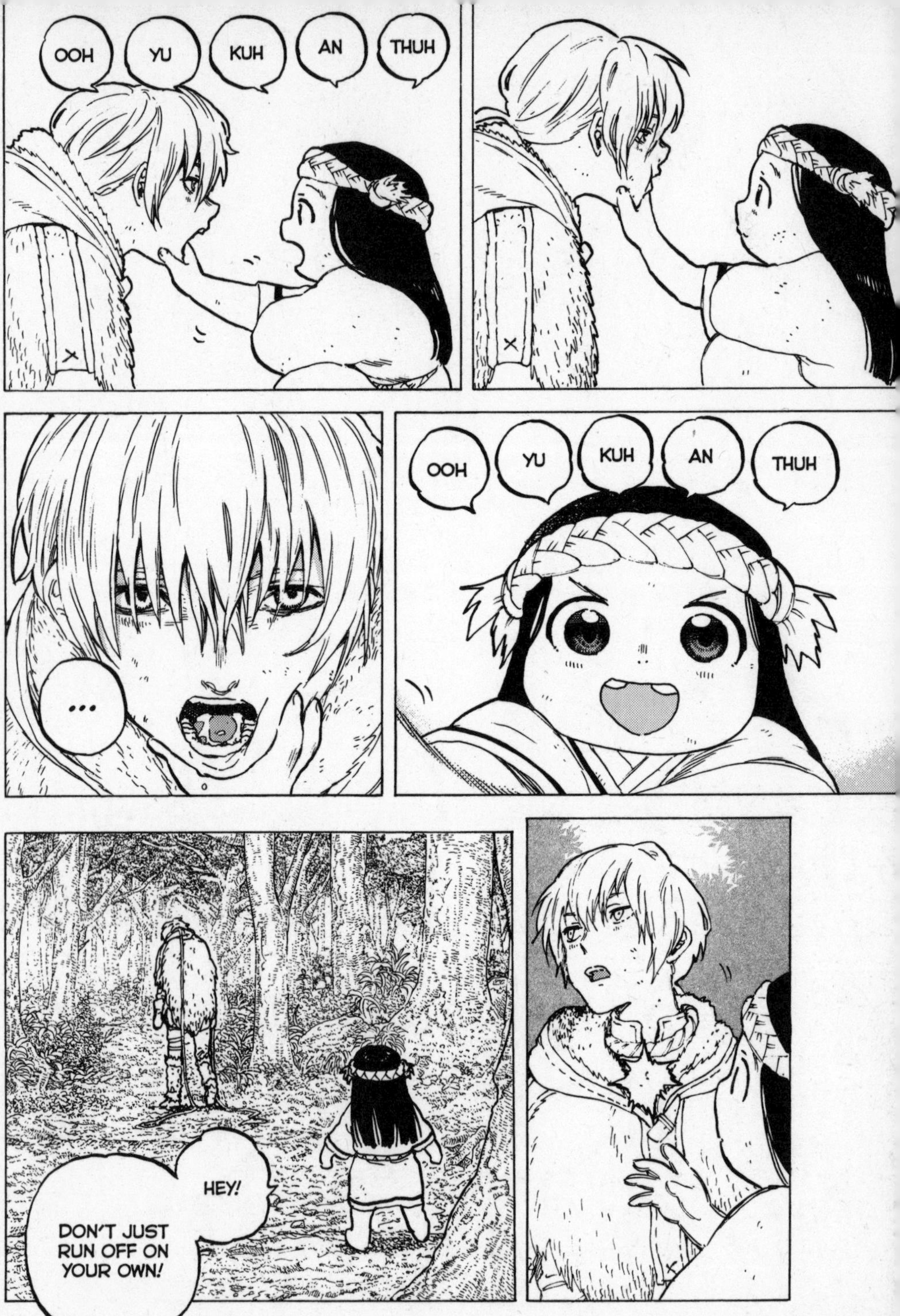
OOH
YU
KUH
AN
THUH
OOH
YU
KUH
AN
THUH
...
HEY!
DON'T JUST RUN OFF ON YOUR OWN!

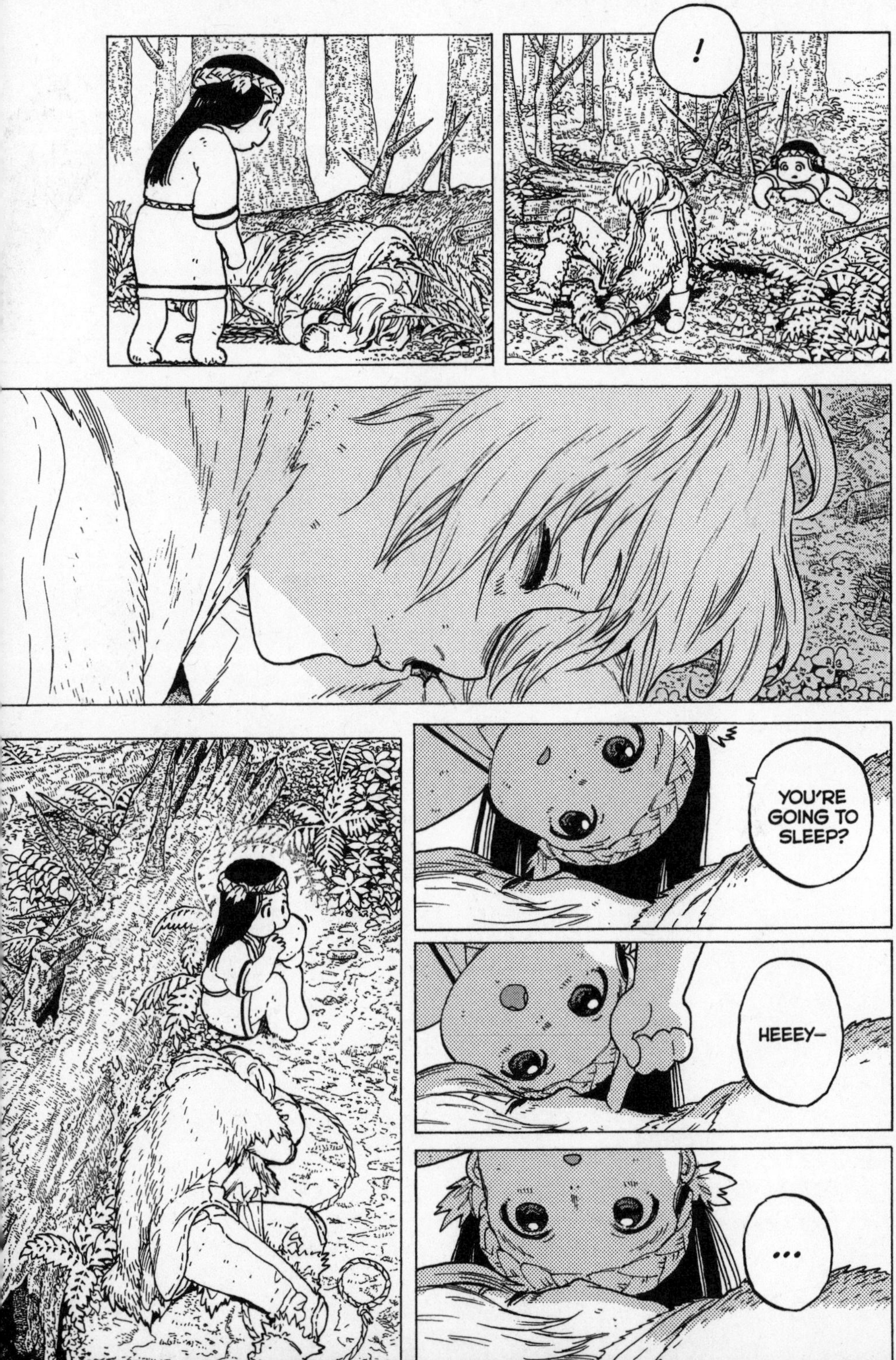
!
YOU'RE GOING TO SLEEP?
HEEEY–
...

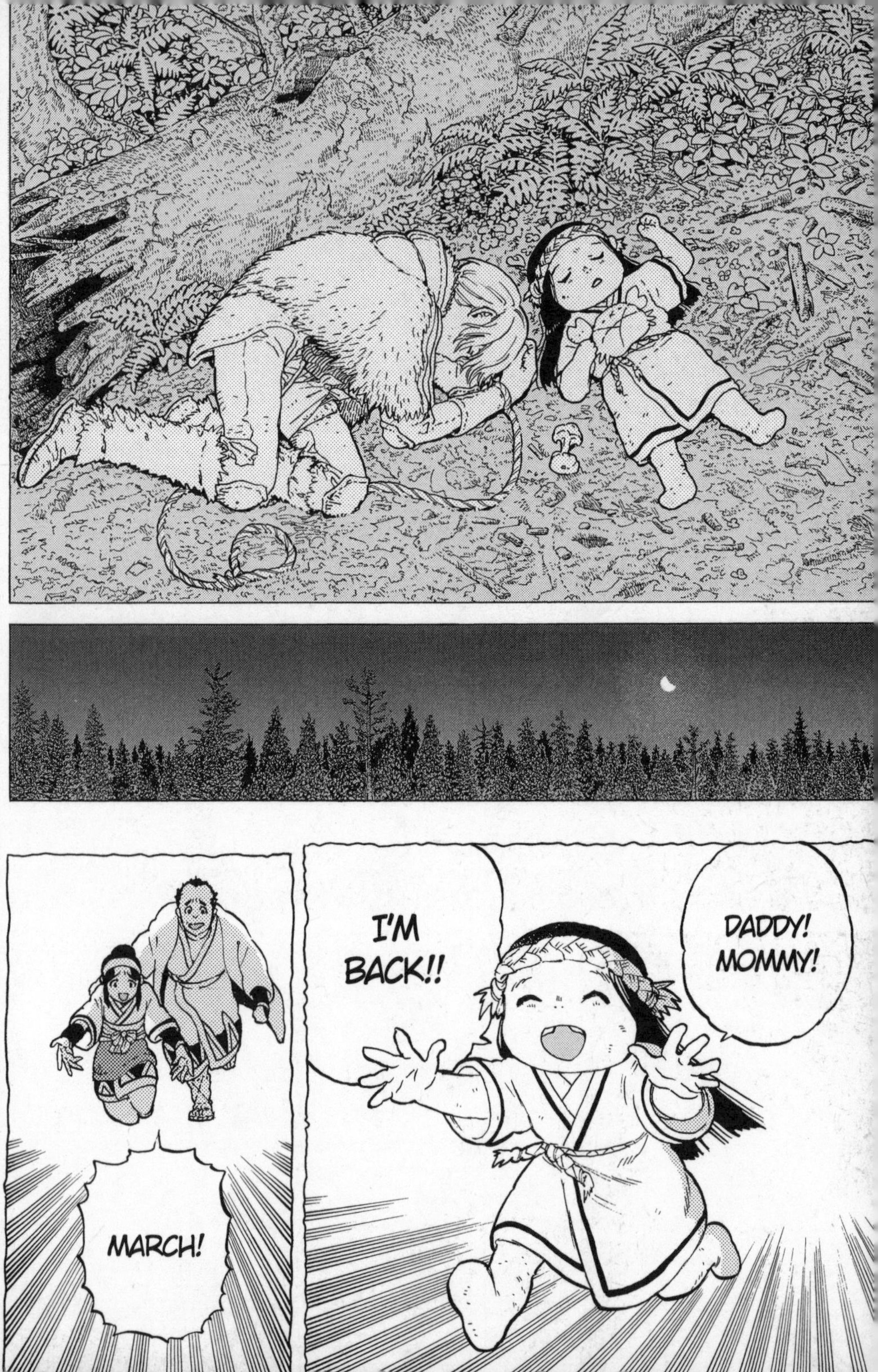

DADDY! MOMMY!
I'M BACK!!
MARCH!

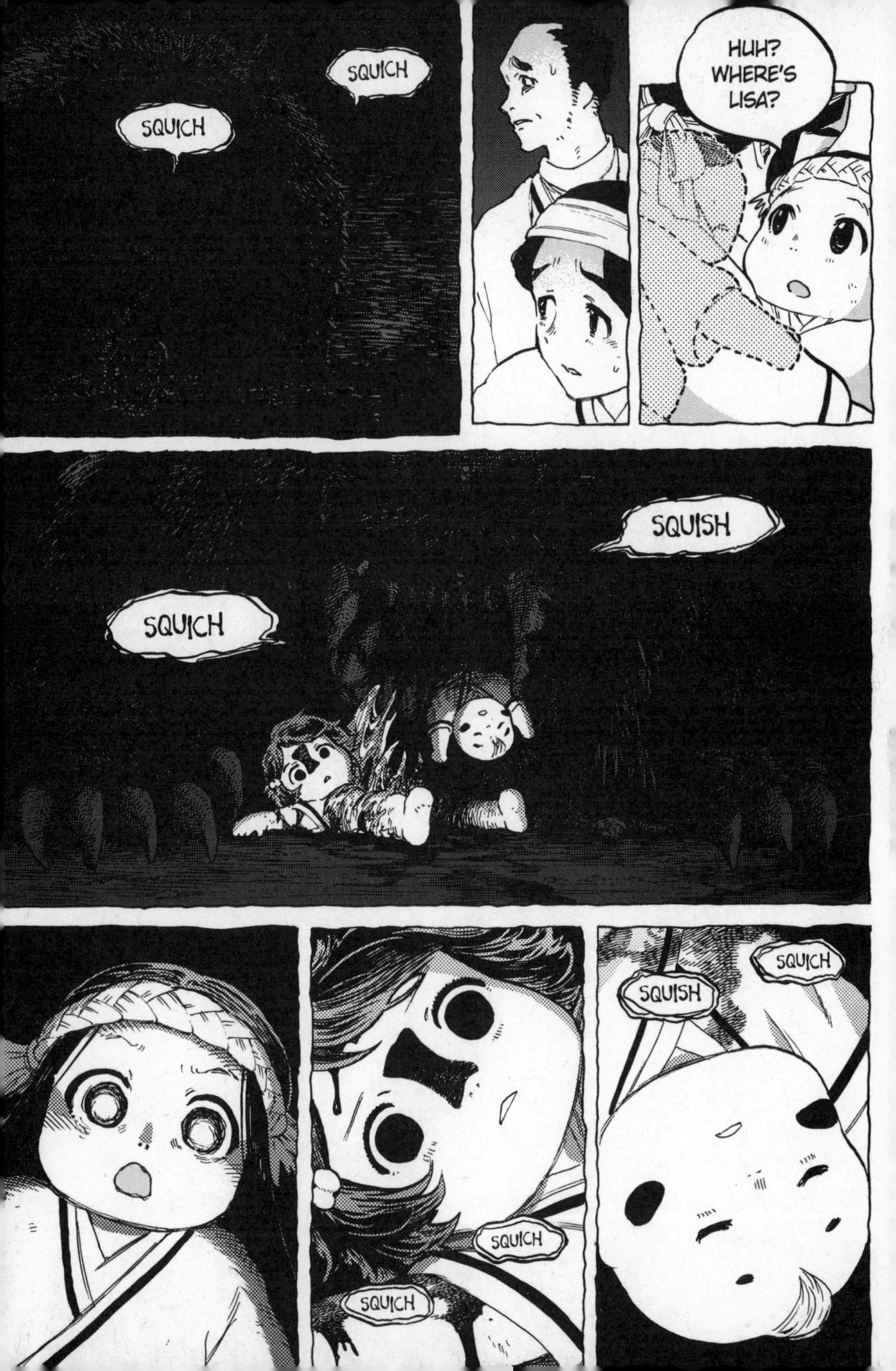
HUH? WHERE'S LISA?
SQUICH
SQUICH
SQUISH
SQUICH
SQUICH
SQUISH
SQUICH
SQUICH

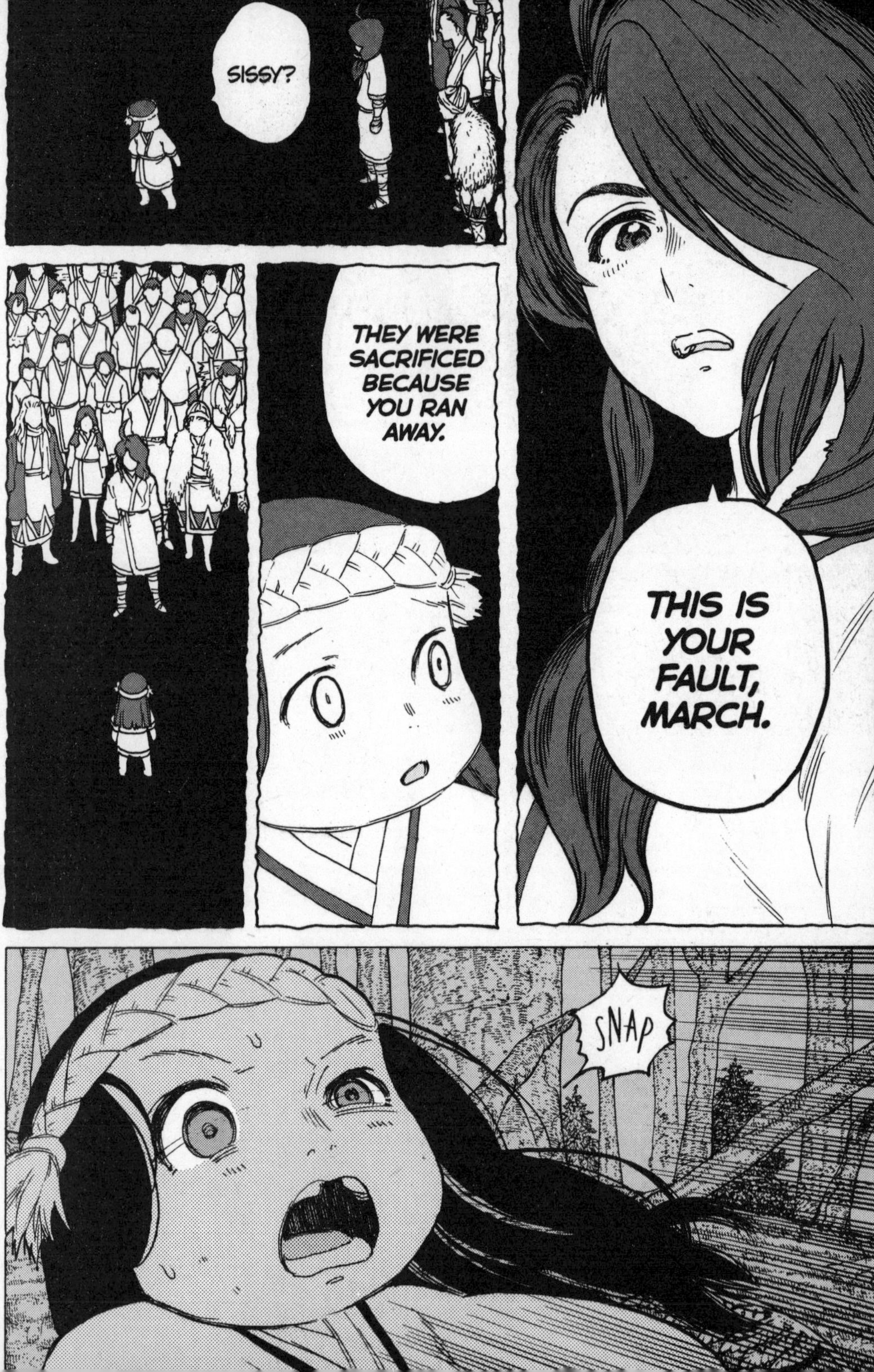
THIS IS YOUR FAULT, MARCH.
SISSY?
THEY WERE SACRIFICED BECAUSE YOU RAN AWAY.
SNAP

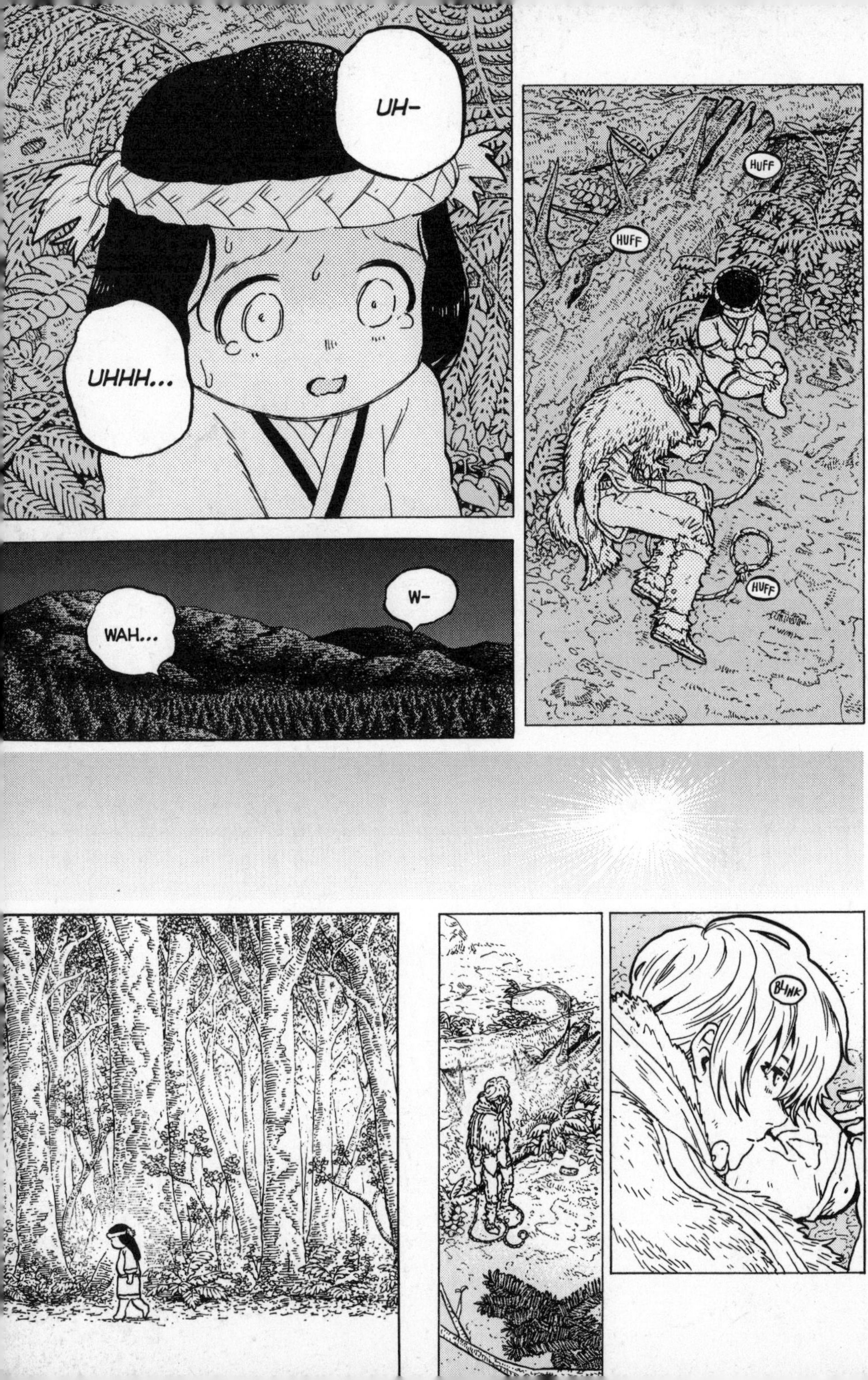
HUFF
HUFF
HUFF
UH-
UHHH...
W-
WAH...
BLINK

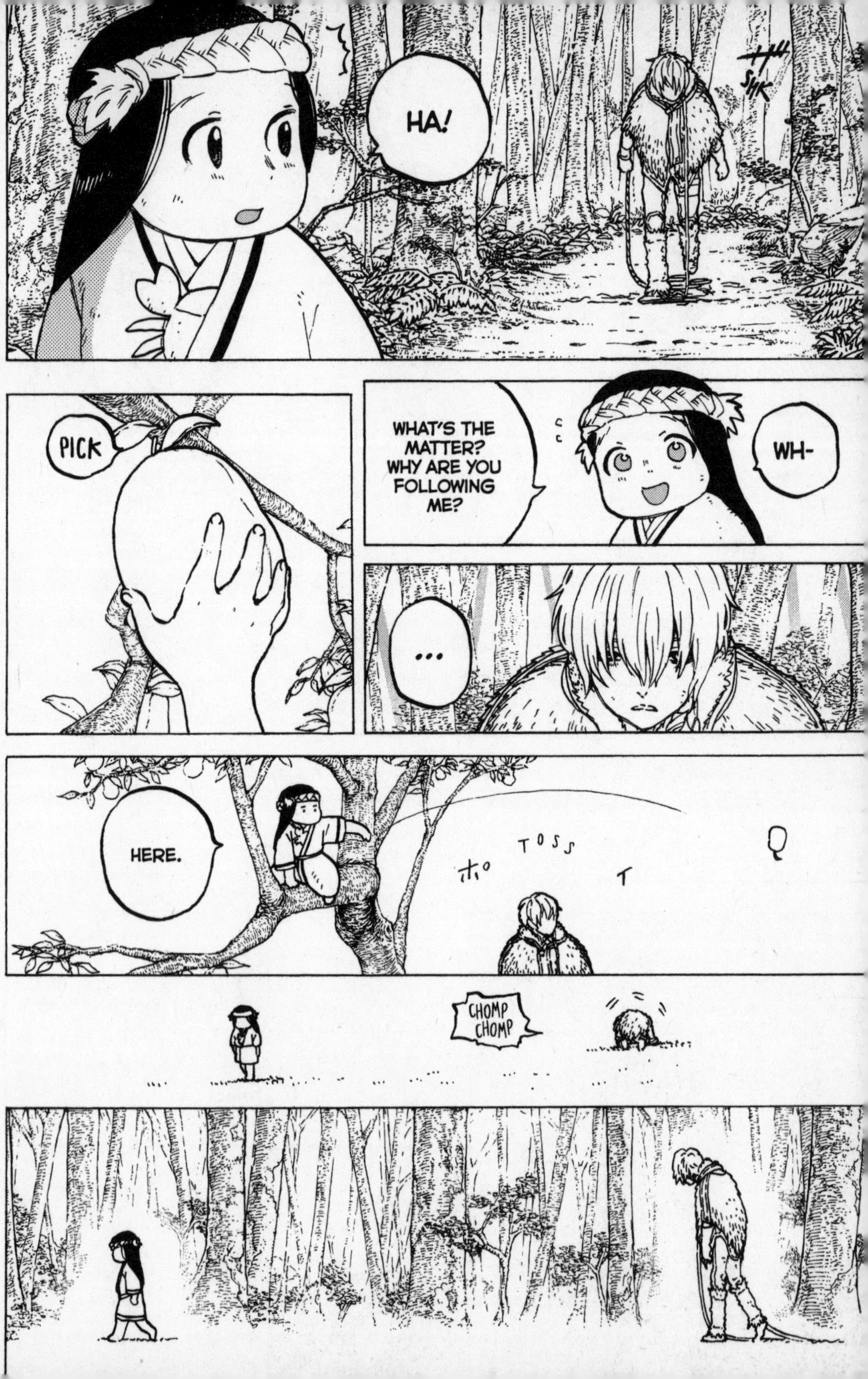
SHK
HA!
WH-
WHAT'S THE MATTER? WHY ARE YOU FOLLOWING ME?
...
PICK
Q
TOSS
HERE.
CHOMP CHOMP

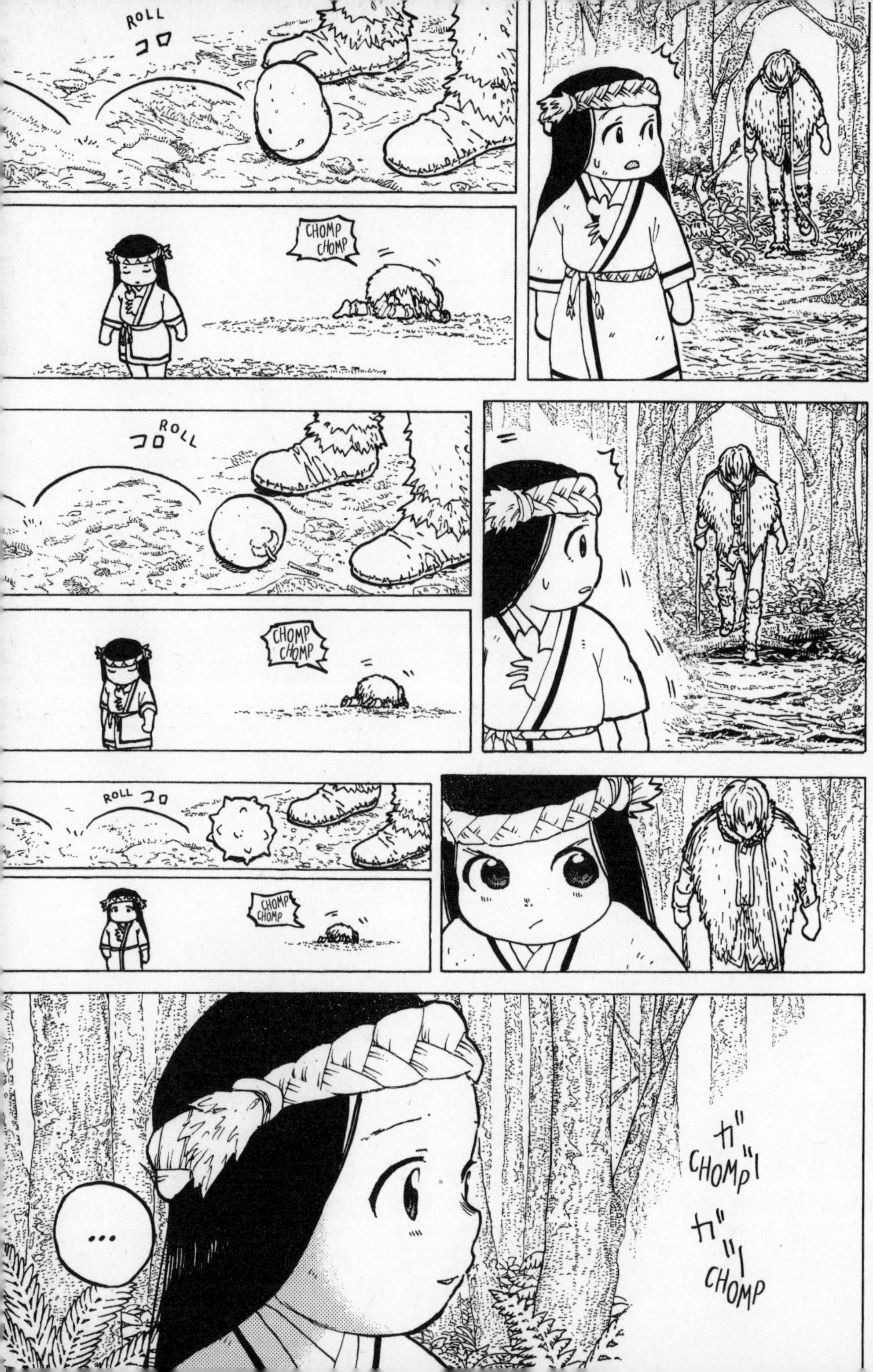
ROLL
コロ
CHOMP CHOMP
コロ
ROLL
CHOMP CHOMP
ROLL
コロ
CHOMP CHOMP
ガリ
CHOMP
ガリ
CHOMP
...

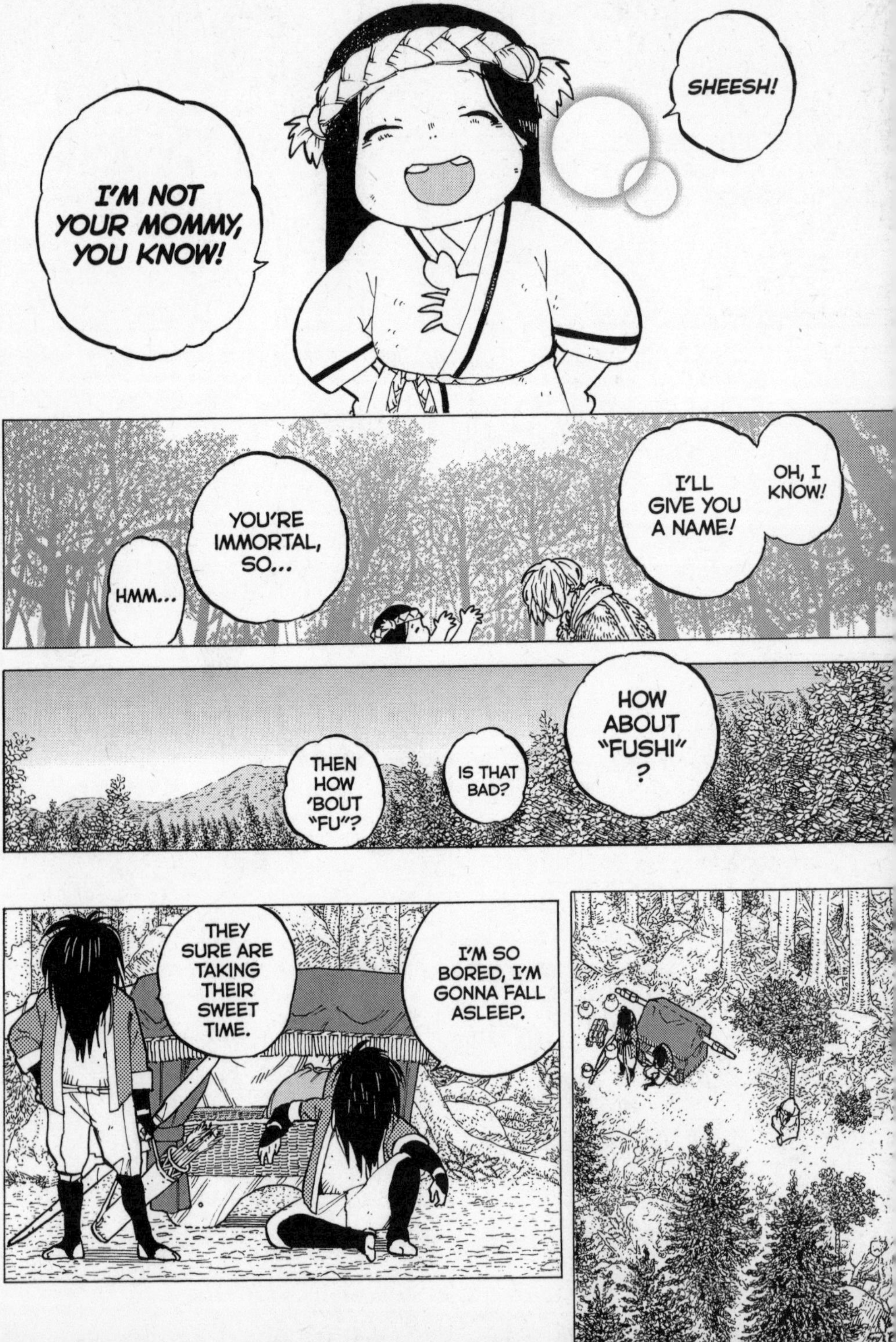
SHEESH!
I'M NOT YOUR MOMMY, YOU KNOW!
OH, I KNOW!
I'LL GIVE YOU A NAME!
YOU'RE IMMORTAL, SO...
HMM...
HOW ABOUT "FUSHI"?
IS THAT BAD?
THEN HOW 'BOUT "FU"?
I'M SO BORED, I'M GONNA FALL ASLEEP.
THEY SURE ARE TAKING THEIR SWEET TIME.

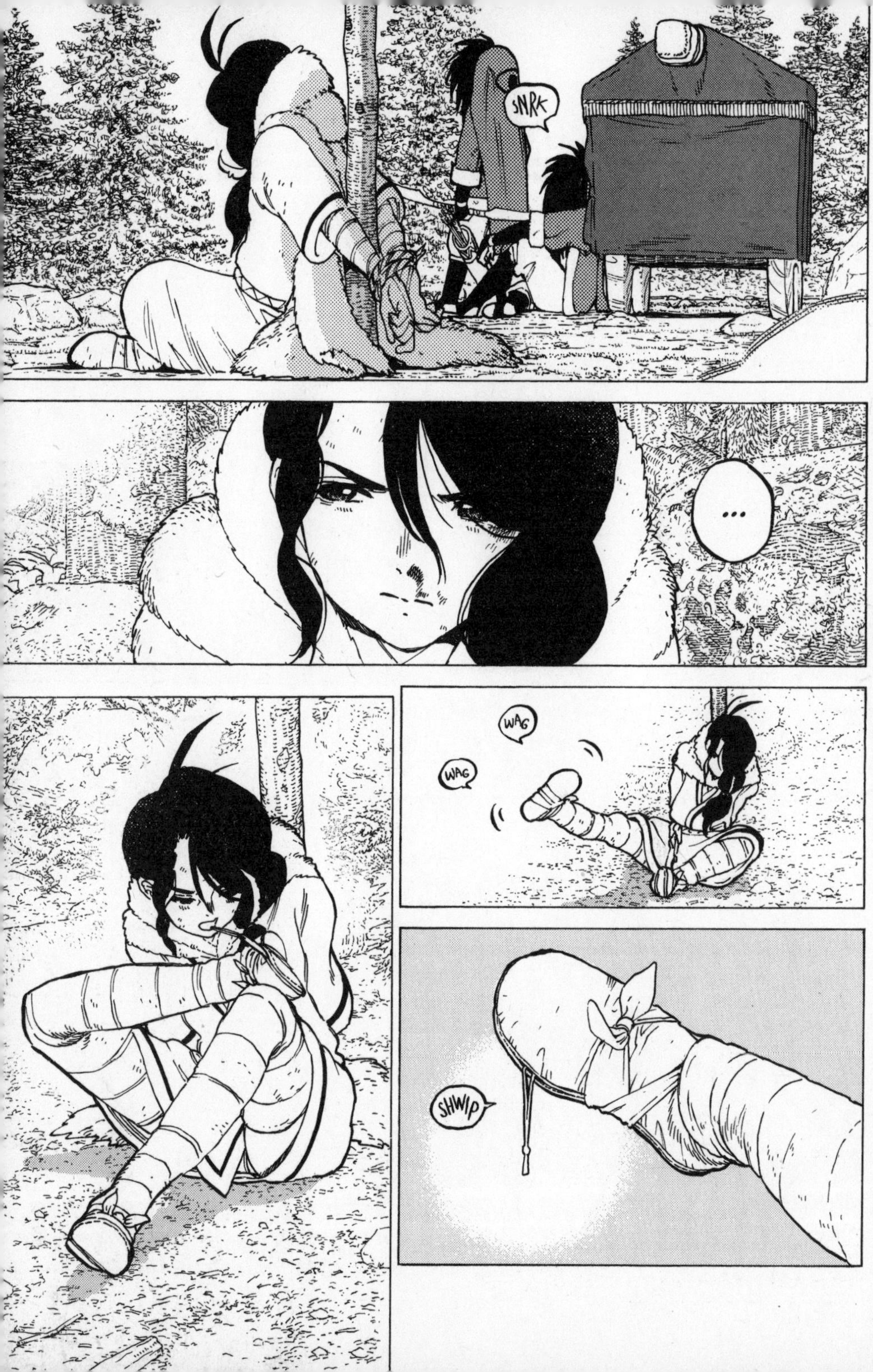
SNRK
...
WAG
WAG
SHWIP

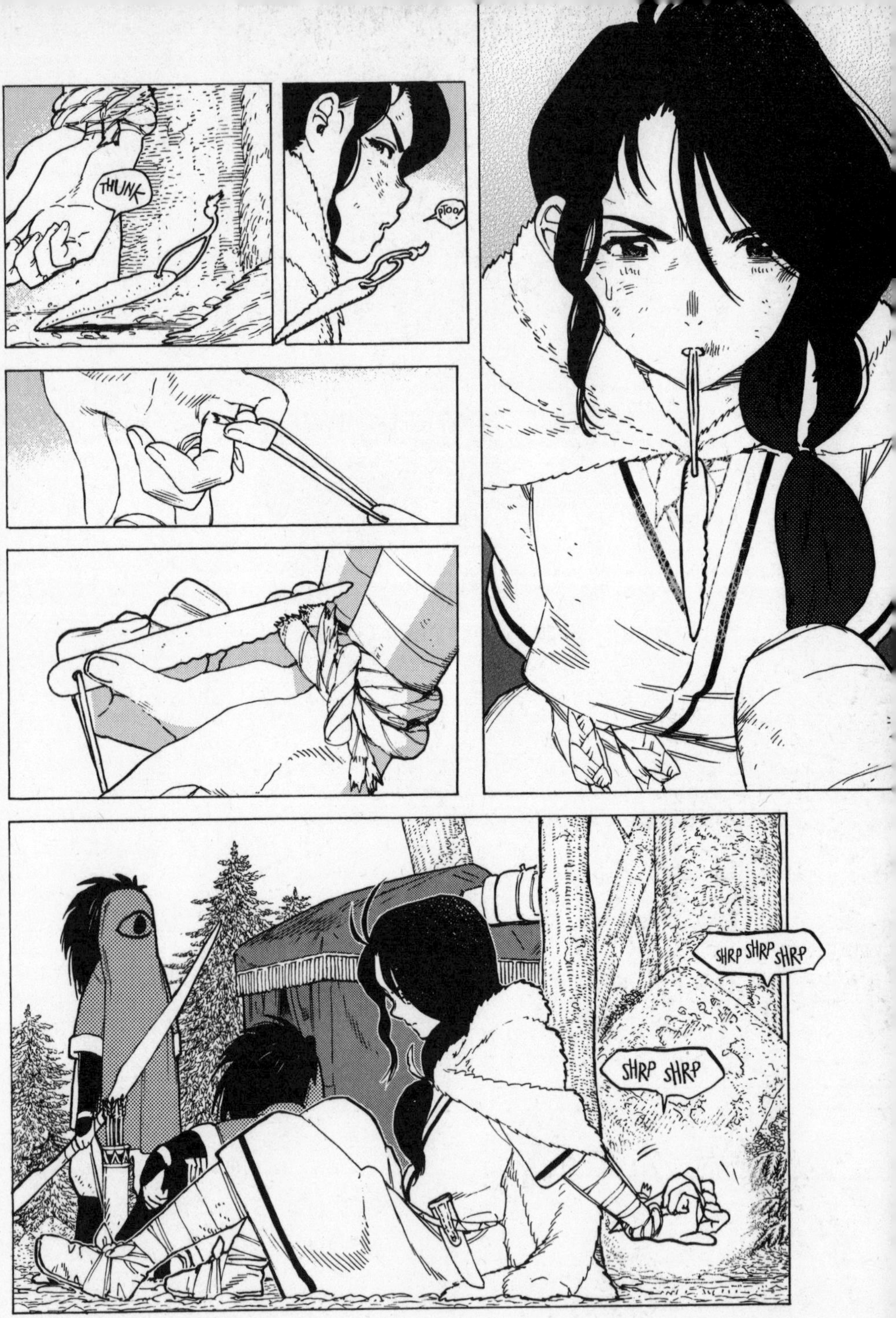
PTOO!
THUNK
SHRP SHRP SHRP
SHRP SHRP

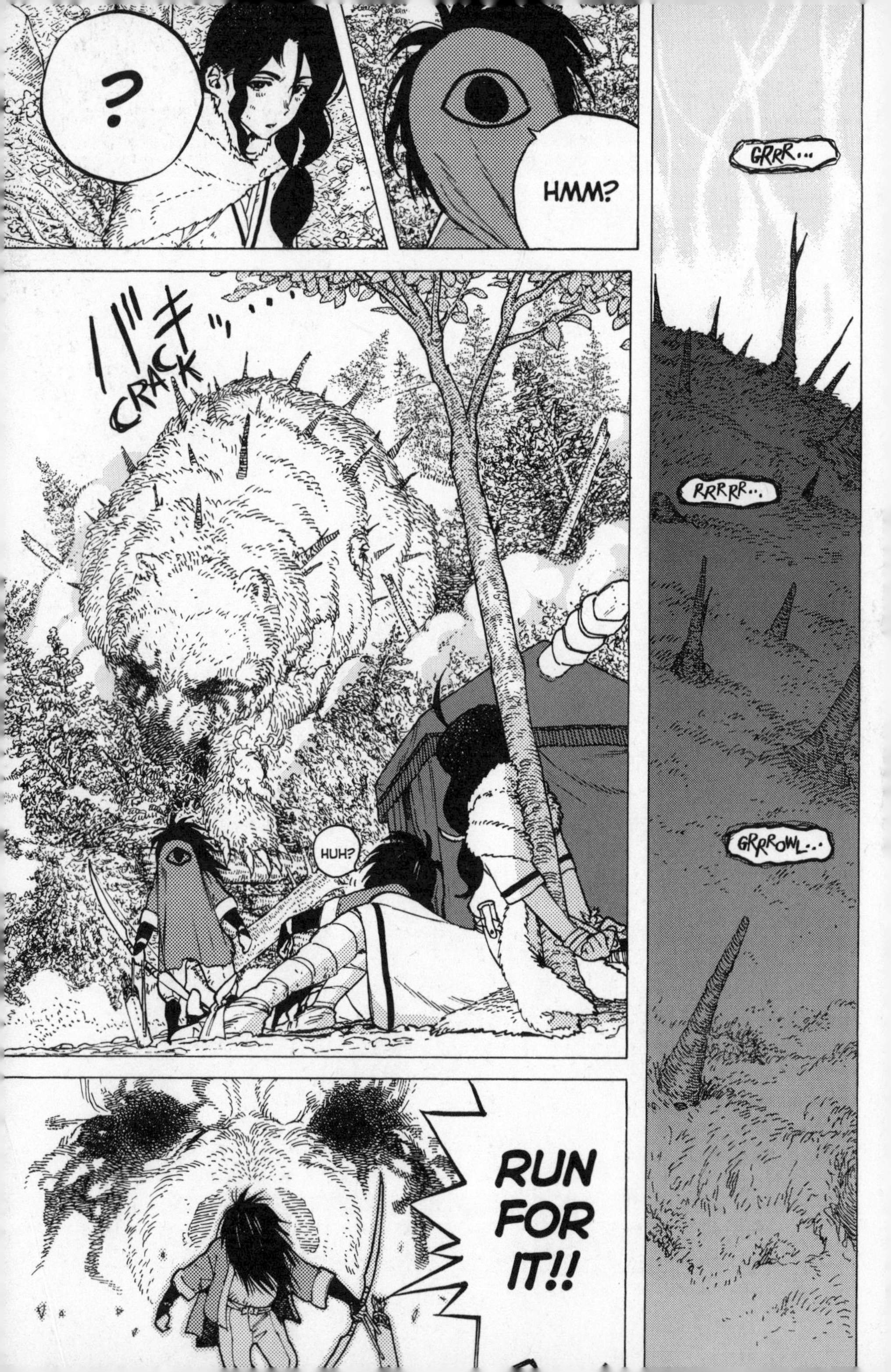
GRRR...
RRRRR...
GRRROWL...
HMM?
?
バキッ…
CRACK
HUH?
RUN FOR IT!!

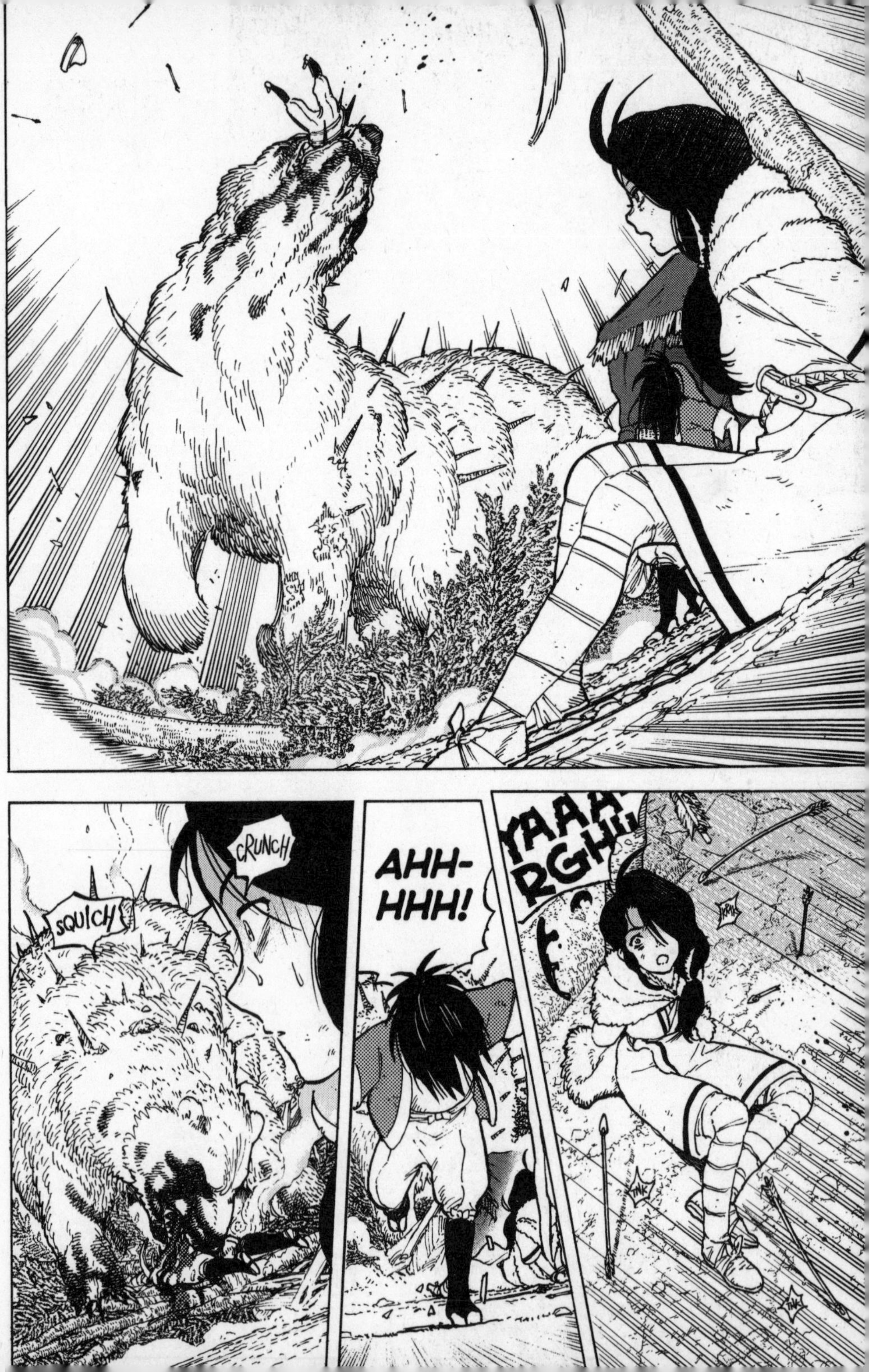
YAAARGH
AHH-HHH!
CRUNCH
SQUICH

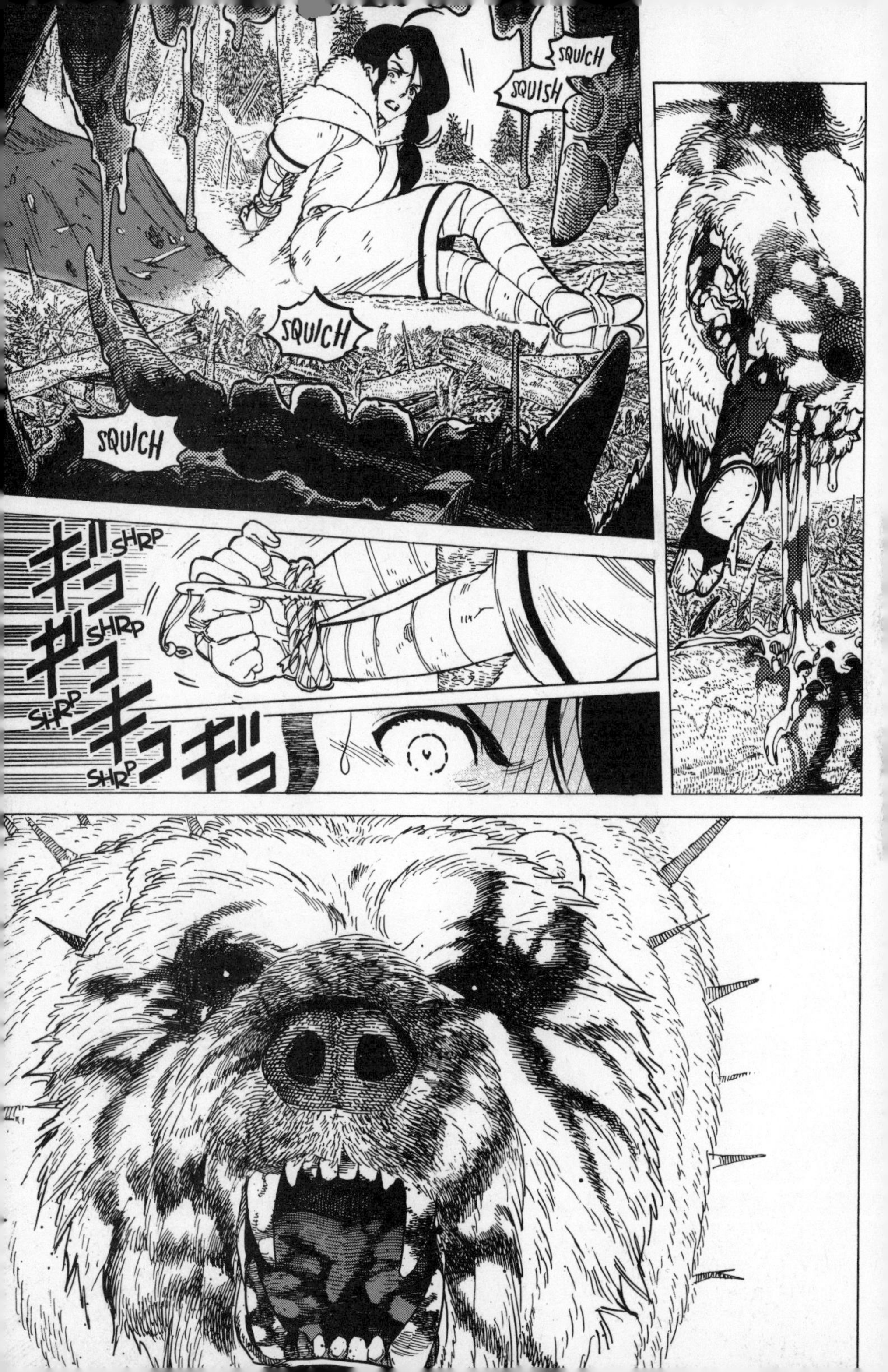
SQUICH
SQUISH
SQUICH
SQUICH
SHRP
SHRP
SHRP
SHRP

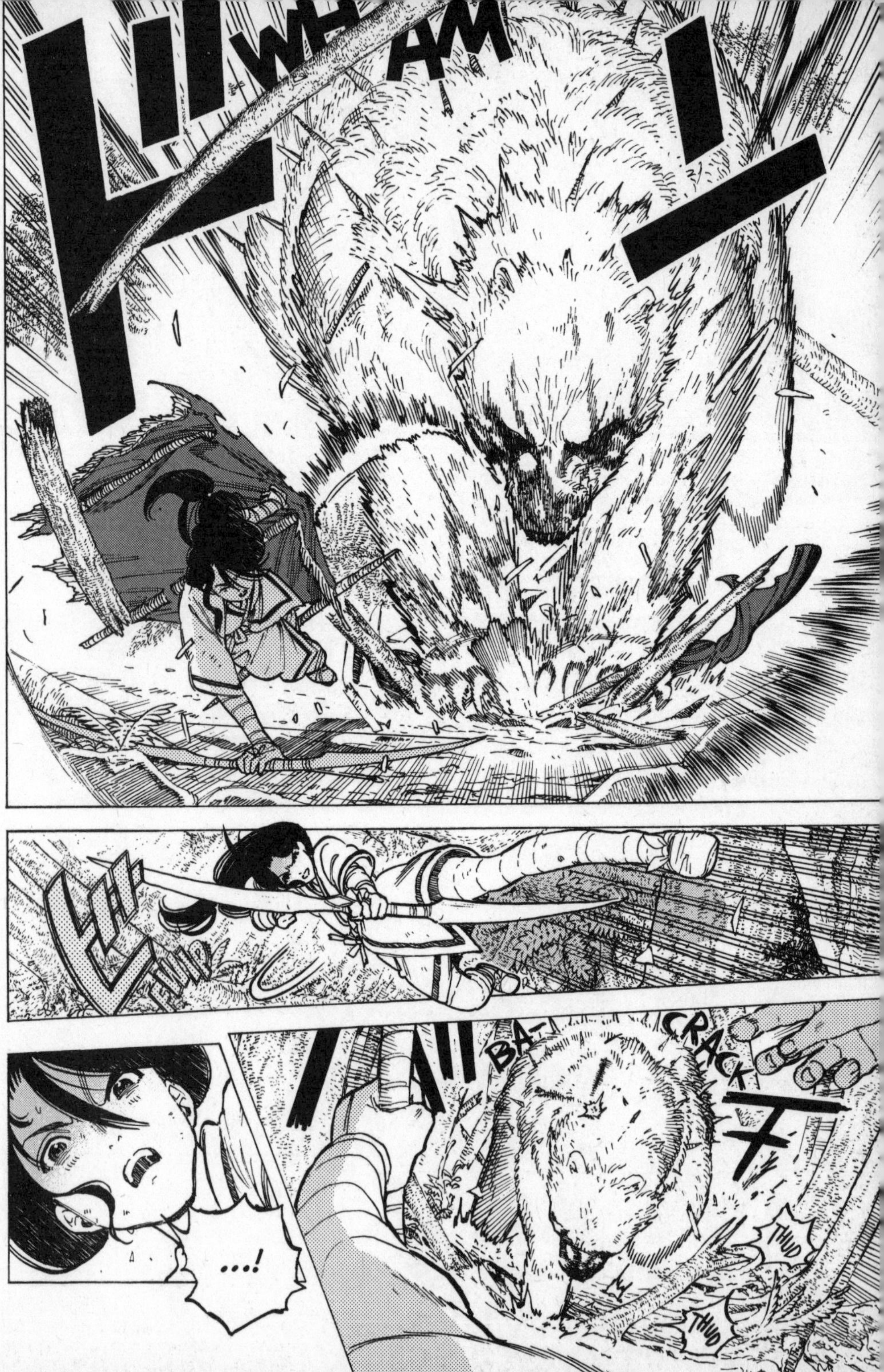
WHAM
WHIP
BA-CRACK
THUD
THUD
...!

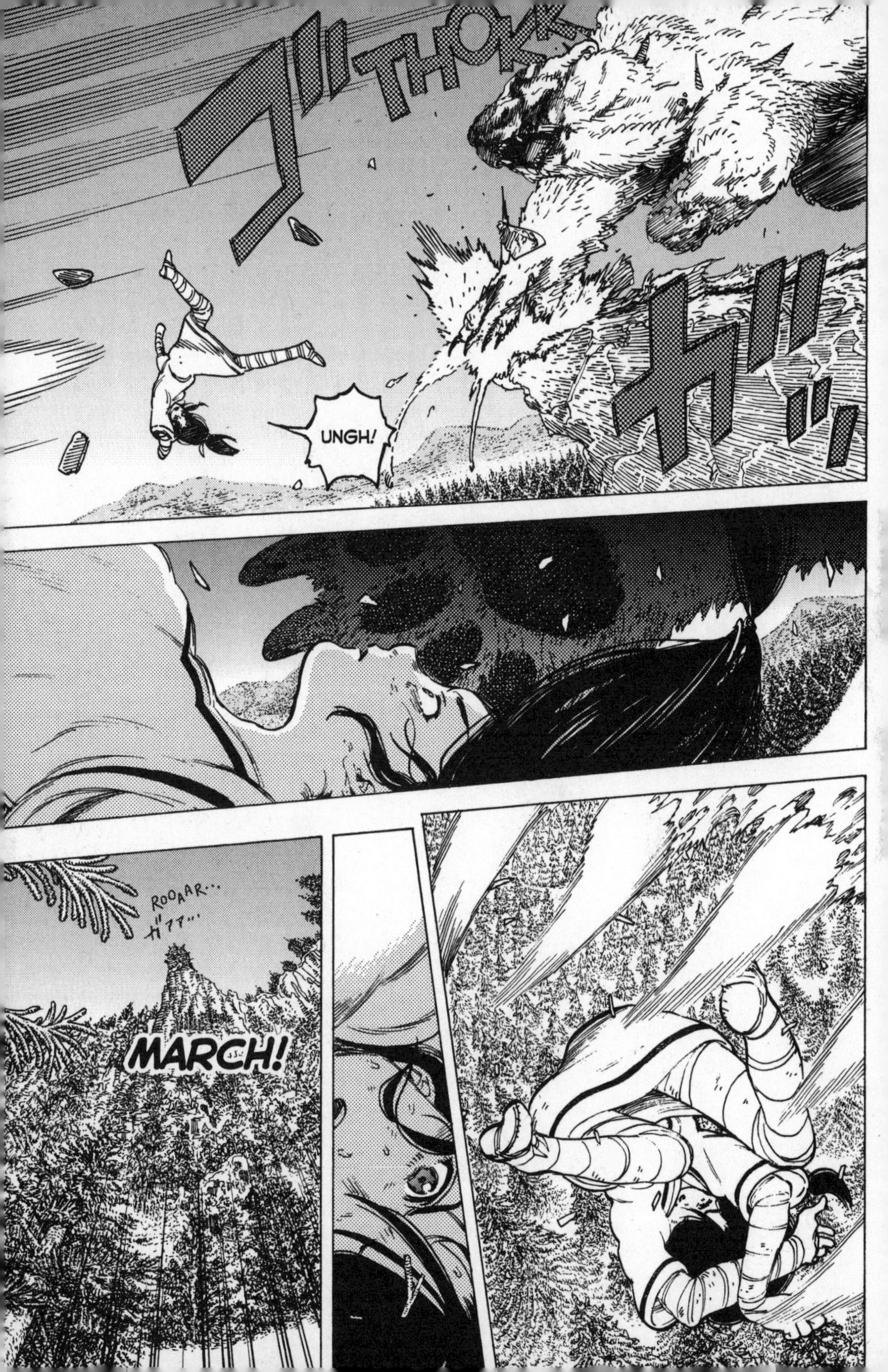
THOK
UNGH!
ROOAAR...
MARCH!

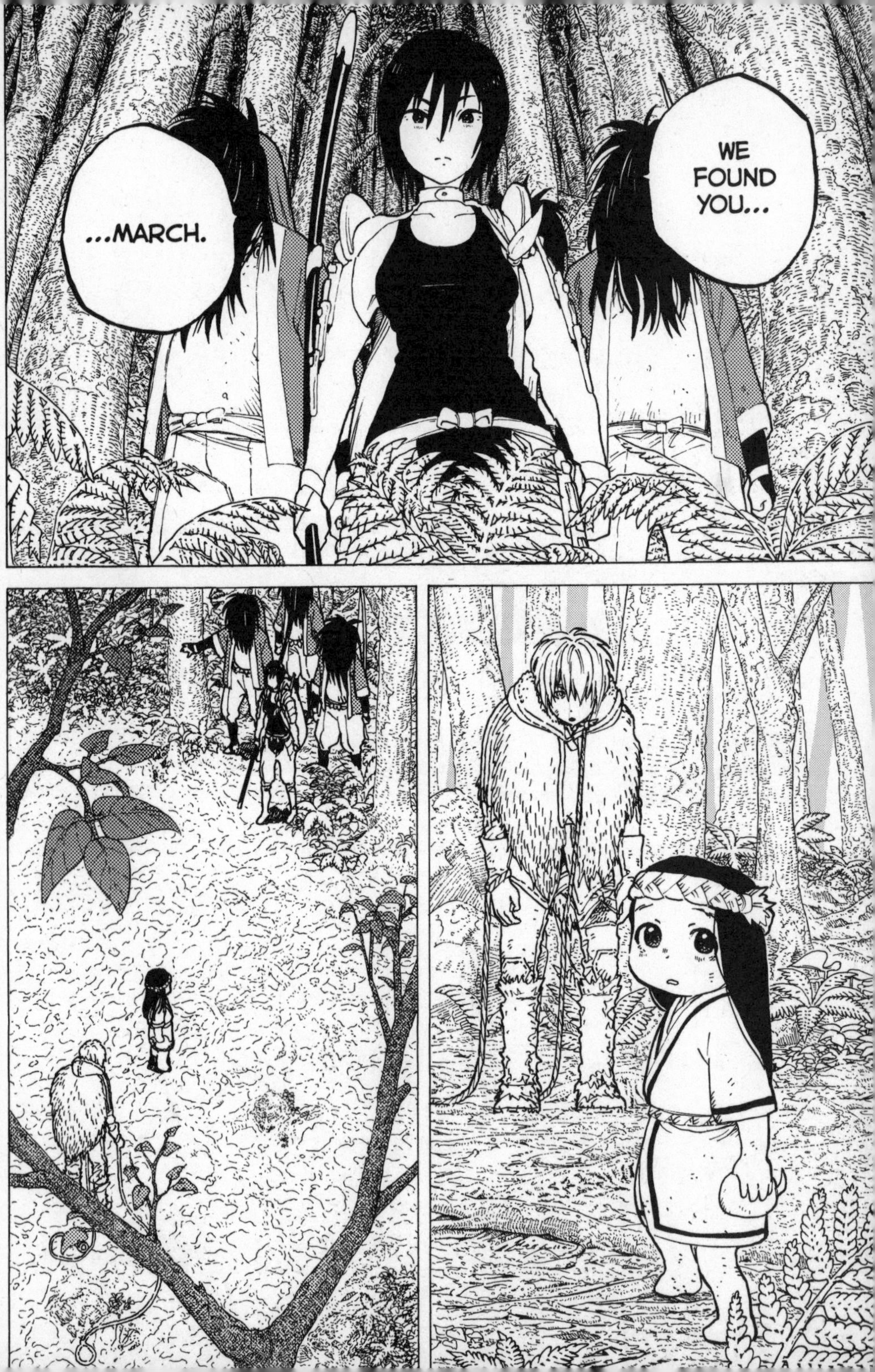
WE FOUND YOU...
...MARCH.

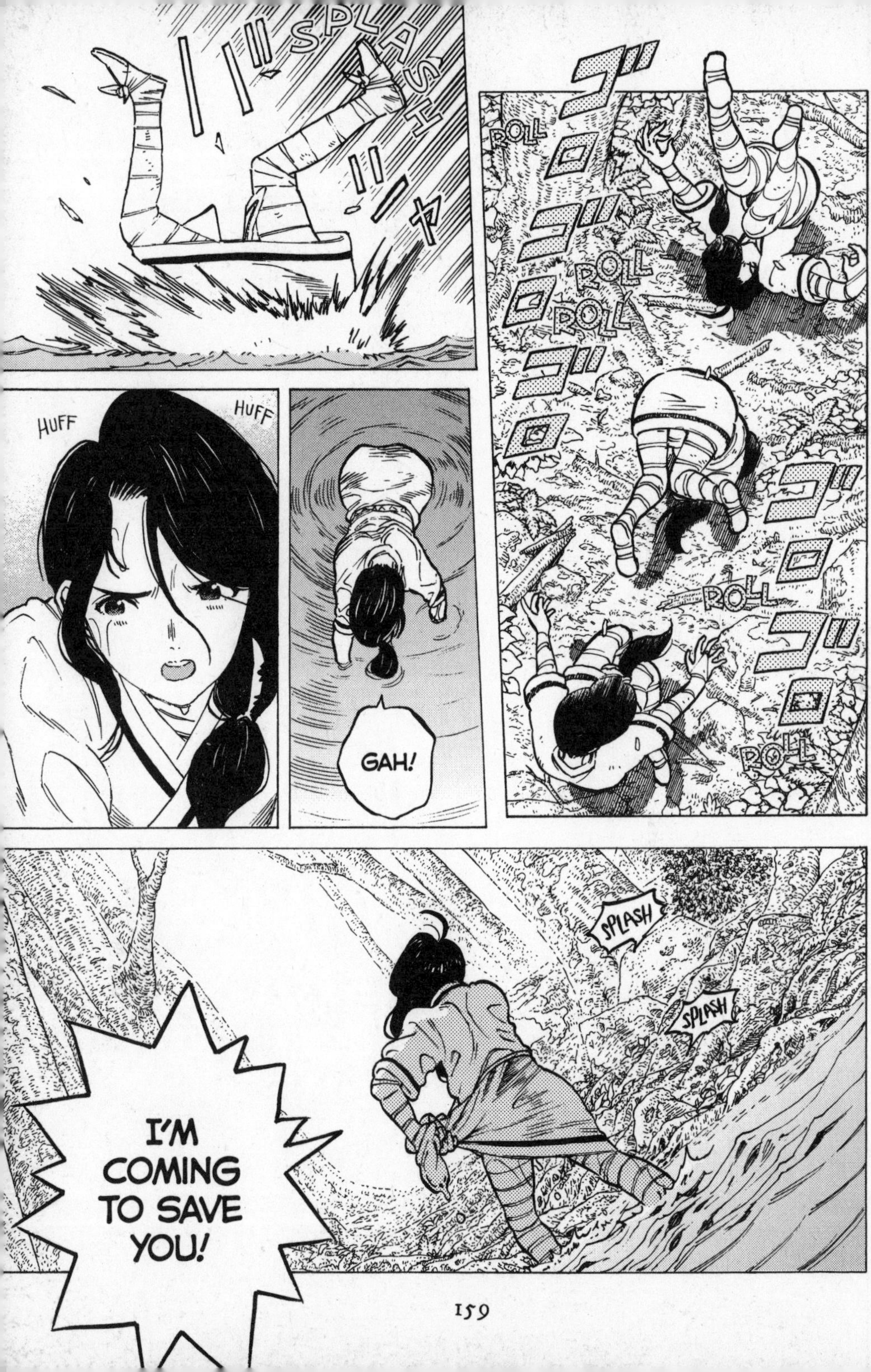
ゴロ
ROLL
ゴロ
ROLL
ROLL
ゴロ
ゴロ
ROLL
ゴロ
ROLL
SPLASH
GAH!
HUFF
HUFF
SPLASH
SPLASH
I'M COMING TO SAVE YOU!

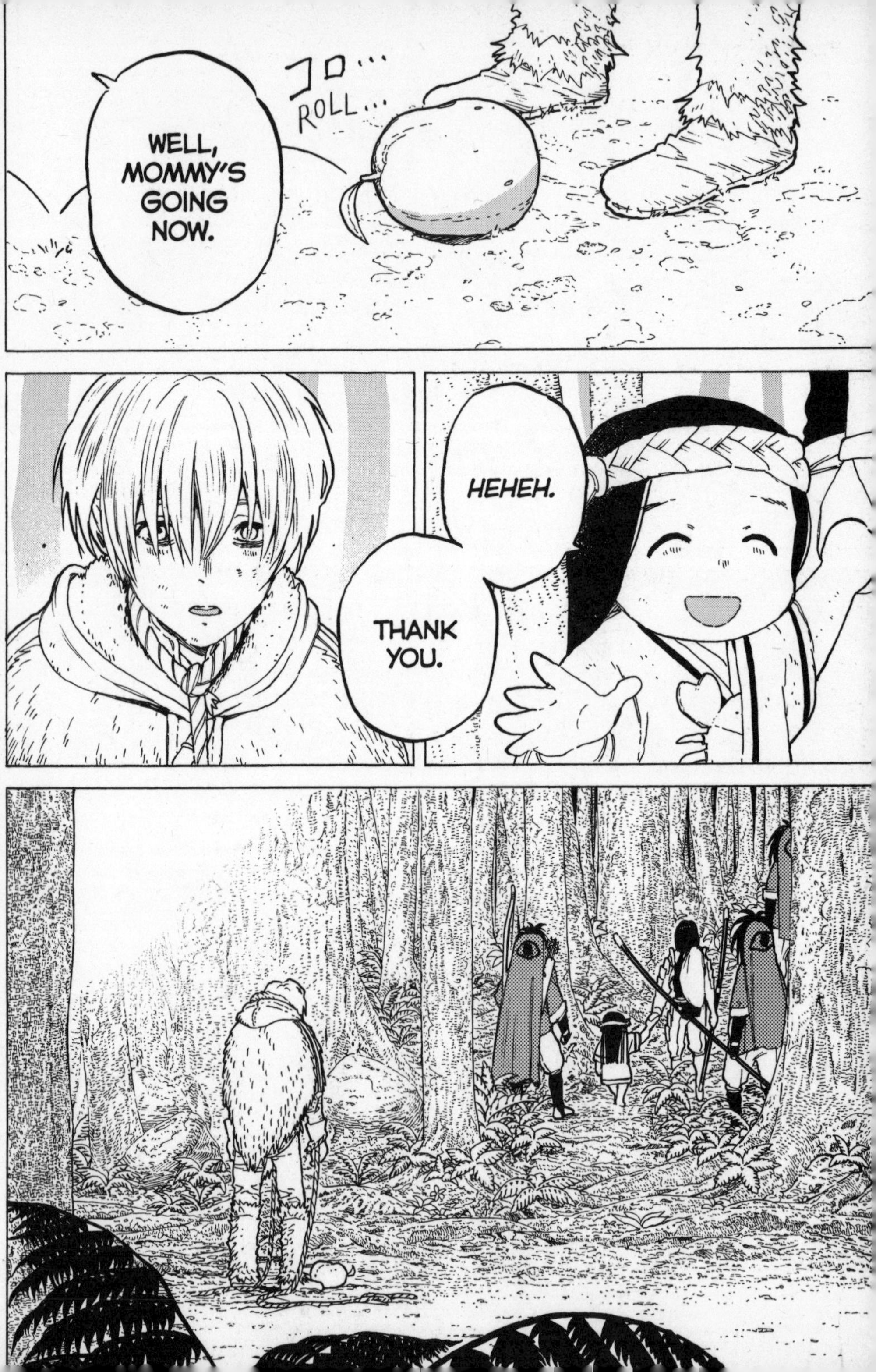
コロ… ROLL…
WELL, MOMMY'S GOING NOW.
HEHEH.
THANK YOU.

#4 A Minor Evolution

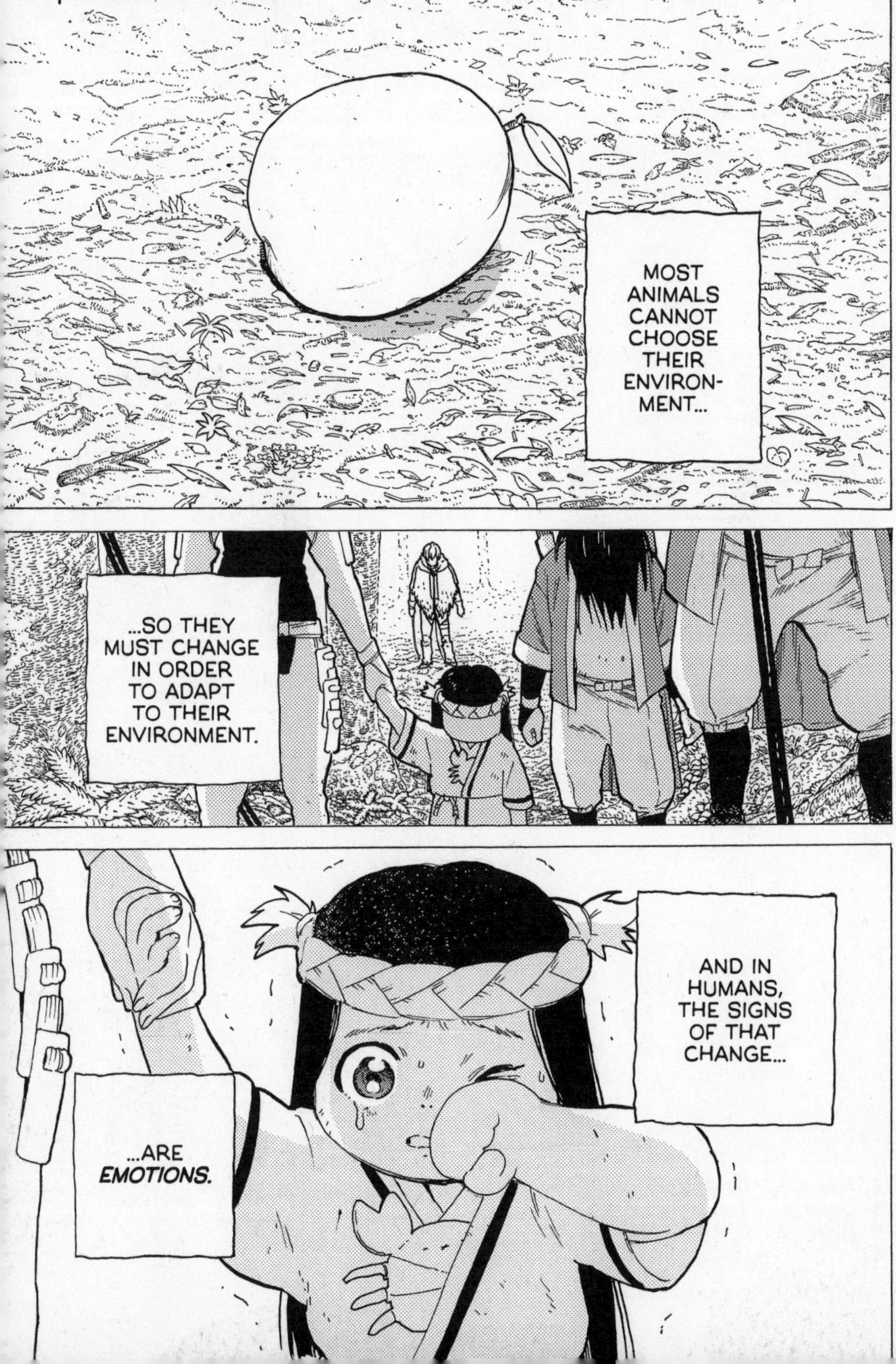
MOST ANIMALS CANNOT CHOOSE THEIR ENVIRONMENT...
...SO THEY MUST CHANGE IN ORDER TO ADAPT TO THEIR ENVIRONMENT.
AND IN HUMANS, THE SIGNS OF THAT CHANGE...
...ARE *EMOTIONS.*

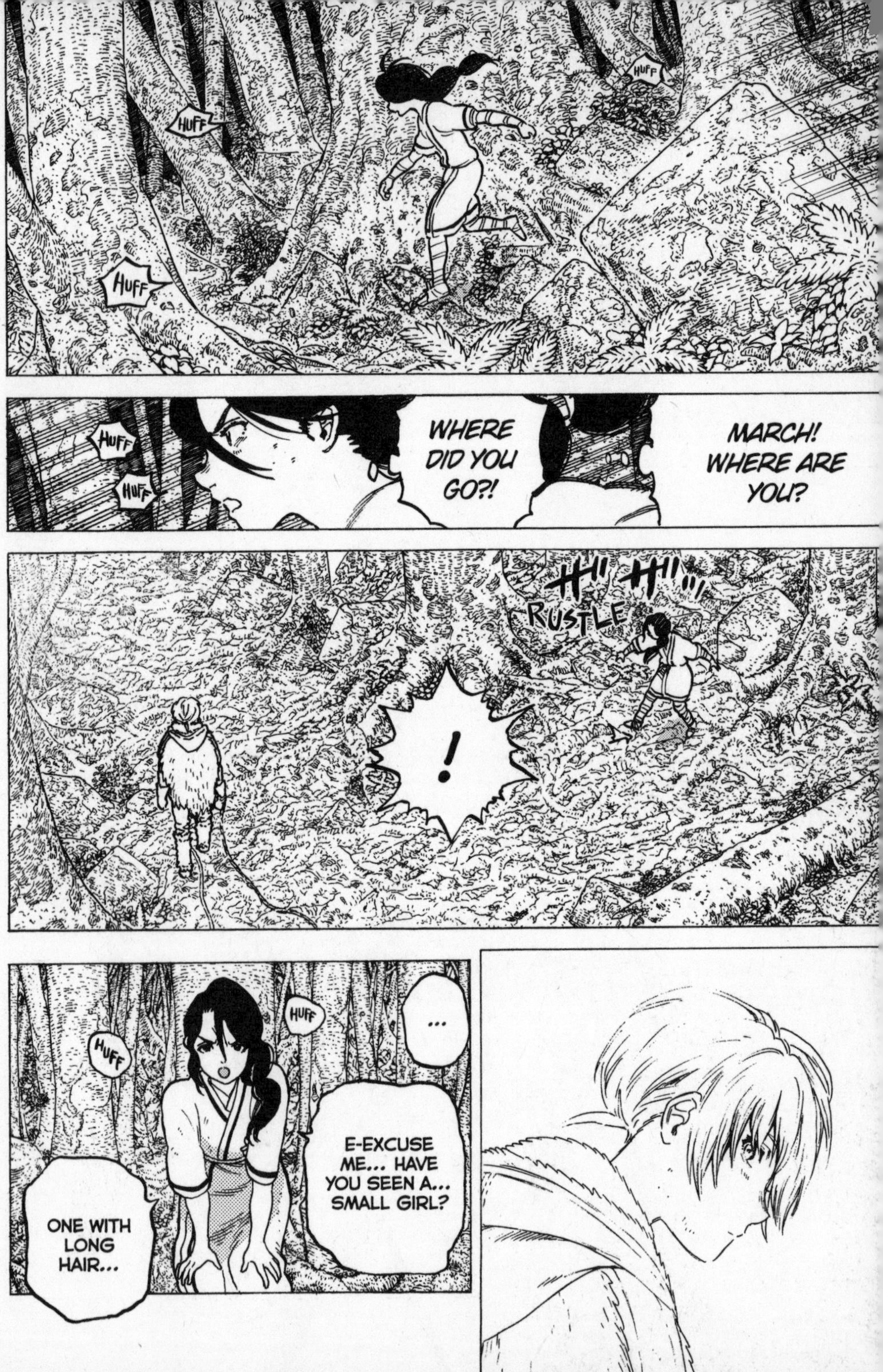

HUFF
HUFF
HUFF
MARCH! WHERE ARE YOU?
WHERE DID YOU GO?!
HUFF
HUFF
RUSTLE
!
...
HUFF
HUFF
E-EXCUSE ME... HAVE YOU SEEN A... SMALL GIRL?
ONE WITH LONG HAIR...

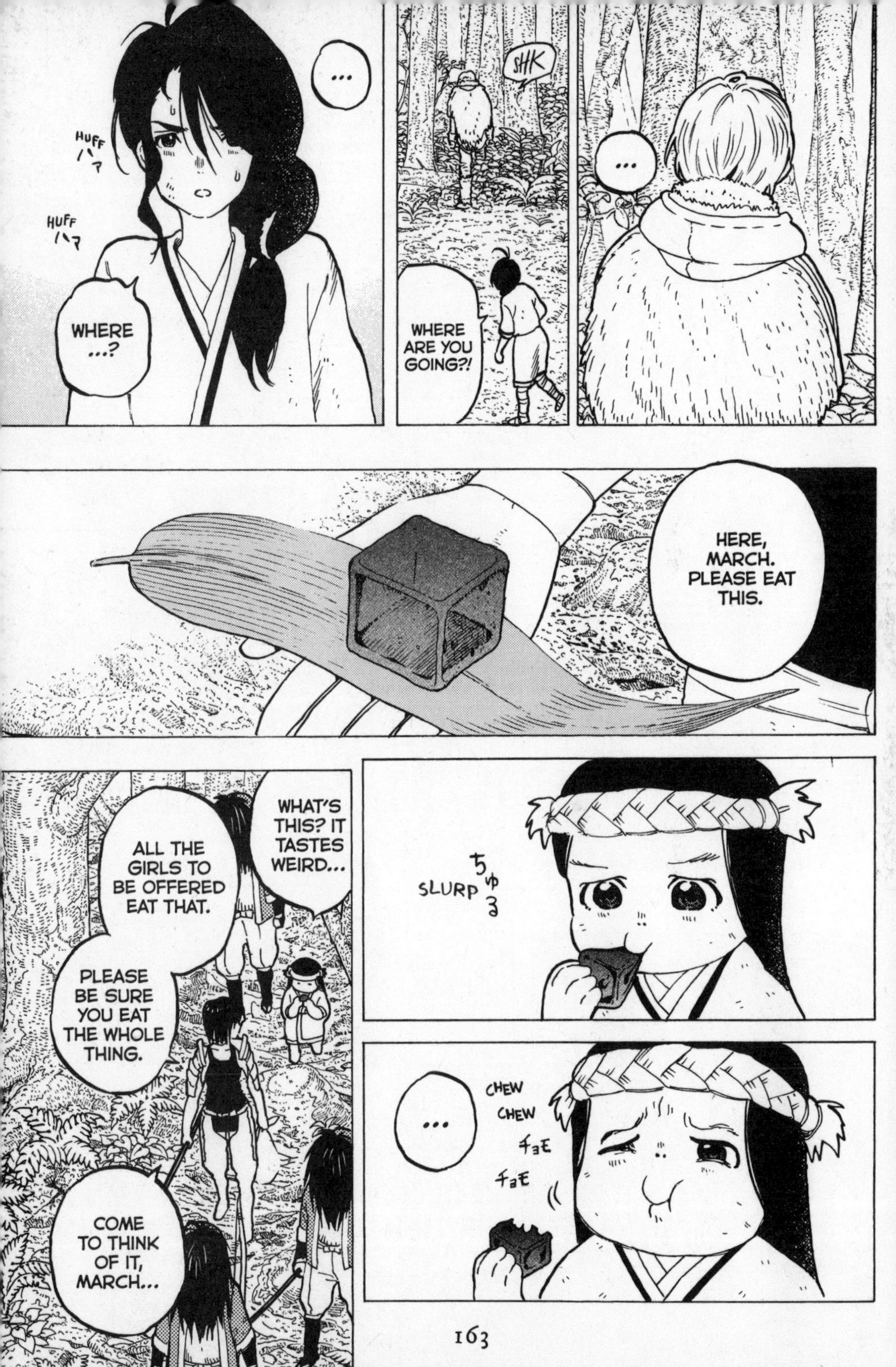

...
SHK
WHERE ARE YOU GOING?!
...
HUFF ハァ
HUFF ハァ
WHERE ...?
HERE, MARCH. PLEASE EAT THIS.
SLURP ちゅる
...
CHEW CHEW
WHAT'S THIS? IT TASTES WEIRD...
ALL THE GIRLS TO BE OFFERED EAT THAT.
PLEASE BE SURE YOU EAT THE WHOLE THING.
COME TO THINK OF IT, MARCH...

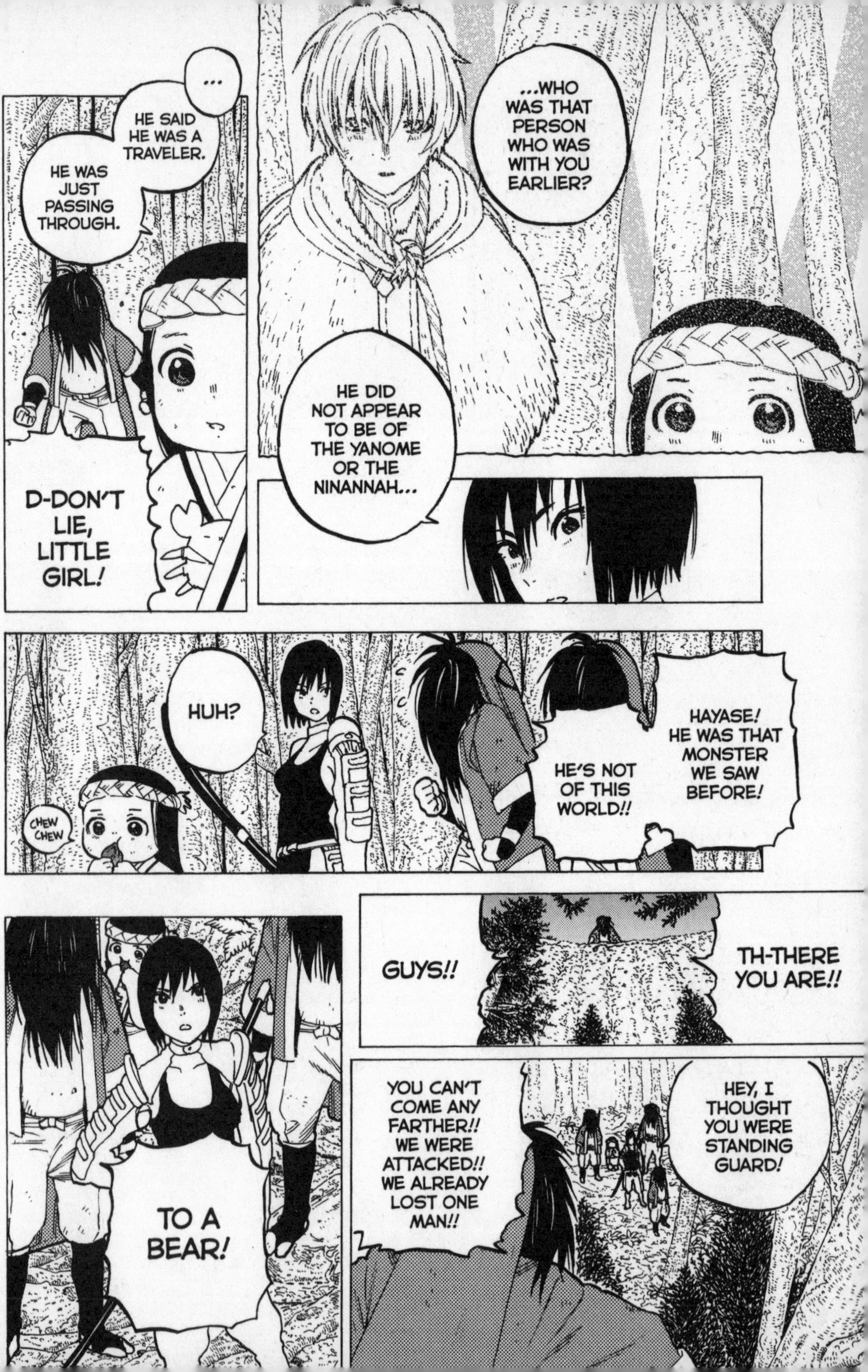
...WHO WAS THAT PERSON WHO WAS WITH YOU EARLIER?
HE DID NOT APPEAR TO BE OF THE YANOME OR THE NINANNAH...
...
HE SAID HE WAS A TRAVELER.
HE WAS JUST PASSING THROUGH.
D-DON'T LIE, LITTLE GIRL!
HAYASE! HE WAS THAT MONSTER WE SAW BEFORE!
HE'S NOT OF THIS WORLD!!
HUH?
CHEW CHEW
TH-THERE YOU ARE!!
GUYS!!
HEY, I THOUGHT YOU WERE STANDING GUARD!
YOU CAN'T COME ANY FARTHER!! WE WERE ATTACKED!! WE ALREADY LOST ONE MAN!!
TO A BEAR!

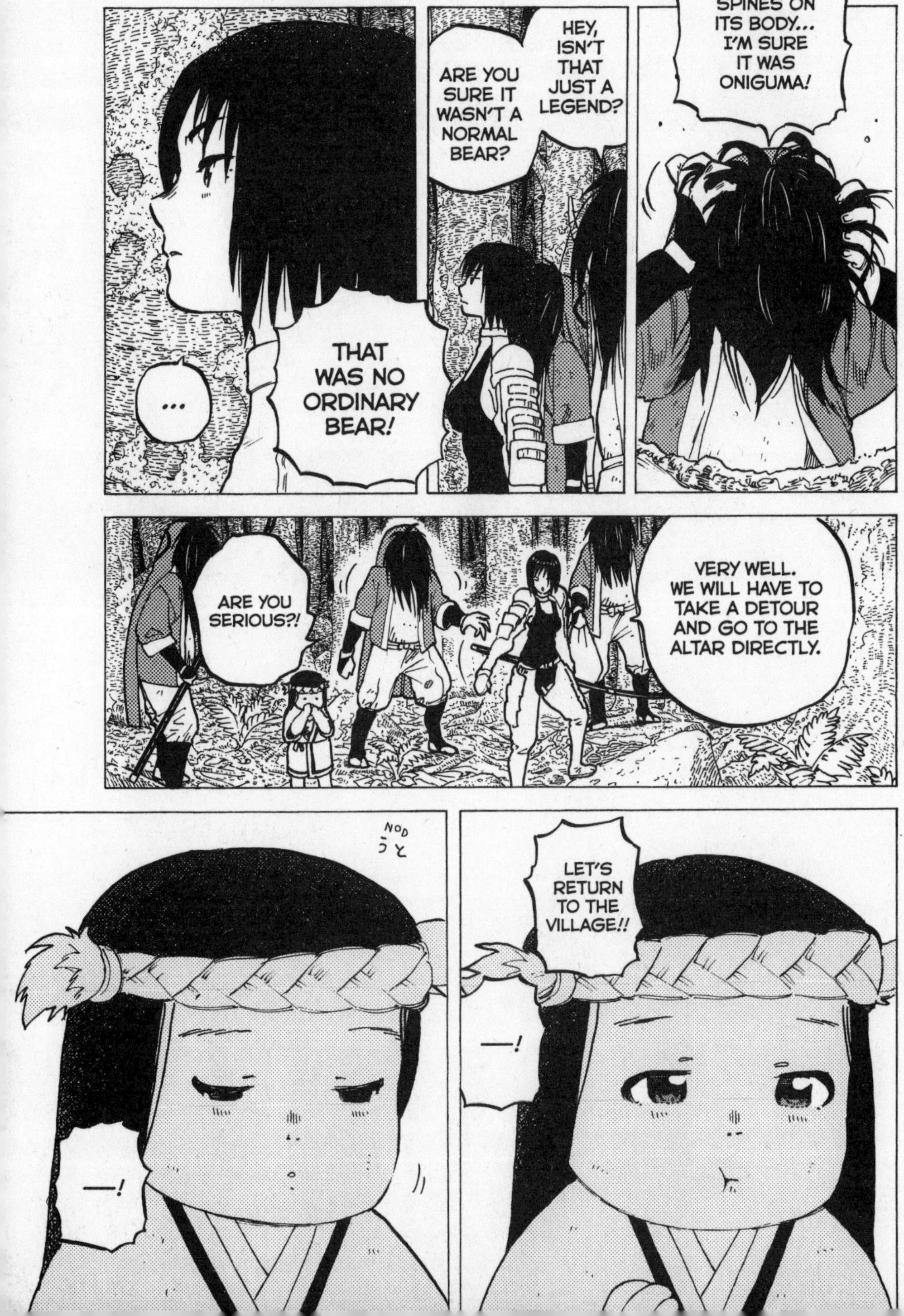
THOSE SPINES ON ITS BODY... I'M SURE IT WAS ONIGUMA!
HEY, ISN'T THAT JUST A LEGEND?
ARE YOU SURE IT WASN'T A NORMAL BEAR?
THAT WAS NO ORDINARY BEAR!
...
VERY WELL. WE WILL HAVE TO TAKE A DETOUR AND GO TO THE ALTAR DIRECTLY.
ARE YOU SERIOUS?!
LET'S RETURN TO THE VILLAGE!!
—!
NOD
うと
—!

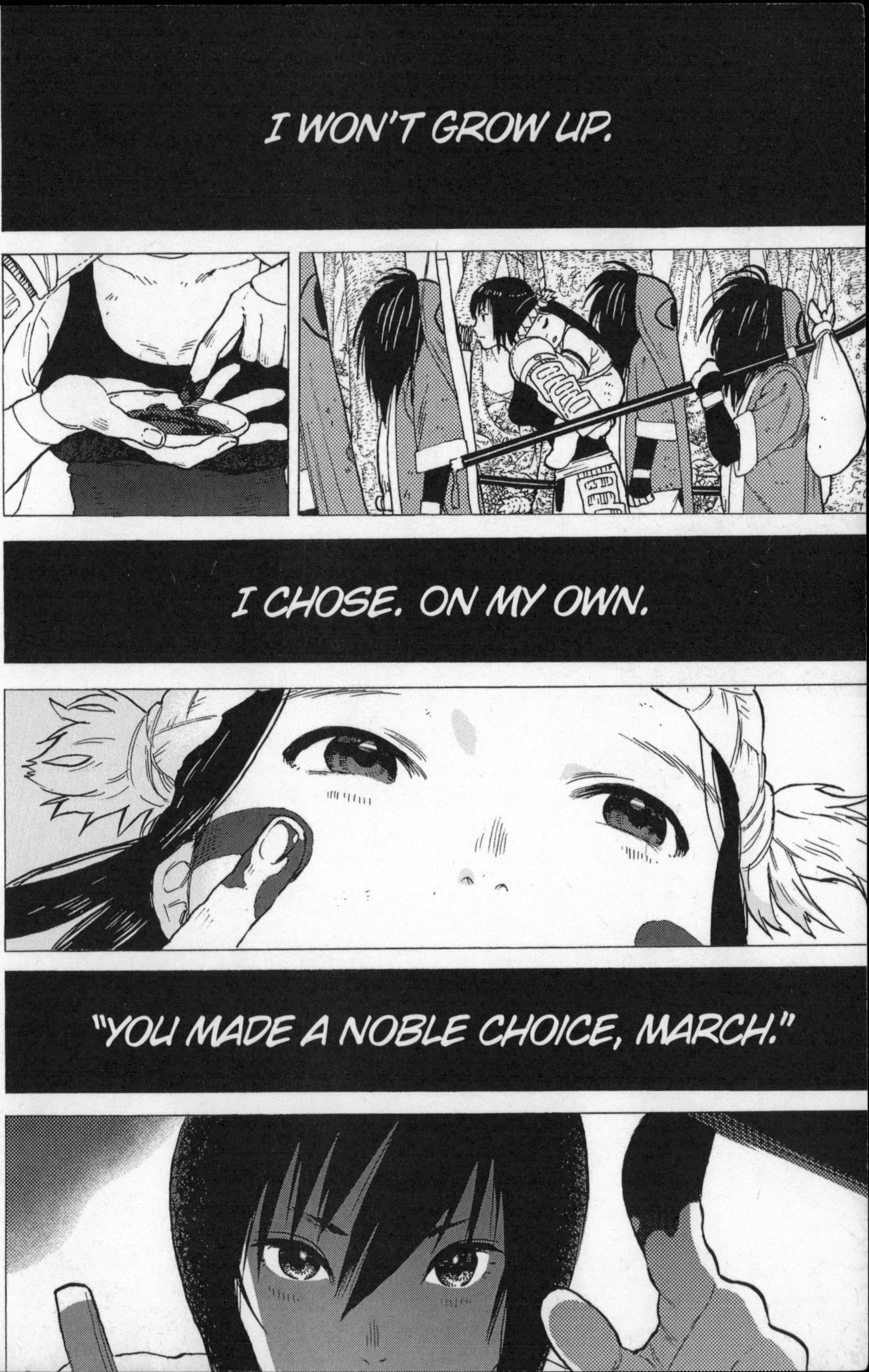
I WON'T GROW UP.
I CHOSE. ON MY OWN.
"YOU MADE A NOBLE CHOICE, MARCH."

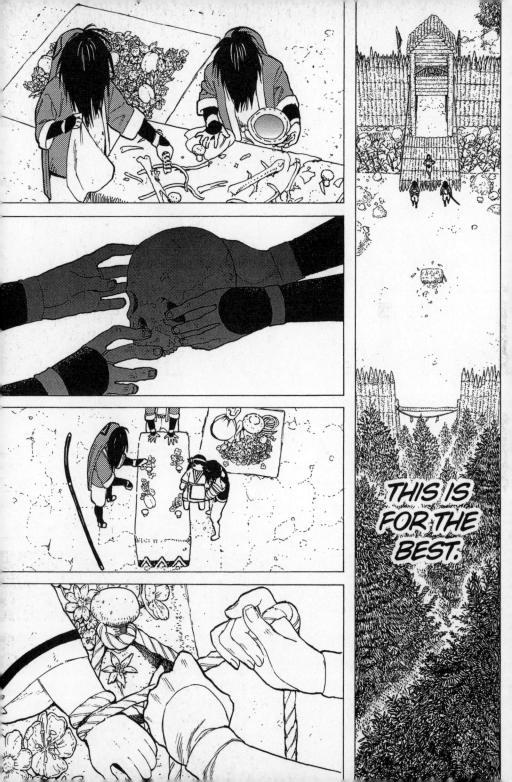

THIS IS FOR THE BEST.

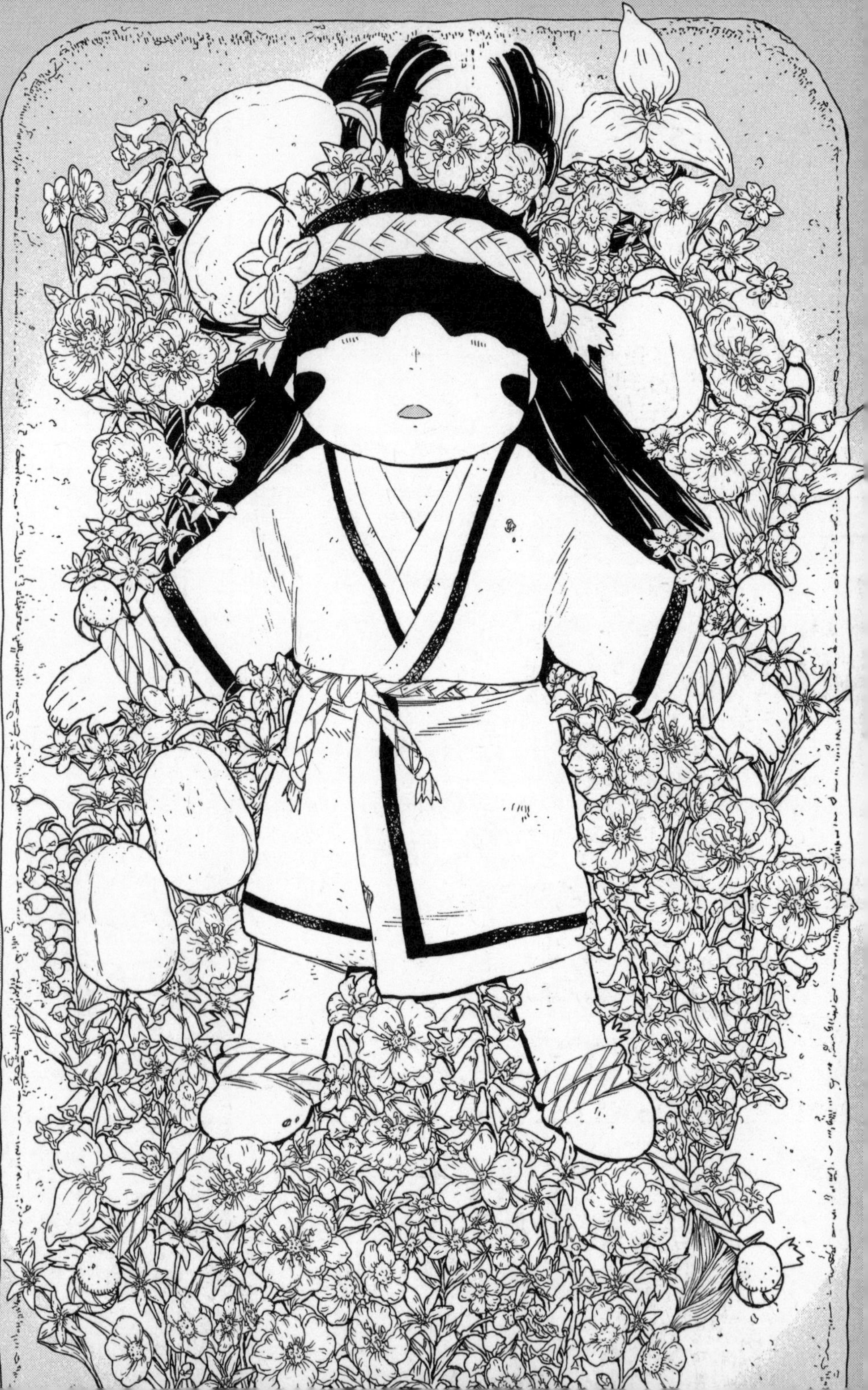

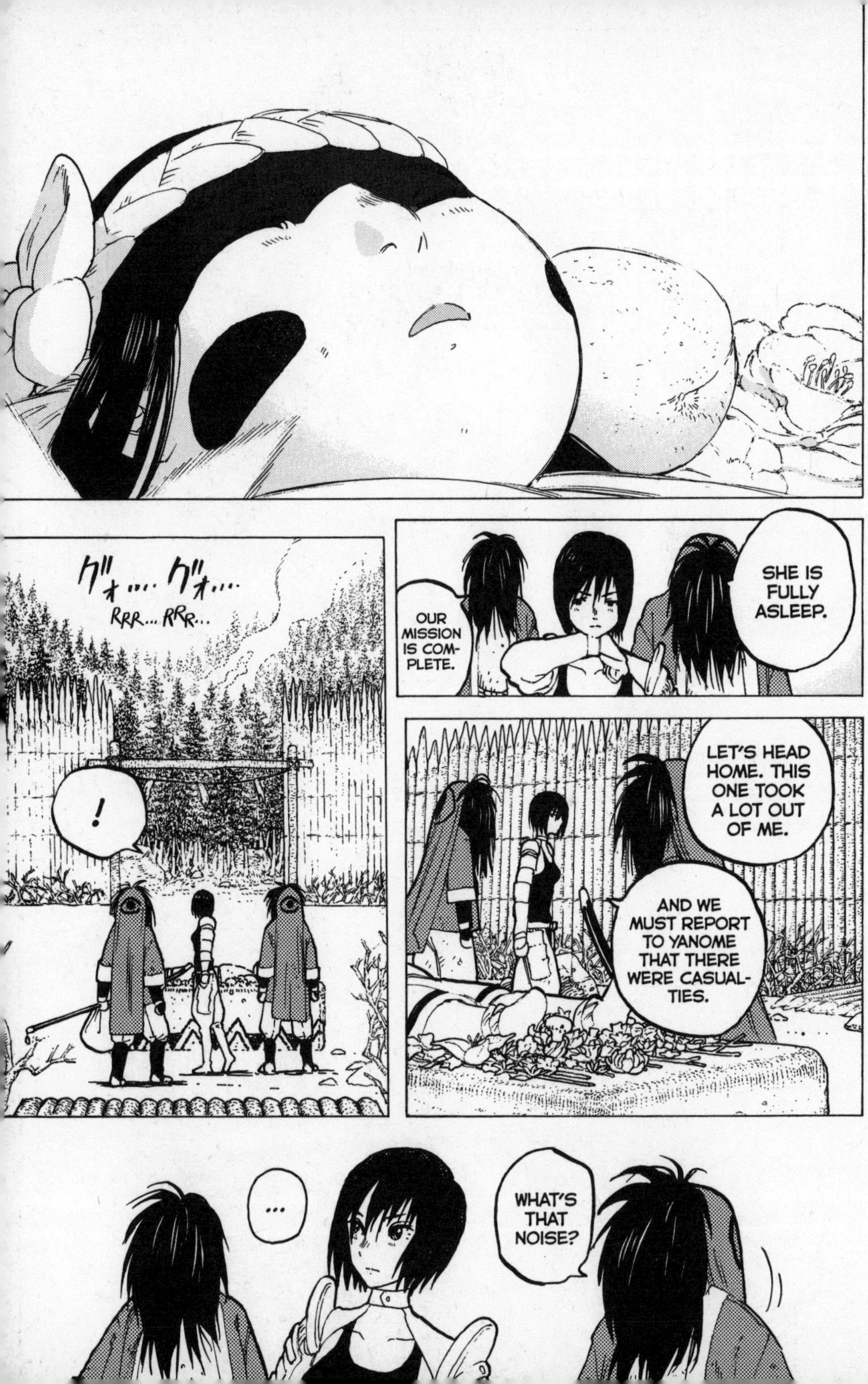
SHE IS FULLY ASLEEP.
OUR MISSION IS COMPLETE.
LET'S HEAD HOME. THIS ONE TOOK A LOT OUT OF ME.
AND WE MUST REPORT TO YANOME THAT THERE WERE CASUALTIES.
...
グォ… グォ…
RRR... RRR...
!
WHAT'S THAT NOISE?
...

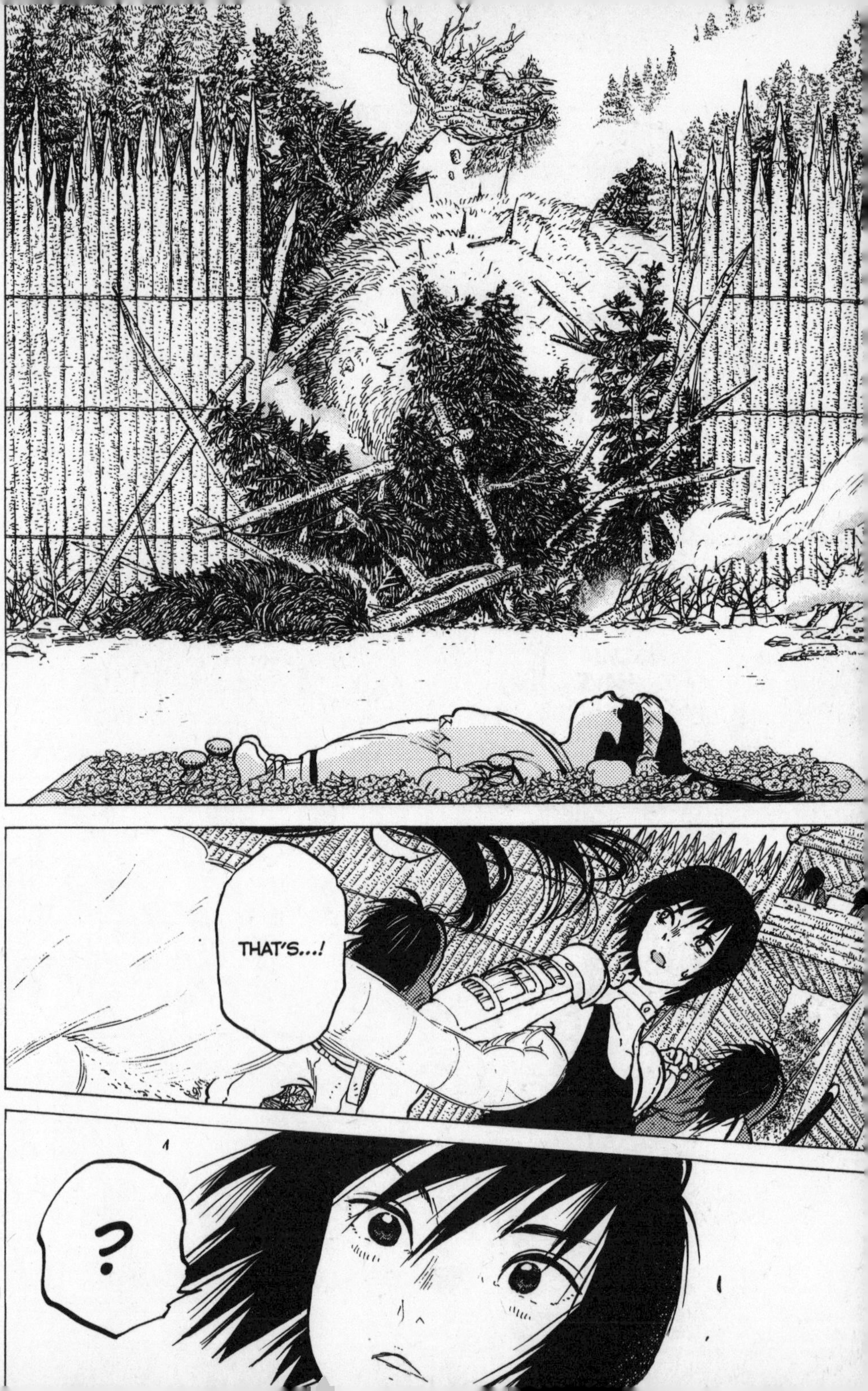
THAT'S...!
?

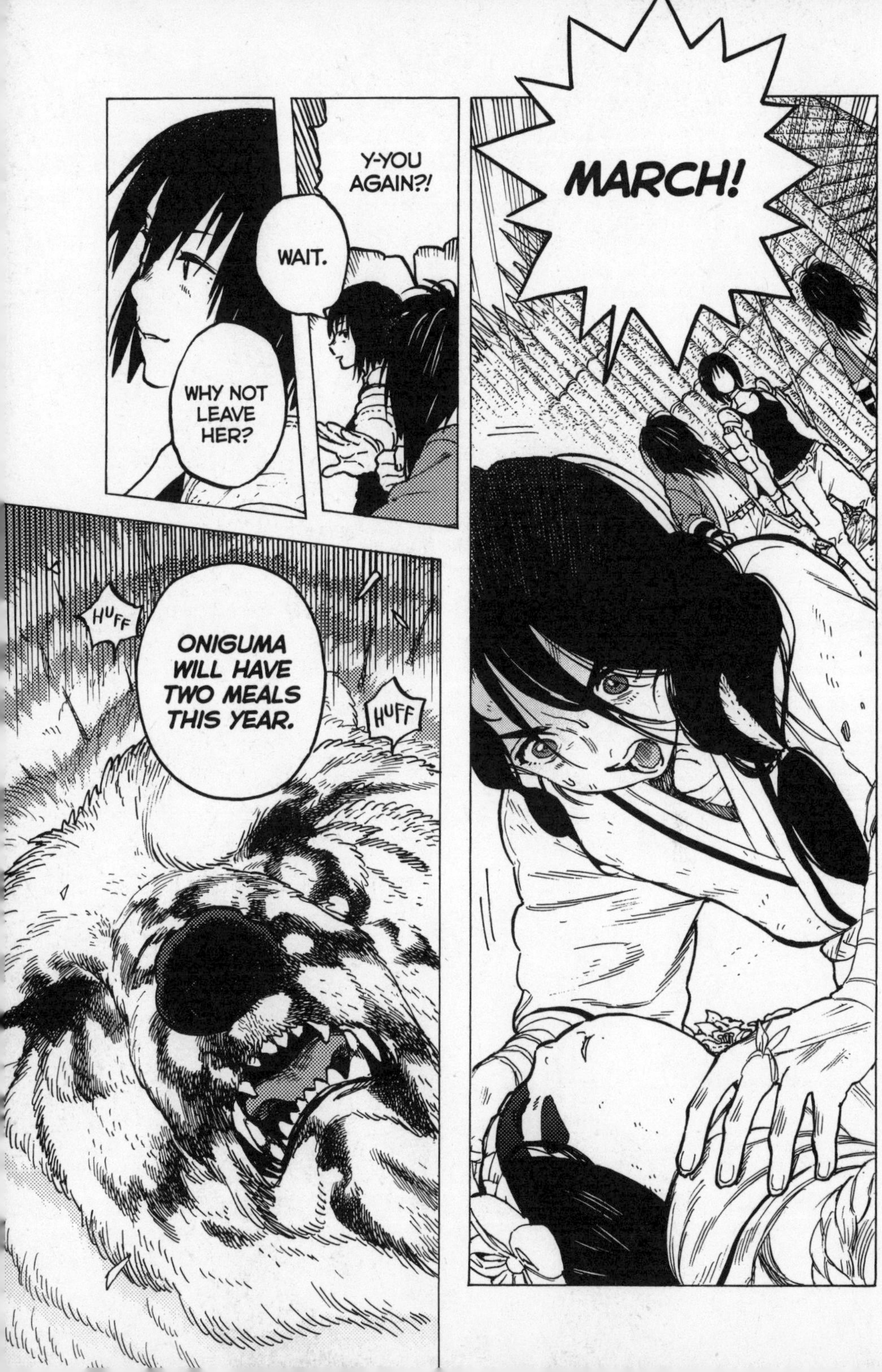
MARCH!
Y-YOU AGAIN?!
WAIT.
WHY NOT LEAVE HER?
ONIGUMA WILL HAVE TWO MEALS THIS YEAR.
HUFF
HUFF

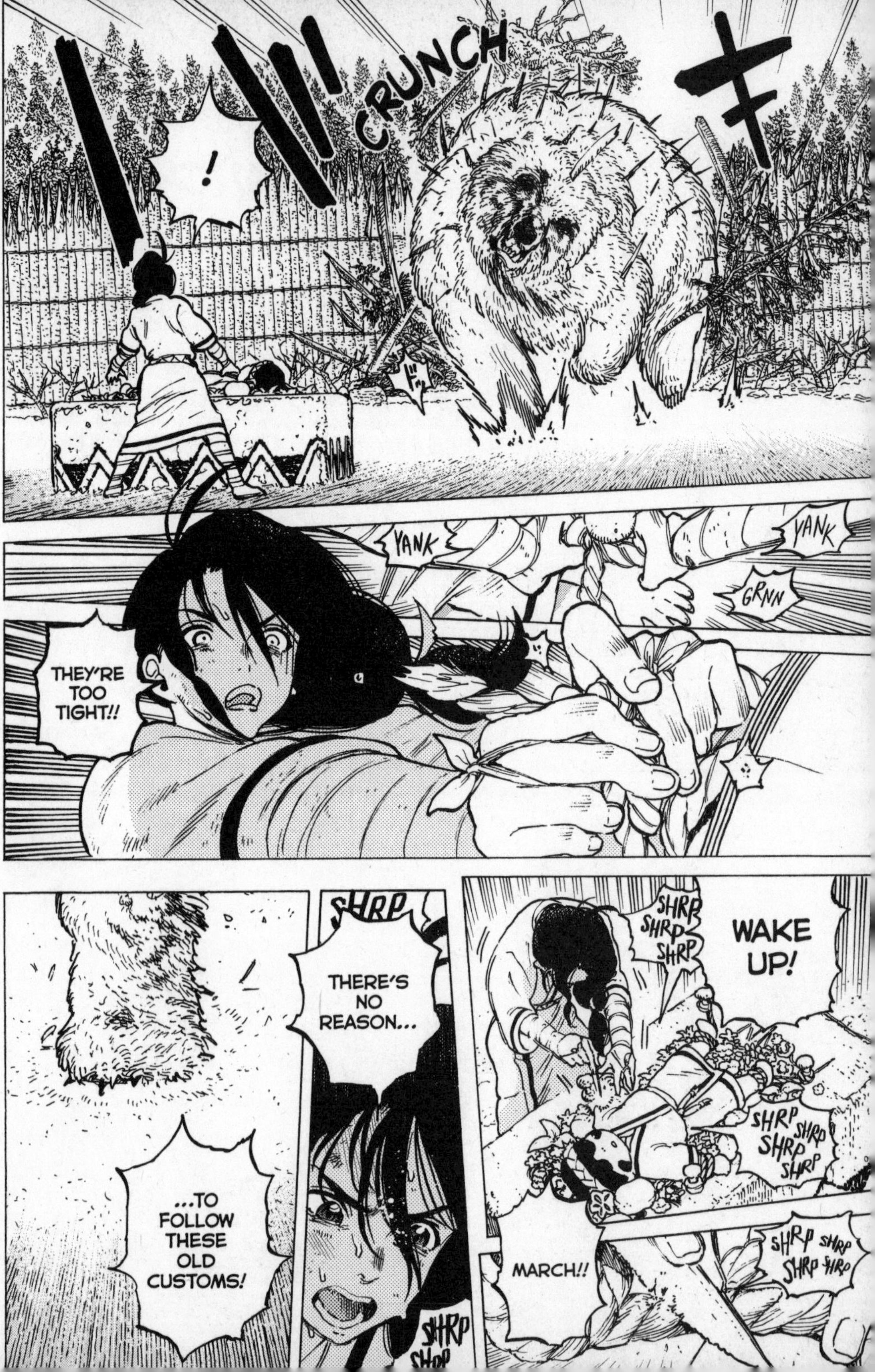
CRUNCH
!
YANK
GRNN
YANK
THEY'RE TOO TIGHT!!
WAKE UP!
SHRP SHRP SHRP
SHRP SHRP SHRP SHRP
MARCH!!
SHRP SHRP SHRP SHRP
SHRP
THERE'S NO REASON...
...TO FOLLOW THESE OLD CUSTOMS!
SHRP

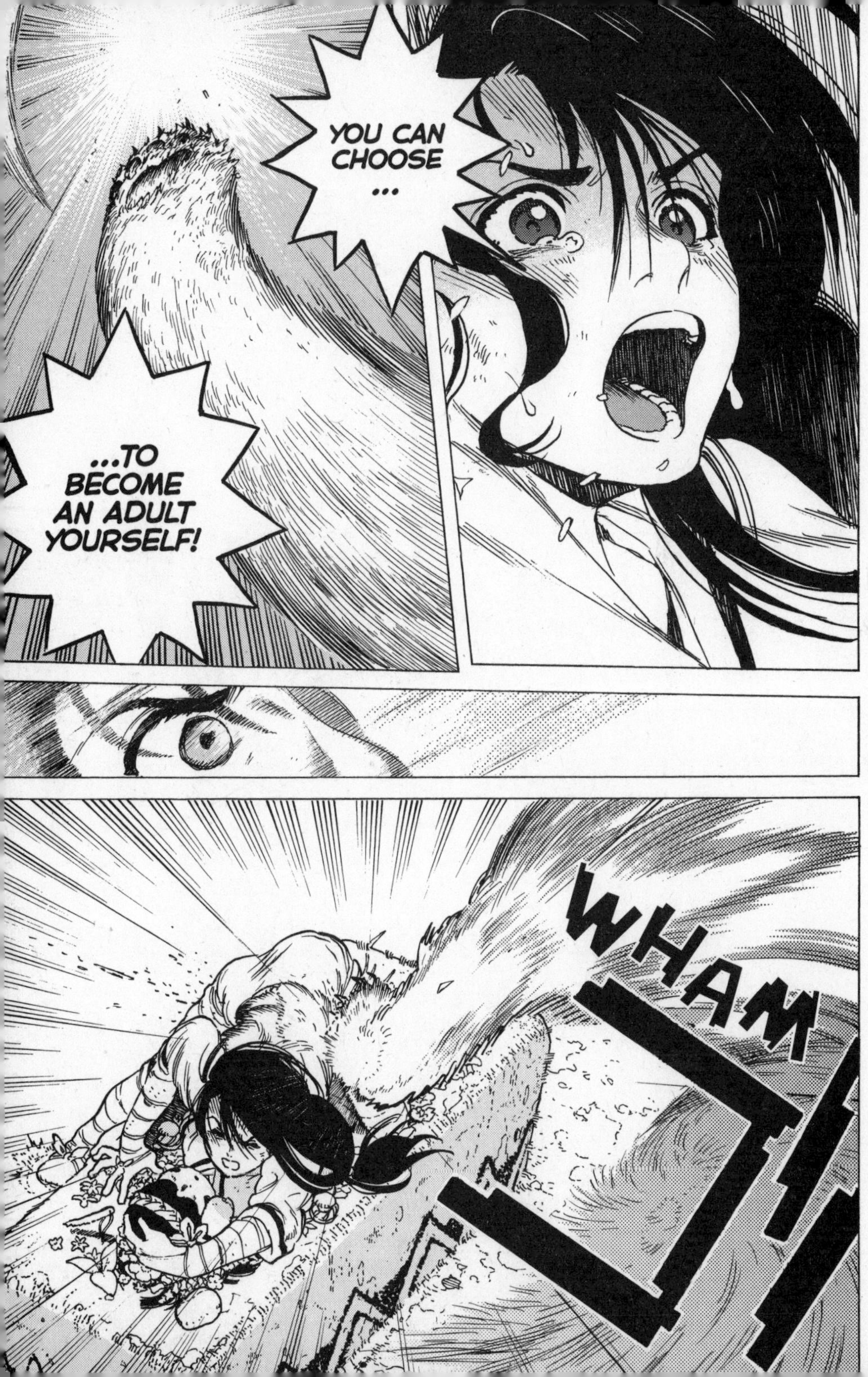
YOU CAN CHOOSE ...
...TO BECOME AN ADULT YOURSELF!
WHAM

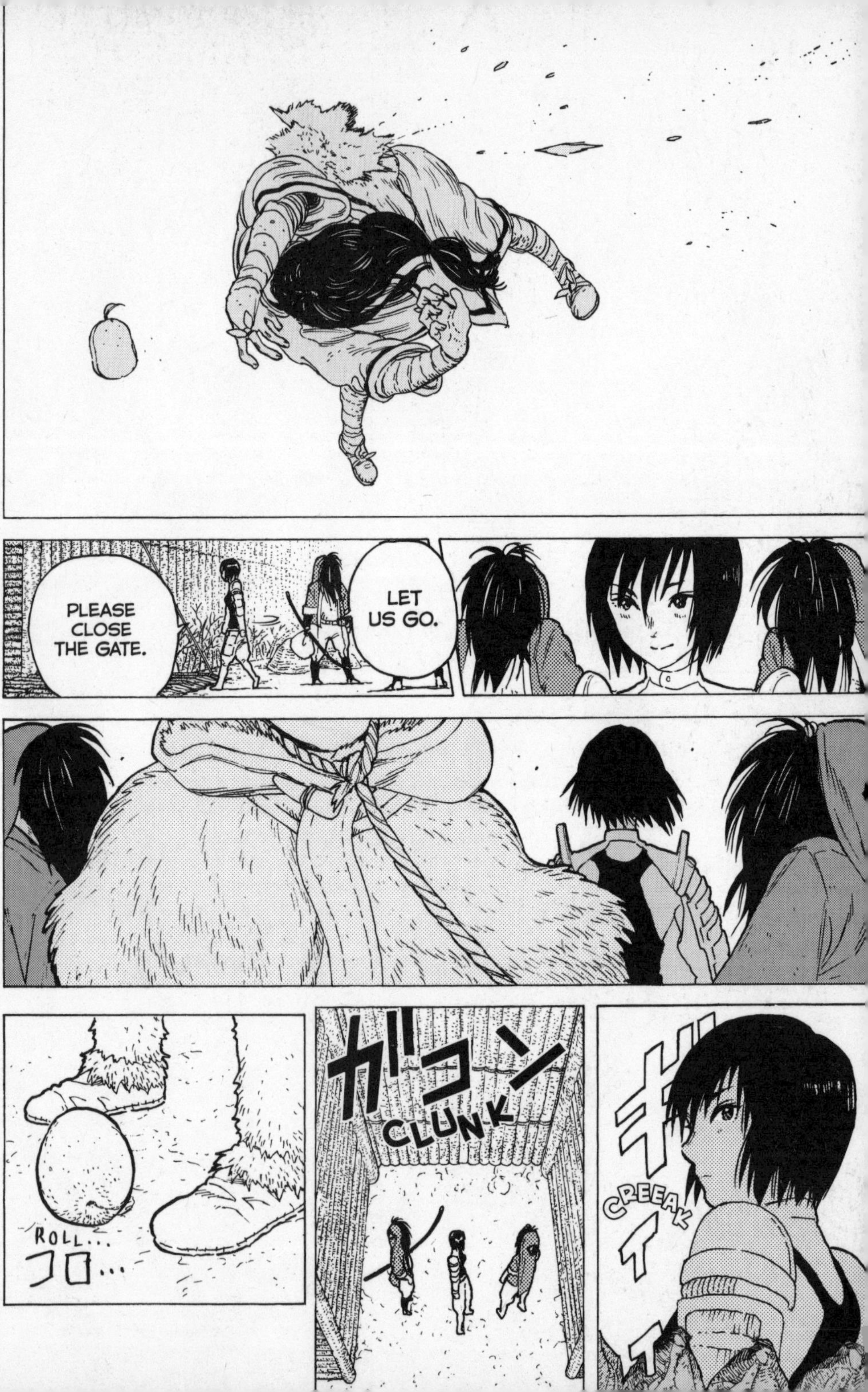
LET US GO.
PLEASE CLOSE THE GATE.
ギィ
CREEAK
ガコン
CLUNK
ROLL...
コロ...

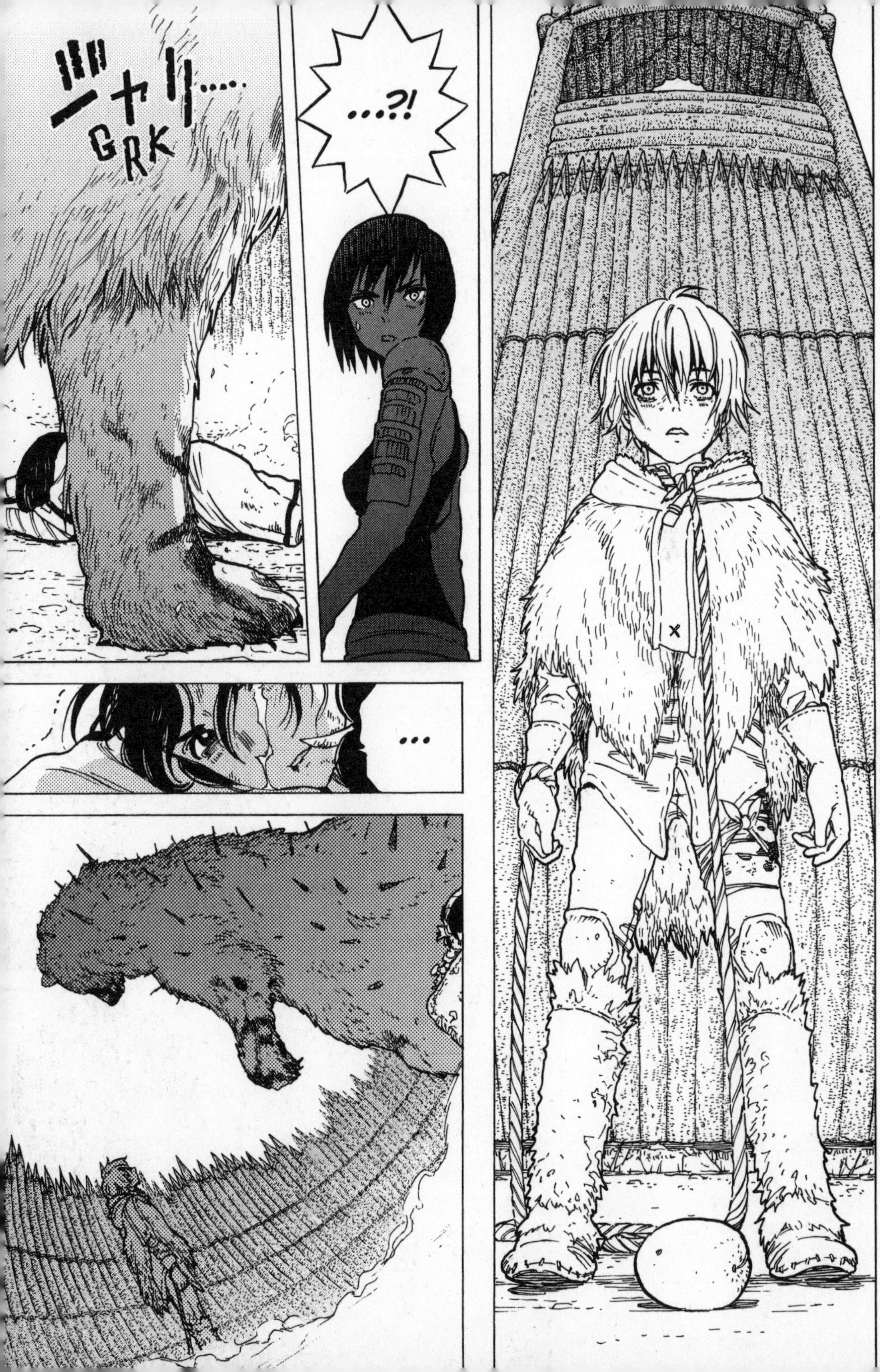
...?!
GRK
...

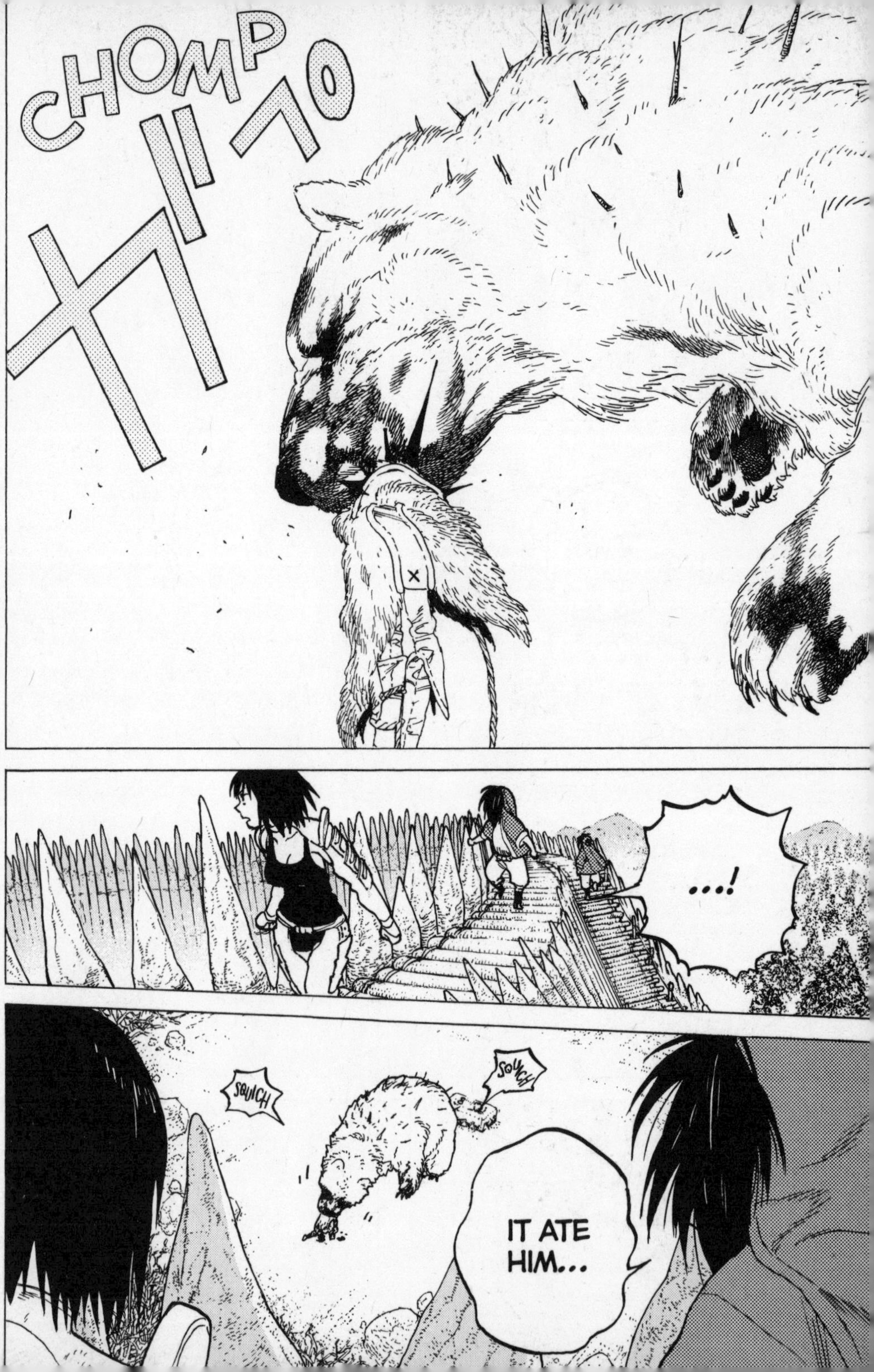
CHOMP
...!
SQUICH
SQUICH
IT ATE HIM...

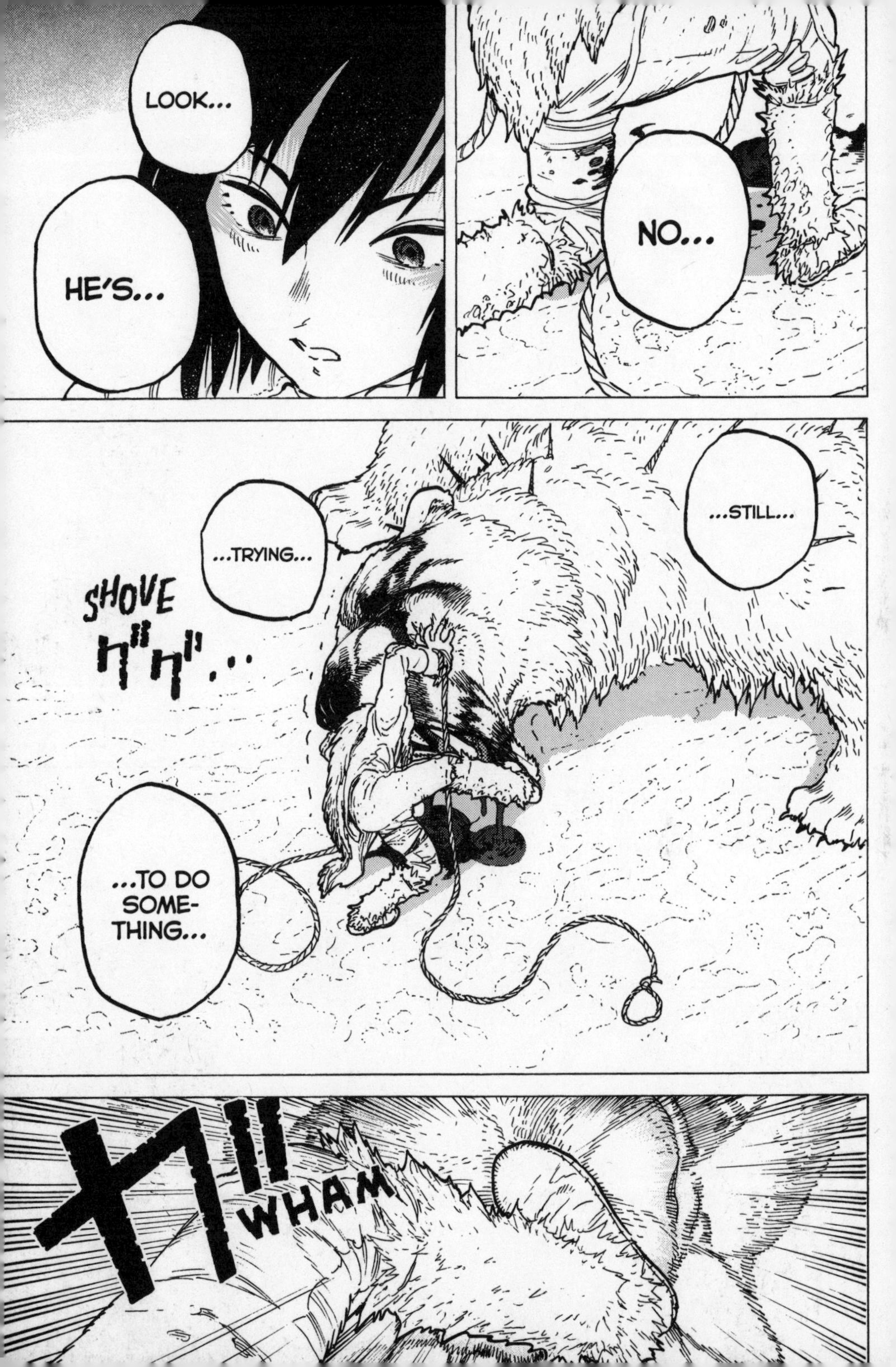
NO...
LOOK...
HE'S...
...STILL...
...TRYING...
SHOVE
...TO DO SOMETHING...
WHAM

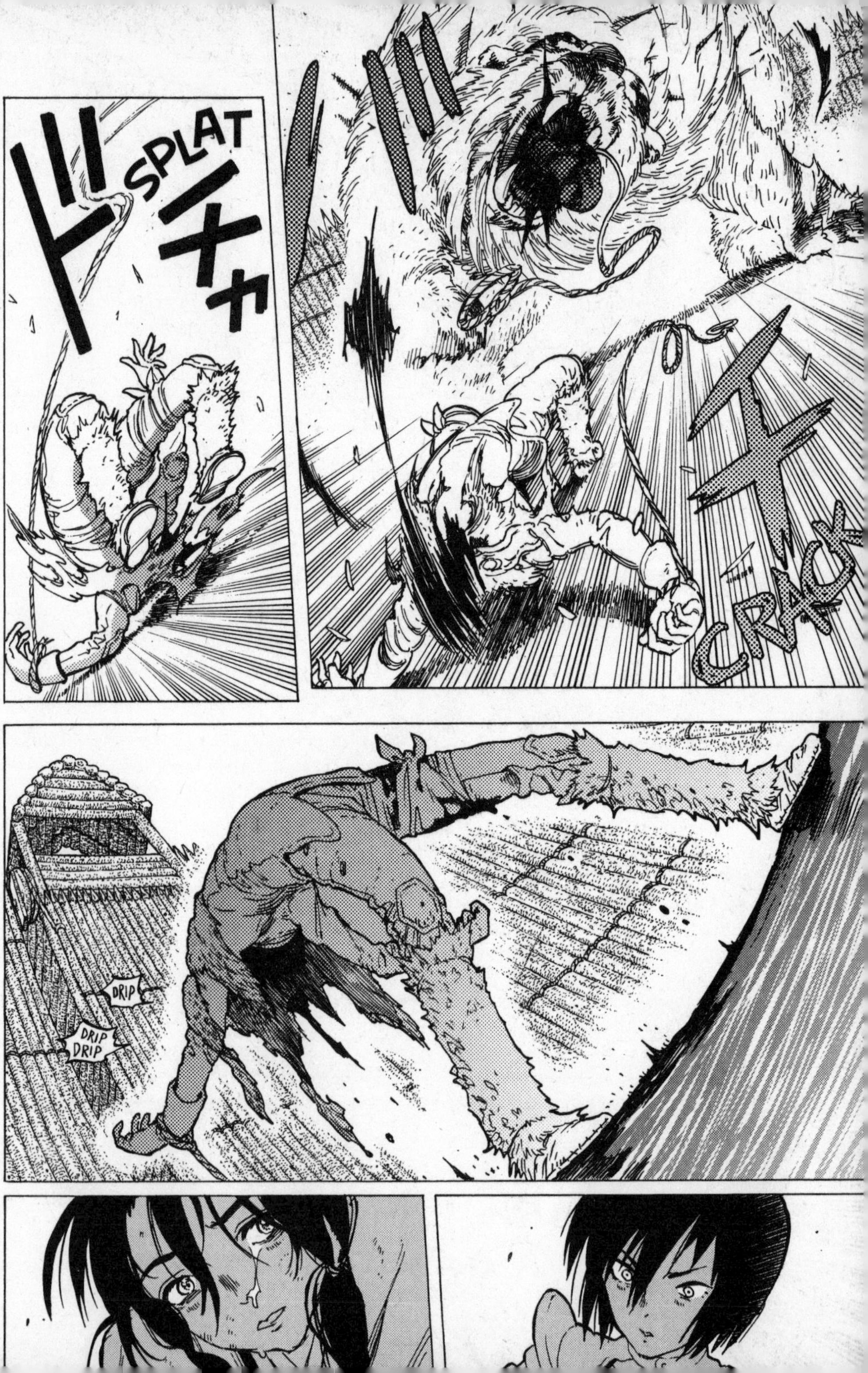
CRACK
SPLAT
DRIP
DRIP DRIP

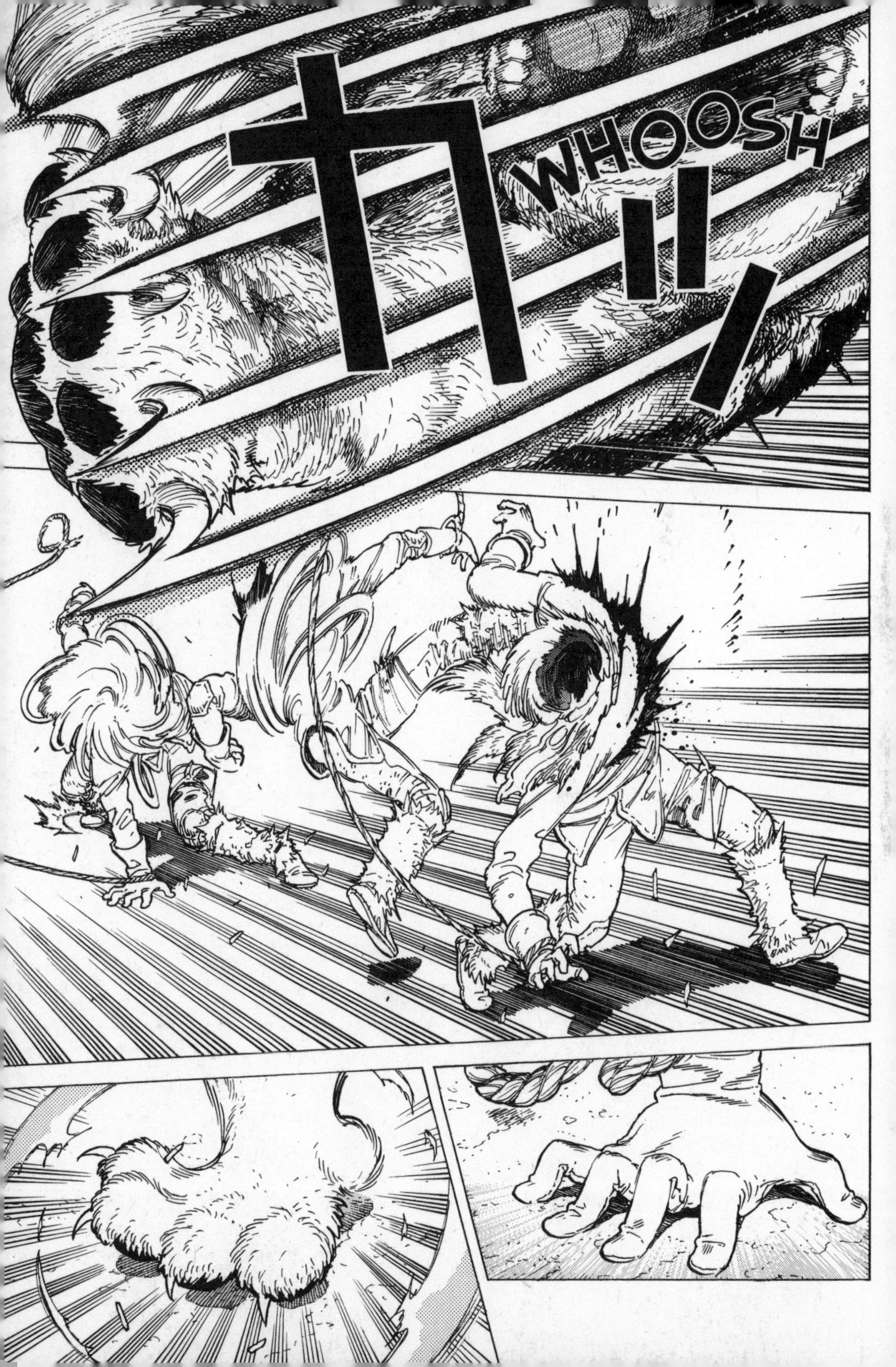
WHOOSH

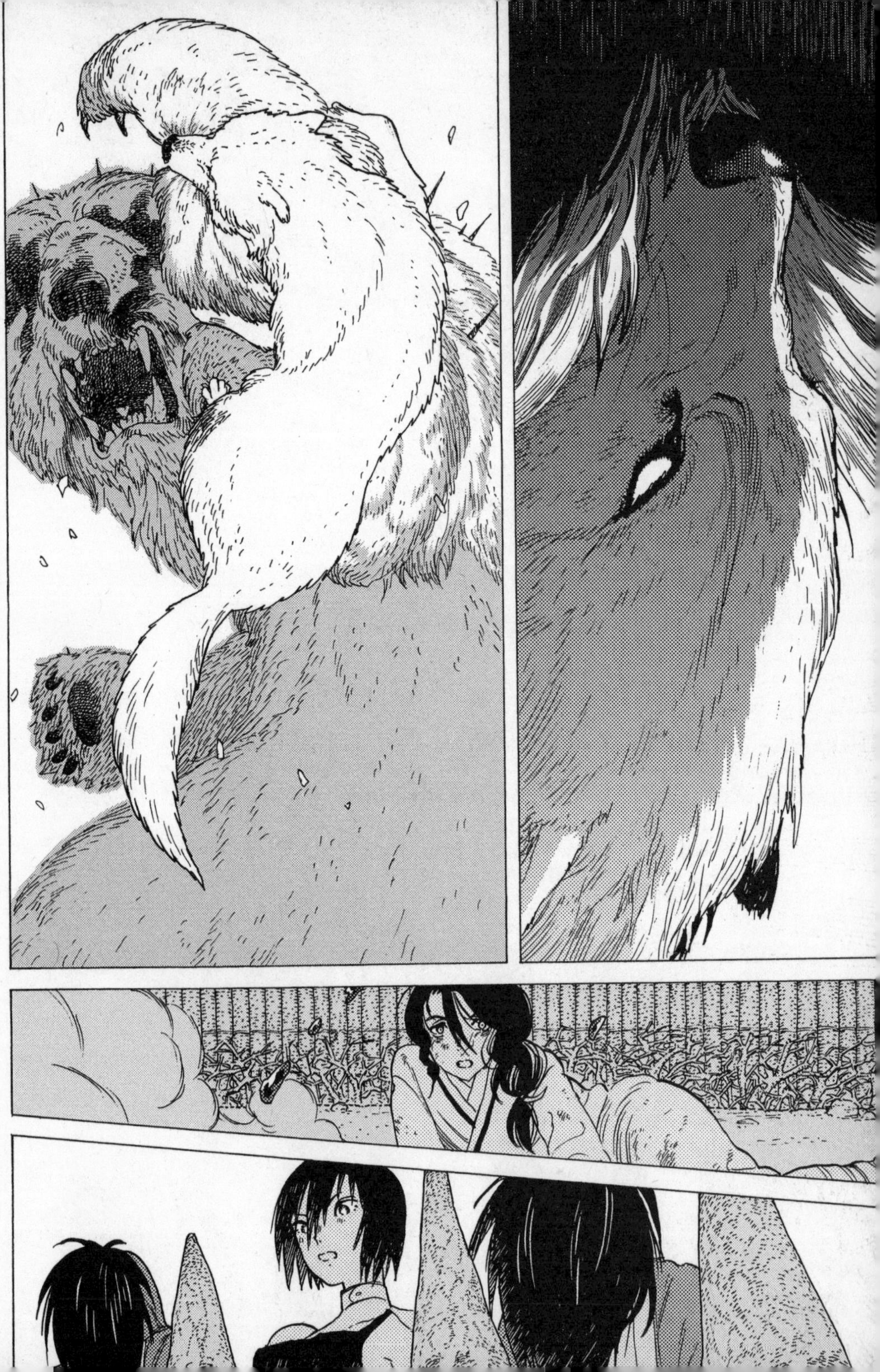

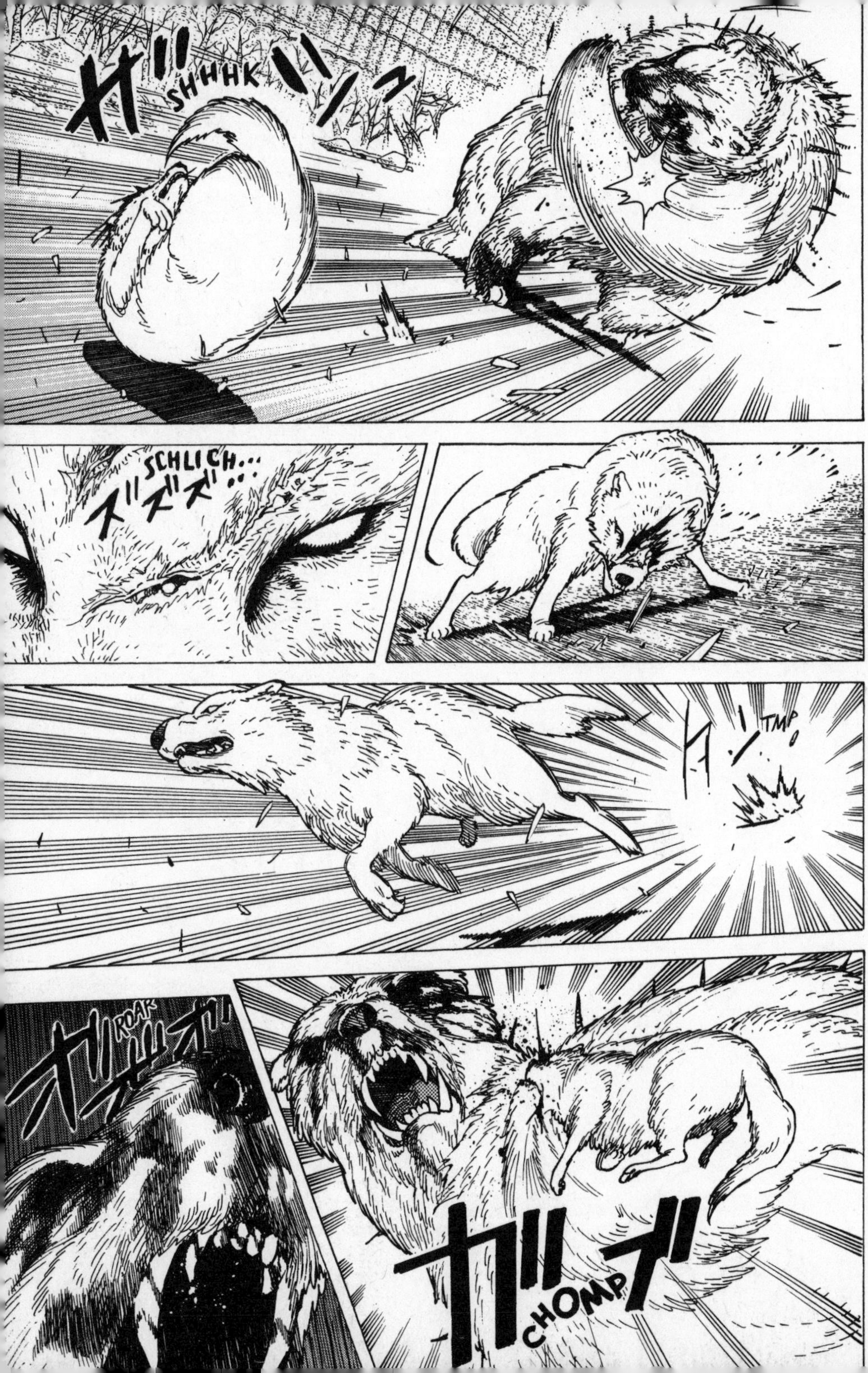
SHHHK
SCHLICH...
TMP
CHOMP
ROAR

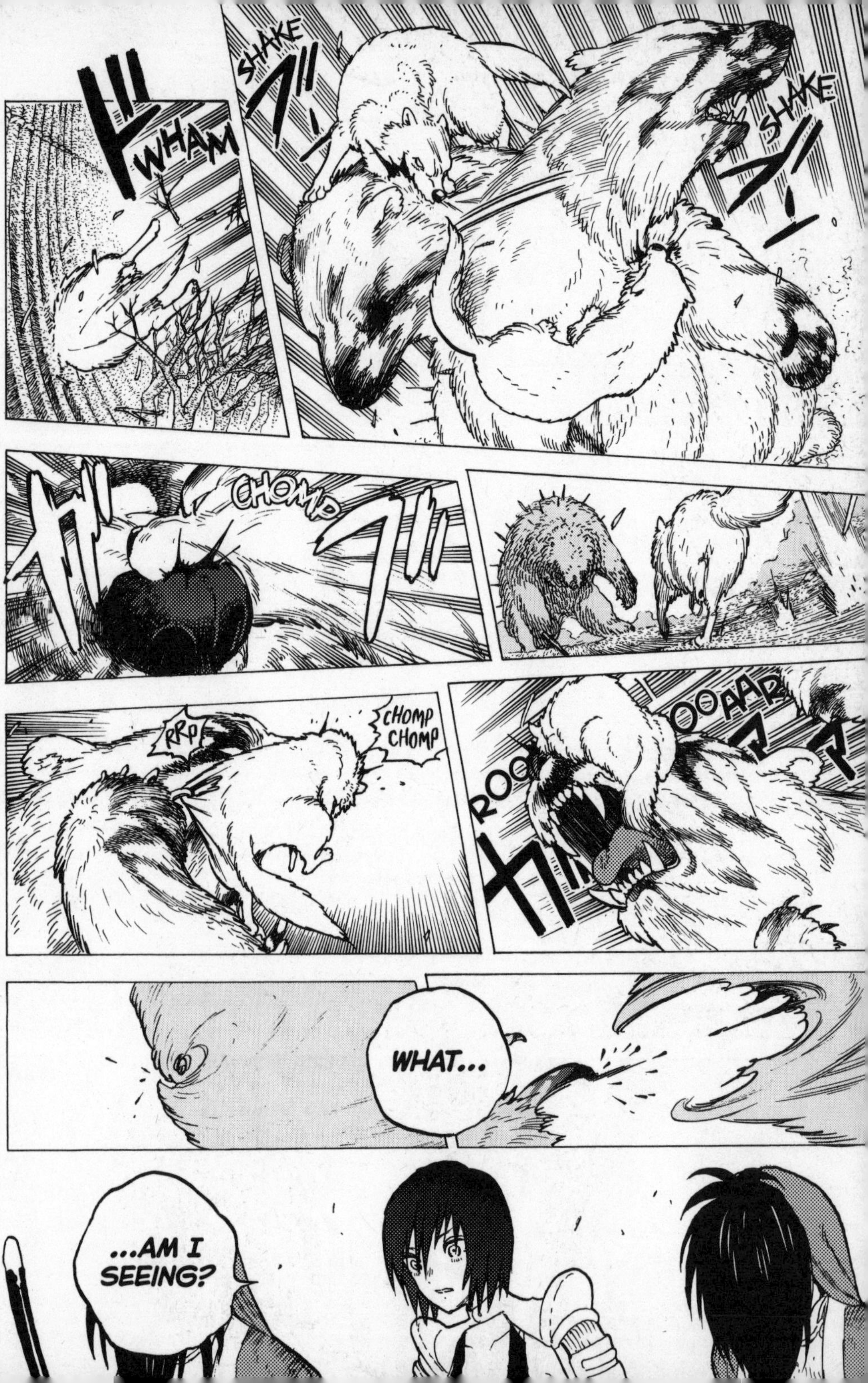
SHAKE
SHAKE
WHAM
CHOMP
ROOOOAAR
CHOMP CHOMP
RRP
WHAT...
...AM I SEEING?

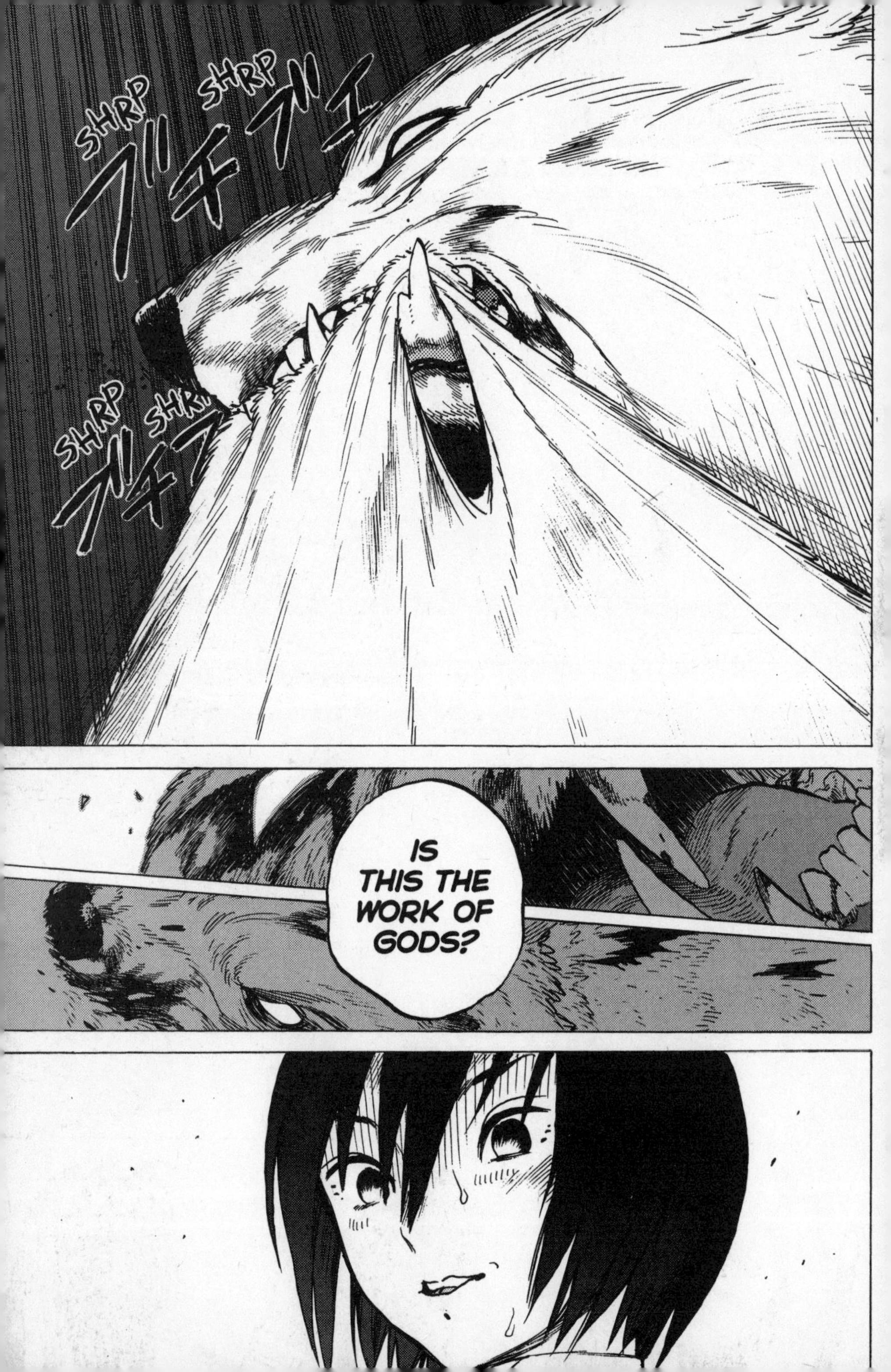
SHRP SHRP
SHRP SHR
IS THIS THE WORK OF GODS?

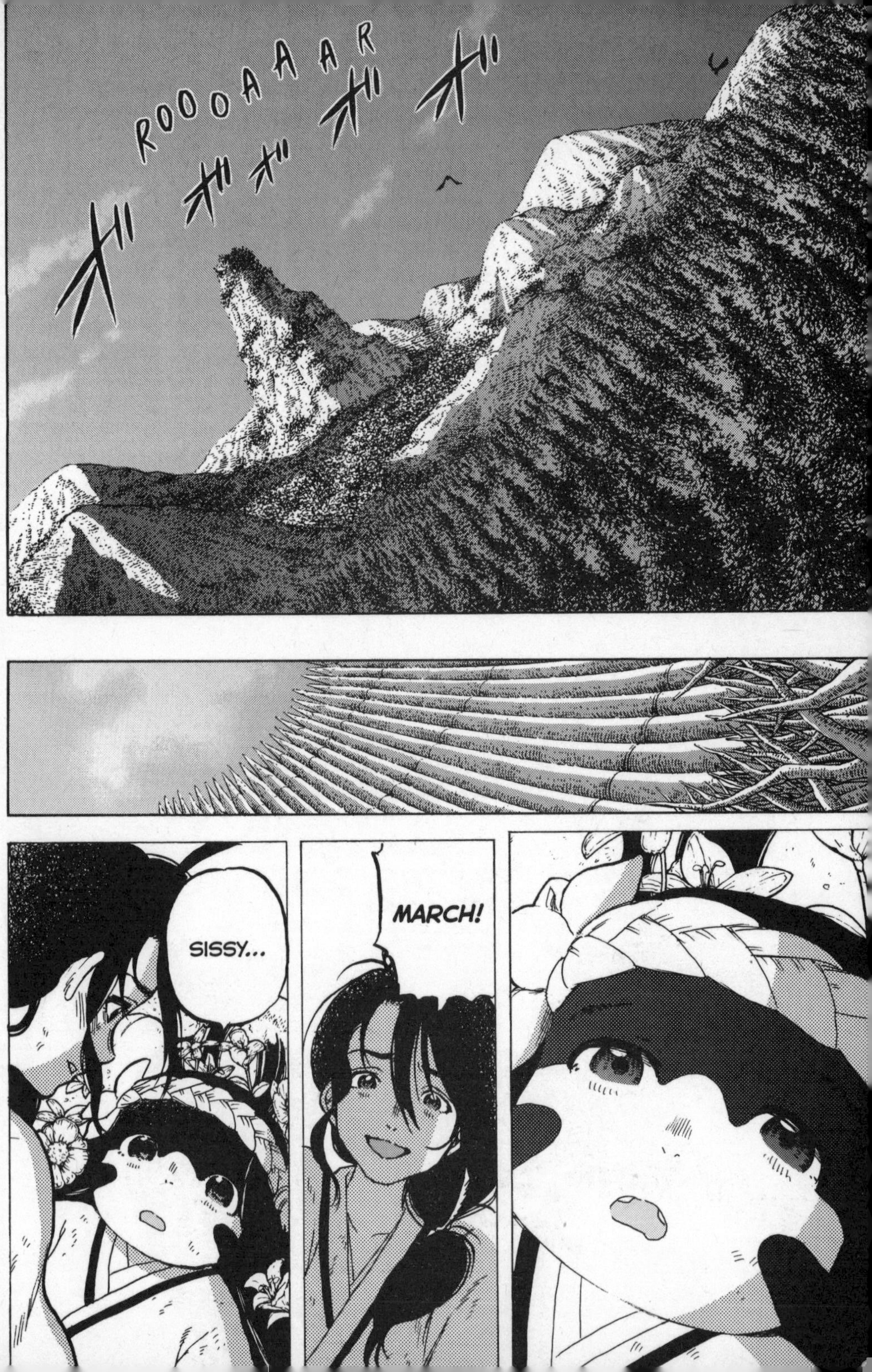
ROOOAAAAR
MARCH!
SISSY...

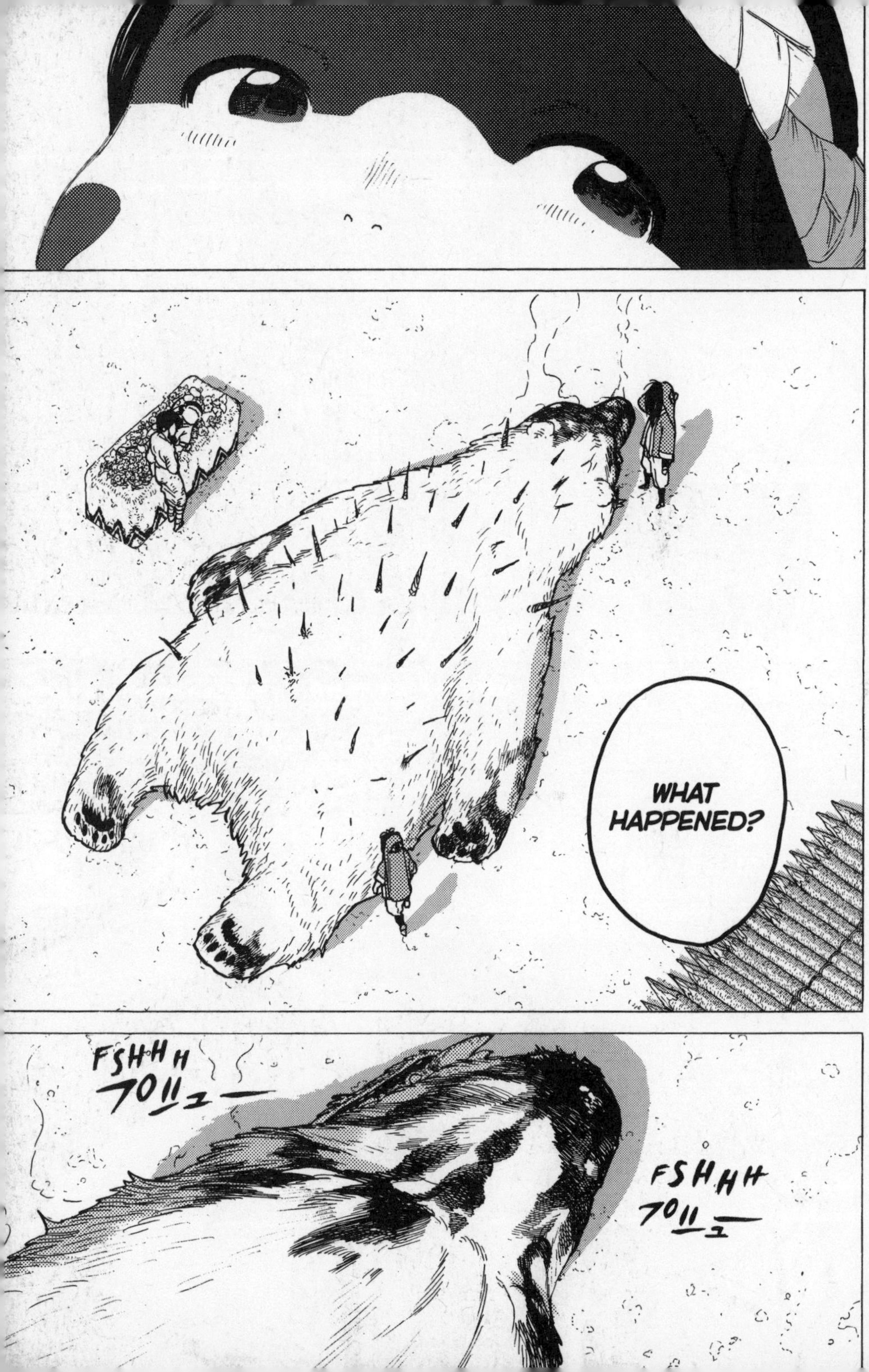
WHAT HAPPENED?
FSHHH
フシュー
FSHHH
フシュー

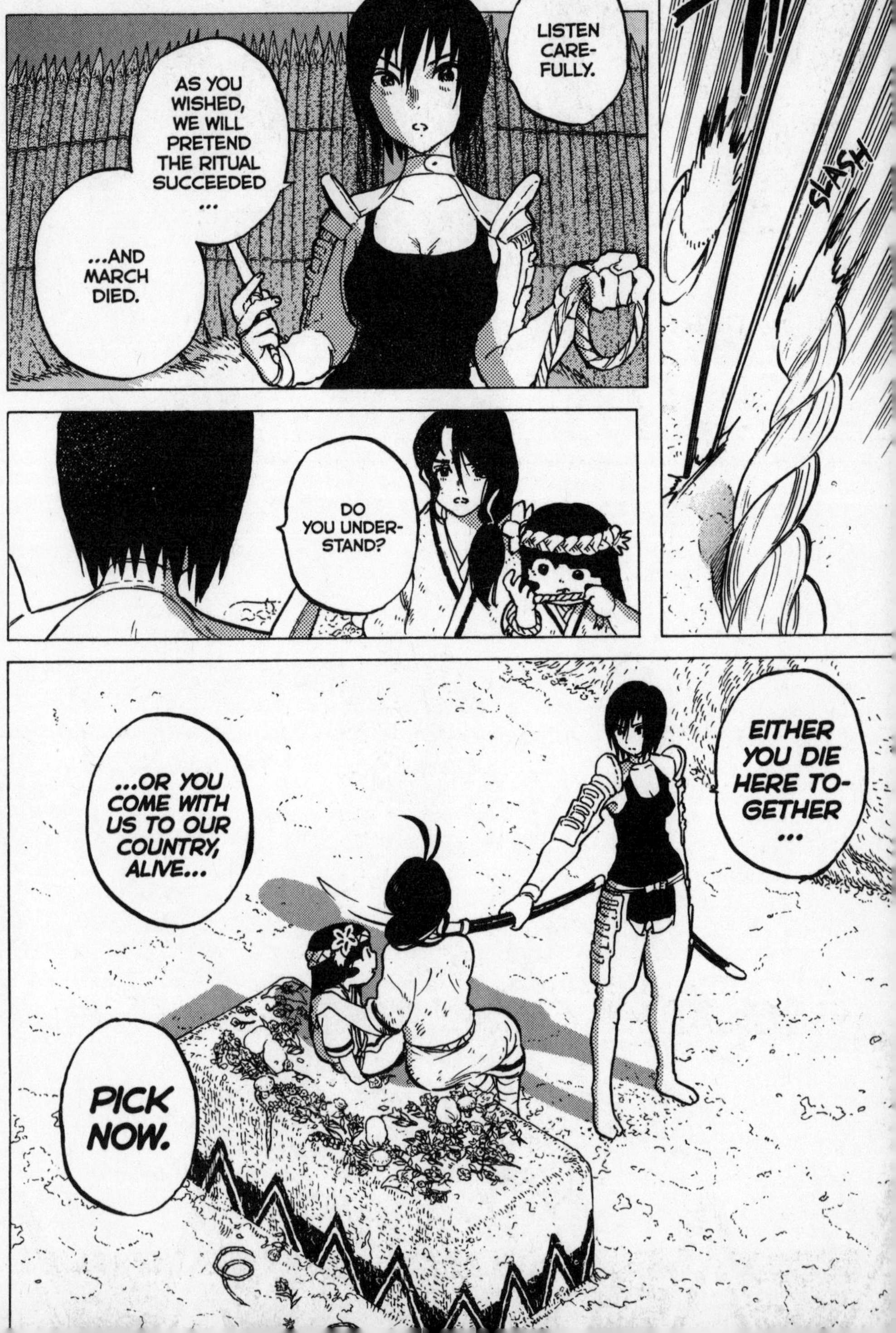
SLASH
LISTEN CARE-FULLY.
AS YOU WISHED, WE WILL PRETEND THE RITUAL SUCCEEDED ...
...AND MARCH DIED.
DO YOU UNDER-STAND?
EITHER YOU DIE HERE TO-GETHER ...
...OR YOU COME WITH US TO OUR COUNTRY, ALIVE...
PICK NOW.

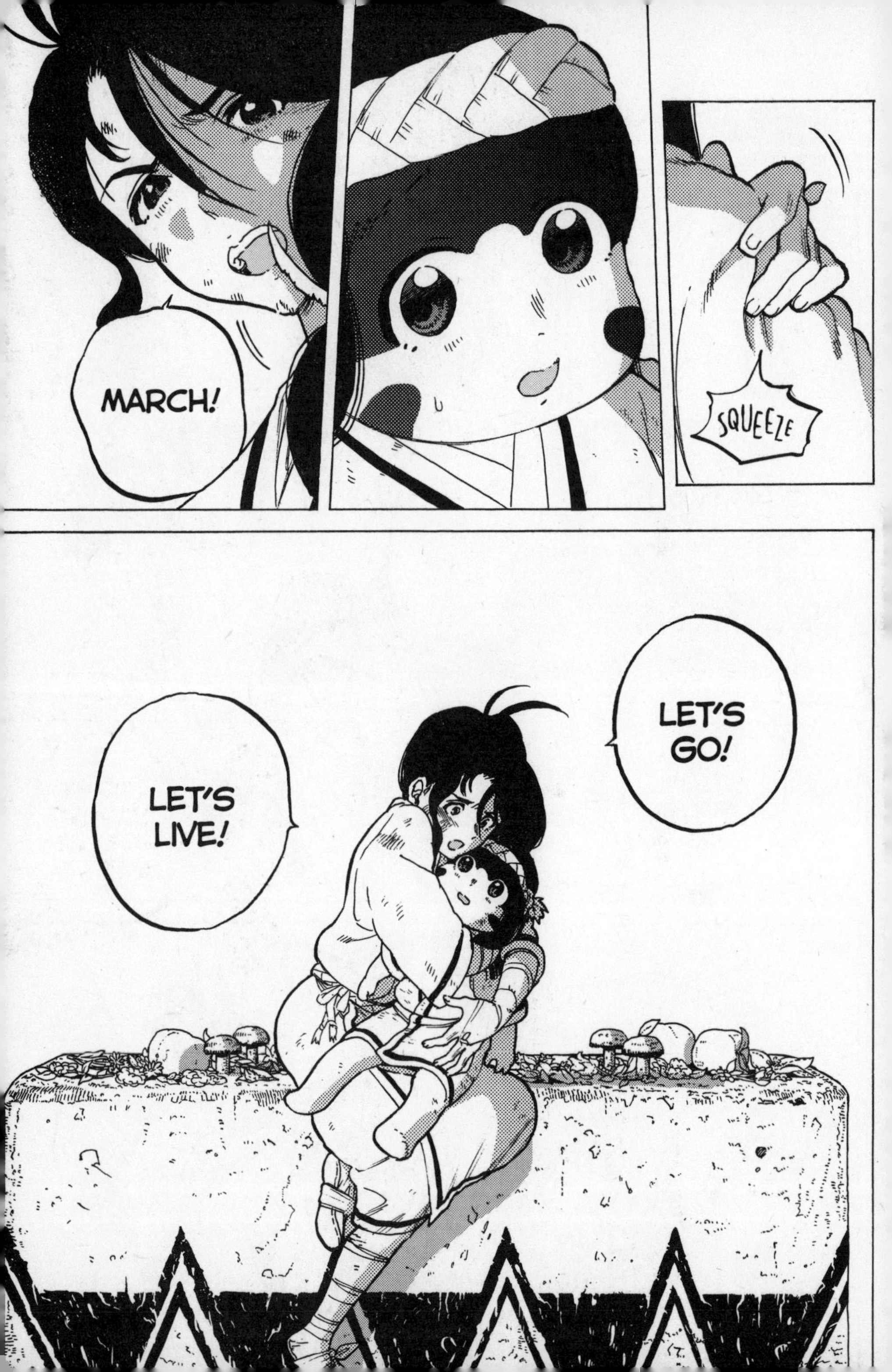
SQUEEZE
MARCH!
LET'S GO!
LET'S LIVE!

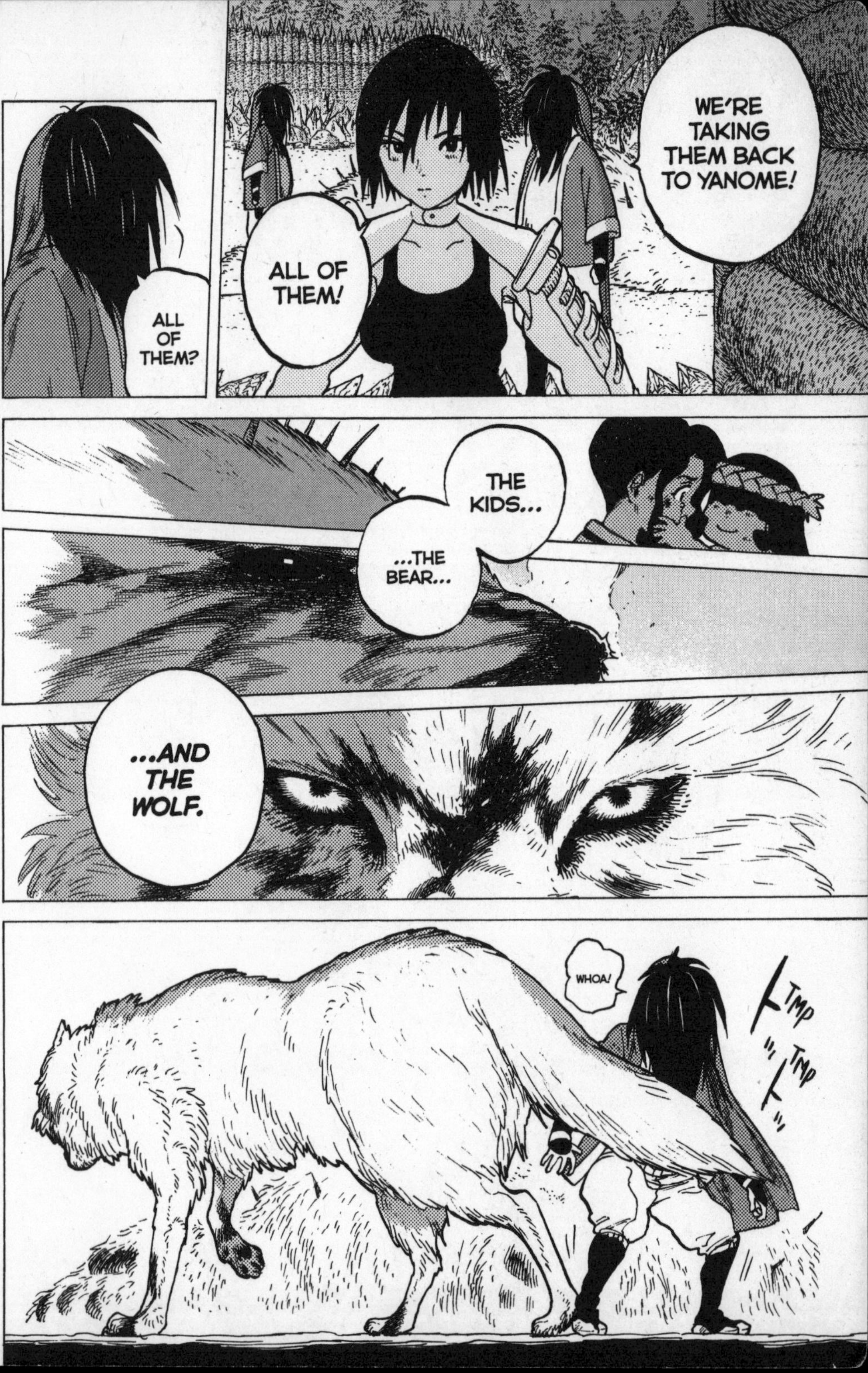
WE'RE TAKING THEM BACK TO YANOME!
ALL OF THEM!
ALL OF THEM?
THE KIDS...
...THE BEAR...
...AND THE WOLF.
TMP
TMP
WHOA!

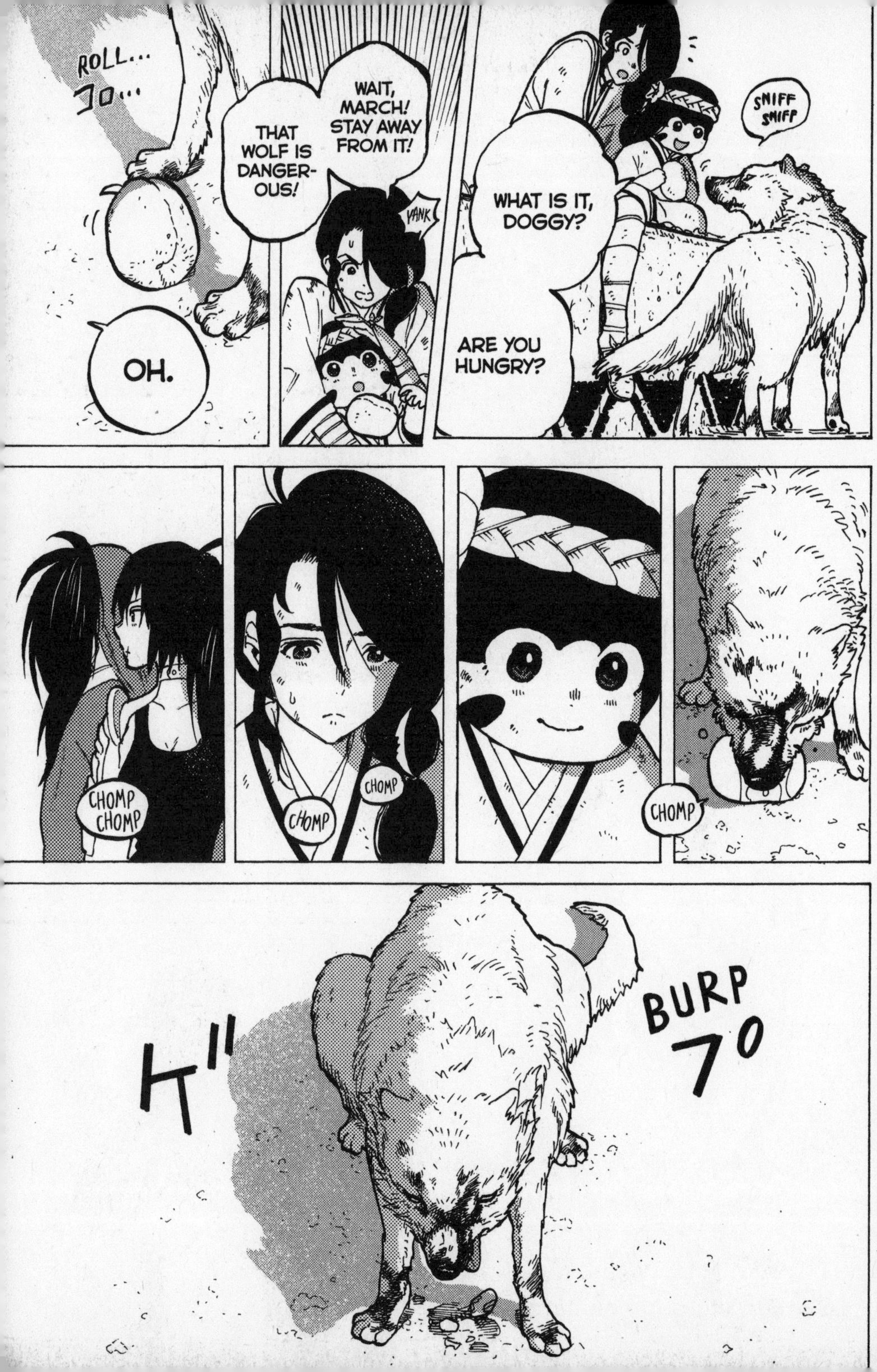
SNIFF SNIFF
WHAT IS IT, DOGGY?
ARE YOU HUNGRY?
WAIT, MARCH! STAY AWAY FROM IT!
THAT WOLF IS DANGER-OUS!
YANK
ROLL...
コロ...
OH.
CHOMP
CHOMP
CHOMP
CHOMP
CHOMP CHOMP
BURP
プ
ド

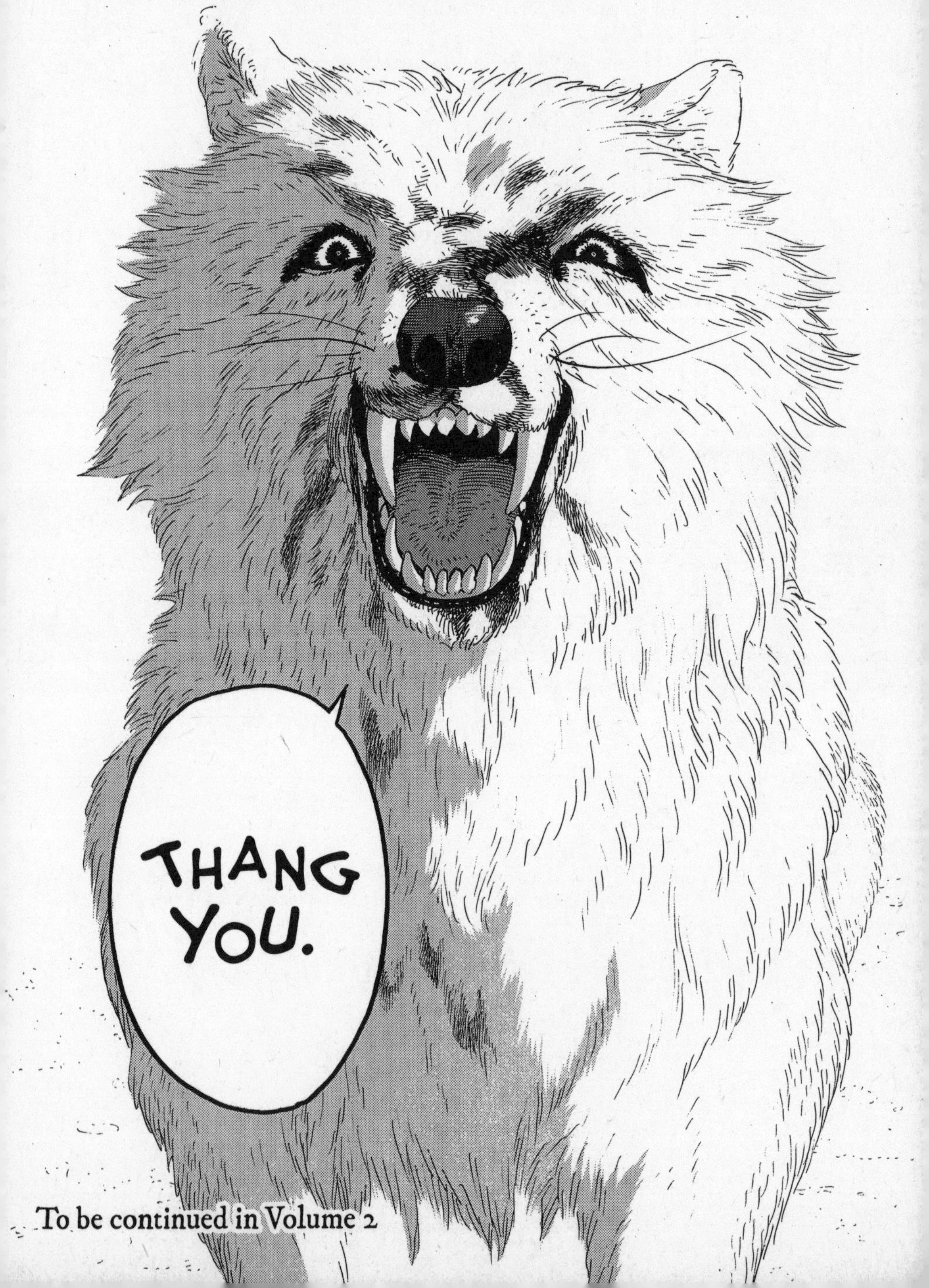
THANG YOU.

To be continued in Volume 2

TRANSLATION NOTES

Kanitaro and Usajiro, p.94-96

In Japanese naming conventions, Taro/-taro and Jiro/-jiro are typical first names or suffixes. They are both traditional masculine names. Taro most commonly means "eldest son" and Jiro means "second son." March's names for her toys is humorous and childlike because *kani* means crab in Japanese, and *usa* is short for *usagi*, or rabbit.

The name Fushi, Fu, p.150

The Japanese word for immortal is *fushimi*. Here, March suggests the name Fushi or Fu for short.

a Silent Voice

"The word heartwarming was made for manga like this."
–Manga Book-shelf

"A harsh and biting social commentary... delivers in its depth of character and emotional strength." -Comics Bulletin

"A very powerful story about being different and the consequences of childhood bullying... Read it."
–Anime News Network

Shoya is a bully. When Shoko, a girl who can't hear, enters his elementary school class, she becomes their favorite target, and Shoya and his friends goad each other into devising new tortures for her. But the children's cruelty goes too far. Shoko is forced to leave the school, and Shoya ends up shouldering all the blame. Six years later, the two meet again. Can Shoya make up for his past mistakes, or is it too late?

Available now in print and digitally!

Japan's most powerful spirit medium delves into the ghost world's greatest mysteries!

Story by Kyo Shirodaira, famed author of mystery fiction and creator of *Spiral*, *Blast of Tempest*, and *The Record of a Fallen Vampire*.

Both touched by spirits called yôkai, Kotoko and Kurô have gained unique superhuman powers. But to gain her powers Kotoko has given up an eye and a leg, and Kurô's personal life is in shambles. So when Kotoko suggests they team up to deal with renegades from the spirit world, Kurô doesn't have many other choices, but Kotoko might just have a few ulterior motives...

IN/SPECTRE

STORY BY **KYO SHIRODAIRA**
ART BY **CHASHIBA KATASE**

KC
KODANSHA
COMICS

New action series from Hiroyuki Takei, creator of the classic shonen franchise Shaman King!

In medieval Japan, a bell hanging on the collar is a sign that a cat has a master. Norachiyo's bell hangs from his katana sheath, but he is nonetheless a stray — a ronin. This one-eyed cat samurai travels across a dishonest world, cutting through pretense and deception with his blade.

STRAY CAT
SAMURAI

By
Hiroyuki Takei

To Your Eternity volume 1 is a work of fiction.
Names, characters, places, and incidents are the products of the author's imagination or are used fictitiously. Any resemblance to actual events, locales, or persons, living or dead, is entirely coincidental.

A Kodansha Comics Trade Paperback Original.

Published in the United States by Kodansha Comics,
an imprint of Kodansha USA Publishing, LLC, New York.

Publication rights for this English edition arranged through Kodansha Ltd., Tokyo.

First published in Japan in 2017 by Kodansha Ltd., Tokyo,
as *Fumetsu no Anata e* volume 1.

Cover Design: Tadashi Hisamochi (hive&co., Ltd.)
Title Logo Design: Shinobu Ohashi

ISBN 978-1-63236-571-2

Printed in the United States of America.

www.kodanshacomics.com

9 8 7 6 5 4 3 2 1

Translation: Steven LeCroy
Lettering: Darren Smith
Editing: Haruko Hashimoto, Alexandra Swanson
Editorial Assistance: YKS Services LLC/SKY Japan, INC.
Kodansha Comics Edition Cover Design: Phil Balsman